Edward Clarke, Thomas Becket, Peter Abraham De Hondt

Letters Concerning the Spanish Nation

Written at Madrid During the Years 1760 and 1761

Edward Clarke, Thomas Becket, Peter Abraham De Hondt

Letters Concerning the Spanish Nation
Written at Madrid During the Years 1760 and 1761

ISBN/EAN: 9783744687294

Printed in Europe, USA, Canada, Australia, Japan

Cover: Foto ©ninafisch / pixelio.de

More available books at **www.hansebooks.com**

LETTERS

CONCERNING THE

SPANISH NATION:

Written at M A D R I D during the Years 1760 and 1761.

By the Rev. E D W A R D   C L A R K E, M. A.

Fellow of St. John's College, Cambridge, and Rector of Pepperharrowe, in the County of Surry.

Quantos payzos, tantos coſtumbres.

L O N D O N:

Printed for T. Becket and P. A. De Hondt, at Tully's Head in the Strand. MDCCLXIII.

TO THE
RIGHT HONOURABLE
GEORGE BRODRICK
LORD VISCOUNT MIDLETON,
OF THE
KINGDOM OF IRELAND;
THESE LETTERS CONCERNING
THE SPANISH NATION
ARE INSCRIBED,
WITH THE SINCEREST RESPECT
AND GRATITUDE,
BY HIS LORDSHIP's
MOST OBLIGED,
AND OBEDIENT
HUMBLE SERVANT,

EDWARD CLARKE.

TABLE of CONTENTS.

TABLE OF CONTENTS.

NEW

NEW BOOKS

Juſt imported by T. BECKET and P. A. DE HONDT, in the Strand.

1. RECUEIL d'Antiquites Egypt, Etrus, Grec. & Rom. par Mr. le Comte de Caylus, avec grand Nomb. des Planches, Tom. V. Paris, 1762.
   ☞ Complete Sets of the above may be had.
2. Egypte Ancienne, par Mr. d'Origny, 2 Vol. Paris, 1762.
3. Elemens d'Agriculture, avec Fig. per Du Hamel, 2 Vol. Paris, 1762.
4. Contes Moraux, par Marmontel, 2 Vol. Paris, 1762.
5. Oeuvres Theatre de Mr. Saint Foix, Nouv. Edit. 4 Vol. Paris, 1762.
6. Etrennes Mignones, pour 1763, Paris.
7. ———— Maritime, avec Fig. pour 1763, Paris.
8. Melanges d'Alembert, 4 Vol. Nouv. Edit. Paris, 1762.
9. Oeuvres Complete de Mr. J. J. Rouſſeau, 8 Vol. 1762.
10. Oeuvres Complete de Mr. l'Abbe Vertot, 13 Vol.
11. Oeuvres Complete de Mr. Voltaire, 19 Vol.
12. Muſhenbroek Introd. ad Philoſ. Exp. 2 Vol. 4to. 1762.
13. Muſhenbroek Comp. Phyſicæ Exp. Conſcriptum in Uſus Academicos, Lugd. Bat. 1762.
14. Principes de la Lect. Orthographie, Paris, 1762.
15. Art de Sentir et Juger en matieres de Gout, 2 Vol. 1762.
16. Recueil de Memoires concernant l'Oeconomie Rurale, par une Societe etablie a Bern en Suiſſe, pour 1760, 1761, 1762, 10 Parts.
17. Memoires et Conſid. ſur le Commerce et les Finances d'Eſpagne, 2 Vol. 1762.
18. Avis au Peuple ſur ſa Sante. Par Tiſſot, 1762.
19. Ecole Militaire, 3 Vols. Paris, 1762.
20. Oeuvres de Monſ. Thomas, contenant, 1. Ode a Monſ. Moreau de Sachelles. 2. Jumonville, Poeme. 3. Epitre au Peuple. 4. Eloge de Comte de Saxe. 5. Eloge de Monſ. Dagueſſeau. 6. Eloge de Dugay-Trouin, Paris 1762.

1

PREFACE.

THE compiler of the following papers having had the honour to attend his Excellency the right honourable GEORGE WILLIAM, Earl of BRISTOL, his Britannic Majesty's Ambassador Extraordinary, and Minister Plenipotentiary to the court of MADRID, in quality of chaplain, for near two years; he made it his business, during his stay there, to collect such informations, hints, and materials relative to the present state of SPAIN, as might either gratify the curiosity of his friends, or prove of some utility to the public in general.

FOR this hath ever appeared to him to be the true and proper design of *Travelling*, to bring back such notices of foreign countries, as may correct any prejudices and errors we have entertained concerning them; such as may improve our present opinions, and contribute to form a just idea of different nations. This employment may be more useful, though, perhaps, not so flattering to the imagination, as that of reading *Virgil* upon the banks of the *Mincio*, *Horace* upon the *Aufidus*, or *Homer* upon the *Scamander*. Writers of authentic accounts of countries, though beneath the attention of elegant genius, and not rising to the higher claims of taste and *virtú*, may notwithstanding be more serviceable to the public, than the purchaser of a decayed *Titian*, the recoverer of a rusty *coin*, the copier of a defaced *inscription*, or the designer of an old *ruin*.

IT is, perhaps, to be wished, that the generality of our young travellers would give more of their attention this way; the subject is not exhausted, and the object is of much greater moment, than the dresses of one country, or the tunes of another; than

a   the

the vineyards of this province, or the kitchens of that. To obferve the variation of manners, the force of cuftoms, the utility of
laws, or the effects of climate, renders a much more effential fervice to your country, than to fet a new fafhion, teach a new air,
or give a new difh.

THE writer, apprehending that his ftay in SPAIN would have
been of much longer duration, had formed his original plan of a
much larger extent, than that which is now laid before the public : but as the war, which unfortunately broke out between the
two courts, prevented his profecuting that more extenfive defign,
the reader will, he hopes, charitably place this defect to the account of that unforefeen event, and not to any want of intention
or induftry in the writer.

HE is very fenfible of the many imperfections and defects of
this performance, and is convinced, that it ftands in need of all
the apologies he is capable of making for it. The reader owes the
perufal of it not to the writer's own fentiment or opinion, but to
the determination of abler judges, who conceived, that with all its
errors it might be of ufe to the public, as relating to a country, the
accounts of which now extant among us are more apt to miflead,
than to inform.

THE following papers would have been much lefs fuperficial
and jejune, if the country, in which they were collected, had
been half fo *communicative* as that in which they are publifhed. In
SPAIN, the want of that general education and knowledge, which
is fo univerfally diffufed throughout this ifland, renders the progrefs of all enquiry very flow and difficult : the referved temper
and genius of the Spaniards makes it ftill more embaraffed; but
the caution they ufe, and the fufpicions they entertain with regard
to hereticks, efpecially priefts, are generally fufficient to damp the
moft induftrious and inquifitive refearcher. Add to this that in-
vincible obftacle to all free enquiry in catholic countries, *the in-*
quifition, and then it is apprehended that the reader will not wonder, that he finds fo little entertainment and information in the
following letters.

BUT

But this is not all; befides the difficulties a foreigner meets with in the dominions of his catholic majefty, *that* of the language is not the leaft. French and Italian are now become fo very fafhionable and common among us, that moft of our young travellers fet out with the *Bocca Romana*, and the accent of Blois. But how few are there of us, that go out Spaniards? that have language enough to afk, Which is the way? or, How many miles are there to the next town? This inconvenience will be fenfibly felt by every enquiring mind. For want of Spanifh, the compiler of thefe papers ufed to endeavour to avail himfelf at firft of that almoft univerfal tongue of mankind, the *Latin:* but in that, befides the difference of pronunciation, he found a much worfe circumftance belonging to it: few of the monks or clergy underftood any thing of it; and ftill fewer were able to fpeak it. Their common anfwer was, *No entiendo Ufte*; *No es Latino por aca, pero es Latino por alla:* that is, " I do not underftand you, Sir: it is not " the Latin of this here country, but of that there country."

Having fairly apprifed the reader of thofe imperfections which he will find in this mifcellany, the writer hopes to be indulged in fubmitting to him what may be modeftly faid in favour of the performance.

The accounts which we have of Spain, may be reduced to *three* forts; the *Romance*, the *Obfolete*, and the *Modern*. With regard to the firft, the author rejoices to fee that abfurd kind of writing fo generally difregarded, that even the very names of the celebrated romances of the laft age are almoft as much forgotten as thofe of their authors: Though it is to be feared, that the wretched tribe of novel-writers, which have fucceeded, have done greater mifchief. The too fublime Clelia and Pharamond were compofitions, perhaps, of lefs pernicious tendency, than fome of our later printed poifons: the former might fill the mind with improbable fictions, but the latter may inflame the heart with probable vice: the apprentice, or young mifs, may be lefs incited by objects of impoffible imitation, fuch as the wandering knight in black armour, or the rambling lady upon a milk-white palfrey,

than

than by the familiar hiftory of the feducer and the feduced, which fill up moft of our modern novels; thefe are fubjects of more probable, and, therefore, more dangerous, imitation.

BUT to return from this fhort digreffion: the *romance*-accounts of SPAIN have had this bad effect upon us, that they have in a manner infufed themfelves into our ideas of that country. The manners of the moft inflexible people, and fuch the Spaniards are, undergo fome alteration in every age; the mad exploits of chivalry, and the extravagant gallantries of the old Spaniards, are now no more: the guittar and gauntlet are both thrown afide. The more refined manners of FRANCE paffed over the *Pyrenees* with the houfe of BOURBON. Even the *Spanifh language* is now making its laft ftruggles againft the more infinuating one of FRANCE; and, if the court did not ftill retain that laudable cuftom of anfwering foreign ambaffadors in their own tongue, it would probably have fallen into great neglect before now. *French politeffe* has given a new air to, and foftened the ferocious features of that country; the muftacho has dropped from the lip, and the cloke from the fhoulders of their nobleffe. Even the *Inquifitors* have fince learned not only the politenefs, but humanity of that people, and have left off roafting heretics *alive:* a cuftom, which, within this century, has been practifed at GRANADA.

THE next accounts which we have of SPAIN, may be called *Obfolete*; and fuch fhould be efteemed all thofe which have not been publifhed within this century. They are accounts, indeed, which were once true, but are now no more a juft defcription of the Spaniards, than an account of ENGLAND in the time of EDWARD III. would be called now: fuch are *The lady's travels into Spain*, a book pirated from a French writer; and many others. The *Delices d'Efpagne*, though a good book, is now quite antiquated; even the defcriptions of places in it are become unlike, becaufe the face of a country will change with time, as well as the manners of a people.

THE third clafs of accounts mentioned above, are the *Modern*; of this fort we have very little that is either tolerably correct or authentic. Mr. WILLOUGHBY's *Travels*, though republished in HARRIS's Collection, are of no moment; it is said the botanical, or natural history part of it is good; which, I suppose, made them appear together with Mr. RAY's. Mr. AP RICE has indeed lately published *A tour through Spain and Portugal, London* 1760, in 8vo; his view appears merely to have been that of exposing the absurd miracles of the Romish church, which indeed he has done effectually: but, in other respects, that book does not seem to have been written by one who actually visited the places themselves.

THE last thing, which I have to offer in favour of these letters, is, that the reader may be assured, that the utmost care was taken, that the accounts should be had from the best hand possible. The account of the *Spanish Money* was examined and approved by DARCY and JOIS, the great bankers at MADRID, and by the gentlemen of the embassy. The state of the *Army, Navy, Finances, and Civil List of the Court*, were transcribed from *an original French MS.* of the greatest authority, which may be seen in the author's possession, and which is a curiosity of no small value. The title of that French MS. which is a thin folio, runs thus, *Bila General des Finances de S. M. C. Don Carlos III. Roi d'Espagne, et. 1760.*

THE writer has inserted nothing, which he apprehends to be either ambiguous or false. And though he makes no doubt, but there are mistakes, yet he is certain, that he hath done all that he could to avoid them. He has made use of all the helps, living or dead, which fell in his way. And as he believes he has availed himself of most of what is *printed* upon this subject; so he is not conscious of having omitted any hints, given him by his friends and acquaintance, either in SPAIN or ENGLAND.

BUT though he has consulted what others have written upon this subject, it has been more with a view of avoiding their observations, than of making himself rich by their spoils: For in this matter he followed, as near as he could, that excellent instruction, which Dr. MIDDLETON hath given to succeeding writers, in his

admirable

admirable preface to the Life of CICERO. ' In writing hiſtory,
' as in travels, inſtead of tranſcribing the relations of thoſe who
' have trodden the ſame ground before us, we ſhould exhibit a
' ſeries of obſervations peculiar to ourſelves; ſuch as the facts and
' places ſuggeſted to our own minds, from an attentive ſurvey of
' them, without regard to what any one elſe may have delivered
' about them : And though in a production of this kind, where
' the ſame materials are common to all, many things muſt necef-
' ſarily be ſaid, which had been obſerved already by others; yet,
' if the author has any genius, there will be always enough of what
' is new, to diſtinguiſh it as an original work, and to give him a
' right to call it his own :' which, he flatters himſelf, will be allowed to him in the following letters.

AS to the form of *Letters*, in which this collection appears, it
was owing to this circumſtance; great part of it was ſent to the
author's friends in ENGLAND, in that dreſs, from MADRID : and
when he came to review the whole, he ſaw no reaſon why he
ſhould alter it; it is the eaſieſt and moſt comprehenſive vehicle
of matter, it allows of more liberty than a ſtiff and formal narrative; it affords more relief to the reader, there being perpetual
breaks, where he may pauſe at pleaſure.

BUT there is one circumſtance in this publication, which affords the author no ſmall ſatisfaction; and that is the giving his
reader a freſh proof of the happineſs, which he enjoys in being
born a Briton; of living in a country, where he poſſeſſes freedom
of ſentiment and of action, liberty of conſcience, and ſecurity of
property, under the moſt temperate climate, and the muſt duly
poiſed government in the whole world. A liberty that cannot
become licentious, becauſe bounded and circumſcribed, not by
the arbitrary will of ONE, but by the wiſdom of ALL, by the due
limits of reaſon, juſtice, equity, and law : Where the prince can
do no wrong, and where the people muſt do right : Where the
lawleſs noble is no more privileged from the hand of juſtice, than
the meaneſt peaſant : Where the greateſt miniſter ſtands accountable to the public, and, if he betrays the intereſts of his country,
cannot bid defiance to the juſt reſentments of the law.

LET

LET an Englishman go where he will, to SPAIN or PORTU-
GAL, to FRANCE or ITALY; let him travel over the whole globe,
he will find no constitution comparable to that of GREAT BRI-
TAIN. Here is no political engine, no bastile, no inquisition, to
stifle in a moment every symptom of a free spirit rising either in
church or state; no familiar, no alguazil to carry off each dangerous genius in arts or-science, to those dark and bloody cells, from
whence there are

—— *vestigia nulla retrorsum.*

THE *Monsieur* is polite, ingenious, subtle, and proud: but he
is a slave, and is starving; his time, his purse, and his arm are not
his own, but his monarch's. The *Italian* has neither freedom,
morals, nor religion. The *Don* is brave, religious, and very jealous of his honour, when once engaged: yet oppression and poverty are his portion under the sway of an arbitrary monarch. And
though he may boast, that the sun never rises or sets but within
the vast limits of the Spanish monarchy, yet he will never see liberty, science, arts, manufactures, and commerce flourish in them
with any vigour. The *Portuguese* is equally a slave, ignorant, and
superstitious. The *German* is continually at war, or repairing
the havock made by it. The *Hollander*, sunk in sloth, and the
love of money, is only active in commerce out of avarice. All
these, weighed in the balance against BRITAIN, in point of
happiness and advantages, will be found light: Let it, therefore,
be considered as no illiberal end of this publication, to inspire the
reader with love of the British constitution.

THE papers, which compose the following *Historical Introduction*, consist of three parts. The *first* contains *An extract from
the works of the Marquis de Mondecar*, a noble, learned, and judicious Spaniard, shewing the rise and origin of the several kingdoms
into which SPAIN was divided, and whose provincial divisions sub-
sist to this day. The *second* is *A short view of the history of Spain
from the death of Charles II. to the present time:* This period was
chosen, as being that of the accession of the BOURBON-family,
which forms a new æra, and is, in the history of SPAIN, what the
revolution is in the history of ENGLAND; our modern politics
hardly

hardly looking farther back than the prefent fettlement in SPAIN,
and the partition of the Italian dominions, which enfued upon it.
The *third* part of this hiftorical introduction is, *A lift of Englifh
ambaffadors, &c. at the court of Spain, with the treaties, &c.* which
it was thought would be no unufeful appendix to the former.

To conclude: Should there be, among the more humane readers, one who, in any remark, circumftance, or reflexion, may imagine that I have heightened or exaggerated this account of the
Spanifh nation, or have been any where too fevere in my animad-
verfions; have *caricatured* the features, or *magnified* the manners
of that people: he will, upon better information, difcover, that
THIS is by far the moft favourable and candid account of SPAIN,
which is not written by a Spaniard. Thofe who will take the
pains to read what the Marfhal BASSOMPIERE, the Countefs
D'AUNOIS, Father LABAT, the Abbé VAYRAC, Madame de
VILLARS M. DESORMEAUX, Don JUAN ALVAREZ DE COLME-
NAR, himfelf a Spaniard, and others have written upon this fubject, will fee the difference between a fair, true, and impartial
account, and one dictated by a heart overflowing with gall, and
penned with the ink of invective. And yet, what is more remarkable, their defcriptions were written by authors of the fame *religious perfuafion* with the Spaniards, by true and zealous *catholics.*
If mine has any merit to claim over their's, it is by fhewing, that
a *proteftant* has written a more favourable account of a *catholic*
country, than *catholics* themfelves have publifhed. Truth and fact
have been throughout the fole objects of my attention. I had
neither ill-nature to gratify, or fpleen to indulge : I abhor all national reflections, and defpife from my heart the little prejudices of
country, or cuftom. Upon many accounts I love and revere the
Spaniards: I admire their virtues, and applaud their valour. All
nations and regions have their refpective merits. But, notwithftanding, I have fteadily kept that juft rule in view,

Ne quid FALSI *dicere aufus, ne quid* VERI *non aufus.*

Hifto-

Hiſtorical Introduction.

(The remarks of the Marquis de MONDECAR *upon the Spaniſh hiſto-rians being judicious, new, and not commonly to be met with, I thought proper to give the reader the following extracts from his work.)*

THE Roman empire in this country laſted ſomething more than 400 years after the commencement of the Chriſtian æra: but the Spaniſh hiſtory is connected with the Roman for near 600, till that empire was utterly extinct. The GOTHS entered about the year 400. HIMERIC, with the SUEVI and ALANS, con-quered GALLICIA, about the year 408. Theſe SUEVI, who gave name to GALLICIA, ſubdued PORTUGAL about 464. REQUI-NA, the ſon of HIMERIC, conquered BISCAY, ANDALUſIA, and took SARAGOÇA and TARRAGONA in 488. RECARET was King of SPAIN in 587, and called a Cortes, at which prelates, as well as ſecular lords, aſſiſted, and granted aids to the crown. Af-ter him came WITTERIC, to whom ſucceeded GUNDEMAR, in 610. In 631, SISENANDO was choſe King, who called a Cortes at TOLEDO.

THE MOORS entered SPAIN about the year 680, conſequently the Gothic government did not laſt 300 years. TARIF ABENZAR-CA came in 713.

THE three moſt principal northern nations which came here, were, the VANDALS, from whom the province of ANDALUSIA received its name; theſe went afterwards into AFRICA: The SUEVI, who remained long in GALLICIA; and the GOTHS, who conquered the whole country, and held it upwards of 200 years. The GOTHS poſſeſſed the whole continent of SPAIN, MAURITA-NIA, AFRICA, and GALLIA GOTHICA, or that part of FRANCE,

b   which

which is now corruptly called LANGUEDOC : but in their turn
they gave place to the MOORS or ARABS, whofe dominion ceafed,
when PELAYO was eftablifhed in his throne. The MOORS conquered all SPAIN, except thofe mountainous parts, whither fome bodies of refolute chriftians fled for refuge. Thefe by degrees plan-
ned and concerted meafures to fhake off the Arabic yoke. The
firft ftand againft them was made by the mountaineers of As-
TURIAS, who elected King the Infant Don PELAYO, fwearing
the nobles over a fhield, and crying out, *Real! Real!* This
PELAYO was a Gothic prince by birth, fo that he in fome meafure reftored again the Gothic monarchy. He recovered GIJON
and LEON; and his fon got poffeffion of part of PORTUGAL, and
all GALLICIA. From this recovery of LEON came the race
of the kings of OVIEDO and LEON. The boldnefs and fuccefs of
thefe chriftians alarming the ARABS, they attacked them in their
different ftrong-holds, in order to cut off their communications
one with another. But this produced a very different effect from
what they expected. The chriftians, to repel the danger that threat-
ned them on every fide at the fame time, chofe different heads in
different places, who being feparate one from the other in their
governments, defended their fubjects independently of one another. This neceffary refolution gave rife to the *different kingdoms*
in SPAIN. Such was their undoubted origin, tho' it is impoffible
to fay, at what exact period each kingdom rofe, as there are no
antient monuments remaining fufficient to prove that point.

THE firft kingdom or monarchy that arofe, after the Moorifh
invafion, was that, as we have faid, of Don PELAYO in the As-
TURIAS, an elective monarchy : and in proportion as the Aftu-
rian princes diflodged the pagans of thofe lands and territories that
lay neareft to them, they changed the ftile of their titles; being firft
called Kings of ASTURIAS, then of OVIEDO, and laftly of LEON
and GALLICIA, until they were incorporated with the Kings of
CASTILE, by the marriage of Queen Donna SANCHA ISABELLA,
fifter of King Don BERMUDO III. its laft prince, both of them defcendants of King Don ALONZO V. who married the daughter of
FERDINAND *the great*, to whom fome give the title of Emperor,
and who was firft King of CASTILE.

OF

OF this long period, in which the chriſtian princes gained ſuch glorious ſucceſſes, and ſingular victories over the infidels, there are ſome ſhort and obſcure accounts in the little chronicles of Don ALONZO III. King of LEON, ſurnamed *the great*, and of ALVEDA, of SAMPIRO, and of Don PELAYO.

COUNTS and KINGS of *CASTILE.*

AT the ſame time with theſe ASTURIAN Princes, aroſe many nobles, who ſigned their deeds and inſtruments, with the titles of Counts or Princes, and, among others, thoſe of CASTILE, which ſtate arrived at ſovereignty in the time of the great Count FERNAN GONZALEZ, by his heroic valour, glorious triumphs, and extended power. The moſt diſtinguiſhed Prince of this houſe was Don SANCHO GARCIA, whoſe violent death was the cauſe, why this houſe united itſelf to the crown of ARRAGON and NAVARRE, by the marriage of the Princeſs Donna SANCHA his ſiſter, with the King Don SANCHO MAYOR, whoſe ſecond ſon Don FERNANDO raiſed CASTILE into a kingdom. CASTILE afterwards became an hereditary crown in his lineage, in preference to all the other kingdoms, altho' inferior in origin to ARRAGON and NAVARRE.

THE ſeries and chronology of the ſeveral counts is much conteſted between the Spaniſh writers, ARREDONDO, AREVALO, SANDOVAL, and others : a diſpute not worth our entering into, ſince it is certain, that from the bravery, ſucceſs, and power with which Don FERNANDO extended his dominion, ſo as to be ſtiled firſt king of CASTILE, his kingdom became ſo famous, that all the Mooriſh princes acknowledged him for their ſovereign. His ſon was Don ALONZO VI. his grand-daughter was the Queen Donna URRACA, with whom ended the barony of NAVARRE : the crown of CASTILE falling back again into the houſe of the Counts of BURGUNDY (who came from the Kings of ITALY) by her marriage with the Count Don RAYMUND, her firſt huſband; from which match came their ſon the great Emperor Don ALONZO VII.

THIS

THIS prince left his estates divided between his two sons: To Don SANCHO, the eldest, whose great virtues and untimely death gained him the name of *the regretted*, he left the kingdoms of CASTILE, and part of LEON: And to Don FERDINAND, the second, the rest of LEON, GALLICIA, and ASTURIAS. He took upon himself the title of King of SPAIN, pretending that the primogeniture of the GOTHS, which was re-established in PELAYO, had centered in himself.

DON SANCHO dying, he was succeeded by Don ALONZO *the noble*, one of the greatest princes of his time. It was he who gained the famous battle of the plains of TOLOSA over the MOORS, destroying 200,000 of them at one time †. He dying without issue-male, the two kingdoms of CASTILE and TOLEDO went to Donna BERENGUELA, his eldest daughter.

ALTHOUGH the royal barony of BURGUNDY ended in the Queen Donna BERENGUELA, it returned and united with the kingdom of LEON, GALLICIA, and ASTURIAS by the marriage of King Don ALONZO, her uncle (who succeeded in those kingdoms to King Don FERNANDO, brother to King Don ALONZO *the noble*, her grandfather) from which match came the King SN. FERNANDO, from whom descended, without interruption, the Kings of CASTILE and ARRAGON, until united in FERDINAND and ISABELLA, they relapsed into the august house of AUSTRIA, by the marriage of the Queen Donna JUANA, their eldest daughter, to the Arch-Duke Don PHILIP I. from which great union sprung the Emperor CHARLES V.

FROM this period downward, the Spanish history is very connectedly written, and well known; I shall now therefore only give a summary view of it from the death of CHARLES II. to the present time.

† Begging the Spanish historian's pardon, this number must be exaggerated: 50,000 slain is full enough for any hero.

A

A CONCISE VIEW of

THE HISTORY of SPAIN,

From the Death of CHARLES II.

To the Prefent Time.

AS CHARLES the fecond of SPAIN had no iffue, ENGLAND, FRANCE, and HOLLAND, formed, in 1699, the famous treaty of partition, for dividing the dominions of the crown of SPAIN, upon his death. Each party had, or, at leaft, pretended to have, the common view, in this treaty, of preventing fuch a vaft acceffion of power from paffing, either into the Houfe of AUSTRIA, or that of BOURBON, already formidable enough of themfelves. This ftep very fenfibly affected the court of SPAIN : CHARLES the fecond was fo much offended thereat, that, on his death-bed, he figned a will, by which he bequeathed all his dominions to PHILIP Duke of ANJOU, grandfon of LEWIS XIV. Though that Prince had before entered into the partition treaty, yet, finding the fucceffion thus left to his family, he paid no regard to any former engagements or renunciations, but on the 18th of February, declared his grandfon, PHILIP, King of SPAIN, who arrived at Madrid on the 14th of April, 1701. This proceeding immediately alarmed the maritime powers and the Emperor ; the former were apprehenfive of Spanifh AMERICA's falling into the hands of the FRENCH, and the latter, befides the injury he imagined done to his own family, dreaded the too great influence of the power of the Houfe of BOURBON. A war enfued ; and CHARLES Arch-duke of AUSTRIA was foon after fet up, in oppofition to PHILIP V. His claim was vigoroufly fupported by the maritime powers, and at firft favoured by many of the grandees of SPAIN. In the third year of this war, the King of PORTUGAL and the Duke of SAVOY joined likewife

3

wife in the alliance againft PHILIP; who, in the following campaigns, was driven from his capital, by the fuccefs of the allied forces, and almoft obliged to abandon SPAIN. In the end, however, his party prevailed, and, at the peace of UTRECHT in 1713, he was acknowledged as King of SPAIN by all the confederates leagued againft him, except the Emperor. The allies then contented themfelves with fuch limitations and reftrictions, as might keep the two monarchies of FRANCE and SPAIN difunited. A treaty of partition may, indeed, be faid to have taken place at the laft; for PHILIP, by the articles of the peace, was only left in poffeffion of SPAIN, its American colonies, and fettlements in the EAST-INDIES; but the Spanifh dominions in ITALY, and the iflands of SICILY and SARDINIA were difmembered from the monarchy, which had alfo loft the ifland of MINORCA and the fortrefs of GIBRALTAR, both of which places were ceded to GREAT-BRITAIN. The Duke of SAVOY was put in poffeffion of the ifland of SICILY, with the title of King; and the Arch-duke CHARLES, who, two years before, had been elected Emperor of GERMANY, held MILAN, NAPLES, and SARDINIA, and ftill kept up his claim to the whole Spanifh monarchy.

THOUGH PHILIP, by the peace concluded at UTRECHT, was left, by the allies, poffeffor of the greateft and moft important part of the Spanifh dominions, yet fome obftinate enemies ftill remained to be reduced, before he could be faid to have fixed the Spanifh crown fecurely upon his head. The inhabitants of CATALONIA refufed to acknowledge him, and, finding themfelves abandoned by their allies, folicited the affiftance of the Grand Signior, in hopes of eftablifhing themfelves into an independent republic. Their blind obftinacy, however, ferved only to heighten the miferies and calamities to which they had been greatly expofed during the whole courfe of the war. After a moft bloody and ftubborn defence, they were entirely reduced by the King's troops, when they were deprived of their antient privileges, and their country was annexed to the crown of CASTILE, as a conquered province.

THE

THE reduction of CATALONIA reftored tranquillity to SPAIN, which had been haraffed for twelve years by a moft cruel and bloody war. PHILIP, by that conqueft, finding himfelf quietly feated upon the throne, began to turn his thoughts to the re-union of the Italian dominions, which he had feen wrefted from him with the utmoft regret. With a view to this re-union, his firft wife being dead, he married ELIZABETH FARNESE, heirefs of PARMA, PLACENTIA, and TUSCANY; which alliance afterwards proved a fource of new diffenfions and wars among the Princes of Europe; and, to this day, ftill leaves an opening for bloody contefts.

THE match was firft propofed, and afterwards negotiated, by the famous Abbé ALBERONI, who, from being a fimple cu-rate in the PARMESAN, rofe, by a furprifing feries of fortunate incidents, more than by any extraordinary talents, to be prime minifter in SPAIN. ALBERONI was the fon of a common gar-dener. In the beginning of the war he had, by his forwardnefs and addrefs, infinuated himfelf into the favour of VENDOME, the French General in ITALY, who brought him with him to FRANCE, and afterwards to MADRID, where, after the Duke's death, he continued as agent for the affairs of PARMA, and laid hold of the opportunity of aggrandifing himfelf, by propofing a match that fuited with the views of the Spanifh court. The new Queen, being a ftranger in SPAIN, was advifed in every thing by ALBERONI, who, being protected and countenanced by her, boldly intermeddled in affairs of ftate, and foon acquired a great degree of favour with the King. A few days after the celebra-tion of the King's marriage with the Princefs of PARMA, his grandfather, LEWIS XIV. died, and left his dominions to an infant fucceffor. Though PHILIP had, before the conclufion of the treaty of UTRECHT, folemnly renounced, for himfelf, and his heirs, all right to the fucceffion of the crown of FRANCE, yet he was now ftrongly urged by ALBERONI, to infift upon the regency of that kingdom, during the minority, as firft Prince of the blood of FRANCE, and next in fucceffion to the prefent monarch. This wild and imprudent counfel, if it had been fol-lowed, would undoubtedly have involved SPAIN in a new war,

I

which

which would have had no other object, than the meer point of honour; and, upon that consideration, and, perhaps, some regard to the oath, it was rejected by the King. It proved, however, extremely prejudicial to SPAIN, and, in the end, occasioned the ruin of ALBERONI; for the Duke of ORLEANS, who had been declared Regent by the Parliament of PARIS, having received intelligence of his designs, conceived an implacable hatred against him; did his utmost to thwart all his projects of government; and never ceased persecuting him till he saw him disgraced. This happened a very few years afterward, the Duke's wishes being seconded by ALBERONI's own conduct; for the same impetuous and intriguing spirit, which had promoted his grandeur, pushed him on to his downfal.

AT this time, however, he was in the height of favour, and continually urged the King, not to delay the renewing of the war in ITALY, against the Emperor CHARLES, who gave just foundation for a rupture, by still retaining the title of King of SPAIN; by creating Spanish grandees; by protecting those who were disaffected to PHILIP; and by punishing those who remained faithful to him, with the forfeiture of their estates in FLANDERS and ITALY. The Queen, who was lately delivered of a son, had now got a great ascendency over her husband, and zealously supporting ALBERONI in all his proceedings, PHILIP, out of complaisance to her, was easily persuaded to commit the whole management of his affairs to him, and weakly suffered himself to be guided, in every thing, by his counsels. ALBERONI, though not declared prime minister, now acted as such, with a most despotic authority, and caused immense military preparations to be carried on in the ports of SPAIN, with the design of attacking the dominions possessed by the Emperor in ITALY. But, to deceive the Pope, from whom he had, for some time, been soliciting a Cardinal's hat, and who, he knew, would be greatly offended with the renewal of the war in ITALY, he, by private letters, professed his abhorrence of disturbing the repose of that country, and alledged, that the naval armaments were designed against the Turks, who had attacked the

Venetian

Venetian territories in GREECE, and even ftruck a terror into the Italians, by making a defcent upon their coafts.

THE great naval preparations kept all EUROPE in fufpenfe, and very much alarmed feveral ftates. The Emperor fufpected an attack upon NAPLES and MILAN; the Duke of SAVOY feared an invafion of SICILY, which ifland, he knew, was not well affected to him; and GEORGE I. of GREAT-BRITAIN, was apprehenfive, that the fleet was defigned to affift the Jacobites, who had been defeated two years before in SCOTLAND.

ALBERONI having, at length, obtained from the Pope, not only the dignity of Cardinal for himfelf, but alfo an indulgence to raife a fubfidy, for five years, upon the clergy in SPAIN and Spanifh AMERICA, immediately took off the mafk, and ordered the fleet to fail againft SARDINIA, which ifland was reduced in lefs than two months. The Emperor being, at this time, engaged in a war againft the Turks in HUNGARY, had left but a very few troops in his Italian dominions, not expecting to be attacked by PHILIP in thofe parts, as both Princes had ftipulated to obferve a neutrality, in regard to them. He had, indeed, done fome things that might be deemed infractions of that neutrality; but the King of SPAIN not having made any formal complaints of thefe, was now generally looked upon as the aggreffor, by the invafion of SARDINIA.

ACCORDINGLY the Pope, who now never mentioned ALBERONI's name but with fome injurious epithet, by a public brief expreffed his refentment againft PHILIP, and he, in return, commanded the nuntio to leave SPAIN. The King of GREAT-BRITAIN and the Regent of FRANCE ordered their ambaffadors at MADRID, to complain of the violation of the neutrality. They even fent ambaffadors extraordinary to SPAIN, to prefs an accommodation between the Emperor and PHILIP. ALBERONI, however, replying, in a very haughty ftile, and continuing his military preparations with more vigour than ever, the powers who offered their mediation entered into a league with the Emperor, which was called the triple alliance; and King GEORGE fent a fleet of 26

c   fhips

fhips of the line into the MEDITERRANEAN, under the command
of Admiral BYNG, who was ordered to maintain the neutrality of
ITALY.

THE Spanifh minifter vainly perfuaded himfelf, that no powers
but thofe who were directly attacked, would interfere in oppofing his wild fchemes, which tended to difturb the fettled tranquillity of EUROPE; and he leaft of all expected to fee an inti-
mate alliance betwixt the courts of GREAT-BRITAIN and FRANCE.
His fuccefs againft SARDINIA, which was but a trifling conqueft,
fo far blinded him, that he thought himfelf fufficient alone to oppofe three of the moft formidable powers of EUROPE united.
He ftill purfued his warlike preparations with the utmoft vigour;
which were greater than any fitted out by SPAIN, fince the time
of the famous Armada againft ENGLAND. He confulted with
nobody; and the Spanifh officers, of the greateft prudence and experience, who ventured to give their advice, were treated by him
with contempt and arrogance.

To counterbalance the power of the triple alliance, he vainly attempted to embroil all EUROPE. He fent an envoy to CON-
STANTINOPLE, to excite Prince RAGOTSKI to renew the war in
HUNGARY, where the Turks had agreed to a truce for four
years; he formed a confpiracy in FRANCE, for depofing the
Regent, which ferved only to heighten the animofity of the
Duke of ORLEANS againft himfelf; he preffed the Czar of Mus-
covy, to attack the Emperor's hereditary dominions; and he offered large fubfidies to CHARLES XII. of SWEDEN, if he would
invade GREAT-BRITAIN.

DURING thefe negotiations, the Spanifh fleet, confifting of
26 fhips of the line, befides frigates, failed from BARCELONA,
having on board 30,000 of the beft troops of SPAIN, moft of
them veterans, who had been in all the actions of the long
war of the fucceffion.

ON the firft and fecond of July 1719, the army landed on SICILY,
and, in a few weeks, made themfelves mafters of a great part of
that

that ifland.   The entire conqueft, in all probability, would very foon have been compleated; but the Spanifh fleet, on the 9th of Auguft, being totally defeated by Admiral BYNG, who took and deftroyed 23 fhips of the line, their land army could no longer receive any confiderable fupplies, while the Piedmontefe garifons were daily reinforced by German troops from the kingdom of NAPLES.

NOTWITHSTANDING the fatal blow the Spanifh marine had received, ALBERONI ftill thought himfelf able to cope with the many enemies his turbulent ambition had raifed againft SPAIN, though he had exhaufted, not only the King's revenues, but thofe of many private perfons.   Being difappointed in his expectations from CHARLES XII. who was killed, on the 10th of December, before FREDERICS-HALL in NORWAY, he fent for the pretender from ROME, and ordered 5000 men to be embarked at the GROYNE, with a view to invade both SCOTLAND and IRELAND.   Only about 1000 of thofe troops, however, landed in SCOTLAND, where they, and about 2000 Jacobites, who had joined them, were quickly defeated and difperfed.   The reft, after fuffering greatly by a ftorm, were obliged to return to SPAIN.   A few fhips, about the fame time, failed from VIGO to the coaft of BRITANY, in hopes of raifing an infurrection in that province, againft the Duke of ORLEANS; but this attempt had no better fuccefs than the other.

THOUGH ALBERONI feemed to triumph in the beginning of his enterprizes, yet he now began feverely to feel the fuperior ftrength of the powers he had to contend with, which, indeed, had been difcovered long before, almoft by every body but himfelf.   The Regent of FRANCE fent a powerful army againft SPAIN, under the command of the Duke of BERWICK, who, in three months, made himfelf mafter of the provinces of GUIPUSCOA and ROUSSILLON, with all their fortified places, and, at PORT-PASSAGE and SANTOGNA, burnt feven fhips of war, and materials for feven others, the lofs of the whole being computed at near 800,000 l. and, a few months after, the Englifh landed, with 4000 men, at VIGO, where, after making them-

felves

felves mafters of the town, they carried off fix fmall veffels. Thefe
invafions, with the bad news from SICILY, where the Spaniards
had been obliged for feveral months to act on the defenfive, at length
opened the eyes of PHILIP, and induced him to hearken to the
reprefentations of his confeffor d'AUBENTON, and the Marquis
SCOTI, the minifter of PARMA, who affured him, that the
allies would never agree to a peace, while ALBERONI continued in
SPAIN.

PHILIP, alarmed with the bad fituation of his affairs, had,
for fome months, expreffed great diffatisfaction with ALBERONI,
and now parted with him without regret. He ordered him to
leave SPAIN in three weeks, declared the Marquis de BEDMAR
and the marquis de GRIMALDO his firft minifters, and recalled
feveral noblemen, who, on various pretences, had been banifhed, during the late adminiftration. ALBERONI left SPAIN
about the middle of December, and retired to ITALY, where
he was fo perfecuted by the Pope, and even by PHILIP, that for
feveral years he was obliged to travel difguifed, and to conceal
the place of his refidence.

A FEW months after the retreat of ALBERONI, PHILIP,
though very unwillingly, acceded to the triple alliance, by which
he engaged himfelf to evacuate both SICILY and SARDINIA.
The Spanifh troops accordingly abandoned thofe two iflands the
enfuing fummer, the Emperor being put in poffeffion of SICILY,
and the Duke of SAVOY of SARDINIA. Soon after, a congrefs
was appointed to be held at CAMBRAY, to fettle all differences
among the contending parties, and treat of a final pacification.
While fome preliminary points were fettling, PHILIP fent the
Marquis de LEYDE, with a confiderable fleet and army, to the
relief of CEUTA, which had been befieged for 26 years by the
MOORS. The Spanifh troops, a few days after their arrival, totally routed and difperfed the MOORS, and made themfelves mafters of their entrenched camp, and all their artillery.

As the Duke of ORLEANS, fince the difgrace of ALBERONI,
had feemingly favoured the pretenfions of SPAIN, PHILIP the following

lowing year, at his folicitation, contracted a double alliance with the branches of the houfe of BOURBON in FRANCE. The Infanta of SPAIN, tho' then only three years of age, was fent to FRANCE as future queen to LEWIS XV. and two of the daughters of the Duke of ORLEANS arrived in SPAIN, to be married to the Prince of ASTURIAS and the Infant Don CARLOS. The fucceffion of this laft to the Dutchies of PARMA and TUSCANY feemed now to be the chief object of the court of SPAIN. This point and many others were to be fettled at CAMBRAY; but as the Emperor, who had no inclination to gratify the Spaniards, purpofely delayed the congrefs, PHILIP this year concluded a particular treaty with the court of GREAT BRITAIN, who having the *affiento*, or contract of fupplying the Spanifh colonies with negroes, renewed, agreed to re-ftore the fhips taken off SICILY.

NOTHING memorable happened in SPAIN during the two fol-lowing years; but in the beginning of the year after, 1724, PHILIP aftonifhed all EUROPE, by publicly abdicating his crown in favour of his eldeft fon Don LEWIS, Prince of ASTURIAS, who was then in the feventeenth year of his age. PHILIP himfelf, tho' he had not reached his fortieth year, had long been fick of regal grandeur. From a weaknefs of body and mind, the leaft application to bufi-nefs had for fome years given him a difguft; his mind was conti-nually filled with religious fcruples, which rendered him timorous and indecifive in every thing; and he falfely imagined that a fcep-tre was incompatible with a life of integrity.

THE Spaniards expreffed great joy upon the acceffion of LEWIS I. who was endeared to them, not only by being born among them, but by his generofity, affability, and many other virtues. The pu-blic joy, however, was foon turned into mourning, by the unexpec-ted death of the King, who died of the fmall-pox, univerfally re-greted, in the eighth month of his reign.

UPON the death of LEWIS, PHILIP was perfuaded to refume the reins of government, and the year following furprifed all the powers of EUROPE, by concluding a particular treaty with the Emperor, upon which the different princes recalled their pleni-potentiaries.

potentiaries from CAMBRAY, where they had trifled away three years merely in feasting and entertainments. By the treaty of VI-ENNA, which was with the utmost secrecy negotiated by the famous RIPERDA, PHILIP resigned all pretensions to NAPLES, SICILY, the LOW-COUNTRIES, and the MILANESE; CHARLES, on the other hand, renounced all claim to SPAIN and the INDIES, and besides, promised to grant the investiture of PARMA and TUSCANY to Don CARLOS. PHILIP soon after entered into an offensive and defensive alliance with the court of VIENNA; to counterbalance which, the courts of GREAT BRITAIN, FRANCE and PRUSSIA concluded a mutual alliance at HANOVER.

THE system of EUROPE by these treaties seemed again changed, especially as PHILIP was at this time greatly irritated against FRANCE, on account of their sending back the Infanta, and now connected himself most closely with the court of VIENNA. The bad understanding betwixt SPAIN and FRANCE was soon followed with a rupture betwixt that court and GREAT BRITAIN. RIPERDA, by concluding the treaty of VIENNA, rose so high in PHILIP's favour, that he was created a Duke and Grandee of SPAIN, and was entrusted with the departments of war, of the marine, the finances, and the INDIES. He enjoyed those honours and offices, however, only a few months; for the different regulations he proposed were so disgustful to the lazy Spaniards, that he was accused of mal-administration, and not only disgraced, but persecuted. To save himself, he took refuge in the house of Mr. STANHOPE, the English ambassador; but the court was so exasperated against him, that they took him from thence by force, and sent him prisoner to the castle of SEGOVIA. The ENGLISH Ambassador, in resentment for the breach of his privileges, protested against their violence, and left MADRID.

THE Emperor, who was offended with the opposition he had met with from GREAT BRITAIN, in establishing an East-India company at OSTEND, fomented the differences betwixt this court and SPAIN, and was so successful at MADRID, that the year following, 1727, in the end of February, the Spaniards laid siege to GI-

.4   BRALTAR.

BRALTAR. They foon found the enterprize, however, above their ftrength, and, after four months of open trenches, were obliged to retire with difgrace. The bifhop of FREJUS, afterwards fo well known by the name of Cardinal FLEURI, was at this time labouring to eftablifh a general pacification among the powers of EUROPE, and had prevailed on the Emperor and King of GREAT BRITAIN, and the States-General to agree with FRANCE in figning the preliminaries for a peace. The Spaniards, who wanted a fair pretence to withdraw from GIBRALTAR, foon after acceded to thefe preliminaries. A general congrefs being then appointed to be held at SOISSONS, PHILIP fent three plenipotentiaries thither, and foon after fent an ambaffador for the firft time to RUSSIA, who concluded a treaty of commerce between the two nations. As the negotiations at SOISSONS met with many interruptions, on account of the various claims of the different princes who had fent their plenipotentiaries thither, PHILIP, the following year, 1729, concluded a particular treaty at SEVILLE, with GREAT BRITAIN and FRANCE, to which the States-General afterwards acceded. By this treaty PHILIP promifed no longer to countenance the OSTEND-company; and the other powers, in return, engaged to guarantee the fucceffion of Don CARLOS to the dutchies of TUSCANY, PARMA, and PLACENTIA, and to affift in introducing 6900 Spaniards into thefe territories. The Emperor, who could not bear the thoughts of feeing Spanifh troops in ITALY, was greatly offended with this treaty, and endeavoured, by artifice, to render it ineffectual. Accordingly, two years after, when the fucceffion to PARMA and PLACENTIA opened to Don CARLOS by the death of the laft Duke of the Farnefe family, the Emperor's troops took poffeffion of feveral fortified places in thofe dukedoms, under pretence that the widow of the late Duke had been left with child by him. CHARLES however, feeing no way of fecuring thofe dutchies by negotiation, and being fenfible that the cheat would foon be detected, agreed at length to fuffer 6000 Spaniards to accompany Don CARLOS into ITALY, and alfo engaged to fupprefs the OSTEND-company, which had given fo much offence : GREAT BRITAIN, on the other hand, promifing to guarantee his dominions in ITALY. Soon after, an Englifh fleet joined that of SPAIN, and conducted the

Infant .

Infant Don CARLOS to LEGHORN, who quietly at length took poffeffion of PARMA, which had been deftined to him as his inhe-
ritance ever fince his birth.

THE fettlement of Don CARLOS being accomplifhed, the court
of SPAIN turned their views to the recovery of ORAN. An army
of 25,000 men was accordingly fent to AFRICA under the command of the Count de MONTEMAR, who totally defeated the
Moorifh army, and in lefs than a month made himfelf mafter of
the place, tho' it was defended by a garrifon of 10,000 men.

THE recovery of their African poffeffions was far from fatisfying
the ambition of the Spanifh court; who now eagerly embraced an
opportunity of breaking with the Emperor, and thereby extending
their dominions in ITALY. The throne of POLAND becoming vacant, by the death of the Elector of SAXONY, the greateft part of the
POLES elected STANISLAUS, who had formerly been their King;
but a few of the moft powerful chofe the new Elector of SAXONY,
and the fon of their late King. STANISLAUS was fupported by
his fon-in-law, LEWIS XV. of FRANCE, who, on this occafion,
entered into an offenfive and defenfive alliance with the Kings of
SPAIN and SARDINIA. The Emperor CHARLES, and the Czarina
zealoufly efpoufed the caufe of the other competitor.

THE war which enfued was very favourable to the Spaniards,
who, in one campaign, made an entire conqueft of the kingdom
of NAPLES. The year following, 1735, Don CARLOS completed
the conqueft of SICILY, and was crowned as King of the Two
SICILIES in PALERMO, the capital city of the ifland. The Emperor, in the mean time, being driven out of almoft all his poffeffions in LOMBARDY and TUSCANY, and being alfo unable to
oppofe the French armies on the RHINE, folicited the mediation of
the maritime powers, who by threatning to take part in the war,
prevailed on the contending parties to agree to a fufpenfion of arms
in the beginning of winter. As the Elector of SAXONY was by this
time fecurely fixed upon the throne of POLAND, and the interceffion
of the maritime powers cut off all hopes from the French and
Spaniards of enlarging their conquefts in ITALY and GERMANY,

3

they

they were obliged to continue the armiſtice, and to negotiate a peace.

THE preliminary articles of the treaty which were ſettled by the courts of VIENNA and PARIS, being publiſhed in the beginning of the year 1736, were far from being ſatisfactory to the court of SPAIN, becauſe, tho' they were allowed to keep NAPLES and SICILY, it was propoſed they ſhould reſtore PARMA and PLACENTIA to the Emperor, and renounce all claim to TUSCANY. The maritime powers, however, acquieſcing in the diſpoſition that had been made, SPAIN was obliged to ſubmit, and the year following upon the death of JOHN GASTON DE MEDICIS, the laſt male deſcendant of that illuſtrious family, the Spaniſh troops evacuated TUSCANY, which by the treaty then negotiating, was given to the Duke of LORRAIN and BAR, who in the beginning of the preceding year had married the Arch-Dutcheſs MARIA-THERESA, the heireſs of the family of AUSTRIA.

THE peace, which had been negotiating near three years, was at length concluded at VIENNA in the month of November 1738. By this treaty, PARMA and PLACENTIA were ceded in full propriety to the Emperor; and his ſon-in-law was declared Duke of TUSCANY; the Duke, in return, ceding his dutchies of BAR and LORRAIN, to the exiled King STANISLAUS, upon whoſe death they were to be annexed to the crown of FRANCE. The fiefs of the FORTONESE and VIGEVANCSA were detached from the MILANESE in favour of the King of SARDINIA, and Don CARLOS was left in poſſeſſion of the kingdoms of NAPLES and SICILY, with ſome places on the coaſt of TUSCANY.

THE treaty of VIENNA was hardly ratified, when SPAIN was threatened with a new war with GREAT BRITAIN, on account of the diſputes, which, for ſome time, had ſubſiſted between the two courts, about the freedom of commerce in AMERICA. The Britiſh court had, for ſome years, made loud complaints of the piracies and hoſtilities committed in the American ſeas, by the Spaniſh guarda-coſtas, who, on trifling and falſe pretences, ſeized

d   the

the Englifh fhips in their paffage to their own colonies, and not only made prize of them, but treated their crews with the greateft inhumanity. The court of SPAIN, on the other hand, alleged, that the Britifh merchants, in violation of folemn treaties, had, for many years, carried on a clandeftine trade with the Spanifh colonies in AMERICA, by which the commerce of SPAIN had been greatly prejudiced; that SPAIN was, therefore, greatly interefted in putting a ftop to fuch an illicit traffic, and that thofe who were feized in carrying it on could not juftly complain of any injury.

BOTH nations infifted loudly on the injuries they had received; but each evaded giving any fatisfaction as to thofe injuries which their refpective fubjects had committed. The Spaniards, indeed, amufed the Englifh with hopes of redrefs; they fent orders to their commanders in AMERICA to ceafe hoftilities; yet they connived at the breach of thofe orders; and returned evafive anfwers to all reprefentations that were made to them on that head. Their prefumption was not fo much owing to a confidence in their own ftrength, as to their opinion of the paffivenefs of the Britifh miniftry, and their knowledge of the violent contentions between the different parties in this ifland.

IT was certainly the intereft of both parties to avoid coming to extremities; but the Spaniards not acting with fincerity, even in their negotiations for a peaceable accommodation of all differences, and aiming by the famous convention concluded in the beginning of the following year, to quiet the complaints, without having the caufes of them fully difcuffed, the court of LONDON was at length provoked to iffue letters of reprizals againft the Spaniards, their veffels and effects. This ftep was foon followed by declarations of war at LONDON and MADRID, and both nations began hoftilities with great animofity. The Spaniards at firft made confiderable advantages by the capture of great numbers of Englifh fhips; but they were foon alarmed with the news of the lofs of PORTO BELLO, which was taken in the beginning of December 1739, by Admiral VERNON. About the fame time, they fuffered very confiderably by the ravages of the Barbary corfairs

8   on

on their coasts, and were threatened with the loss of their richest provinces in AMERICA, by a conspiracy formed by one CORDOVA, who pretended to be descended from the antient Incas of PERU. The conspiracy however was happily discovered before it took effect, and the author of it put to death.

THE following year the Spaniards sent a fleet of 18 ships of the line to the WEST-INDIES, with a design, as it was supposed, of attacking JAMAICA. The French likewise, though they still professed a neutrality, sent two squadrons to the American seas, to act defensively in favour of the Spaniards, being bound by treaty to guarantee their territories. The English, in the mean time, blind to their own internal strength, suffered themselves most absurdly to be alarmed with the rumour of an invasion from SPAIN, and neglected sending succours to Admiral VERNON, who had bombarded CARTHAGENA, and taken CHAGRE, a town on the river of that name, the head of which is but a few miles distant from PANAMA, on the South Sea.

ABOUT the same time, General OGLETHORPE, Governor of GEORGIA, attacked Fort ST. AUGUSTINE, the capital of Spanish FLORIDA; but, after lying some weeks before the place, he was obliged to withdraw, with loss. In the end of OCTOBER 1740, the English, at length, sent out a most powerful fleet, as a reinforcement to Admiral VERNON, who, the following year, in the month of March, invested CARTHAGENA by sea and land, with a fleet of 29 ships of the line, and an army of about 12,000 men. The Spaniards, however, by the dilatoriness of the English ministry, having had leisure to reinforce the garrison, and the season of the year being very unfavourable to troops in the field, the English, after a siege of some weeks, were obliged to retire, with the loss of several thousand men. The neglect of timeously supporting Admiral VERNON was very fortunate for SPAIN, for, if he had commanded but half that force the preceding year, when he made the first attack upon CARTHAGENA, he would, in all probability, have reduced that city as well as CHAGRE; and, as the passage from this last place to

d 2   PA-

PANAMA is but very fhort, the land troops might alfo have reduced that town, which would have enabled them to co-ope-
rate with Commodore ANSON, who had failed round CAPE-
HORN, and this year began to act offenfively againft the Spanifh
fettlements on the South Sea.

THE bad fuccefs of the Englifh arms in the WEST-INDIES
occafioned great joy in SPAIN; and PHILIP, as a reward for the
bravery of the Marquis de ESLABA, Governor of CARTHA-
GENA, promoted him to the rank of Captain-general, and created him Viceroy of PERU. PHILIP, fome months before, had
publifhed a memorial, claiming the fucceffion of the hereditary
dominions of his rival CHARLES VI. who had died at VIENNA
in the month of October, and was fucceeded by his eldeft daughter, MARIA THERESA, who took the title of Queen of HUN-
GARY. All that the Catholic King aimed at by this claim, was
the fecuring of LOMBARDY for his third fon, Don PHILIP,
which, he thought, would, at this time, be an eafy prize, as
the Queen of HUNGARY was unexpectedly attacked by the King
of PRUSSIA, and alfo by the Elector of BAVARIA, who was affifted
by the Kings of FRANCE and POLAND. However while the
fate of CARTHAGENA depended, the Spaniards made not the
leaft efforts againft their new enemy; but, upon receiving the
news of the repulfe of the Englifh, they affembled a body of
forces at BARCELONA, which failed for NAPLES in the month
of November, under the command of the Duke de MONTE-
MAR. Thofe troops were reinforced the following year 1742 from
SPAIN, and, being joined by the Neapolitans, formed an army
of about 60,000 men, MONTEMAR then advanced through the
ecclefiaftical ftate as far as the Bolognefe: but the King of SAR-
DINIA declaring for the Queen of HUNGARY, and joining the
Auftrian army, the Spaniards were obliged to retreat, in the end
of fummer, to the kingdom of NAPLES, where, foon after their
arrival, they loft their Neapolitan allies, Don CARLOS being
forced to agree to a neutrality, by an Englifh fquadron, which
threatened to bombard his capital. This was a great difap-
pointment to the Spaniards, for they depended upon being fuperior in ITALY before the end of the campaign, as Don PHI-
LIP,

LIP, after marching through FRANCE at the head of 30,000 men, had now entered SAVOY, and taken poffeffion of CHAMBERRY. PHILIP expected to conquer this dutchy, while the King of SARDINIA was oppofing MONTEMAR; but, to his great furprize, the Piedmontefe, who had left purfuing MONTEMAR, quickly attacked him, and obliged him to retreat to FRANCE.

THE Spaniards, notwithftanding the bad fuccefs of their arms, were ftill bent upon purfuing their ambitious views in ITALY, where they fupported their armies at a great expence for feveral campaigns, the detail of which is of no great importance. The Count de GAGES, and their other generals, inftead of having any profpect of making conquefts in that country, found themfelves every year obliged to ftruggle with new obftacles; and any flattering fucceffes they met with were more than counterbalanced by the advantages gained by their enemies. Their perfeverance in the unfuccefsful war in ITALY was chiefly owing to the Queen, who having gained a great afcendancy over her hufband, prevailed upon him to facrifice every thing to procure a fettlement for her fon PHILIP; and her views were feconded by the prime minifter, the Marquis ENSENADA, who having been firft raifed from an obfcure ftation, by the favour of the Count de GAGES, was very active and zealous in furnifhing him with fupplies, which, however, were feldom adequate to the neceffities of the army.

FORTUNATELY for SPAIN, the attention of the Englifh was alfo drawn off to an unnational object, which exhaufted their revenues, and prevented them from profecuting the war in AMERICA with any vigour. King GEORGE, who had efpoufed the caufe of the Queen of HUNGARY, not only affifted her by large fubfidies, but moft imprudently tranfported his troops to FLANDERS, and maintained a large army on the continent, at an immenfe expence, while naval armaments were almoft wholly neglected. Becaufe one enterprize in AMERICA had proved unfuccefsful, the Englifh feemed to conclude, that it would be in vain to hope for fuccefs in any other. Admiral VERNON, after his return from CARTHAGENA, made a defcent upon CUBA near ST. JAGO; but the troops.

troops, inftead of attacking that place, were fuffered to remain feveral months inactive in their camp, where the greateft part of
them were cut off by fickness.

In the beginning of this year, a fmall reinforcement arriving at JAMAICA, Admiral VERNON again failed for PORTO
BELLO, General WENTWORTH, who commanded the land troops,
propofing to crofs the ifthmus, and attack PANAMA: but when
they arrived at the Spanifh coaft, it was agreed, that the enterprize was impracticable. They accordingly failed back to JA-
MAICA, and in the end of the year returned to ENGLAND. The
Spaniards at St. AUGUSTINE in the mean time had made an attempt
upon GEORGIA, with two frigates and 30 other veffels, on board
of which were 3000 land-forces: but General OGLETHORPE
quickly obliged them to retire.

THE following year, 1743, the Spaniards were fo intent upon
fupporting their arms in ITALY, that they wholly omitted profecuting the war againft ENGLAND, unlefs by their privateers,
who made a great many prizes both in EUROPE and AMERICA.
The affairs of the empire in the mean time chiefly engroffed the
attention of the Englifh, who marched into GERMANY under the
command of the Earl of STAIR; and after King GEORGE had
joined them, defeated the French at DETTINGEN on the 27th of
June. One of their fquadrons, under the command of Commodore KNOWLES, made an attack upon LA GUIRA and PORTO CA-
VALLO, two fortreffes on the north coaft of SOUTH-AMERICA;
but were repulfed by the Spaniards with confiderable lofs.

THE Spaniards were chiefly annoyed by the Englifh fquadron
in the Mediterranean under Admiral MATTHEWS, who greatly
difturbed their trade, and rendered it extremely difficult for them
to fend fupplies to their armies in ITALY. The following year,
on the 11th of February, that admiral attacked the Spanifh and
French fleets united off TOULON; this engagement was prevented
from becoming general, by the French declining to come into the
line, on one hand, and the backwardnefs of admiral LESTOCK on
the other; but the Spanifh fhips that engaged were defeated by
                                                            the

the Englifh. The Spanifh fleet might have been attacked three days after, at a great difadvantage; but a bad underftanding that fubfifted between the Englifh admirals prevented them from improving the favourable opportunity.

FROM this time nothing very memorable happened relative to the affairs of SPAIN, till the 11th of July, 1746, when PHILIP died at MADRID, in the 63d year of his age, and was fucceeded by the only furviving fon of his firft marriage Don FERDINAND. By his fecond Queen ELIZABETH of FARNESE, who is ftill alive, PHILIP left three fons, Don CARLOS, then King of the Two SICILIES. Don PHILIP at prefent Duke of PARMA and PLACENTIA, and Don LEWIS, who was created archbifhop of TOLEDO when an infant, but fince has refigned that benefice, and obtained leave to quit the church. Three daughters by the fame Queen likewife furvived him, MARIA ANNA VICTORIA, at prefent Queen of PORTUGAL; MARIA THERESA, married the year before to Dauphin; and MARIA ANTONIETTA; MARIA THERESA the Dauphinefs died in child-bed, a few days after her father.

FERDINAND VI. who was about 33 years of age, when he afcended the throne, began his reign with feveral acts of popularity. Among others, he affigned two days in the week to receive in perfon the petitions and remonftrances of his fubjects. He appointed the famous Don JOSEPH DE CARVAJAL Y LANCASTRE his firft minifter, and foon after publifhed an edict, declaring, that he would fulfil the engagements of his predeceffors with his allies. It might rather have been expected at this time, that an alteration would have taken place in the fyftem of the court of SPAIN; for the war in ITALY, which for five years had been very burthenfome, and was plainly an unnational object, was now very unfuccefsful; and the war with GREAT BRITAIN feemed to have no other confequence but to interrupt the Spanifh commerce, and to heighten the price of Englifh commodities in SPAIN, where they are always much wanted. The Spaniards, this campaign, had been twice defeated in LOMBARDY, with the lofs of upwards of 20,000 men killed and prifoners, and had been forced by the Auftrians to abandon ITALY, and retire into PROVENCE.

FER-

FERDINAND, however, ftill continued the war, and imputing the difgrace of his arms to the mifconduct of the Count de GAGES, recalled him, and gave the command to the Marquis de las MINAS. In the end of the year, indeed, he allowed the chamber of com- merce to enter into a private treaty with the Englifh South-Sea company, for fupplying the Spanifh AMERICA with negroes; but he could not be prevailed upon by the King of PORTUGAL to agree to a feparate peace with GREAT BRITAIN. His allies the French, however, fuffering greatly the following year, 1747, by the deftruction of their fleets, the ruin of their commerce, and a general famine, which induced them to folicit a congrefs, he alfo gave his confent for a peace, as it was vain to expect to continue the war with any fuccefs, either in ITALY or againft GREAT BRI- TAIN, after the French had laid down their arms.

WHETHER this was agreeable to the Queen Dowager is uncer- tain; but as fhe had for feveral years interfered in the direction of ftate-affairs, in behalf of her children, to the great prejudice of the kingdom, and had treated him, when Prince of ASTURIAS, in a difrefpectful manner, and on many occafions very defpitefully, FERDINAND now ordered her to leave MADRID, and to refide ei- ther at TOLEDO, or VALLADOLID, or BURGOS, or SARAGOÇA; and he alfo gave orders, that her fon Don LEWIS fhould retire to his diocefe.

SOON after, the plenipotentiaries began to affemble at AIX LA CHAPELLE, the place appointed for the congrefs; and the fol- lowing year, after they had agreed upon the preliminary articles, a ceffation of hoftilities was publifhed in the month of May. The definitive treaty was concluded on the 7th of October, and con- tained twenty-four articles, of which the treaties of WESTPHALIA, MADRID, NIMEGUEN, RYSWICK, UTRECHT, BADEN, LONDON and VIENNA were declared the bafis. By this treaty the Queen of HUNGARY ceded to the Infant Don PHILIP the duchies of PARMA, PLACENTIA, and GUASTALLA; but with this referve, that if PHILIP fhould die without male iffue, or he or his pofte- rity fhould fucceed to the throne of SPAIN or SICILY, thofe du- chies fhould revert to the houfe of AUSTRIA. As the King of

SAR-

SARDINIA had some pretensions to PLACENTIA and the PLA-CENTINE, his cession was likewise necessary, which he gave in the amplest manner; on this condition, however, that the territory should again revert to him, if PHILIP should die without male issue, or his brother Don CARLOS succeed to the crown of SPAIN. At this day, therefore, the treaty is plainly violated by PHILIP, in regard to the King of SARDINIA, tho' not in regard to the Empress Queen; for though Don PHILIP has not succeeded to the throne of NAPLES, yet Don CARLOS has succeeded to the throne of SPAIN. Thus the foundation of a new war is already laid in ITALY, as it is not to be expected, that the King of SARDINIA will without expressing his resentment suffer himself to be robbed of his right; and perhaps the Empress Queen will also look upon herself as injured, as the clause of reversion of those duchies was the same, in the preliminary articles, in regard to AUSTRIA as SARDINIA. By other articles of the definitive treaty, the King of SARDINIA, the Republic of GENOA, and the Duke of MODENA were reinstated in their former possessions; and the assiento, or contract for negroes with the English merchants, was granted for four years, as an equivalent for the same number of years which had been interrupted by the war.

BUT not the least mention was made in the treaty of the right claimed by the Spanish guarda-costas, of searching foreign ships that approach their American colonies, nor of their privilege of fishing on the banks of NEWFOUNDLAND, nor of their exclusive right to the Bay of CAMPEACHY, where the English had formed settlements before the year 1670. These disputed points, which had too precipitately hurried the Spanish and British nations into a war, were now referred, with some others of less consequence, to be settled amicably by commissaries. If the national interest on both sides had been equitably consulted, the differences might easily have been adjusted in that manner before the war; but each nation, from narrow views, had wanted solely to engross certain advantages, which it claimed as peculiar to itself, tho' a mutual communication of them would have been no detriment to either.

THE

THE peace of AIX-LA-CHAPELLE feemed to have reftored tranquillity to EUROPE : FERDINAND, neverthelefs, ftill kept up all his land-forces, and gave orders for augmenting his marine with the utmoft diligence. The Marquis de ENSENADA, who was now prime-minifter, being fenfible of the great prejudice the Spanifh commerce fuftained by the clandeftine trade carried on by foreigners with their colonies, gave orders for guarding the American coafts more ftrictly than ever. Thefe orders being obeyed with the utmoft vigilance, were not only difagreeable to the trading nations of EUROPE, but to the Spanifh colonifts themfelves, who, the following year, rofe in arms in the province of CARACCAS, obliged the Spanifh troops to retire into the fort of LA GUIRA, and declared for a freedom of commerce. Upon the news of this infurrection 1500 men were embarked at CADIZ, who, upon their arrival at AMERICA, were fo fuccefsful as to quell the rebellion.

FERDINAND, in the mean time, applied his chief attention to regulate the internal policy of his kingdom, and infpire his fubjects with a fpirit of induftry. He particularly aimed at promoting and encouraging agriculture, the trueft fource of the riches of a ftate poffeffing an extenfive territory ; he granted charters for eftablifhing manufactures of fine woollen cloth, and gave great encouragement to fome Englifh fhip-carpenters and weavers, who had been tempted to go and fettle in SPAIN ; he ordered no lefs than 20,000 vagrants to be apprehended in the different provinces, and to be employed in tillage and country improvements; and in the end of fummer, he opened the communication between the two CASTILES, by a fine road, forty-fix miles in length, on which were no lefs than 283 aqueducts, and 7 bridges of fine architecture, the whole being begun and finifhed in five months, under the direction of the Marquis de ENSENADA. The King was enabled to profecute his defigns by the immenfe wealth which at this time poured into SPAIN ; for as the Englifh, towards the end of the war, had acted with great vigour at fea, the colonifts waited for a peace, before they would embark their treafure for EUROPE, and it now arrived to a great amount, and likewife during the two following years.

THE

THE Spanish and British commissaries, in the mean time, were employed in negotiating the disputed points betwixt the two courts, which were at length finally settled by a treaty concluded at MADRID on the 5th of October 1750. By this treaty the King of GREAT BRITAIN gave up his claim to the four remaining years of the assiento-contract, and to all debts the King of SPAIN owed to the English company on that account, for an equivalent of 100,000 l. sterl. His Catholic Majesty engaged to require from British subjects trading in his ports, no higher duties than they paid in the time of CHARLES II. of SPAIN, and to allow the same subjects to take salt on the island of TORTUGA. All former treaties were confirmed, and the two princes promised to abolish all innovations that appeared to have been introduced into the reciprocal commerce of both nations. These innovations, however, not being specified, it was the same thing as if no mention had been made of them at all. Thus the most material differences being suffered to remain undecided, most unhappily gave rise to another war; whereas, if the controverted claims had been clearly and candidly discussed, and the differences settled by a friendly communication of mutual advantages, which no ways excluded precision and distinctness as to the extent of those advantages, the two nations might have lived in amity without interruption, and thereby promoted each other's prosperity. Tho' gold be the idol of traders, yet it is far from always contributing to render a state flourishing and happy; and if the English merchants shall violate treaties in search of it, it would be more for the honour and interest of this nation to punish the offenders, than to enter into a new war in their defence.

THE remaining years of FERDINAND's reign, after the signing of the treaty of MADRID, were very barren of events. The English court were jealous of his attempts to introduce the woolen manufacture in SPAIN, and reclaimed their workmen in that branch, who had passed over thither. New disputes likewise arose betwixt them, on account of the English trafficking with the Indians of the Moskito-shore, who had never submitted to SPAIN, and claimed to act as a free nation. FERDINAND, at the same time, had the mortification to find it impossible to introduce a spirit of industry among his subjects, the favours and encouragements of the court

e 2 being

being like rain falling upon a fandy defart, where there was not a feed or plant to be enlivened by it: In the year 1754, the marquis de ENSENADA was unexpectedly difgraced, and the department of the INDIES, one of the places he enjoyed, was conferred on Don RICHARD WALL, fecretary of ftate for foreign affairs, who had lately returned from an embaffy in ENGLAND. About two years after, a war breaking out betwixt GREAT BRITAIN and FRANCE, FERDINAND declared, on that occafion, that he would adhere to the ftricteft neutrality; but he was far from obferving the neutrality he profeffed, and partially favoured FRANCE in a great number of inftances.

HIS queen dying in the end of the year 1758, he was fo affected with grief, that he entirely abandoned himfelf to gloom and melancholy; and neglecting both exercife and food, threw himfelf into a dangerous diftemper, which, after preying upon him for feveral months, put a period to his life the year following, on the 10th of AUGUST. As FERDINAND left no iffue, he was fucceeded by his brother, Don CARLOS, King of the TWO SICILIES, who refigned that kingdom, and disjoined it from the monarchy of SPAIN by a folemn deed, in favour of his third fon, Don FERDINAND; fetting afide his eldeft fon on account of his weaknefs of mind or idiocy, and referving his fecond fon for the fucceffion of SPAIN. Don CARLOS, or CHARLES, arrived in SPAIN in the month of NOVEMBER, and foon after entered MADRID in great pomp and ceremony.

IT would neither be prudent nor decent in me to enlarge on the tranfactions of the prefent reign, thofe particularly relating to GREAT-BRITAIN, which are recent in every one's memory. I fhall only obferve, that whoever will perufe the letters lately laid before the parliament, relating to SPAIN, will plainly perceive the candour of the court of GREAT-BRITAIN, and the ability of her minifters; and that the SPANIARDS artfully, and with the greateft injuftice, fought a rupture, for which they have fince paid very dear, by being obliged to defift from their pretenfions to a fifhery at NEWFOUNDLAND, and likewife to cede to us all FLORIDA, and to allow us to cut logwood in the Bay of CAMPEACHY.

An

An account of the Ambaſſadors, Miniſters, and Envoys, from the Court of GREAT-BRITAIN *to the Court of* SPAIN, *from the year* 1600 *to the breaking out of the preſent war, with the titles of the Treaties and Conventions during that period. The treaties prior to that, may be found in the* Corps Diplomat. *tom.* IV.

Kings of GREAT-BRITAIN and SPAIN.	Ambaſſadors.	Treaties; years.	Where ſigned, and by whom.
JAMES I. PHILIP III.	Earl of NOTTINGHAM and Sir CHARLES CORNWALLIS, the latter left ambaſſador, 1605.	Auguſt, 1604.	LONDON. Earl of DORSET, VELASCO, &c.
	Sir JOHN DIGBY, ambaſſador, 1618. See *Ruſhworth*.		
	Sir WALTER ASTON, 1620.		
	Lord DIGBY, ambaſſador extraordinary, 1621.		
	Prince CHARLES, Duke of BUCKINGHAM, Earl of BRISTOL, employed in negotiating the Spaniſh match, which had been then ſeven years in agitation. N. B. *See an account of this match at the end of this liſt.*	April, 1622.	
PHILIP IV.	Sir WALTER ASTON, ambaſſador, 1623.	Concerning the Palatinate, 1623.	

Kings

Kings of GREAT-BRITAIN and SPAIN.	Ambassadors.	Treaties; years.	Where signed, and by whom.
CHARLES I. of GR. BRITAIN.	Sir FRAN. COT-TINGTON, ambassador.	November, 1630.	MADRID. COTTINGTON. COLONA, DE ROSAS, PHILIP.
	Mr. FANSHAW, resident.	1643. Cedulas granted to ENGLAND, March 1645. See the *British Merchant*, v. iii.	
The Protector.	Mr. ASCHAM, envoy, killed in his lodgings at MADRID, by some English cavaliers.	May, 1653.	
CHARLES II. of GR. BRITAIN, during his exile.		A leagúe, 1657 *.	
	Lord CLAREN-DON. Lord COTTING-TON †.		
CHARLES II. of GR. BRITAIN, restored.	Sir RICHARD FANSHAW, 1662‡.		

* This was a league made between CHARLES II. of ENGLAND, and the Archduke LEOPOLD, Governor of the LOW COUNTRIES, which gave King CHARLES liberty to reside at BRUSSELS, with the promise of 6000 men, 6000 livres pension, and 3000 to the Duke of YORK. An amazing treaty to be made by a poor and banished Monarch.

† They stayed two years, but effected nothing; and were at last sent away, lest they should see the pictures which formerly belonged to CHARLES I. of ENGLAND, and had been bought by the Spanish ambassador.

‡ He died at MADRID, 1666. The letters and papers relating to his embassy were printed in octavo, LONDON, 1702.

Kings of GREAT-BRITAIN and SPAIN.	Ambassadors.	Treaties; years.	Where signed, and by whom.
CHARLES II. of SPAIN.	Earl of SAND-WICH, 1665.	Treaty of May 23, 1667 *.	MADRID. SANDWICH. NIDHARD. D'ONATA. PENNERANDA.
	Sir WILLIAM GODOLPHIN, ambassador in 1668 †.	Treaty of July 8, 1670. ‡	MADRID. PENNERANDA. GODOLPHIN.
		League of 1680.	WINDSOR. D. PEDRO DE RONQUILLO. SUNDERLAND. Lord HYDE. JENKINS. GODOLPHIN.
JAMES II. of GR. BRITAIN.	None.		
WILLIAM III. of GREAT-BRITAIN.	Count SCHONEN-BERGH, minister from GREAT-BRITAIN and the STATES GENERAL, 1699. §		

Kings

* This treaty was contrived by Sir WILLIAM GODOLPHIN, then secretary of the embassy, and has been the basis of all the treaties since.

† This gentleman continued at MADRID many years after his embassy expired, and died there in 1696, leaving an estate of 80,000 pounds sterling. The heirs were cheated out of the greatest part of it, which went to found the church of St. George in MADRID. See *Cole's Memoirs*, p. 20. He died a Roman Catholic. During the Popish plot, the house of Commons addressed the King to recal him, as he was accused by OATES of being concerned in that plot; but he did not chuse to venture himself home.

‡ This is the American treaty, and the only one we have for settling disputes there. It chiefly relates to the freedom of our navigation to the Spanish West India-Main; but is not confirmed by the treaty of 1750. That point remains still unsettled.

§ His name was BELMONT: he had been agent for the Prince of ORANGE before the Revolution, and was by no means acceptable to that court. From a letter

Kings of GREAT-BRITAIN and SPAIN.	Ambaſſadors.	Treaties; years.	Where ſigned, and by whom.
	ALEXANDER STANHOPE, envoy, 1699. *		
Queen ANNE of GR. BRITAIN. CHARLES and PHILIP, contenders for the crown of SPAIN.	Earl of PETER-BOROUGH, ambaſſador extraordinary, 1706. General STANHOPE, envoy extraordinary, 1706. Both to King CHARLES of SPAIN. †		

Kings

ter of his, to the Earl of MANCHESTER, dated September 23, 1700, in which he mentions a memorial he gave to the Spaniſh miniſters, both in the name of the King his maſter, and of the States, I conclude that he acted as Engliſh miniſter after Mr. STANHOPE left MADRID.

* He was ten years in SPAIN in a private character; but was ſoon recalled from his public one, becauſe the court of GREAT-BRITAIN had deſired the Spaniſh ambaſſador, the Marquis de CANALES, to leave LONDON, on account of an inſolent memorial delivered to the Lords Juſtices, September, 1699.

† General STANHOPE, taking advantage of the broken ſtate of King CHARLES's affairs, concluded with the Count d'OROPEZA, Prince LICHTENSTEIN, and the Count de CORDOVA, Admiral of ARRAGON, his plenipotentiaries, a treaty of commerce, which, had that Prince gained poſſeſſion of the crown of SPAIN, would ſoon have indemnified ENGLAND for the expence we were at on his account. The ſubſtance of the treaty was,

1. A ſincere peace between the two crowns. 2. All treaties of friendſhip and commerce renewed, and all royal cedulas and privileges formerly granted, particularly thoſe of PHILIP IV. confirmed by the treaty of May, 1667. 3. All priſoners on both ſides ſhall be ſet at liberty, without ranſom. 4. All merchandize brought into SPAIN by the ſubjects of GREAT BRITAIN, for which cuſtom, under the name of conſumption, or other tolls, are uſually demanded, ſhall not pay ſuch toll till ſix months after unlading, or ſale and delivery. 5. The ſubjects of GREAT BRITAIN may bring into SPAIN the produce of the dominions of MOROCCO, and ſhall not pay greater duties than uſual. 6. Books of rates, containing an exact account of the cuſtoms agreed on, by the commiſſioners from the Queen of GREAT BRITAIN and the King of SPAIN, ſhall be adjuſted and eſtabliſhed within a year after the ſigning of this treaty, and be publiſhed thro' all the Spaniſh dominions; nor ſhall the Britiſh ſubjects be obliged to pay greater duties than what is therein ſet down; and for all other goods not mentioned in thoſe tables, the rate of 7 per
cent.

Kings of GREAT BRITAIN and SPAIN.	Ambaſſadors.	Treaties; years.	Where ſigned, and by whom.
Queen ANNE of GREAT BRITAIN. CHARLES and PHILIP, contenders for the crown of SPAIN.	Mr. WALPOLE, in 1707, brought from SPAIN a treaty of commerce, probably that above mentioned. *Cole's Mem.* p. 472.		

Kings

cent. ſhall be demanded on the credit of the inſtrument, declaring the charge and prices of the merchandize and goods, which ſhall be exhibited by the merchant or factor, confirmed by witneſſes on oath. 7. All prize goods, taken by the Queen's ſhips of war, or privateers, ſhall be eſteemed as goods the produce of GREAT BRITAIN. 8. The Queen of GREAT BRITAIN and the King of SPAIN ſhall ratify theſe articles within ten weeks.

To this treaty was annexed a ſecret article, whereby it was agreed, that a company of commerce to the INDIES ſhould be formed, conſiſting of the ſubjects of GREAT BRITAIN and SPAIN, in the dominions of the crown of SPAIN in the INDIES. The forming of this company was reſerved till his Catholick Majeſty ſhould be in poſſeſſion of the crown of SPAIN: but, in caſe unforeſeen accidents ſhould prevent the forming ſuch company, his Catholic Majeſty obliged himſelf and ſucceſſors to grant to the Britiſh ſubjects the ſame privileges and liberty of a free trade to the INDIES, which the Spaniſh ſubjects enjoyed, a previous ſecurity being given for the payment of the royal duties. His Catholic Majeſty likewiſe obliged himſelf, that from the day of the general peace, to the day the ſaid company of commerce ſhould be formed, he would give licence to the Britiſh ſubjects to ſend to the INDIES annually ten ſhips, of 300 tons each, provided that they pay all the royal duties, and be regiſtered in ſuch port of SPAIN as his Catholic Majeſty ſhould appoint; and give ſecurity to return from the INDIES to the ſame port of SPAIN, without touching elſewhere. That his Catholic Majeſty would likewiſe permit the ſaid ten ſhips of trade to be conveyed by Britiſh ſhips of war, provided the ſaid ſhips of war do not trade: And that he would not demand any *indulto* or donative on account of the ſaid trade, contenting himſelf with the royal duties only. And the Queen of GREAT BRITAIN promiſed, that the ſaid ſhips of war ſhould, in going to, and returning from the INDIES, convoy the ſhips of his Catholic Majeſty: And his Catholic Majeſty engaged never to permit the ſubjects of FRANCE to be concerned in the ſaid company of commerce, nor in any wiſe to trade to the INDIES.

After the ſigning of this treaty, King CHARLES was made ſenſible, that the conceſſions granted therein to the Engliſh were ſuch as would not eaſily paſs with his own ſubjects, ſhould he ever be poſſeſſed of the SPANISH throne; and therefore it was not without reluctance, and merely in compliance with the neceſſity of his affairs, that he ratified the articles of it, on the 9th of January 1708, ſix months after

f   ic

Kings of GREAT BRITAIN and SPAIN.	Ambaſſadors.	Treaties; years.	Where ſigned, and by whom.
Queen ANNE of GREAT BRITAIN. CHARLES and PHILIP, contenders for the crown of SPAIN.	Mr. CRAGGS, ſecretary in SPAIN in 1708. *Id.* p. 544.		
	Duke of ARGYLE, ambaſſador, plenipotentiary and general in SPAIN, 1710.		
	Lord LEXINGTON arrived at MADRID, 1712, to take PHILIP's renounciation of the ſucceſſion of FRANCE.	Convention, March 1713.	MADRID. LEXINGTON, BEDMAR.
(		Aſſiento, 1713*.	MADRID. LEXINGTON, ESCALERA.
		General Pacification, July 1713†.	UTRECHT. J. BRISTOL, Duke D'OSSUNA. MONTELEON.

it was ſigned. The perſon who was entruſted to carry this treaty to LONDON having embarked at BARCELONA, on board a ſmall veſſel for GENOA, was unluckily taken by a French frigate: the expreſs, as is uſual in ſuch caſes, threw his diſpatches over-board; but they were taken up by ſome divers, and tranſmitted to the Marquis de TORCY at VERSAILLES, who took care to ſend privately a copy of the treaty to the States General, in order to excite their jealouſy of the Engliſh, who were endeavouring, by that tranſaction, to engroſs the trade to the WEST INDIES. See *Tindal's Continuation of Rapin*, Vol. 4. B. 26.

   * This contract (for *Aſſiento* in Spaniſh ſignifies a contract) was to commence May 1713, and end in 1743. It was a ſource of iniquity, and a depoſit in the hands of the Spaniards for our good conduct, to ſeize on at pleaſure.

   † By this treaty King PHILIP yielded *for ever* to GREAT BRITAIN, GIBRALTAR and MINORCA.

Kings of GREAT BRITAIN and SPAIN.	Ambaſſadors.	Treaties; years.	Where ſigned, and by whom.
GEORGE I. of GREAT BRITAIN. PHILIP V. of SPAIN.	BENSON, lord BINGLEY, ambaſſador, 1713.		
	Sir PAUL METHUEN, October 1714.		
	Mr. CRAGGS, Mr. BUBB, miniſters, December 1715.	Treaty, December 1715 ‡.	MADRID. BEDMAR, GEORGE BUBB.
		Convention for explaining the Aſſiento, May 1716.	MADRID. BEDMAR, GEORGE BUBB.
	JOHN CHETWYND, envoy extraordinary, 1717.		
	WILL. STANHOPE, envoy, 1718.	Treaty of 1718.	HAGUE. Lord CADOGAN. Marquis de PRIE.
	Colonel STANHOPE, miniſter, 1720.	Treaty, June 1721 *.	MADRID. STANHOPE. GRIMALDI.

‡ This treaty is very ſhort, contains little new, confirms the former, but revokes the three articles ſo injurious to GREAT BRITAIN, which were tacked to the treaty of UTRECHT, and called *explanatory*. Theſe were the III. V. and VIII.

† This ſettled the reſtitution of the ſhips taken by lord TORRINGTON and Sir GEORGE WALTON in 1718. The Spaniards are perpetually objecting to us, the injuſtice and illegality of that meaſure of attacking their fleet in the time of profound peace, and without any declaration of war; but thoſe who will take the trouble to peruſe CORBET's account of that matter, will find that Sir GEORGE BING ſent an officer to the Spaniſh miniſter, to acquaint him with the deſign and deſtination of his fleet; and that the miniſter ſent him word back, that he might go and execute whatever commiſſion the king his maſter had given him. See alſo, for the ſame purpoſe, *the memoirs of the Marquis* ST. PHILIP.

Kings

Kings of GREAT BRITAIN and SPAIN.	Ambaſſadors.	Treaties; years.	Where ſigned, and by whom.
	BENJ. KEENE, eſq; (afterwards Sir BENJAM. KEENE, knight of the BATH) was appointed his Majeſty's conſul at MADRID, March 1724.		
	He was appointed his Majeſty's miniſter plenipotentiary to the King of SPAIN, Aug. 1727.		
GEORGE II. PHILIP V. ℂ	BEN. KEENE, A. STURT, Jos. GODDARD, commiſſaries.	Convention, May 1728.	PARDO. STANHOPE, KEENE, M. de la PAZ, D. J. PATINHO.
	Col. STANHOPE, Lord HARRINGTON.	Treaties of 1729 and 1731 *.	SEVILLE. STANHOPE.
		Treaty of 1731.	VIENNA. Duke of LIRIA. Sir THOMAS ROBINSON.
	BEN. KEENE, envoy, 1733.		
	He was appointed his Majeſty's envoy extraordinary to the King of PORTUGAL, May 1745.		

* Theſe two treaties related to the neutral garriſons in ITALY, and were owing to our being tired of the congreſs at SOISSONS. The quadruple alliance ſtipulated, that *Swiſs*, and not *Spaniſh* troops, ſhould be ſent into ITALY, to maintain Don CARLOS; but the treaties of SEVILLE changed it for Spaniſh, and not Swiſs troops. That is to ſay, the court of SPAIN carried its point.

Kings of GREAT BRITAIN, and SPAIN.	Ambaſſadors.	Treaties; years.	Where ſigned, and by whom.
	He was appointed his Majeſty's ambaſſador extraordinary and plenipotentiary to the King of SPAIN, October 1748.		
	WILL. FINCH, brother to the Earl of WINCHELSEA, envoy extraordinary, 1732.		
		Convention of 1739 *.	PARDO. M. de VILLARIAS. Sir BEN. KEENE.
FERDINAND VI. of SPAIN.		Treaty of 1748 †.	AIX LA CHAPELLE.
		Treaty of 1750 ‡.	MADRID. FERD. ENSENADA. Sir BEN. KEENE.
	Sir B. KEENE died.		

* The Aſſiento ſuſpended at this time. The balance between ENGLAND and SPAIN was 96,000 pounds; but the ſecret article took away 36,000 pounds. The difference could not be adjuſted, and the war broke out.

† By the tenth article of the preliminaries, and the XVI. of this treaty, ENGLAND was to be paid 100,000 pounds reimburſement, and the right to the remaining four years of the Aſſiento was ſettled; but it was afterwards ſold by a convention, and occaſioned the treaty of 1750.

‡ In this the 100,000 pounds were again ſettled and agreed on, the *explanatory* articles of the treaty of UTRECHT again aboliſhed, and the Aſſiento and the annual ſhip given up. All former treaties confirmed.

Kings of GREAT BRITAIN and SPAIN.	Ambassadors.	Treaties; years.	Where signed, and by whom.
CHARLES III. of SPAIN. GEORGE II. and GEORGE III. of GREAT BRITAIN.	His Excellency the right honourable GEORGE WILLIAM, earl of BRISTOL, ambassador extraordinary, and minister plenipotentiary from his BRITANIC Majesty to the court of MADRID †.		

✿✿✿✿✿✿✿✿✿✿✿✿✿✿✿✿✿✿✿✿✿✿✿✿✿✿✿✿✿✿✿✿✿✿✿✿

An ACCOUNT *of the* SPANISH MATCH.

HERE it may not be improper to give a short account of that strange affair, the *Spanish* Match; because the court of SPAIN hath been frequently charged with the breaking off that matter; but in the following relation, extracted from Mr. *Howell's Letters,* who was upon the spot at that time, it will appear probable that the fault lay on the other side, and not at PHILIP's, but King JAMES's door.

In December 1622, Lord DIGBY and Sir WALTER ASTON went out joint ambassadors under the great seal of ENGLAND, especially commissioned about the *Spanish Match;* Mr. HOWELL, afterwards clerk of the council, soon followed their Excellencies; Mr. GEORGE GAGE came likewise from ROME to MADRID, to treat about it. The match was first set on foot by the Duke of LERMA, but was not so warmly adopted by his successor the Count d'OLIVAREZ. GONDOMAR at this time left ENGLAND,

† He arrived there, September 8th, 1758, and left that court, December 17th, 1761, without taking leave, because his Catholic Majesty did not chuse to give an explicit answer to the court of GREAT BRITAIN, but only said, *Muy bien esta,* (*Very well, Sir*) on which the rupture ensued.

re-

returned to MADRID, and brought with him Lord DIGBY's patent, that made him Earl of BRISTOL. The bufinefs of the match went on very brifkly for near four months, when, to the furprize of the Earl of BRISTOL, who knew nothing of the matter and of every one elfe at MADRID, the Prince of WALES, and the Marquis of BUCKINGHAM, arrived on the latter end of March 1622, at the Earl of BRISTOL's houfe, late in the evening. The Prince went by the feigned name of THOMAS SMITH, and the Marquis by that of Mr. JOHN SMITH.——They were attended by the Lords CARLISLE, HOLLAND, ROCHFORT, DENBIGH, the Knights Sir FRANCIS COTTINGTON, Sir LEWIS DIVES, Sir JOHN VAUGHAN of the GOLDEN GROVE, and his fon, comptroller to the Prince, Sir EDMUND VARNEY, Mr. WASHINGTON page to the Prince, Mr. PORTER, and others.

THE arrival of the Prince of WALES in MADRID was like the reft of his father's politics, and inftead of forwarding the match, marred the whole bufinefs. The Spaniards having fuch a pledge in their hands, rofe in their demands, and thought they had it in their power to *treat* juft as they pleafed. Befides this, the Spanifh court took a difguft at BUCKINGHAM, and he and the Earl of BRISTOL difagreed extremely about the conduct of that bufinefs. The nobility in SPAIN were very much averfe to this alliance; the Bifhop of SEGOVIA wrote againft it, but was banifhed from court for fo doing; the common people in SPAIN were ftrongly for it. In ENGLAND, the parliament and commons would never confent to it.

Upon the arrival of the Prince, the court of SPAIN fent back the difpenfation to the court of ROME, in order to be better modelled. When the difpenfation was returned to MADRID, it came back clogged with new claufes: the Pope required a caution to be given for the performance of the articles: this made a difficulty: the King of SPAIN, however, offered to give the caution, but defired to confult his divines upon it, who, after a tedious debate, gave his Majefty permiffion. Upon this, the King of SPAIN and the Prince mutually fwore to, and ratified the articles of marriage; and the 8th of September following, 1623, was fixed for the betrothing her to him. But foon after, *Pope Gregory*, who was a friend to the match, died, and *Urban* fucceeded; whereupon PHILIP declared, he could not proceed in the match unlefs the new Pope confirmed the difpenfation which was given by the former. This created fresh delays; the Prince remonftrated warmly, and infifted on the neceffity of his departure. The King of SPAIN confented to his going, provided he would leave him and Don CARLOS *proxies* for the match: this was accordingly agreed on: and thus the Prince, after feven months ftay, and a fruitlefs errand, fet out for ENGLAND in the month of Auguft 1623, without his Infanta. The Lord RUTLAND waited for him at fea with the fleet, on board of which he embarked at BILBOA. The Infanta in particular, and the Spaniards in gene-ral, were very much afflicted at this Prince's returning without her. The King of SPAIN and his two brothers accompanied him as far as the ESCURIAL, and on the fpot where they parted PHI-LIP erected a pillar, which remains to this day. The Prince, in his paffage, very narrowly efcaped fhipwreck, Sir SACKVILLE TREVOR having the honour of taking him up.

NOTWITHSTANDING this abrupt departure of the Prince, the ENGLISH at MADRID, and at home, were ftill perfuaded the match would be effected at laft; and not without good grounds; for the Infanta learned Englifh, took the title of the Princefs of WALES; the ladies and officers that were to go with her were named. But there was one very extraordinary circumftance, which happened at this juncture: The Prince of Wales, juft before he embarked, fent a letter to the two ambaffadors, de-firing them, in cafe the ratification came from ROME, not to de-liver the proxies he had left in their hands to the King of SPAIN, till they had heard further orders from ENGLAND.—But this both the ambaffadors very wifely refufed to do, as the Prince could not fufpend their commiffion from King JAMES under the great feal of ENGLAND; on the contrary, they both made extra-ordinary preparations for the match, the Earl of BRISTOL laying out 2400 pounds in liveries only, upon that occafion. At length the ratification came from ROME; the marriage day was ap-pointed; but juft a day or two before it drew on, there came *four* Englifh meffengers to the Earl of BRISTOL, commanding him not to deliver the proxies till full fatisfaction was made for

4   the

the furrender of the Palatinate. This ftep of King JAMES's put
an entire end to the bufinefs of the match. The King of SPAIN
faid very truly, that the Palatinate was none of his to give; but
that he would fend ambaffadors to recover it by treaty, or an
army to regain it by force; and in proof of his fincerity in thefe
promifes, he offered to pledge his Contratation-houfe at SEVILLE,
and his Plate fleet. This not being thought fatisfactory, the
Earl of BRISTOL took his leave, when the King of SPAIN gave
him a ring off his own finger, and plate to the value of above
4000 pounds. This Earl of BRISTOL, by far the moft eminent
of the DIGBY family, was a very extraordinary character, and a
truly great man; he furprized the Spaniards with his virtues as
well as talents: the rewards and honours paid him by PHILIP
were but equal to his deferts; for he even aftonifhed that Prince,
when he found, that neither the bribes of one monarch, nor the
menaces of another, could in the leaft fhake the fteady temper of
that ambaffador.

THUS ended the affair of the Spanifh match, that had been
near ten years in agitation. It is certain, that the breaking of it
off was the work of the Duke of BUCKINGHAM: whether he
did right or wrong will now perhaps be difficult to fay; but I
am of opinion, that we could not have been fo much prejudiced
by having MARIA of SPAIN for our Queen, as we were afterwards by taking HENRIETTA of FRANCE. The women of the
MEDICIS line do not appear to me to have done the world much
good. As for the deferted Infanta, fhe married afterward to the
Emperor.

E R R A T A.

In the Introduction, p. 27. for *timeously*, read *timely*. Laſt line, for CAMPEACHY, read HONDURAS. P. 221. l. 1. for *El* Aventurarara, read *La* Aventurarara. Ib. l. 19. for *El* Venganza, read *La* Venganza. P. 220. l. 21. for *El* Nueva, read *La* Nueva. P. 214. l. 20. for *Eſtramadura*, read *Eſtremadura*. P. 208. l. 16. for *ſtruck*, read *ſtuck*. P. 198. l. 4. for 1661, read 1061. P. 188. l. 12. for *called them*, read *called him*. Dele the Note at bottom. P. 182. Laſt line but one, for LICINIUS LARIUS, read LARTIUS LICINIUS. P. 295. for BAGER, read BAYER. P. 297. for *eundem*, read *eandem*. P. 300. for *Chaldic*, read *Chaldee*. Ib. for *Clevard*, read *Clenard*. Ib. for *Vergera*, read *Vergara*. P. 303. for *Honoretes*, read *Honoratus*.

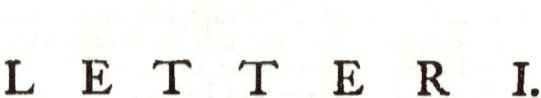

LETTER I.

Journey from LONDON to MADRID.

I LEFT London, in company with two other gentlemen, on Saturday the 10th of *May*, 1760, set sail from Falmouth on the 20th, and arrived at Corunna on the 26th of the same month.

The harbour of Corunna presents you with a fine prospect as you sail into it; on your right are *The Tower of* Hercules, the fort, and the town; before you the shipping; all terminated by an agreeable view of the country: On your left you see Cape Prior, the entrance of Ferroll, and a ridge of barren mountains, with a large river running between them. Corunna is well built and populous, but, like most other Spanish towns, has an offensive smell. Their method of keeping the tiles fast, on the roofs of houses, is by laying loose stones upon them. The Spaniards, to my great mortification, have quitted that old dress, which looks so well on our English stage: The men wear a great flapped hat, a cloke reaching down to their feet, and a sword, generally carried under the arm: The women wear a short jacket of one colour, a petticoat of another, and either a white or black woolen veil. We stayed at Corunna a whole week, because we could not procure a vehicle to convey us to Madrid, nearer than from Madrid itself: Nor could we travel on the streight road to Astorga by any other convenient method, than riding on mules or horses, for we rejected the *litter*, as disagreeable and fatiguing, and no other carriage could pass the mountains that way: We wrote therefore to Madrid for a coach to meet us at Astorga, which is about 150 miles from Corunna.

B

THE

THE Spaniards call the Tower of HERCULES by a wrong name: It is amazing, when the *inscription* still remains as an evidence, that it was the Tower of MARS, that they should be so perverse as to give it to HERCULES. The words are:

MARTI. AVG.
SACR.
C. SEVIUS. LVPVS.
ARCHITECTVS.
A. F. DANIENSIS.
LVSITANVS. EXVL.

It is very plain, that the *Romans* intended this for a watch-house, or *speculum*, and the *Spaniards* use it as a light-house now.

THE poorer sort, both men and women, at CORUNNA, wear neither shoes nor stockings. We lodged at the best inn; but all inns throughout SPAIN afford miserable accommodations: It was kept by an Irishman named OBRIEN. We were well entertained by the Spanish Governor DON LOUIS DE CORDOUVA, and the English consul Mr. JORDAN. The town is pretty, and supplied with water by an *aqueduct*. Our route from CORUNNA to ASTORGA and MADRID was as follows:

ROUTE FROM CORUNNA TO MADRID.

		Leagues
To PATANSOS,	First day,	— 3
JETERIS,	} Second day,	— 5
VAMONDE,		— 2
LUGO,	} Third day,	— 4
GALLEGO,		— 6
FUENFRIA,	} Fourth day,	— 4
SERRARIAS,		— 5
	Carried over,	— 29
	Brought	

		Leagues 29
Brought over,		
VILLA FRANCA,	} Fifth day,	— 4
PONFERRADA,		— 4
RAVANAL,	} Sixth day,	— 6
ASTORGA,		— 3

Leagues, 46

From ASTORGA to BANEZA,	} Seventh day,	— 4
To LA VENTA,		— 3
To BENEVENTE,	} Eighth day,	— 3
To VILLALPANDO,		— 5
To VILLAPRAIS,	} Ninth day,	— 4
To VEJA,		— 3
To MEDINA DEL CAMPO,	} Tenth day,	— 6
To ARTIQUENES,		— 3
To OVEJA,	} Eleventh day,	— 5
To LABAJOS,		— 3
To ESPINAL,	} Twelfth day,	— 5
To GUADARAMA,		— 3
To LAS ROSAS,	} Thirteenth day,	— 6
To MADRID,		— 3

Leagues 102

THE extent of this ROUTE is called 450 miles; but their computation by leagues is very uncertain, like the miles in CORNWALL, guessed at from one town to another. The only way to know the true distance in SPAIN is by your watch. The *Spanish* league is computed equal to about three miles and three quarters *English*.

WE set out from CORUNNA the 3d of June, being honoured with a discharge of guns from the packets in the harbour. You must carry your provisions and bedding with you in SPAIN, as you are not sure of finding them in all places. We seldom met with any thing to eat upon the road, or a bed fit to lie upon. After having passed the fertile mountains of GALLICIA, and the barren rocks of LEON, we came to ASTORGA the 8th of June.

Here

Here we refted till the 11th, and then fat out in a clumfy coach, drawn by fix mules, with *ropes* inftead of *traces:* This furprifed me at firft, but I found afterwards, that the *grandees*, and people of rank in MADRID, ufe ropes conftantly at the *Prado* and *Promenade*, places of airing fomewhat refembling the old ring in *Hyde Park*.

AFTER paffing over the immenfe plains of OLD and NEW CASTILE, which feem more like feas than plains, we arrived at MADRID the 18th of June, being the 7th day from our leaving ASTORGA. Though we travelled fo long a tract of country, we faw few cities or towns, that were confiderable for their extent, ftrength, riches, manufactures, or inhabitants. VILLA FRANCA in LEON is extremely beautiful, and ftands high; PONFERRADA neat, anciently called *intra fluvios*, becaufe it was between the rivers SIL and BOEGA, afterwards ftiled *Pons Ferratus*, from its bridge on the hard rock. MEDINO DEL CAMPO in CASTILE is an agreeable fituation; there is a large fquare in the middle of it, and fome of the nobility refide there.

LUGO in GALLICIA is a remarkable ancient city, furrounded with a moft fingular fortification; as near as I could judge, a fquare; and at the diftance of about every twenty feet a circular *baftion* of thick and lofty walls: The city fortified on every fide in the fame manner, having rather a tremendous appearance, and muft have been extremely ftrong, before the ufe of that villainous *faltpetre*, as SHAKESPEARE calls it. It ftands near the fource of the MINHO; the turnips here are faid to be fo large, as to weigh fifty pounds each: But who can believe it? Its ancient name was *Lucus Augufti*, and thence corruptly called LUGO.

THE city of ASTORGA in LEON is fituated in a wide plain; the moft remarkable thing in it is the *Cathedral*, which is a noble Gothic building; a *bafilica*, confifting of fix pointed arches, fupported by tall, light, neat pillars, in a good tafte; the portal a large round arch, with a vaft number of mouldings; there are feven or eight fine altars, but the *High Altar* is exceedingly magnificent;

nificent; it confifts of twenty compartments of marble-fculp-
ture in alto relievo, the figures as large as life; the fubject the hiftory of our SAVIOUR; at the fummit GOD the Father crowning
the Bleffed Virgin. The *glory* is well expreffed; for being cut
through the frame, and a lamp placed behind it, the light
fhews the *rays.* We happened to attend at the Vefpers; the
mufic of the organ was fine; the number of tapers, the rich-
nefs of altars, in fhort, the whole fcene was ftriking. This city
gives the title of *Marquis* to the family of *Oforio*, inferior to
few, either for antiquity or valour.

BENEVENTE in LEON is encompaffed by three rivers, and remarkable for little more than giving the title of Earl to the family of PIMENTEL. VILLALPANDO is in a pleafing plain, has a
large fquare, and contains a palace of the *Conftable of Caftile*, to
whom the town belongs. The only river we paffed of note was
a branch of the MINHO; a noble current, almoft as broad as the
Thames at Windfor, and to appearance deep; finely wooded on
each fide, the trees larger and taller than you ufually meet with in
SPAIN. The place where we paffed it was called HOSPITAL DE
Efchemofo.

THE *florks nefts* upon the tops of the *churches*, with the birds
hovering over them, or juft peeping out, are pleafing as you pafs.
It was fo in old ROME: The *florks* built their nefts in great numbers on the fummits of their *temples,* as their poets often tell us.
—Thus JUVENAL fays of the Temple of *Concord:*

Quæque falutáto crepitat *Concordia* nido.

It was cruel to kill fuch focial birds as thefe; and yet we find by
HORACE, that the Epicures of his times could not keep their
knives from them; though it was an abfolute violation of hof-
pitality. Speaking of the luxurious difhes of thofe days, he
fays, their anceftors never eat *turbots* nor *florks:*

Tutus erat *rhombus*, tutoque *ciconia nido.*

This bird is often mentioned in Scripture. In the Pfalms,—*The
fir-trees are a dwelling for the ftork:* And in JOB, *Who giveth the
ftork*

nificent; it confifts of twenty compartments of marble-fculp-
ture in alto relievo, the figures as large as life; the fubject the hiftory of our SAVIOUR; at the fummit GOD the Father crowning
the Bleffed Virgin. The *glory* is well expreffed; for being cut
through the frame, and a lamp placed behind it, the light
fhews the *rays*. We happened to attend at the Vefpers; the
mufic of the organ was fine; the number of tapers, the rich-
nefs of altars, in fhort, the whole fcene was ftriking. This city
gives the title of *Marquis* to the family of *Oforio*, inferior to
few, either for antiquity or valour.

BENEVENTE in LEON is encompaffed by three rivers, and remarkable for little more than giving the title of Earl to the family of PIMENTEL. VILLALPANDO is in a pleafing plain, has a
large fquare, and contains a palace of the *Conftable of Caftile*, to
whom the town belongs. The only river we paffed of note was
a branch of the MINHO; a noble current, almoft as broad as the
Thames at Windfor, and to appearance deep; finely wooded on
each fide, the trees larger and taller than you ufually met with in
SPAIN. The place where we paffed it was called HOSPITAL DE
Efchemofo.

THE *ftorks nefts* upon the tops of the *churches*, with the birds
hovering over them, or juft peeping out, are pleafing as you pafs.
It was fo in old ROME: The *ftorks* built their nefts in great numbers on the fummits of their *temples*, as their poets often tell us.
—Thus JUVENAL fays of the Temple of *Concord:*

Quæque falutáto crepitat *Concordia* nido.

It was cruel to kill fuch focial birds as thefe; and yet we find by
HORACE, that the Epicures of his times could not keep their
knives from them; though it was an abfolute violation of hof-
pitality. Speaking of the luxurious difhes of thofe days, he
fays, their anceftors never eat *turbots* nor *ftorks:*

Tutus erat *rhombus,* tutoque *ciconia nido.*

This bird is often mentioned in Scripture. In the Pfalms,---*The*
fir-trees are a dwelling for the ftork: And in JOB, *Who giveth the*
ftork

ftork food? She buildeth her neft on high. It delights in the moft lofty fituations. All the nefts, which we faw, were in the higheft places the bird could find.

WE paffed fome forefts; but the trees are dwarf and poor, not refembling the timber of GREAT-BRITAIN; you will in vain look for thofe ftately woods, which not only afford fuel, fhade, and wealth to their owners, but fend forth fleets, which give laws to the ocean. Though I loft my watch on the top of one of the higheft mountains near the ZEBREROS, yet, by extraordinary good fortune, it was found by the *Marigatti*, or mule-drivers, and carried to the Padre Abbad of ZEBREROS, who fent it me in lefs than a month.

THE new STONE-CAUSEWAY, which joins the two CAS-TILES, and extends to GUADARAMA, is a moft magnificent public work: It was done by an order of FERDINAND VI. the late King, as appears by the following infcription on a pillar erected on the caufeway: FERDINANDUS VI. PATER PATRIÆ. VI-AM VTRÆQUE CASTELLIÆ SUPERATIS MONTIBUS FECIT. ANN. SALUTIS M DCC XLIX. REGNI SUI IV. It is really a noble road, and feems owing rather to the labour and activity of a *Roman*, than to the flow induftry of a *Spaniard*.

SOME parts of the CASTILES are pleafant; they are ill cultivated; have no wood of any moment; this makes fuel incredibly dear in MADRID; the expence of one fingle fire there for the winter has been known to coft fifty pounds; an amazing article! The charcoal confumed in their kitchens, and braziers, comes chiefly from GALLAPAGAR, at the diftance of 30 miles, which is far enough in that country to make the carriage of it very expenfive. The principal *timber* they ufe, is *fir*, the growth of the country; their houfes, churches, carriages, and furniture, are chiefly of *deal*; there are fometimes no lefs than fourteen large girders, in the cieling of a fmall apartment. One would not imagine from this circumftance, that timber was fcarce. As to the *water* in this country, I do not think it in general good; that of MADRID is excellent, which is plain by the court's being at much expence to have it conveyed to diftant places. There are two fine rivers in the CASTILES, the TAGUS, and the GUADIANA; as to the MANSANARES, which runs clofe by MADRID, it is but a poor ftream, and falls into the XARAMA, about 6 leagues diftant from the TAGUS. I was told in LONDON, that the fituation of MADRID was upon a plain, but it is a great miftake: It is built upon a chain of little hills, and, becaufe there are higher mountains round it, at a diftance, has been fuppofed to be in a plain.

THE Spaniards erect pillars at proper diftances upon the caufeways, to direct travellers during the fnows; we faw feveral of them in LEON, and other parts. The firft comer to a *Spanifh* inn, be his rank what it may, has the firft choice of the accommodations; this occafions a fort of conteft between the travellers in this country, who fhall get firft to the inn. It is a common practice to fend a man on an hour or two before: We diftanced one DON JOSEPH, a Bifcayner, in this way; finding that he was going to the fame *Pofada*, or inn, we detached our faithful ANTONIO, who, as fleet as an *Arab*, ran over the mountains in bye-paths, and arrived at the inn long before the DON and we came to it. This conteft arifes from there being feldom more than one inn in a village; at which, if difappointed, you muft probably ride 8 or 10 miles before you can find another, which, at the end of a long day's journey, and in the dark, would be fatiguing, and perhaps dangerous.

UPON a review of the whole country from CORUNNA to MADRID, one may fay, that GALLICIA is a fine fertile province; that fome parts of it are equal to many in ENGLAND; but as to LEON, it is a naked, dreadful, barren rock, except where it is covered with a few pitiful firs, or fhrubs, fuch as are about BENEVENTE and VILLALPANDO, and except fome few plains after you have paffed ASTORGA. I turned round to take a view of LEON from one of the higheft mountains, and was almoft frightened at the fight; a brown horror, as Mr. POPE expreffes it, was fpread over the whole; fands, rocks, and craggy precipices, formed as favage a profpect, as can be imagined. And yet this country was probably once fought for; the inhabitants furely muft find a charm in it unknown to us. In one of thefe villages we
found

found a set of people, dreffed in a whimfical manner, dancing to
rude mufic; the whole appearance was entertaining and grotefque;
the dance artlefs and odd; its natural fimplicity fhewed the people
in their true character.

THE road from CORUNNA to MADRID is certainly not fo bad,
as it is generally thought in ENGLAND. The mountains of GAL-
LICIA are very paffable; the only difficult parts which I faw, were
the defcent at LA FAVA, and about 12 miles, as you come out
of SERRARIAS. The mountains of LEON are rather difagreeable
than dangerous, and all the reft is eafy. Be it as it may, our
Englifh meffengers find no difficulty in it. The accommodations,
indeed, are miferable: I have faid you muft abfolutely carry your
provifions and bedding along with you; and even then, unlefs
you can bear fatigue well, lye down in your clothes, eat eggs,
onions, and cheefe; unlefs you can fleep while your mules reft,
rife the moment you are called, and fet out early in the morning, before the heat comes on, you will fare ill as a traveller in
SPAIN. It is a good method to carry dried tongues with you, hard
eggs, not hams, for they will not keep, as we found by experience; fome portable foup; tea, fugar, and fpirituous liquors;
not forgetting even pepper and falt; and whenever you meet
with good bread, meat, fowls, or wine, always to buy them,
whether you want them or not, becaufe you know not what
to-morrow may produce. A knife, fork, and fpoon, are abfolutely neceffary, for you will find none; nor fhould you omit a
pair of fnuffers, a candleftick, and fome wax-candles. Take care
only not to carry any tobacco or rum; for they are all contraband, and may occafion the detention, if not the feizure of your
baggage. Particularly bring with you as few *books* as poffible;
for the inquifition will feize them. My baggage was detained a
fortnight on account of my books; and THE EARL of BRISTOL
was obliged to fpeak twice to GENERAL WALL, before he could
releafe the captives. Many of thefe circumftances feem *trifling*,
but they are fo material, that thofe who happen to travel without them in this country, will find, by dear-bought experience,
that all thefe *trifles* have their ufe, and if neglected,

————Hæ nugæ feria ducent
In mala.

LETTER

LETTER II.

The STATE of RELIGION in SPAIN.

WITH regard to ancient religious rites or customs in this country, there was probably in early times a great mixture of all sorts. The first accounts of SPAIN, that are clear and authentic, are, I believe, those in STRABO and LIVY. The face of it then was certainly very savage and barbarous. It could have no religious notions besides its own, but from GAUL, ITALY, or AFRIC, from the PHOENICIANS, CARTHAGINIANS, GAULS, or ROMANS: and what those were, are well known.

MARIANA tells us, that Christianity was first preached in SARAGOÇA by St. JAMES, 42 years after CHRIST: and for this he quotes ISIDORE, bishop of SEVILLE. With all due deference to the authority, though episcopal, I must beg leave to deny the fact; for St. LUKE says expresly, that St. JAMES was killed at JERUSALEM. The SPANIARDS have likewise another tradition concerning this apostle; which, though believed by themselves, will hardly find credit among Protestants. It is, that St. JAMES, by birth a SPANIARD, has been often seen armed in the air, going before the van, and protecting the SPANISH armies: Which circumstance you may read in Boldonius, if you like it. Whether it be for these reasons, or others, I cannot say, however this fact is certain, that SAN JAGO, or St. JAMES, hath from the earliest times been ever revered and worshipped as the guardian, and tutelar saint of SPAIN.

C

WHAT innovations, or changes their religious worſhip underwent from the firſt planting of *Chriſtianity* to the arrival of the
GOTHS, or the invaſion of the MOORS, would perhaps be impoſſible to ſay : That the *Gothic* princes embraced the *Chriſtian*
faith, is clear from many evidences ſtill remaining, not in SPAIN
only, but in ENGLAND and other countries : That the MOORS
would never receive *Chriſtianity* among them, appears but too
plainly from the enmity that hath ever ſubſiſted between the two
people, from their final expulſion under PHILIP III. and the
odium with which they purſue them to this day.

THAT the JEWS have always ſubſiſted here in ſuch numbers
was probably owing to this circumſtance : when TITUS carried
back with him to ROME ſo many thouſand captive JEWS, the
ſhattered remnants of that devoted people, and diſperſed them
afterwards throughout the world ; as SPAIN lay convenient for
their paſſage out of ITALY, and being a wide and extended country, multitudes of them probably fled for an aſylum there : Tho'
great numbers remained at ROME and in ITALY, as appears by
the edicts againſt them afterwards, and by the religion of the
captives ſpreading ſo much among their conquerors : A circumſtance which RUTILIUS has finely lamented ;

> Atque utinam nunquam Judæa ſubacta fuiſſet
> Pompeii bellis, imperioque Titi.
> Latius exciſæ gentis contagia ſerpunt,
> Victoreſque ſuos natio victa premit.

That the JEWS had in ſome parts of SPAIN, and at ſome periods, the free exerciſe of their religion, and worſhip, is an undoubted fact : There is an *Hebrew* Temple ſtill remaining at To-
LEDO, which I have ſeen, as a ſtanding proof of it to this day.

WHAT is of more moment to us is, as may be collected from
Dr. GEDDES's ſeveral tracts, that no weſtern church has preſerved
ſo many, and ſuch authentic monuments and records, as the SPA-
NISH church hath down to the VIIIth century. It was antiently exactly the ſame with the preſent church of ENGLAND, had
the ſame NICENE CREED, and appealed to the ſame general councils :

cils : And their Prince, as well as ours, was defender of the faith and head of the church. The Bifhop of ROME had no more authority there, than any other prelate. The *Spanifh* Church had no dependence on that fee till the VIIIth century. Till after the *Moorifh* times, it had no image-worfhip ; no prayers addreffed to faints, or angels ; no purgatory ; it did not maintain feven facraments ; it knew not tranfubftantiation, which certainly is of no older date than the time of Pope INNOCENT III. in the *Lateran* council, held after the year 1200 ; by confequence the cup was always given to the laity, and never refufed till after that doctrine prevailed in the beginning of the XIIIth century. There was likewife no adoration of the hoft, no auricular confeffion. They had no prayers then in an unknown language. The antient *Gothic* Liturgy, then in ufe, was called *Mozarabic*, or *Mufarabic*, from thofe chriftians, who lived under the *Moorifh* government in SPAIN. It was firft printed by Cardinal XIMENES. And there is to this day, an annual *Mozarabic* mafs celebrated with great pomp and folemnity, in the metropolitan church of TOLEDO, at which the prefent King of SPAIN has affifted in perfon. Every one knows, that the term *mafs* came from the cuftom of difmiffing the people with the—*Ite*—*miffa eft.*

As the SPANISH Church certainly remained pure, uncorrupted, and unpapiftical till towards the VIIIth century ; fo from that period downwards, Paganifm artfully, and by almoft imperceptible infinuations, gradually ftole in, wearing that mafk or vizor, which we now call *Popery*. Whatever triumphs Chriftianity may formerly have gained over the Gentile worfhip ; Paganifm, in all catholic countries, is now entirely revenged ; fhe triumphed in her turn from the moment fhe eftablifhed herfelf in the form of Popery. Concealed under this drapery, fhe prefides in the very tabernacle and fanctuary of chriftians, and is worfhipped fitting between the horns of the altar. When you enter a Roman catholic, apoftolic, papiftical, chriftian temple, at your firft view you fee that all is *Pagan*. The late Dr. MIDDLETON hath very learnedly, elegantly, and effectually proved this point to demonftration. But I never relifhed that ingenious performance fo much, as when my own eyes bore teftimony to the truth of his obfervations. The

refemresemblance is so striking between the use of the ancient *Thura*, and the modern Incense; their *aspergillum, lavacrum,* &c. and the present holy water; the blessing of horses, and the ancient benediction of cattle; the same profusion of lamps and wax-lights; between the ancient *votivæ tabulæ,* ἀναθήματα, and the modern votive limbs, offerings, and pictures: the multitude of shrines, crosses, and altars in the churches, roads, hills, and high places; and particularly of *images,* which have often brought to my mind that satirical joke of PETRONIUS, who said he never walked the streets, but he could much more easily meet with a god than a man.

>   Facilius est deum, quam hominem invenire.

And I am sure, if you spit out of a window in SPAIN, 'tis ten to one but you spit upon a saint. The *Spanish Flagellantes,* by PYTHAGOREAN transmigration, are exactly the old, self-lashing priests of JOVE, or the AJAX MASTIGOPHORUS on an *Athenian* stage: and are indeed a most shocking spectacle. The custom of churches being permitted as sanctuaries for villains, prevailed at ROME in the time of the Emperor TIBERIUS: For the senate very justly exclaimed against it. See TACITUS. Annal. III. CESTIUS's opinion was,

>   Neque quenquam in urbis templa perfugere, ut eo subsidio
>   ad flagitia utatur.

And yet, what a ROMAN Senator blushed at, is sanctified by a *Roman-catholic Pope.* The quires of churches in all popish countries are a sort of religious fairs or markets, where people continually come and go in succession, and masses are constantly said till twelve o'clock at noon, but not after. The mass for the dead is exactly copied from the parentation of the heathens. The dress of the officiating priest has constantly put me in mind of those remarkable words:

>   Tanquam vestis illa prophetica, quæ licet vera ederet mira
>   cula, operanti ornamentum potius quam adjumentum
>   videretur *.

The present King of SPAIN, while he was at NAPLES, sent orders to the officiating priest on St. JANUARIUS's day, that the

---

* See TACITUS.

blood

blood fhould be made to liquefy in fuch a precife number of mi-
nutes, for he would ftay no longer. This is exactly the old quack
experiment mentioned by Horace, which he faw at Gnatia:

Dum flammâ fine thura liquefcere limine facro
Perfuadere cupit——

There is one reafon why the Church of Rome ought not to
make fo free with the argument of miracles: becaufe if they
maintain *theirs* to be as genuine as thofe of the Apoftles, it will
be an eafy matter to prove thofe recorded of the Emperor Vespasian (who is faid to have healed a withered hand, and reftored
the blind to fight) to be at leaft of equal authority: A *Roman*
hiftorian records the one, and a *Roman* catholic writer maintains
the other: *Utri creditis*, Quirites! This folly of theirs, inftead
of ftrengthening their own caufe, tends evidently to weaken it,
and it faps the rotten foundations of popifh policy. If the mifchief ended there, it would be well: but it tends alfo to fubvert
the great proofs of Chriftianity, and to affift the gates of hell,
inftead of oppofing them. The character of the prefent Papifts
is exactly that which Tacitus hath given of the old Germans,

De actis deorum credere, quam fcire.

The number of holydays enjoined by the Pope is become fo
exceffive, as to be a fcandalous encouragement to idlenefs. If it
was thought defpicable by the bufy minds of the *Roman* people, to fee the Jews, from the inftitutions of Moses, give but
one day in feven to complete indolence, though for the caufe of
religion: If their active virtue abhorred to fee, as one of them
calls it, *feptima quæque lux quieti data*; what would he have faid,
had he feen fuch a number of days confecrated in his own Rome
to the fame purpofe? But this practice likewife had its birth in
Paganifm; and made Cassius fay in the reign of Nero, that if
they were to decree fuch a vaft number of feftival days, the gods
would take up the whole year in being thanked, *coque oportere di-
vidi facros, et negotiofos dies, queis divina colerentur, et humana non
impedirent.*

THE abfurdity of their *Reliques* is beyond meafure ridiculous; fuch as the thigh of St. LAWRENCE, with the fkin burnt, and marked with the prongs, which he was turned with on the gridiron. There are faid to be the heads of two thoufand martyred virgins in the convent of our Lady of ATOCHE near MADRID, where the *Britifh* ftandards, taken at the battle of ALMANZA, ftill remain.

IT is certain, that their blind zeal in matters of religion has deftroyed many fine remains of heathen learning, and claffic antiquity: It ftill continues the fame ravage under the direction of monks and inquifitors; leaves are cancelled, prefaces torn, and books prohibited, fecreted, or burnt, becaufe they are againft the Catholic faith. As they formerly thought the Bible would appear to more advantage, when the pagan poets were deftroyed; fo they are ftill of opinion, that popery will always appear beft, when every evidence of its impofture is fuppreffed or fpirited away. Thefe are lengths in which the zealots of the church of ROME have certainly gone too far: And on the other hand LUTHER himfelf, when he began the reformation, went too far in burning the canon law. This fuperftitious zeal of theirs againft Pagan writers, and modern heretical authors, cannot be placed in a more ridiculous light, than they have placed it themfelves in one of the pictures, which I faw at the ESCURIAL: where feveral angels were flogging St. JEROM for the wicked delight he had taken in reading the works of that vile heretic MARCUS TULLIUS CICERO.

As the feveral pagan gods were multiplied by being worfhipped as different deities, though in reality they were the fame: as a JUPITER, an HERCULES, &c. were fet up in almoft every country: So where popery prevails, and particularly in SPAIN, the Bleffed Virgin MARY, the mother of our Lord, is multiplied into almoft as many diftinct divinities, as there are feparate diftricts and places. Thus there is our Lady of ATOCHE, our Lady of ALCALA DE HENARES, our Lady of TOLEDO, &c. And the little pictures or images of thefe are worn as *Amulets* by the common people, who have as much faith in them, as the antients
had

had in a *Talisman*, or *Abraxas*. I have seen one of these last, which Prince EUGENE himself wore, a strange instance of human weakness in one who rose so much above the common level, and made such a shining figure as a hero on the theatre of EUROPE. The Spaniards have marvellous superstitions relating to the different properties of those different Virgin MARIES: If you pray to *this*, she is a good preservative against thunder and lightning; if you pray to *that*, an admirable specific against the cholic and rheumatism. But the Blessed Virgin of PILAR, or our Lady of the Pillar, MARIA DE COLUMNA, in SARAGOÇA, is the most capital Virgin MARY, the greatest object of devotion in all SPAIN.

THERE cannot be much *simony* in the Church of ROME, because the Pope, or the King, disposes of all church-preferments; for there can be no traffic supposed between the inferior ecclesiastics and his Holiness, or his Majesty. Statutes of mortmain are highly requisite and necessary in this country. The present King of SPAIN hath, it is said, attempted something like them, by taxing all donations to religious uses ever since the year 1730. These were anciently such a grievance in ENGLAND, that it became a form in some wills: *dentur, assignentur, vendantur—exceptis Religiosis & Judæis.*

PHILIP V. in 1716, obtained of the Pope an indulto for raising money upon the clergy. The Pope granted him one for five years, that is to say, a million and a half in the Indies, and a million on the churches in SPAIN. It is a mistake to call this the *los millones*, which is a different tax, as will appear in the account of the Spanish Revenue. This is called *subsidio*.

THE Crusade against the followers of WALDO (a merchant of LYONS) or the *Albigenses*, in 1160, gave birth probably to the INQUISITION. Pope GREGORY IX. first devised that horrid tribunal, but INNOCENT IV. was the first, who had abilities and courage sufficient to bring it to a due maturity, and give it a just establishment. The form of it, and the number of its members, differ greatly in different countries. * In SPAIN it was established chiefly by Cardinal XIMENES, who knew perfectly well what political use could be made of it. The Spaniards still sup-

* See more upon this article in the next Letter.

C 4

port it, not fo much with an intention to burn Jews or Heretics, as they do in PORTUGAL, but to enjoy the benefit of one religion, the want of fuch uniformity being, they apprehend, a great inconvenience to other ftates.   Monf. VOLTAIRE indeed is of another opinion; he tells us, that if there was but one religion in ENGLAND, the government would foon become defpotic; if there were, two, they would cut each others throats; but as there are fo many religions amongft us, things go on very quietly.   To fpeak however of the Inquifition in the mildeft terms, it is at beft but a *Roman, Turkifh,* or an *Arabian* perfecution in a Chriftian drefs. The inquifitors perhaps may fay,   "·We only perfecute in this " manner the very worft of heretics, fuch as *Jews.*"   It may be anfwered, " And what have the Pagans done more ? thofe whom " they perfecuted, they accounted heretics, and thefe very Jews " did the fame thing." The Dominican will reply, " But can you " as a *Chriftian* fpare and tolerate the perfecutors of CHRIST ?" We anfwer, I think juftly, That we have no authority to punifh them; but we may tolerate their worfhip, or not, as we think proper.   Becaufe fome people, called Jews, crucified the founder of our religion, JESUS CHRIST, above 1700 years ago, that is no reafon why you fhould crucify all thofe who go under that name at this day.   Where is your warrant, your authority, your commiffion delegated from the Almighty for this purpofe ? Is it any where faid, " Go forth, my difciples, with fword and fire, torment, rack, and burn all thofe who will not embrace the Chriftian faith; or, what is much lefs, the Roman Catholic faith ?" Though GOD himfelf may punifh the fins of the fathers on the children to the third and fourth generation; thefe people are at prefent at leaft the *fiftieth* generation from the murderers of Chrift.   Thus you feem to me not only to fnatch the thunder of the ALMIGHTY out of his hands, but to dart it unwarrantably, and even launch the bolt much farther than He ever declared he fhould do himfelf.   Can the GOD of all mercy be delighted with fo cruel a facrifice of human blood ?   There is an undoubted refemblance between a SPANISH INQUISITOR, and a DIOCLESIAN, a CALED, or a MUSTAPHA ; you now act the part of the Pagan princes, as they formerly acted yours.   Such a tribunal, fhocking as it is to humanity, has nothing but falfe political ends to plead in its excufe : And where nature and religion
must

2

muſt be ſacrificed, ſuch a policy is only worthy of a MACHIA-
VEL, a XIMENES, or an Emperor of JAPAN. The principles of
toleration are founded in nature, reaſon, humanity, juſtice, and
true policy. If in a well civilized ſtate the majority are of one
religious perſuaſion, the moſt that you can lawfully do is, to lay
thoſe who are diſſentient, under ſuch reſtrictions, as ſhall prevent
their diſturbing, or ſubverting the civil or religious harmony of
that ſtate. This is all that appears to me allowable ; and of this
nature are the laws in England and Ireland againſt the Papiſts.
But when you come to moleſt innocent ſubjects, to take from them
theĭr poſſeſſions, to expoſe them to tortures and cruel deaths, or drive
them to ſeek ſettlements in other countries, you then exceed your
power, play the part of a Syracuſan tyrant, and it becomes *Perſecution* ; like the expulſion of the Moors, or the revocation of
the edict of Nantz.

But after all, why are the Jews ſingled out, as the worſt of
heretics? In one light they are the moſt pardonable. They are
the only people, beſides the Chriſtians, who have received the glorious depoſit of a true, a divine revelation : They had theirs from
God himſelf; we received ours from his Son : They are, no doubt,
in a dangerous and incorrigible ſtate of error, by not acknow-
ledging the true MESSIAH ; but we are not to be the puniſhers
of that error : A very ſevere part of that puniſhment ſeems already
to have paſſed upon them ; they have been deprived of their country and temple; their exiſtence, as a nation, deſtroyed ; they have
been ſold, and carried captive into all lands; driven as wretched
fugitives and vagabonds throughout the world : Let the intolerant
ſpirit of bigots exclaim as loudly againſt them as it may, there is
not a Roman-catholic in the world but will join in the cry : which
very circumſtance ſhould awaken all the ſuſpicions of us Proteſtants. The next ſtep from excluſion out of community, is
perſecution. But to a humane mind, conſidering the ſufferings
of theſe people, the moſt natural concluſion will probably be that,
which was made by the firſt outlaw of the human race, at a time
when ſociety or communion had not thoſe ſweets and advantages
which they now enjoy. The concluſion meant is, *That their puniſhment is greater than they can bear.* The Spaniards have

D   always

always found, that this violent way of making profelytes has had
but indifferent fuccefs. It may make men temporize, diffemble,
or perhaps perjure themfelves. Fire and fword, famine and torture will never cure Jewifh blindnefs; when miracles wrought by
a divine power have had no effect, what is to be hoped for from
any human means? TITUS reafoned with them in this way much
more forcibly than any one, either before or fince his time; the
SENNACHERIBS, and NEBUCHADNEZZARS fell far fhort of him
in this method of argument. But what was the confequence?
They fought ftill more defperately for their civil and religious liberties, and obftinately expired, as they ftill do in the inquifitor's
flames, in the defence of their faith..

UPON the whole we may fafely fay, that the Roman-catholic
fyftems of *morality*, as treated by jefuitical cafuifts, are truly
l'art de chicaner avec Dieu; that their religion, as dreffed out with
the trappings of popery, difcovers in its folds the pagan wardrobe
from whence it was taken. From a view of it one cannot help
coming at this obvious truth: That as the admiffion of all error is
dangerous, it is moft fatally fo in matters of religion; the avenues
of which fhould therefore be guarded with the greater vigilance.
In other cafes the error is removable, or the remedy at worft but
difficult: But here error is generally uneradicable, permanent, and
the remedy impracticable. All attempts to alter what has once
been facred, are imagined to border fo near to facrilege or impi-
ety, that few in any age or country have had firmnefs and difcretion enough to undertake the tafk. This is the great ftronghold
of popery, and all other corrupt religions. For as the Roman
conful judicioufly faid upon a like occafion,

> Nihil enim in fpeciem fallacius eft, quam prava religio. Ubi
> Deorum numen prætenditur fceleribus, fubit animum timor,
> ne fraudibus humanis vindicandis divini juris aliquid im-
> miftum violemus. LIVIUS, lib. xxxix. cap. 16..

ERRORS in learning commonly ferve for our amufement; as
abler men will fet them right; errors in politics occafion at worft
but temporary evils; but errors in religion are everlafting, too

obftinate

obftinate to be fubdued. Learned and political controverfies, tho'
often managed with much heat and rancour, produce generally
new lights for the ufe of the public; but religious controverfy is
for the moft part pernicious, and ferves only to poifon the minds
of men. When bigotry prompts, and enthufiafm inflames, and
the zealous fury once rifes, the worft of all plagues is then begun :
for, more human blood has been fhed by this blind religious zeal,
than by the dagger of the affaffin, the fword of juftice, or all the
artillery and implements of war.

FROM the firft century, Spain had bifhoprics, and was divided
into the provinces *Carthaginienfis, Tarraconenfis, Betica, Lufita-
nica,* and *Gallaica.*

THE firft bifhops were, according to the Spanifh writers, difciples of St. James the Apoftle. The epifcopal government was
fomewhat interrupted by the *Moors,* who ravaged part of the peninfula : but the *Mauritanians* in ANDALUSIA were mote inclined
to conquer Spain than to change its religion from the chriftian to
mahometanifm. By this means, the kings of OVIEDO and LEON,
together with the counts of CASTILE and the kings of NAVARRE,
having recovered ftrength to conquer the SARACENS, re-eftablifh-
ed the bifhops who had retired, and founded feveral churches and
monafteries.

SPAIN had eleven archbifhoprics, and fifty-four bifhoprics, including thofe of PORTUGAL.

LIST

LIST of the ARCHBISHOPRICS and BISHOP-RICS of *SPAIN*, with their valuation.

I. *TOLEDO*. Archbifhop and Metropolitan.

His Eminence, Don LUIS DE CORDOVA, *   *L.* 50,000

SUFFRAGANS.

1. CARTHAGENA	Don Diego de Roxas,	-	8000
2. CORDOUA	Don Martin de Barcia,	-	5250
3. CUENÇA	Vacant, -	-	6250
4. SIGUENZA	Don Francifco Dias,	-	7500
5. JAEN	Don Fran. Benito Marin	-	5000
6. SEGOVIA	Don Manuel Murillo	-	4250
7. OSMA	Vacant -	-	3250
8. VALLADOLID	Don Ifidro de Coffio,	-	2500

II. *SEVILLE*. Archbifhop, &c.

Don FRANCISCO SOLIS DE CARDONA,   15,000

SUFFRAGANS.

1. MALAGA	Don Jofeph de Franquis Lafo,	7500
2. CADIZ	Don Francifco Thomas del Valle,	2000
3. CANARIA	Don Francifco Valentin Moran,	
4. CEUTA	Don Jofeph de la Cuefta.	

III. *SANTIAGO*. Archbifhop, &c.

Don BATHOLOME RAJOY Y' LOSADA,   15,000

SUFFRAGANS.

1. SALAMANCA	Don Jofeph Zorila	-	3000
2. TUY	Don Juan Manuel Caftannon,		2000
3. AVILA	Don Romualdo Velarde,	-	2500
4. CORIA	Don Juan Jofeph Garcia Alvaro,		3250
5. PLASENCIA	Vacant, -	-	6875
6. ASTORGA	Don Francifco Xavier Cabezon,		1875

* The valuation of thefe preferments is taken from a Spanifh book lately publifh-ed at MADRID: It makes the revenues of TOLEDO greater than the common eftimation of them: But I doubt if the account is exaggerated.

7. ZAMORA

7. ZAMORA	Don Iſidro Cavanillas,	2500
8. OXENSE	Don Franciſco Auguſtin de Euro,	1500
9. BADAJOZ	Don Manuel Perez Minago,	3250
10. MONDONNEDO	Don Carlos de Riomol,	1250
11. LUGO	Don Fr. Franciſco Izquierdo,	1500
12. CIUDAD RODRIGO	Don Joſeph Viguezal,	1250

IV. *GRANADA.* Archbiſhop, &c.

Don PEDRO ANTONIO BARROETA,	6250

SUFFRAGANS.

1. GUADIX	Don Franc. Alexandro Bocanegra,	1000
2. ALMERIA	Don Franciſco Gaſpar de Molina,	1125

V. *BURGOS.* Archbiſhop, &c.

Don ONESIMO SALAMANCA,	3750

SUFFRAGANS.

1. PAMPLONA	Don Gaſpar de Miranda,	3500
2. CALAHORRA	Don Andres de Porras,	3000
3. PALENCIA	Don Andres de Buſtamante,	2500
4. SANTANDER	Don Franc. Xavier de Arriaza	1500

VI. *TARRAGONA.* Archbiſhop, &c.

Don JAYME DE CORTADA Y' BRU',	3250

SUFFRAGANS.

1. BARCELONA	Don Aſſenſio Sales,	1500
2. GERONA	Don Manuel Antonio Palmero,	1250
3. LERIDA	Don Manuel Macias Pedrejon,	2000
4. TORTOSA	Don Luis Garcia Mannero,	2500
5. VIQUE	Don Fr. Bartholomè Sarmentero	750
6. URGEL	Don Fr. Chathalan de Ocón,	1000
7. SOLSONA	Don Fr. Joſeph de Mezquia,	625

VII. *ZA-*

VII. *ZARAGOZA.* Archbiſhop, &c.

Don FRANCISCO DE ANOA Y BASTA.   7500

SUFFRAGANS.

1. HUESCA	Don Antonio Sanchez,	1500
2. BARBASTRO	Don Fr. Diego de Rivera,	1000
3. XACA	Don Paſqual Lopez,	750
4. TARAZONA	Don Eſtevan de Villanova,	1875
5. ALBARRACIN	Don Juan Navarro,	1000
6. TERUEL	Don Fr. Rodriguez Chico,	2250

VIII. *VALENCIA.* Archbiſhop, &c.

Don ANDRES MAYORAL.   13,750

SUFFRAGANS.

1. SERGOVE	Don Fr. Blas de Arganda,	2000
2. ORIHUELA	Vacant,	3750
3. MALIARCA	Don Lorenzo Deſpuig,	2750

In AMERICA.

I. *SANTO DOMINGO.* Archbiſhop.

Don PHELIPE RUIZ DE AUSMENDI.

SUFFRAGANS.

1. PUERTO RICO	Don Pedro Martinez de Oneca.
2. CUBA	Don Pedro Aguſtin Morel.
3. CARACAS	Don Diego Diez Madronnero.

II. *MEXI-*

II. *MEXICO.* Archbifhop, &c.

Don MAN. RUBIO DE SALINAS.

SUFFRAGANS.

1. PUEBLA DE LOS AN-GELES	Don Domingo Alvarez de Abrea,
2. OAXACA ——	Don Ventura Blanco.
3. MECHOACAN. ——	Don Pedro Sanchez de Tagle.
4. GUADALAXARA ——	Don Francifco de Texada.
5. YUCATAN ——	Don Fr. Ignacio de Padilla.
6. DURANGO ——	Don Pedro Tamaron.

III. *MANILA.* Archbifhop, &c.

Don MANUEL ANTONIO ROXO.

SUFFRAGANS.

1. CEBU' ——	Vacant.
2. NUEVA SEGOVIA —	Don Juan de la Fuente.
3. NUEVA CACERES. —	Don Fr. Manuel de Matos.

IV. *GUATEMALA.* Archbifhop, &c.

Don FRANCISCO DE FIGUEREDO.

SUFFRAGANS.

1. CHIAPA ——	Don F. Jofeph Videl de Montezuma,
2. NICARAGUA ——	Don Fr. Mato. Navia Bolano.
3. COMAYAGUA —	Don Diego Rodriguez Rivas.

V. *LIMA.* Archbifhop.

Don DIEGO DEL CORRO.

SUFFRAGANS.

1. AREQUIPA ——	Don Jacinto Aquado y' Chacón.
2. TRUXILLO ——	Don Francifco de Luna Victoria.

3. QUITO

3. Quito   ——   Don Juan Nieto Polo del Aquila.
4. Cuzco   ——   Don Juan de Caftonneda.
5. Guamanga   ——   Don Phelipe Manrique de Lara.
6. Panama   ——   Don Man. Romani y' Carrillo.
7. Chile   ——   Don Man. de Alday.
8. Concepcion de Chile Don Jofeph de Toro.

VI. *CHARCAS*. Archbifhop.

Don Cayetano Marcellano y' Agramont.

SUFFRAGANS.

1. Nra. Sra. de la Paz Don Diego de Parada.
2. Tucuman   ——   Don Pedro de Argadona.
3. Sta. Cruz de la Sierra Don Fern. Perez de Oblitas.
4. Paraguay   ——   Don Manuel de la Torre.
5. Buenos Ayres   ——   Don Jof. Anto. Bafurco y Herrera,

VII. *SANTA FÉ*. Archbifhop.

Don Joseph Xavier de Arauz.

SUFFRAGANS.

1. Popayan   ——   Don Geronymo de Obregon.
2. Cartagena   ——   Don Manuel de Sofa y Betancur.
3. Santa Marta   -   Don Nicolas Gil Martinez.

These were formerly in the nomination of the King, and afterwards the Concordate. This is not the cafe now. The Pope, the King, and the Archbifhop of Toledo divide the patronage. The *concordate* was an old council. or junto' for that purpofe ; but is lately abolifhed.

The bifhoprics in Spain have very fine revenues. The bifhops always go in the following drefs : A long robe and a
purple

purple rochet. They generally carry a crucifix, wear a crofs upon their breafts, and a ring.

THE clergy of Spain who are not of any particular monaftic order wear the regular drefs, confifting of a caffock, and a hood of flannel or filk. The caffock has a cape; and their hats are tucked up on both fides. The ecclefiaftical eftates are very confiderable.

LETTER III.

Of the GOVERNMENT of SPAIN, the *Cortes,* or PARLIAMENT, its LAWS, TRIBUNALS, COURTS of JUDICATURE, *&c.*

THE government of SPAIN was, by its ancient conftitution, a limited monarchy, of hereditary fucceffion, both in males and females. The male line ended in FERDINAND, who united CASTILE and ARRAGON, by marriage with ISABELLA of CASTILE. That Princefs dying at MEDINA DEL CAMPO, in 1505, left iffue, I. JOHN, who married MARGERITE, daughter

E of

of the Emperor MAXIMILIAN. 2. ISABELLA, married firſt to
Prince ALPHONZO, ſon of JOHN II. and afterwards to EMANUEL
óf PORTUGAL. 3. JOAN, who was afterwards Queen of CAS-
TILE. 4. MARY, who married EMMANUEL of PORTUGAL.
5. CATHERINE, who married ARTHUR Prince of WALES, and
afterwards HENRY VIII. of ENGLAND.

ISABELLA appointed her heirs by will, the Princeſs DONNA
JUANA her third daughter, conjointly with her huſband the
Archduke PHILIP, of BURGUNDY, ſon of the Emperor MAXI-
MILIAN, who was firnamed PHILIPPE LE FLAMAND. In conſequence of this teſtamentary diſpoſition, PHILIP claimed the
crown of CASTILE againſt his father-in-law FERDINAND. This
diſpute was however amicably adjuſted by an agreement in 1506,
that both parties ſhould have equal power and authority. But
PHILIP dying that ſame year, the power and crown of SPAIN
reverted entire into the hands of FERDINAND, who dying in
1516, was ſucceeded in the throne of SPAIN by his grandſon
CHARLES Vᵗ. who was the ſon of PHILIP by Donna JUANA,
ſtiled the *Fool*, who was the mother of two Emperors. And
thus the crown of SPAIN came into the houſe of AUSTRIA.
This monarchy was limited by its *Cortes*, or Parliament, compoſed of repreſentatives ſent from the cities and towns, each of
which, according to the old *Gothic* plan, ſent procurators,
or deputies, choſen by and out of the aldermen of their reſpec-
tive cities. The eldeſt member for BURGOS always acted as
ſpeaker of the houſe; though TOLEDO was a rival to BURGOS
for that privilege. In order to adjuſt amicably their two claims,
the King uſed to ſay on opening the ſeſſion of the *Cortes*, " I
" will ſpeak for TOLEDO, which will do what I order : But
" let BURGOS ſpeak *firſt*;" becauſe BURGOS was anciently the
capital of CASTILE. No act could paſs in this parliament by
majority of voices; it required the unanimous aſſent of all the members. All its acts were afterwards carried to the King to be confirmed. The members of this parliament were always aſſembled
in a *Cortes*, by letters convocatory from the King and privy council;

cil; and it was diffolved by a notification from the prefident of that council. But notwithftanding its diffolution, a committee of eight members ftill remained at court. This *Cortes* has rarely been called fince the year 1647, when they gave PHILIP IV. the *millones*, or general excife, and will probably never be affembled any more, as their power is great, and they can call minifters fo feverely to an account. The laft meeting of it that I know of, was in May 1713, when it affembled to receive the renunciation of PHILIP V. to his rights upon the crown of FRANCE. This affembly was antiently the keeper of the revenues of the crown. But CHARLES V. and his minifters firft laid them afide, becaufe they could get no money from them : And having obtained a grant of the fale of the bull of the *crufado* from the Pope, they found they could get money without the help of a *Cortes*, and fo took their leave of an affembly which few princes or minifters are fond of feeing.

THIS antient Spanifh *Cortes* undoubtedly refembled OUR ENGLISH *Parliament :* For all the northern nations had originally a like form of government, which was a limited monarchy, and the legiflative authority was fo commixt in the King and the eftates, that no laws could be made, repealed, or fufpended, nor any money raifed upon the fubject, but with their common confent. But now this *Cortes* is laid afide; SPAIN is no longer a mixed monarchy, but entirely abfolute; the whole government being folely in the hands of the King and his minifters, and the councils, which are altogether at their devotion. This change from mixed to abfolute monarchy was occafioned by the timidity of the commons of CASTILE, who having in their laft ftruggle for expiring freedom, fupported for fome time a war againft the crown, on a fingle defeat deferted the noble caufe of liberty in the moft abject manner. This war began in the year 1520, and lafted only two years : At which time CHARLES V. carried his point with a high hand, and told the *Cortes*, he would always have the fupplies granted firft, and then he would pafs the bills they petitioned for, and not before; to which they timidly fubmitted, and voted him four millions of ducats (about 480,000 *l.* fterling) to be paid in three years.

E 2.   THE

THE writ antiently fent to each city, as a fummons to parliament, convened all the prelates, mafters of the military orders of knighthood, earls, rich men, nobles, and procurators of the cities and towns throughout the realm, in the following manner : (take notice, that this is for CASTILE only, as CATALONIA and ARRAGON had a feparate *Cortes.*)

From the City of	Members.		Members.		Members.
BURGOS	8	TORO	4	TRUXILLO	2
TOLEDO	5	CALAHORRA	2	CANERES	2
LEON	5	OVIEDO	1	CADIX	2
SEVILLE	3	XEREZ	2	XERIZ	4
CORDUBA	3	ASTORGA	1	BEJAR	3
MURCIA	2	RODRIGO	1	VILLA REAL	3
JAEN	3	BADAJOX	1	CUELLAR	3
ABULA	2	CORIA	2	TARIFF	1
SALAMANCA	8	GUADALAJARA	2	HUETE	2
ZAMORA	4	CORUNNA	1	ANDUJAR	2
SEGOVIA	2	MEDINA DEL		ATIENCA	3
SORIA	4	CAMPO	2	MADRID	2
VALLADOLID	4	CUENZA	3	ALCARAZ	2
PLACENTIA	2	CARMONA	2	St. SEBASTIAN	2
BAEZA	3	EZIJA	2	SATIAGUN	2
UBEDA	3	VITORIA	2	FUENTE RU-	
		LOGRONNO	1	BIA	1

THIS is copied from a writ inferted in Dr. GEDDES's tracts, fent by Don HENRY II. of CASTILE in 1390, and fummons 125 members to the *Cortes,* which was afterwards affembled in the church of St. SALVADOR at MADRID. I am told, the oath, which the Kings of SPAIN take at the *Jura* on their acceffion, is as follows: " I do promife and fwear to maintain, and to caufe to " be maintained, to all the nobles, prelates, churches, and mafters " of the military orders; and to all the cities, towns, and villages, " all the fame privileges, grants, franchifes, exemptions, good " ufages and cuftoms, which they enjoyed in the reigns of my an- " ceftors, and in the fame manner."

THEIR Kings, according to the laws of SPAIN, are declared of age, or out of their minority, on the completion of their four-
teenth

teenth year. In regulating the fucceffion, after the death of
CHARLES II. a medium was obferved between the *Salic law*, and
the ufage of CASTILE; namely, that any *male* heir, howfoever
diftant, fhould inherit before a *female*, who was to have no right
but after the extinction of every male-branch.

SPANISH LAW, TRIBUNALS, and COURTS OF JUSTICE.

THE Laws of SPAIN are compounded chiefly of the *Roman*
civil law, the royal edicts, and probably certain provincial
cuftoms. Where they thought the *Roman* law was not fufficiently
extenfive, they have made large additions of their own. Thefe
are called the *Leyes de Partidas*; and form at prefent a fyftem
of modern *Spanifh* Law, and have been publifhed by BERNI and
CATALA in fix volumes octavo. The name *Partidas* comes from
the divifion of them into chapters. As to what we call Common
Law in ENGLAND, the SPANIARDS have no fuch thing; their
provincial cuftoms have fome refemblance to it, but their laws
are LEGES SCRIPTÆ. Much, however, of the *feudal* and *Gothic*
conftitutions ftill remain: Thus the grandees have ftill their vaffals, and very extenfive powers over their perfons. The ftudy of
the Spanifh lawyers confifts chiefly in that of their old *Gothic*
code, or the *Fuero Jufgo*, as they call it, which I apprehend to be
a more complete body of *Gothic* law than any thing of that fort
ever publifhed. It was compiled by SIJENARDO a *Gothic* prince,
in 631, was printed in 1600. It would have been a very confiderable addition to *Lindenbrogius's Gothic* Code, who has omitted
the *Gothic* laws made in SPAIN. Then the Code of Don SAN-
CHO, in the year 1000; then the *Fuero Royal* of ALPHONSO X.
in the year 1255: The *Roman Codes*, digefts, pandects, &c. and
after thefe the *Leyes de Partidas*, the *Pragmatica*, the royal edicts,
mandates, &c. Thofe who would know minutely and accurately the ftate of the Spanifh law, fhould read *Apparatus Juris Publici Hifpanici: Valentiæ*, 2 vol. 8vo. and *Sacra Themidis
Hifpanicæ*, 4to. and *L'Hiftoire du Droit Royal d'*ESPAGNE.

E 3   THEIR

THEIR great court of civil law is divided into the two chance-ries of VALLADOLID and GRANADA, which include the whole kingdom. Tho' ARRAGON, VALENTIA, and CATALONIA loſt their old privileges; yet they ſtill retain a court of chancery among themſelves in audiences held in the capital of each of thoſe king-doms, whoſe determinations are ſubjeſt only to the ſupreme council of CASTILE. If it be a caſe of property, the ſuit is commenced in that chancery to which the plaintiff belongs, and then the affair is referred to the *Conſejo Real y Supremo*, at which the King may order, if he pleaſes, all the deputy-councils to aſſiſt. The deter-mination here is not final, becauſe an appeal ſtill lies to the *Sala de Mil y Quinientos*; but that is final, and beyond it is no dernier reſort. The tribunals of VALLADOLID and GRANADA were inſtituted by Don HENRY of CASTILE, enlarged by Don JOHN I. and put on their preſent footing by FERDINAND and ISABEL-LA in 1499.

ALL other cauſes go before the reſpeſtive courts to which they belong, (whether civil, criminal, or commercial, which are as follow:

I. *The Royal or ſupreme Council of* CASTILE.

This and the following council are frequently aſſembled as one, to determine appeals made from the chanceries of *Valladolid* and *Granada:* And ſometimes affairs of the police are referred to them by the King.

II. *The ſecond Hall of Government.*

The determinations of theſe are not final, but the ultimate appeal lies to the following court.

III. *The Hall of the Mil y Quinientos.*

So called, becauſe the parties muſt firſt depoſite here *one thouſand five hundred doblas,* (about 223 *l.*) before the appeal can be lodged, which is not a large ſum, conſidering law-expences. This is nothing elſe but a committee of the ſupreme council.

IV. *The Hall of Juſtice.*

This is a court for matters purely litigious, and is a part of the ſupreme council.

V. *The*

V. *The Hall of the Province.*

This is a court of matters chiefly relating to the police.

VI. *The Fiscal: the Office of the Attorney General for the Royal Council.*

VII. *The Hall of the Alcaydes de la Casa y Corte.*

This hall was instituted by ALPHONZO X. to superintend the lodgings for the court, and to provide them. As every house in the kingdom was subject to this inconvenience, the landlords of houses made a composition with the crown to get rid of this grievance : and this composition is said to amount to 150,000 ducats *per annum*. This council was established to preserve this prerogative : and this court antiently found lodgings for all foreign ambassadors, as may be seen in Sir RICHARD FANSHAW's account of his embassy at the court of MADRID.

VIII. *The Supreme Council of War.*

This determines all causes relating to the army ; excepting what belongs to the council of the Indies.

IX. *Council of the Inquisition.*

This consists of an inquisitor-general ; of five counsellors, whereof one must always be a *Dominican* ; of a procurator ; two secretaries of the chamber ; two secretaries of the council ; an *Alguazil*-mayor ; a receiver ; two reporters ; two qualificators, and consultors, and a legion of *familiars*, or spies.

THE supreme office of this *Holy Tribunal*, as they call it, is at MADRID ; but there are also inferior holy tribunals, or inquisitionary offices, placed in the great cities almost all over SPAIN. These are the great state-curbs that hold the people in such an implicit religious obedience, and preserve their boasted uniformity of faith. " Among you ENGLISH," they cry, " you have as ma-" ny religions as districts ; but here all is undividedly Roman-" catholic." 'Tis true, we ENGLISH are enemies to all persecutive principles ; we breathe the spirit of toleration and humanity, and are unwilling to roast any man into Protestantism, or convince by racks, instead of Bibles. I remember 1 saw at SEGOVIA the tragic footsteps of the inquisition, which once was there, but is

4   now

now removed, in the badges of 5co Jews, who had been burnt in that single office only. The inquifitor *Torquemada* (according to Madame D'Aunois's account) in the time of Ferdinand and Isabella, tried above 100,000 souls, of which 6000 were burnt in lefs than 14 years time.

This court was erected in the XIIIth century, about the year 1251. Pope Innocent IV. authorized the *Dominicans* as perpetual inquifitors: Clement IV. confirmed thefe powers, and enlarged their privileges and tribunals in the year 1265. It was eftablifhed in Castile under Ferdinand and Isabella, and in Portugal by John III. in the year 1557. In 1483 Ferdinand obtained a bull to conftitute the inquifition in Arragon and Valentia from Sixtus IV. who afterwards extended it all over the catholic dominions.

This *holy office* ufed antiently to acknowledge only the power of the Pope above it, and bad defiance to all other controul. It raifed itfelf far above the authority of their Kings, who were often bridled, humbled, and even punifhed by it. It then was truly formidable, when fupported by the united force of papal and royal authority. Their *auto de fe's*, or folemn acts of faith, ufed to be exhibited commonly when their princes came of age, or at their acceffion.

In the year 1724, there was printed in London in 12°. *An Account of the Trial and Sufferings of* Mr. Isaac Martin, *who was put into the Inquifition in Spain, for the fake of the Proteftant Religion.*

This man, a native of London, a member of the church of England, kept a *pofada*, or inn, at Malaga, and traded as a merchant with fuch captains of merchant-fhips as touched there; taking their adventure, and giving them the product of the country in return, fuch as wine, fruit, oil, &c. He came, with a wife and four children, to fettle at Malaga in the year 1714, and having ftayed there four years, was accufed by a fet of Irifh papifts, who envied his better fuccefs in trade, in the bifhop's court, of fuch crimes as they commonly charge Proteftants with ; fuch as
                                                                his

his being a Jew, and an heretic, and having given too much fcandal, by his difcourfe and actions, to the *Malagans*, in regard to religion and matters of faith.   This was fufficient to accomplifh his ruin, which was the end they aimed at.   In the year 1718, he was taken up by order of the holy office, and conveyed to the inquifition of GRANADA, from whence after eight months imprifonment, and many vain attempts, by threats and hard ufage, to make him turn catholic, he was releafed in the following manner: As the man was an Englifh proteftant, refiding there under the protection of treaties fubfifting between the two crowns, his commitment and detention were a manifeft violation of thofe treaties, and of the law of nations : accordingly the Englifh Conful at *Malaga* reprefented the cafe in a proper manner to the Englifh minifter, and the minifter in confequence laid the affair before one of the fecretaries of ftate; who immediately reprefented the matter to his majefty GEORGE I. who was gracioufly pleafed to fend a very fpirited remonftrance to Cardinal ALBERONI, PHILIP V.'s firft minifter, claiming his own fubject, and infifting upon the immediate releafe of the faid ISAAC MARTIN from the prifon of the inquifition, and defiring that he might be fent back to England.   The cardinal, upon this, applied to the inquifitor-general to know how the cafe ftood : This gentleman, whofe name was Don JACINTO DE ABRANA, fent to the inquifitors at Granada for a true account of the cafe; and then wrote a letter to the cardinal, ftating the matter to him; upon which the cardinal gave orders for his releafe.   The original letter, which the inquifitor-general wrote to cardinal Alberoni upon this fubject, accidentally fell into my hands: It is manifeftly a letter written defignedly to be fhewn to the Englifh miniftry, in order to juftify the inquifition in fo illegal and inhuman a procedure.   There was, no doubt, another *private* letter written by the fame inquifitor to the cardinal, ftating the real injuftice and indefenfible circumftances of this imprifonment; otherwife had the account given in this publick letter been ftrictly true, the poor man had never been releafed at all.   What the inquifitor in this letter fays, indeed, was true enough, that feveral witneffes of *Malaga* had laid fuch charges againft the faid ISAAC MARTIN.   But he conceals what was equally true, that thefe witneffes were a fet of Irifh papifts, who,

F   out

out of envy to the man as a more fortunate trader, accufed him before the *inquifition*: that thefe were not only envious witneffes, but falfe witneffes, and had crouded into their charge many lies and little truth. A religion muft be grounded upon very flimfy evidence, that has recourfe to fuch wretched fhifts, to fuch low artifices for its fupport. The interceffion of GEORGE I. did indeed releafe this unhappy object; but how was he releafed? He received, upon his enlargement, two hundred lafhes, was whipped and pelted for three quarters of an hour through the ftreets of GRANADA, ftripped and plundered of all his effects, fent back to MALAGA, and then put aboard a fhip, with his wife and children, to fhift for themfelves.—— Upon a view of this cafe, I think one cannot help faying, that *the tender mercies* of the inquifition *are cruel*; and if this be the juftice of a chriftian country, let my lot be thrown among barbarians. The letter, which the Inquifitor-general wrote to cardinal Alberoni, upon this occafion, is an original piece never before publifhed, and is as follows:

＋.

Emminentiſſimo Senor.	Moſt Eminent Sir.
SENOR,	SIR,
EN cumplimiento del prezepto de Vueſtra Emminencia acerca dela priſſion, que ſe hizo, por el Santo Offizio de la Inquiſition de Granada, de la perſona de Iſaac Martin vezino de la ciudad de Malaga; Debo decir a Vueſtra Emminencia, que eſte Reo fue teſtificado en la Inquiſition por nueve teſtigos, de que ſe jactaba de ſer obſervante de la Ley de Moyſes; y que con eſcandalo de muchos decia, eſtabamos enganados los Catholicos en la creencia de nueſtra ſagrada Religion: y que ſiendo aſſi	IN obedience to the commands of your Eminence concerning the imprifonment, by order of the holy office of the inquifition of Granada, of the perfon of Ifaac Martin, inhabitant of Malaga: I ought to inform your Eminence, that that criminal was proved in the inquifition by nine witneffes to have boafted, that he was an obferver of the law of Mofes; and to the fcandal of many he faid, that we Catholics were in an error in the belief of our moft holy religion:
6	And

que muchos *Yngleses Protestantes hacian reverencia al santissimo sacramento, quando passaba por las calles, ó entraban en las yglesias, no solo no la hazia este Reo, sino que volvia las espaldas, y serraba las ventanas de sus casas, quando passaba alguna Procession, para que sus hijos y familia no hiziessen adoracion : Que ha hablado con Catholicos malamente de el summo Pontifice, y de las santas Imagenes, y articulos del Purgatorio : Y que haviendo embiado a sus hijos a la escuela, tubo un disgusto con el maestro, por que los ensennaba a persignar se, y las oraciones ; y por esto los saco de dicha Escuela : Y que hospedo a un Judio que passaba a Liorna, haviendo graves indicios de que se vino huyendo de Portugal, por temor de que se prendiesse aquella inquisition.*

And altho' many English Protestants did reverence to the most holy sacrament, when it passed along the streets, or when they entered into the churches : Yet this criminal did not only not do this, but turned his back upon it, and shut the shutters of his windows when any procession passed by, in order that his children and family might not worship the Host. And that he hath spoken defamatory words to catholics of the Pope, of the holy images, and our articles of faith relating to purgatory. And that having sent his children to school, he was disgusted with the master, because he taught them to cross themselves, and to say prayers : And that for this reason he took them from the said school : And that he lodged a Jew in his house, who was going to Leghorn, there being strong proofs, that that Jew fled from Portugal for fear of being apprehended by the inquisition of that kingdom.

C O N esta informazion fue mandado prender, y esta confesso en casi todos los cargos, negando solo el ser Judio. Y estando determinaao por los sagrados canones y leyes de estos reynos, y por los capitulos de Pazes entre esta y la corona de Yngalaterra, que el

With this information orders were given by the Inquisition for apprehending the person of the said Isaac Martin, and he hath confessed almost all the articles of the charge against him, but absolutely denies his being a Jew. It being however de-

*santo officio pueda y deba proze-
der contra los Yngleses que dieren
escandalo en punto de religion ; no
solo no ha contravenido en la prif-
sion de este Reo a ello, sino que el
procedimiento es en su conformi-
dad y obserbancia : Por lo qual,*

determined by the sacred canons,
and the laws of these kingdoms,
and by the articles of our treaties of peace between this crown
and that of England, that the
holy office may and ought to
proceed against such Englishmen, as say any thing scandalous
in matters of religion : The holy office has not only not done
any thing contrary to the said
canons, laws, and treaties of
peace, in the imprisonment of
this criminal, but the *procedimus*
is in conformity to them, and
observance of them. Wherefore,

*SUPPLICO a Vuestra Emmi-
nencia se sirva mandar responder;
que el santo officio prozede justa y
lexitimamente. O como Vuestra
Emminencia fuere servido.*

I SUPPLICATE your Emi-
nence to give for answer *(to the
English minister, I suppose)* that
the holy office hath proceeded
lawfully and rightly in this matter : Or that your Eminence
hath been obeyed.

*DIOS guarde a Vuestra Em-
minencia los muchos anos, que
puede y le supplico. MADRID,
y Abril 25 de 1718.*

GOD preserve your Eminence
many years, which I pray that
he may. MADRID, the 25th
of April, 1718.

*Emminentissimo Senor,
  Beso los manos de Vuestra Em-
    minencia,
     Su mas rendido Servidor*
       Jacinto de Abrana.

Most eminent Sir,
  I kiss your Eminence's hands,
    Your most truly
     and affectionately
      Jacinto de Abrana.

Al Emminentissimo Senor Cardenal *Alberoni.*

To his Eminence Cardinal Alberoni.

BUT

BUT now, thank God, thefe fanguinary acts of faith feem to be growing out of vogue in SPAIN. There has not been, I am told, an *auto de fe* at MADRID for thefe twelve years; which was owing to this circumftance: A *Jew*, and his wife, and a daughter of about thirteen years of age, being condemned to be burnt; while the father and mother were burning, they fet the child loofe from its fetters, and the priefts got round it, with a view of converting it by the united force of their rhetoric, and the terrors of imme-diately undergoing the fame cruel death. The child, after feem-ing to liften a while to their oratory, gave a fudden fpring, and vaulted into the midft of the fire; giving a fhining example of the force of early piety, of an heroic fortitude equal to that of the moft refolute Roman, or the moft unfhaken martyr.

THE power of this tribunal is now declining very vifibly, and feems haftening to its fall; for the prefent King of SPAIN has taken a bolder ftep to humble the inquifition, than any of the PHI-LIPS or CHARLES's who went before him. The inquifitor-ge-neral having thought proper, laft year, to prohibit a liturgy which the king had licenfed, without confulting his majefty about it; the king, with a very proper fpirit, put the inquifitor under an ar-reft, and immediately fent him, guarded with a file of grenadiers, into exile, in a convent, at a great diftance from MADRID. So determined and refolute a meafure as this, alarmed the whole body of the clergy; they moved heaven and earth to obtain the inqui-fitor's recal; but for fome time their endeavours had no effect: The king was inflexible. The common people were taught by their priefts to fay, that his Catholic Majefty was no good catho-lic in his heart. At length, however, the king reftored the inqui-fitor to his liberty: but in fuch a manner, as that prelate had no reafon to triumph; for his majefty, at the time of releafing him, publifhed at Madrid the following edict, which I fhall here give in the original Spanifh, and fubjoin to it a tranflation.

HAviendo confiderado qᵉ. no puede fatisfacer mi religiofo Celo los finceros defeos qᵉ tengo de proteger en todas occafiones las de-

HAving confidered that my re-ligious zeal cannot fatisfy the fincere defire I preferve for protecting on all occafions either the

terminaz[n] de la Santa Sede, ni las del Tribunal de la Ynquifiz[n]. de eftos Reynos en los graves, é importantes affumptos, que eftan encomendados a fu ciudado, y que con tanto Celo procura defempennar, fi antes que todos mis vafallos no tengo previa notiz[a] de las mifmas determinaz[n] y fino fe eftablecen las mas feguras reglas para évitar antes de fu promulgazion todos. riefgos de émbarazo, é incomben[te] hé refuelto defpues de una madura deliberazion, y confulta de mi Confejo, q[e] en adelante toda Bula, Breve, Refcripto, Exortation, o Carta Pontifizia fobre qualquiera affumpto que fea, que trate de eftablecer Ley, Regla, u óbfervanzia gen[l] que venga dirigida, ya fea en particular, ó general a los Tribunales, Juntas, Arz̃pos, Obifpos, ó Prelados de eftos Reynos, no fe haya de publicar, y obedezer, fin que primero confte haverla Yo vifto, y Examinado, y q[e] el Nuncio App[co] fi viniefe dirigida por fu mano la haya pafada a las mias por la via refervada de Eftado; que qualquier Bula, ó Breve de negozios entre partes, ó perfonas particular[s] ya fuere de gracia, ó juftiz[a] fe prefente, y examine en el Confejo de Caftilla, pueda verfe, fi de fu égecuz[n] puede refultar algun perjuicio al Concordato, a las Leyes, buenos ufos, y coftumbres, y quietud

the determinations of the holy-fee, or thofe of the inquifition of thefe kingdoms in the ferious and important bufinefs committed to their care, and which is executed with fo much zeal by that tribunal, unlefs I fhould be acquainted with thofe fame determinations previous to any notice given of them to my vaffals, and unlefs the moft fecure regulations fhould be eftablifhed for avoiding before the publication thereof every danger of embaraffment or inconvenience; I have refolved after mature deliberation, and with advice of my council, that henceforwards neither pontifical bulls, briefs, refcripts, exhortations, nor letters upon any fubject whatfoever, treating to eftablifh a law, regulation, or general obfervance, whether directed in particular, or in general to the tribunals, juntas, magiftracies, archbifhops, bifhops, or prelates of thefe kingdoms, fhall be publifhed, or obeyed, unlefs it appears to have been firft feen, and examined by Me; and if ever they fhould be addreffed to the apoftolic nuncio, he muft. pafs them to my hands by the fecretary of ftate's office: And that all bulls or briefs for bufinefs between private perfons or parties, whether they be of grace or juftice, fhall be

del Reyno, ó perjuicio de terzero, exceptuando unicam.ᵗᵉ de esta presentaz.ⁿ las dispensas, y Breves, que se expiden por la sacra Penitenziaria para el fuero interno de la conzienz.ᵃ que el Ynq.ᵒʳ general no publique edicto álguno dimanado de Bulla, ó Breve Pontifizio, sinque se le pase de mi orden a este fin, supuesto que todos los ha de entregar el nuncio à mi persona ó a mi primer secretario del despacho de estado, y que si perteneciese à prohibizion de libros, observe la forma prevenido en el Auto àcordado 14. titulo 7ᵘ· lib. 1ᵒ· haziendolos examinar de nuebo, y prohibiendolos si lo merecieren por propia potestad, y sin insertar el Breve: Que tampoco publique el Ynq.ᵒʳ general edicto alguno, ó expurgatorio en la corte ni fuera de ella sin darme parte por el secretario del despacho de grazia y justiz.ᵃ ò en su falta cerca de mi persona por el de estado, y que se le haya respondido que lo consiento, y finalm.ᵗᵉ que antes de condenar el Ynq.ᵒʳ general y el tribunal de la Ynq.ᵒⁿ qualq.ᵒ libro, ò papel, oiga las defensas, que quisieren hazer los interesados citandolos para ello conforme à las reglas prescriptas a la Ynquisiz.ⁿ de Roma por el Papa Benedicto XIV. en la Constituzion App.ᶜᵃ que empieza, solicita ac provida. En Buen Retiro à 27 de Nov. de 1761.

be prefented to, and examined by the council of Caftile, in order to difcover, if any prejudice can refult from its obfervance, either to the concordatum' or to the laws, good cuftoms and practices, or to the tranquillity of the kingdom, or to the prejudice of any third perfon, excepting folely from this prefentation, the difpenfations and briefs difpatched by the holy penitenciary for the internal forum of confciences: And that the inquifitorgeneral fhall not publifh any edict, proceeding from any pontifical bull, or brief, unlefs it be tranfmitted to him by my order; for they muft all be delivered by the nuncio to my perfon, or to my firft fecretary of ftate; and that if they belong to the prohibition of any books, the formality muft be obferved, as exprefled in the 14th Auto, tit. 7. book I. caufing the books to be examined again, and then, if they fhould deferve it, prohibiting them by his own authority, and without inferting the brief: And likewife that the inquifitorgeneral fhall net publifh in the court, or out of it, any edict, or expurgatory, without firft giving notice thereof to me, by the fecretary of difpatch, of grace, and juftice, or in his abfence, from my perfon, by the fecretary of

ftate;

ftate; nor without obtaining in anfwer my confent: And finally, that before any book or paper be condemned by the inquifitor-general, or by the tribunal of the inquifition, they fhall hear the defence that the concerned may defire to make, citing them for that purpofe, according to the regulations prefcribed to the inquifition of Rome by Pope Benedict XIV. in the Apoftolic Conftitution, which begins, *Solicita ac provida*, &c. Buen Retiro, the 27th November 1761.

X. *The Royal Council of the Indies.*

The Duke of Alva is chancellor of it.   This is juridical only.

L E T T E R

LETTER III. PART II.

COUNCILS, HALLS, and TRIBUNALS.

XI. *Royal Council of the Orders of Knighthood.*

Inftituted for the regulation and government, and to preferve the privileges of thofe orders, by FERDINAND the Catholic, in 1489. As thefe Spanifh orders feem not to be very well known in England, I will now give fome account of them. They are,

1. The Order of the GOLDEN FLEECE.
2.   Of ST. JAMES, or SAN JAGO.
3.   Of ALCANTARA.
4.   Of CALATRAVA.
5.   Of MONTESA.
6.   Of THE HABIT OF CHRIST.

I. *The Order of the Golden Fleece* came originally from the houfe of BURGUNDY. PHILIP *the Good,* Duke of BURGUNDY, inftituted it in 1429. The collar of this order has a lamb hanging to it, with this motto, *Pretium non vile laborum.* The prefent members of this order are as follow :

LIST *of the* KNIGHTS *of the* GOLDEN FLEECE; *as it ftood in the Year* 1760.

The KING, *Chief, and Sovereign of the Order.*
The MARQUEZ DE GRIMALDO, *Chancellor.*
CONDE DE CANILLAS, *Regifter.*
D. MANUEL MUNOZ Y' HESTARTE, *King at Arms.*
G   *KNIGHTS.*

KNIGHTS.

1. Duc de Noialles, March 7, 1702.
2. Conde del Montijo, December 9, 1713.
3. Duc de Sully, December 31, 1714.
4. Marquez de Arienzo, March 16, 1719.
5. The Serene Duke of Parma, May 27, 1723.
6. Comte de Coigni, July 22, 1734.
7. The Serene Infant Don Luis, October 24, 1735.
8. Duque de Sora, October 21, 1736.
9. Don Miguel Reggio, December 18, 1737.
10. Marquez de las Minas, January 23, 1738.
11. Duc de Penthievre, April 27, 1738.
12. Prince Albert of Poland, November 28, 1738.
13. The King of France, March 13, 1739.
14. The Most Serene Dauphin, March 13, 1739.
15. Conde de Jablonewski, January 20, 1740.
16. Elector of Bavaria, January 20, 1742.
17. Duc de Belleisle, April 5, 1742.
18. Duc de Lauraguais, June 19, 1745.
19. Duque de Alva, May 26, 1746.
20. Comte de Noailles, May 27, 1746.
21. Duque de Medina Coeli, April 9, 1748.
22. Serene Prince of Asturias, January 3, 1749.
23. Duke Clement of Bavaria, June 11, 1749.
24. Marquez de la Ensenada, April 12, 1750.
25. Duque de Bejar, April 12, 1750.
26. Prince of Parma, February 2, 1751.
27. King of Naples, February 2, 1751.
28. Serene Infant Don Gabriel, June 9, 1752.
29. Serene Duke of Orleans, June 9, 1752.
30. Prince Masseran, September 22, 1752.
31. Principe de San Nicandro, September 22, 1752.
32. Duque de Bournombile, December 18, 1753.
33. Marquez de Villa Franca, December 18, 1753.
34. Duque de Medina-Sidonia, December 18, 1753.
35. Serene Duke of Burgundy, March 27, 1754.
36. Constable Colonna, December 16, 1755.

L.

37. Se

37. Serene Infant Don Antonio, January 16, 1756.
38. Conde de Aranda, April 13, 1756.
39. Serene Infant Don Francisco, March 11, 1757.
40. Marquez de Monte Alegre, September 5, 1758.

Created since, on the Rupture between England and Spain.

Duc de Choiseul.
Conde de Fuentes, &c.

The grand mastership of this order was made hereditary in the Kings of Spain, of the house of Austria: consequently the present King of Spain has no right to it.—The rest were instituted to encourage a spirit of cruzading.

II. *The Order of San Jago, or St. James,* is divided into twelve governments. It was instituted in the twelfth century, and confirmed by Pope Alexander III. in the year 1175. Its revenues, arising from 87 commanderies, are computed at 230,000 ducats, (28,750 pounds.) Each knight is obliged, by his feudal tenure, to furnish the King yearly with 368 lances, to make war against the infidels. They compound for this with the King, and pay a certain yearly sum.

III. *The Order of Alcantara* was called *the noble*; because, to be a knight, you must prove your nobility for four generations past; whereas the other orders required only a proof through two descents. The knights of *Alcantara* have 38 commanderies, worth 200,000 ducats, (25,000 pounds.) These furnish only 138 lances to the King.

IV. *The Order of Calatrava,* instituted in the twelfth century, for the defence of that city against the Moors in 1158, and Pope Alexander III. confirmed it. They have 54 commanderies, worth 110,000 ducats revenue, (13,750 pounds.) They furnish 300 lances to the King.

V. *The Order of Montesa* is only worn in Valentia, and was established in 1317. It has 9 commanderies.

The King of Spain is grand master of these orders.

Be-

BESIDES thefe the prefent King of SPAIN has now introduced the Neapolitan order of St. JANUARIUS: And has ordered that to be worn in his court above the French order of the *St. Efprit*, or that of the *Golden Fleece*.

XII. *Royal Council of the Hazienda, or Treafury.*

This is not properly the treafury, but rather a court of exchequer: All the King's revenues are received by an annual treafurer, who is generally a member of this body. This council was inftituted by PHILIP III.

XIII. *The Hall of the Millones.*

Here are paid in the impofts called *Alcavalas* and *Millones*, the firft of which are the moft ancient revenues of the crown of SPAIN, eftablifhed originally by the Moors. They were at firft a fifth, afterwards a tenth part of the value on goods bought or fold. They are now about 14 *per cent.* and are exacted alfo on private confumption, as if you kill your own meat, &c. you pay the *Alcavala*. The *Millones* are a fort of general excife given by the *Cortes* to PHILIP IV. in 1647, are the heavieft tax in all SPAIN, and renewed every fix years.

XIV. *The Hall of Juftice and Grace.*

This is an office, through which all commiffions and grants of the crown pafs.

XV. *Tribunal of the Greater Chamber of Accompts.*

This is a check upon the King's treafurers; for the gentlemen of this office audit all their accounts, and can reject any part of them. It was eftablifhed in 1574, by PHILIP II.

XVI. *General Commiffion of Crufade.*

When CHARLES V. grew tired of afking money of his *Cortes*, and was willing to free himfelf from their controul; in order to become abfolute, he had recourfe to other expedients of getting money, and fet himfelf at work to find other fources, for his

his royal revenues. With this view he petitioned CLEMENT VII. to grant him the profits arising from the sale of those indulgences, which are contained in the *bull of the crusado.* The Pope very complaisantly granted the request; and the contrivance compleatly answered that prince's expectation: For indulgences have always sold better in SPAIN, than in any other country. There are four *bulls* granted by the see of ROME to SPAIN exclusively; these are,

I. *The Bull of the Crusado,* which grants plenary indulgence to all who shall serve personally for the space of one year in war against the infidels; or if they send soldiers to that service; or if they contribute *two rials of plate* (about the value of an English shilling) for that purpose. In the INDIES, where money was to be had in greater plenty, the price of this bull was prodigious; it has been sold for a pound of gold. Those that purchase this bull twice in one year, have a *double* indulgence or absolution: For it lasts only for the space of one year, so that a new one must be bought annually by every individual. The next bull is,

II. *The Bull for the Dead.* This being bought for any dead person, it ensures them absolution from all sin, and sets them free from purgatory.

III. *The Bull of Composition.* This entitles the purchasers to a right to any stolen goods, or such effects as they may be unlawfully possessed of; for by buying this indulgence, they compound with the Pope for them. How much shorter a process is this, than our English method of hearings in the King's Bench, or a tedious chancery-suit! One twelve-penny indulgence adjudges the property to the thief himself. This the Pope does by virtue of his being supreme lord of all *temporal,* as well as spiritual goods.

IV. The last is *the Bull of Milk.* This is an indulgence to eat flesh, butter, cheese, and eggs in Lent.

THUS you see the business of this council, or *general commission of Crusade,* is to distribute those bulls; to raise a revenue to the
crown,

crown, under a pretence of levying a tax for crufading: Its great object is the maintenance of CEUTA, for that is the *fole tenure* by which they hold the grant of thofe bulls: For were they to lofe CEUTA, they would lofe all pretenfions to this tax, which would revert to the fee of ROME. In this council all books of religion are examined; no breviary nor miffal can be printed without its licence. It is the depofitary of ftolen goods unowned. It was erected in the year 1525. All the King's fubjects are obliged to buy the indulgence belonging to the *bull of the Crufado*, to enable them to go to confeffion, receive abfolution, and to communicate; for if they bring not this bull, the priefts will neither abfolve them, nor give them the wafer. This very confiderable part of the crown revenues was given in confequence of Cardinal XIMENES's expedition into AFRICA. All the benefices in SPAIN are taxed for the crufade. TOLEDO alone pays 50,000 ducats yearly, (6250 pounds;) the contribution of the clergy is great, but of the laity ftill more: Thefe bulls are faid to produce yearly, in SPAIN only, 1,200,000 ducats (above 57,000 *l.* fterl.) and about double that fum in AMERICA. Thofe who die without having bought them, die excommunicated.

XVII. *Board of Works and Forrefts.*

XVIII. *Council of Commerce, Money, and Mines*; or a board of trade.

XIX. *Junta de Facultades y de Viudedades.*

What the nature of this board is, I cannot fay, having made feveral enquiries in vain about it: Tho' I am inclined to believe, that it relates to cafes of property and perfonal eftates, and particularly widows jointures.

XX. *Apoftolical Junta.*

To appoint miffionaries.

XXI. *Junta of Tobacco.*

To manage the farm of the tobacco.

XXII. *Junta*

XXII. *Junta of the Provisions.*

This is a council of persons of rank and property, who are obliged to furnish MADRID with bread and all other provisions at a fixt price. It has the preference of the first purchase at all markets.

XXIII. *Tribunal of the first Physician.*

DON JOSEPH SUNOL, of the Council of his Majesty, and first Physician of the Chamber, *President.*

DON MIGUEL BARBON, of the Council of his Majesty, and his Physician of the Chamber, *Vice-president.*

DON JOSEPH AMAR, Physician to his Majesty, and first Physician.

DON ANDRES PIQUER, Physician of the Chamber of his Majesty, and first Physician.

DON MATTHIAS DE LA RUBIA, *Assessor.*

DON FR. ANT. DE VERGARA, *Fiscal.*

DON FR. XAVIER DE QUESADA, *Secretary.*

XXIV. *Tribunal of the Nonciature, or Concordate.*

This related, among other articles, to the disposal of *ecclesiastical preferments.* It was abolished by an agreement between the courts of ROME and SPAIN, in 1753.

ACADEMIES ERECTED

In this Court under the Royal Protection.

XXV. ROYAL SPANISH ACADEMY.

HIS EXCELLENCE THE DUKE OF ALVA, Dean of the Council of State, *Director.*

DON FRANCISCO DE ANGULA, *Secretary.*

XXVI. ROYAL ACADEMY OF HISTORY.

D. AUG. DE MONT. Y LUYANDO, perpetual Director for his Majesty, and Secretary of the Chamber of Grace and Justice, and Estudo of Castille.

D. EUG.

D. Eug. de Llaguno Amirola, *Secretary* *.

XXVII. Royal Academy of the Three Noble Arts, Painting, Sculpture, Architecture, with the Title of San Fernando.

His Excellency D. Ricardo Wall, Protector and Counfellor of State.

D. Tib. de Agirre, *Vice Protector* of the Council of the Orders.

D. Ig. de Hermositta, Secretary.

XXVIII. Royal Academy of Physic at Madrid.

Don J. Sunol, *Counfellor* of his Majefty, and his firft Phyfician, perpetual *Prefident* for his Majefty.

Don A. Piquer, Phyfician of his Majefty, *Vice Prefident,* and firft Phyfician.

Don J. de Ortega, *Secretary.*

---

* The Academy of Hiftory at Madrid was founded in 1713, by the Duke de Escalona, who is well known to the republic of letters. There is another Academy at Seville, chiefly relating to the Mathematics.

LETTER

LETTER IV.

STATE of LITERATURE, LETTERS, and
MEN of LEARNING in SPAIN.

IN regard to learning, and the belles lettres, SPAIN evidently
labours under two material difadvantages; which are, the
want of a liberty of the prefs; and the being fubjected to the cenfure of the inquifition. It is eafy to imagine how many valuable
works of wit, humour, fatire, and genius are entirely rendered
abortive for want of this liberty; and though it may be attended
with fome evils and inconveniencies, yet its advantages are evident,
from the many entertaining and ufeful productions, which in our
ifland folely owed their birth to it: for, as one well faid, Is it not
better for the public, that a million of monfters fhould come into
the world, which are fure to die as foon as they are born, than
that one *Hercules* fhould be ftrangled in his cradle? Let us bear
patiently with the infamous productions of infidelity and faction,
as long as we can receive from the fame channel, the admirable
difcourfes of a SHERLOCK, or a HARE; the political writings of
a BOLINGBROKE, or a BATH, and the various mafterly and elegant compofitions of a LYTTLETON. What would have become of the wit and buffoonery of Dr. SWIFT, the elegant obfervations of Mr. ADDISON, and the genteel humour of Sir RICHARD
STEELE, if their free and unfhackled fpirits had been chained down
like thofe of the *Spaniards?* Where would have been thofe many
pleafing and inftructive writings which daily fprung up, thro' this
liberty, at different periods, in the many controverfial wars which

H   we

we have had upon fubjects of party, politics, learning, and even religion? Would not all thefe have been deftroyed in the bud, if
we had feen, as Mr. POPE fays, under the throne of Ignorance or
Superftition,

> Beneath her footftool Science groan in chains,
> And Wit dread exile, penalties and pains.
> There, foam'd, rebellious Logic, gagg'd and bound ;
> There, ftript, fair Rhet'ric languifh'd on the ground ?

It is a matter of much more furprize to me, when I confider
things in this light, to find that the *Spaniards* are advanced fo far
as they are in arts and fcience, than to wonder, that they are got
no farther. If we add to this the power and uncontrouled licence, which the Inquifitors or Dominicans have to cenfure all
works printed there, and if they pleafe, to chaftife and punifh the
authors, it would furely make a full apology for SPAIN in this
article. I know not well how many *licences* a book muft have
before it can actually pafs the prefs, but I think at leaft three. It
is ufually read by as many cenfors, and is carefully cleanfed by
the Catholic fpunge, before it falls under the eye of the public.
The inquifition never grants any licence, referving to itfelf the
freedom of condemning or abfolving afterwards, as it may judge
expedient. The art of this management is apparent. The index of the *Libri Probibiti* publifhed by the holy office is now
increafed to two large volumes in folio; and a man muft fairly turn
over all that work, before he can well know what he dare read.
The claffics that I opened in the royal library at MADRID were
anathematized in the title with thefe words, *Auctor Damnatus*,
and many whole prefatory difcourfes were erazed and blotted
out, becaufe, as the librarian told me, *Ils font contre notre religion*. I have been told by a Spaniard, a friend of mine, that the
Dominican library, confifting only of books which they have feized, and which of courfe are forbidden, is one of the largeft and
fineft in MADRID. I have heard many of them own, that the
prohibited books were generally the moft worth reading. One in
particular told me, that as Father PAUL's hiftory of the council of
TRENT was forbidden to be read any where upon earth, he took it
with him, and read it at fea. It is no uncommon thing here to fee
the

the works of our LOCKE, NEWTON and BACON, thofe immortal glories of human nature, fhut up in durance. But how fhould it be otherwife, when, as BAYLE tells us, in an extract from JOHN of SALISBURY, that Pope GREGORY VI. not only banifhed mathematics from the court, but burnt a library of heathen learning, in order to give the Scripture more authority. ERASMUS found the weight of this millftone upon the neck of fcience almoft infupportable at the time that he was making fuch noble efforts for the revival of letters: And the ignorance and indolence of the monks, which he fo much exclaims againft in thofe days, is very little altered for the better in the prefent. Few of them, even now, either underftand or talk the Latin tongue; and fewer ftill are employed in ftudies of real or ufeful learning: they are chiefly confined to the narrow limits of the fcholaftic writers, the polemic divines, and Thomaftic or Auguftin theology. I fpeak only in general, for doubtlefs there are fome exceptions, fuch as a FLORES, a PONCE, a BURRIEL, or a FEIJO; but thefe are rare, and fhine, like lamps in fepulchres, amidft the numerous cells of thofe ufelefs ecclefiaftics. Great part of this dearth of fcholars is certainly owing to the want of a due encouragement, a reftriction of the liberty of the prefs, and their fubjection to the yoke of the inquifition. And how much they have fuffered from thefe curbs may be eafily gathered from a few facts that have paffed in SPAIN only. Poor MIGUEL CERVANTES, the inimitable author of *Don Quixote*, underwent many fevere fufferings in combating thofe triple monfters, prejudice, ignorance, and fuperftition. The incomparable JOHN DE MARIANA, whofe labours and ftudies have done fuch lafting honour to himfelf, and to his country, was confined twenty years in prifon, and when he wrote his Hiftory, he dared not to bring it down any nearer to his own times, for fear of giving offence. And even within thefe two or three laft years, Dr. ISLA, who wrote that pretty fatire, *Frey Gerundio*, upon the monks and preachers of thefe times, has been perfecuted and filenced by the inquifition for his impertinent wit.

SUCH being then the true ftate of the cafe, we are certainly much obliged to thofe wits and geniufes in SPAIN, who have had firmnefs enough to break through all thefe obftacles, and have

pro-

produced works, which have made their names the theme of their own countrymen, and refpected and efteemed abroad. The Com-PLUTENSIAN Bible* has undoubtedly been the beft monument to the memory of Cardinal XIMENES, and would atone, if any thing could atone, for the fhare which he had in eftablifhing the inquifition. This certainly doubles the merit of fuch writers, who have been fo hardy as to ftep forth in this country: fuch as, CER-VANTES, COVARRUBIAS, FAXARDO, ZURITA, CABRERA, SAN-DOVAL, MARIANA, ANTONIO PEREZ, GARCILASSO DE LA VE-GA, LOPEZ DE VEGA, CARPIO, ANTONIO DE GUEVARA, CAL-DERONI, ANT. DE SOLIS, HERRERA, &c. It makes us regard in a much higher light fuch men as ANTONIO AUGUSTINO, VIL-LALPANDO, L. RAMIREZ DE PRADO, SANCTIUS, and others.

BUT in order to fet this point in a clearer view, I will now make fome general remarks upon the prefent ftate of Divinity, Hiftory, Phyfic, and Poetry in this country, and then fubjoin a lift and account of the moft remarkable writers in each branch.

IN regard to Divinity, it confifts much, as it formerly did, in the ftudy of the fathers, councils, the decrees of the popes, and their canons, and in fyftems of Thomaftic and Auguftine theology. The knowlege of the learned languages, and explication of the text of the facred writings, has very little to do with it. In this track of criticifm they are almoft utter ftrangers; and I cannot find any thing of late years publifhed in this way: It is holy ground, and therefore dangerous to be approached. In cafuiftry indeed they are very well verfed, and this makes a conftant part of the ftudies of their paftoral office: I fuppofe it is in fome meafure ne-ceffary to fuch as muft be confeffors; but whether it is fo far re-quifite, as to run into fuch obfcene difquifitions, as refine, and re-duce finning to a fyftem, it will be difficult to perfuade our divines.

* This was the firft *Polyglot* ever printed, and was done at the expence of the cardinal, then archbifhop of Toledo. It was about four years in printing, from 1514 to 1517, but not publifhed till 1520, when it came out in 6 volumes, including the Lexicon: It was printed in four languages, the Hebrew, Chaldee, Greek, and Latin. This ferved as a model to that of Mr. Walton, which is more ufeful and exact, and to that of Mr. Le Jay, printed at Paris with many expenfive ornaments.

But

But that this kind of cafuiftry is too infamoufly ftudied, appears from the many tomes that have been publifhed in this country, and particularly in that curious refearch of *Sanchez de Matrimonio*. When I fay the fathers, take notice I mean the Latin fathers; for as to the Greek, there are very few amongft them, who are able to undertake that tafk : for the ftudy of the learned languages is here but at a low ebb; Hebrew feems to be rather the moft culti-vated. It may not be improper to obferve, that I am told there is a MS. of St. AUGUSTINE in the Bodleian library at Oxford, in which there is a paffage allowing the clergy to marry; which paffage is not extant in any Roman-catholic copy that was ever heard of.

THE lawyers in this country get as much money as the practi-tioners in other countries; and whatever may be faid of the flow-nefs of our chancery fuits, the tedioufnefs of theirs will at leaft equal them : A friend of mine, a great merchant at CADIZ, has juft obtained a caufe at MADRID, after *nine* years attendance; and I could mention fome others, which are at this time depending, which probably will never be determined at all. Bribery ope-rates too much in this country; and to do the *Spaniards* juftice, they do not difown it. It appeared very plainly in the famous caufe of the ANTIGALLICAN privateer, in which the late Sir BENJAMIN KEENE took fuch patriotic and difinterefted pains; and in many others, which might be mentioned.

IN Hiftory, the Spaniards have many valuable writers. The detail of particular wars, as that of GRANADA, between PHILIP IV. and the MOORS, by MENDOSA, faid to be a mafterly work; the relation of the fucceffion-war, or partition of the Spanifh mo-narchy, by SAN FELIPPE, &c. the ecclefiaftical hiftory of SPAIN by Father HENRY FLORES, in fifteen volumes 4to. &c. the hi-ftory of particular cities, fuch as *Toledo, Seville*, &c. Their great antiquarians are FLORIO OCAMPO, AMBROSIUS MORALES, MA-RIANA; REQUESENDIUS for thofe of PORTUGAL. But I can-not find, that any writer of credit (for fome have attempted it) has been yet bold enough to take up the thread of their gene-ral hiftory, where MARIANA left it off, that is to fay, with FER-DINAND and ISABELLA (for the fupplement and continuator

Mi-

MINIANA I don't confider) and bring it down to thefe times. Perhaps they do not care to attempt it, for fear of offence ; and another reafon may be, that the King has abfolutely forbid any of his fubjects to write the hiftory of CHARLES V.; which, I fuppofe, is owing to fome circumftances relating to religion and that prince, which might be too delicate to touch upon. Tho' it would be both a curious and ufeful tafk to trace the fecret fprings and caufes that fet a prince of his active and aduft complexion upon fuch various and great enterprizes ; who made vaft advances towards univerfal monarchy, and perhaps was nearer to it than any other man ever was fince ALEXANDER and CÆSAR; who was not contented to reign while living, but left a political teftament for his fon's direction after his death; and, what was more extraordinary, a teftament, which that fon religioufly obferved and copied from. What can be more aftonifhing, than to fee this fame active and reftlefs fpirit, all at once, in a fit of difguft, retire to the narrow cell of a poor monk, and there amufe himfelf with acting over the approaching fcene of his own death! For this, however odd it may feem, was certainly done; and tho' alive, he had the fame preparations made, of proceffion, mournings, coffin, &c. as if he really was dead, and was at the fame time, what no man ever was before, or will be probably again, the fubject, actor, and fpectator, all at once, of his own funeral. PHILIP of MACEDON's fo much talked of *Memento Mori* was poor to this. This was a fight, which, I believe, few people's curiofity would not wifh to have feen. But this was not all : tho' CÆSAR was his model, tho' he conquered all things, he could not, like that Prince, conquer himfelf : for he foon repented that he ever had refigned the world and his crown, and died at laft of chagrin, at the folly of having done that act, which he could never revoke.

LETTER

LETTER IV. PART II.

STATE of PHYSIC, POETRY, &c.

IN Phyſic and Chirurgery this country is at leaſt two centuries behind the Engliſh. But as thoſe arts are much out of my province, I ſhall give what I have to offer upon them in the words of one of their moſt eminent writers. There is ſcarce any ſtudy that takes in ſuch a variety of knowledge as Phyſic doth, and therefore it is no wonder, that the Spaniards, who are ſlow in all things, have made ſuch a ſmall progreſs in this part of ſcience. But perhaps the people may be perſuaded that they have leſs occaſion for it; where they believe that ſaints, miracles, and charms, can cure the moſt inveterate diſeaſes, there muſt be much leſs inclination to have recourſe to art: They may be willing to leave the more feeble reſources of meer human aſſiſtance to thoſe, who are ſo unhappy as to want faith. Not but they have their regular profeſſors in this part of ſcience. Dr. SANGRADO's maxims ſtill prevail among them, notwithſtanding they are ſo finely ridiculed by Monſ. LE SAGE, in his GIL BLAS. There cannot be a more ſtriking proof of their want of ſkill, than the epidemical prevalence of the venereal diſeaſe all over this country; tho' poſſibly they may not deſire to have it quite ſubdued. Give me leave to relate part of a converſation, which I had with a chirurgeon upon that ſubject. He was ſent for by a nobleman to cure him of that diſtemper, who told his excellency, that if he would follow ſuch a regimen and diet, and regularly take what he preſcribed, that he would cure him in a month's time entirely: " Cure me entirely!" replied the nobleman; " no not for the " world; I only want you, ſir, to correct and leſſen it a little; but " I would not be cured entirely upon any account: a little of it " is the beſt thing in nature for the health."—" Sir," replied my
friend,

friend, " if your excellence only wants *palliatives*, a Spanish chi-
" rurgeon will answer that purpose as well as me: my business is to
" cure, not to continue distempers.—Good morning to your ex-
" cellence."

As to dispensaries, and accounts of the *Materia Medica*, they
may have them, but I met with none. Botany is much studied
here, and is well understood: And I am told that the provinces
of GALLICIA and VALENTIA afford great plenty of very excellent shrubs and plants.

Part of Father F E I J O o's Discourses upon PHYSIC.

Translated from the Original Spanish.

[The Physicians he chiefly quotes, are, MICHAEL ETMULLER, GEORGIUS BAGLIVIUS, THOMAS SYDENHAM, LE FRANÇOIS, DON MARTIN MARTINEZ.]

THE Spanish physicians follow the system of GALEN, and LA-
ZARUS RIVERIUS: It is from GALEN they have taken the
practice of *bleeding* so profusely. But some of the *Spaniards*, such
as MARTINEZ, have declared against this practice, and would not
admit of it even in putrid fevers; and he said, that the lancet had
killed more men, than ever were shot by a train of artillery. FEI-
JOO seems to be of this opinion: he says, he believes in some cases
it may be proper, but difficult to say *when*; that you cannot judge
of the goodness or badness of blood by any symptoms, because it
alters immediately on coming out of the veins; because every individual's blood is different, and let it appear ever so bad to the
doctor, the patient cannot live without it. It is for this reason he
condemns all transfusion of blood from one patient to another, as
arrant nonsense: and affirms that experiments upon blood confirm
this doctrine. Our author is likewise no friend to purging, as he
says it carries off the good as well as the bad, the nutricious as well
as the pernicious juices; and that it forces the excrements sometimes thro' improper passages. As to saying, that it purges away
the

the choler, or *the phlegm*, that is all imaginary ; becaufe purges carry
off all things indifcriminately ; and becaufe they give the different
colours to the voided excrements by their different tinctures : *Epi-
thymy* will give a black dye ; and it is well if this be the worft of it :
Phyficians fhould take care left they kill their friends as well as
their enemies, as the Turks did at the fiege of Rhodes. In common cafes you fhould never purge ; never in the beginning of fevers, except in cafes of turgency, and even then in the beginning
it is inexcufable, and in the end doubtful : It is an effort of nature ;
leave Her to herfelf : for purges never affect the morbid matter,
unlefs it happens to be in the *primæ viæ*, and then there is no
doubt of the ufefulnefs of purging. Thofe purges which gripe the
moft are the beft, becaufe the griping comes not from the purge,
but from the acid matter they put in motion. And as to vomits
and clyfters, by the authority of SYDENHAM, I reject them in all
fevers. In fine, there is nothing certain in medicine. One phyfician admires one remedy, which another abhors. What has been
faid for and againft *hellebore ?* for and againft *antimony ?* With
thefe they are *panaceas*, with thofe poifons. What a rout has been
made about medicinal ftones ! the *bezoar*-ftone and many others ?
Cordials are much the fame. Coftly medicines and exotics are juft
as futile ; all, all a fable. One houfe-medicine is worth them all.
A French phyfician I have read of ufed to give all his patients
coffee ; tho' I am perfuaded neither coffee nor tea are of any fervice. The moft known fpecifics begin to be called in queftion ;
the *bark* has many enemies ; and *mercury* begins to be declaimed
againft, though it certainly is the moft generous medicine in the
whole world. I appeal to experience. Englifh falts are hurtful,
becaufe they purge too gently. Too much, too many medicines
certainly do a patient more hurt, than any other miftaken practice.
All phyficians abufe remedies ; none obferve the *crifis* of diftempers ; they fhould never difturb nature : and to apply many medicines, when nature is fighting with a diftemper, is to weaken the
patient's force, when he moft wants it, and taking fide with the
difeafe, inftead of taking part with nature. As to ignorant prac-
titioners, it is in vain to diffuade them from giving much phyfic :
but if any phyfician of real knowledge does it for the fake of af-
fifting the apothecary, and of vending his medicines, the foul of

I   that

that phyfician is in a much more deplorable ftate, than any patient's body. No view of retaining patients, no reafons of convenience, honour, or of being well with the apothecaries, fhould
induce them to this practice : as they will certainly be culpable
in the fight of GOD for whatever damage they may do their
patients.

As to phyfical or medicinal obfervations, there is great infin-
cerity in them, becaufe a phyfician gives ONE cafe in which fuch
a prefcription fucceeded, and conceals *two*, in which it did not.
Every body knows the obfervations of *Riverius*, which have gained great applaufe; and tho' they amount to 400, there is fcarce
one which is not defective : It is very entertaining to fee the author boaft, that he cures a *bilious cholic* with four bleedings, and
four purges mixed up with affiftant emollients, anodynes, and
other remedies : A prefcription, which muft take up many days;
whereas in the natural courfe of the diftemper it feldom lafts fo
long. To make ufeful obfervations requires great knowledge,
great fincerity, and great fagacity ; and thefe qualities are not the
lot of every phyfician.

I KNOW not whether this difcourfe, which I am now publifhing, will be agreeable to the gentlemen of the faculty, or not ; they
may be afraid, perhaps, if the world fhould grow out of conceit
with *phyfic*, it may become out of conceit too with its profeffors,
and then fome would certainly be difcarded, who are now in vogue.
But they need never fear, they are fafe as to this point ; the world
will always remain juft as it has done. No genius was ever able
to turn the courfe of thofe impetuous rivers, prejudice, and cuftom.
How much have QUEVEDO in SPAIN, PETRARCH in ITALY, in
FRANCE firft MONTAIGNE, and then MOLIERE, declaimed
againft all phyficians and phyfic ? and with a great deal of truth.
Their writings are read, and celebrated. But things remain juft
as they were. I fhall content myfelf with perfuading fome few to
follow the beft means they can for the recovery of their health.
Some phyficians have fo much generous candor, as to own publicly the infufficiency of medicine, and the perplexity of their art :
And it is no wonder to fee thofe, whofe minds are not fo noble,
con-

8

confiding in phyſic more than it deſerves. Some doctors, out of mere policy, conceal the weakneſs of their art; BAGLIVIUS was one of theſe. But ſays another; " It is very well for phyſicians " to confeſs the impotency of phyſic to one another, becauſe they " are judges, and they know it. But there is no occaſion to tell all " this to the vulgar, who believe always that a doctor knows much " more, than he either does, or can know." But I ſay on the contrary, that the common people would reap great benefit by ſuch acknowledgements, and the phyſician receive no great damage: becauſe if theſe poor people knew how little ſecurity there was in phyſic, and that there is ſcarce a remedy which is not dangerous; that even the greateſt and moſt knowing phyſicians commit various blunders; that many of thoſe patients, who recover, owe their recovery only to their natural ſtrength, and they owe to the phyſician the obligation of retarding that recovery : Did they know theſe things, they would have much leſs recourſe to phyſic; they would preſerve their entrails more entire, and would not ſpend that money in bottles of phyſic, which they wanted for other uſes. They would content themſelves with taking ſome ſlight things in their habitual indiſpoſitions, which are born with them, and which are inſeparable from their conſtitution, and which no phyſician in the world can cure, notwithſtanding their boaſted *radical cures*, which are not to be found *in rerum natura*. With this management many delicate ladies would ceaſe to be troubleſome to their huſbands and families ; many men would be uſeful ſervants to the public, who are now rendered uſeleſs by phyſicking themſelves. Theſe, and many other advantages, with the knowledge of how little hope is to be repoſed in phyſic, moved me to give this advertiſement to the public : and phyſicians ought in conſcience to concur with me in undeceiving the public.

AND indeed this would be no damage to the faculty themſelves ; at leaſt to the learned part of them, and who have acquired reputations as ſuch. For, to theſe, employment and fees would never be wanting. Becauſe the caſe would never happen, nor the motive for baniſhing all phyſicians out of the world, as they were once from ROME. The fine lady would not always ſend for the doctor to feel her pulſe; nor the imaginary madman, as in the

I 2   comedy

comedy of MOLIERE, fhriek when nothing ails him; nor the decrepit old fool imagine the apothecary's drugs can remove him fome leagues from his grave. By this means the phyficians would have more time for ftudy, and reflexion upon their ftudies and their experiments, as well as to affift at anatomical diffections. The moft eminent of the profeffion would be at leifure to write books : by this means phyficians would become more learned, and phyfic advance daily towards perfection, to which it wants many a good journey ftill. Phyfic is indeed recommended in Scripture, but not the phyfic of thefe modern times; when we are in really imminent danger, I confefs it is prudent to have recourfe to it; and that, generally fpeaking, the quicknefs and immediate application of the remedy is the moft important point. *Opium, Quinquina*, vomits, and very active medicines, may here be of great fervice, becaufe they induce changes, which nature herfelf would never produce. If I have expreffed myfelf too ftrongly in fome places about the danger even of cures and phyfic; it is becaufe I would remove the prejudices of the vulgar, who will follow the blind dictates of even the moft ignorant empyric : And I had rather incline them to the other extreme. In all that I have faid in this difcourfe, I have faid it under the fhade of the moft illuftrious medicinal writers, and fupported by the greateft authorities.

I CONCLUDE with exhorting all, who would choofe their phyfician, to choofe one with thefe qualities. *Firft*, Let him be a good Chriftian; becaufe knowing himfelf accountable to GOD for all his fteps, he will take them more ferioufly and warily, and will really apply himfelf to the ftudy of his profeffion. The *fecond* is, That he be judicious, but of a cool, not warm temperament. The *third*, That he fhould not be boaftful in fhewing the power and fafety of his art; for thofe who are fuch, are either ignorant, or difingenuous. The *fourth* is, That he follow no philofophic fyftem of practice, be addicted to no one fet of rules, but guided only by his own experience, and that of the beft writers. The *fifth* is, That he be not a giver of many remedies, efpecially the dangerous ones; holding it as for certain, that all thofe, who write and prefcribe much, are bad phyficians, altho' they know all that

has

has been wrote about phyfic. The *fixth* is, That he informs himfelf exactly of the fymptoms of diftempers, which are many, and
drawn from various fources. The generality of phyficians, when
they have felt the pulfe, looked at the urine, peeped into the clofe-
ftool, inftantly call for pen, ink, and paper—to *prefcribe*. The
pulfe is a fymptom very obfcure, the urine very fallible : and one
cannot be certain of the diftemper and its caufes (except in a few
cafes, where they are vifible) without attending to the complexion of many circumftances, both confequential and antecedent.
The *feventh* is, That his fuccesses fhould in general anfwer his
prognoftications ; I fay, in general, becaufe always to do it, they
muft be angels and not men ; for that circumftance will excufe
many others that preceded ; and becaufe it is the only means by
which the moft ignorant man can difcern, who is a phyfician of
fkill, and who is an ignorant one : for the certainty of prognofti-
cation is a clear proof, that he knows the prefent ftate of the diftemper ; becaufe by that only which is now, one can know what
is to come. On the other hand, that which thefe prognofticators
commonly fay, plainly fhews they do not know one word of phyfic.
Some think the art of foretelling a feparate faculty from phyfic ;
and thus fome phyficians are celebrated for foretelling, others for
curing : But this is a miftake, for it is impoffible, that the cure
fhould be right, and the prognoftic wrong, and *vice verfâ*. Indeed there is one difference, a phyfician, who misses of the cure
may be blamed, but one who fails in his prophefy may be damned.
In a dangerous cafe, an ignorant phyfician being called in, faid it was
only a light crudity of the ftomach, which would go off the next
day. With this affurance the people about the patient never fent
for the priefts : Soon after the man was feized with a delirium,
and died like a Pagan, or brute. The crime commonly attributed
to phyficians, is, killing the body ; but, in this cafe, they kill the
foul.

OTHER phyficians, more cautious, and more artful, take the
oppofite fide ; and whatfoever the diftemper is, they always fay it
is a very dangerous one ; they give out many orders, put the whole
family in a fright, offer their attendance, and their art. So that
if the patient dies, they are fure to praife the fkill of the phyfician,
who

who faid fo from the firft : If he lives, then the fkill of the phyfician is praifed, that he cured fo terrible a diforder, and God is
thanked that the patient fell into fuch good hands.   One good
thing comes from this, that the fick never die without the facraments.   But one evil is, that the fright they are put into fometimes increafes the diforder, and kills them.   All thefe ways are
full of evil; altho' the firft is the greateft; but however, gentlemen, ye will find one day the angels, to whofe cuftody the fick
are committed, accufing you before God, and placing thofe before you, who died thro' your fault, or your ignorance.

DISCOURSE VI.

Physicians know but little of healing the fick; they know
as little what ought to be the proper regimen for thofe in health;
at leaft they can give no rules for eating and drinking. This pro-
pofition, however abfurd it may appear to phyficians and others,
is proved by the evident variety of habits of body, to which is precifely commenfurate the variety of food, both in quality and quantity. One kind of food is hurtful to one, that is good for another ;
a quantity that is great for one perfon is hurtful to another. The
proportion of the quantity and quality of food to the habit of each
individual can only be known by experience : This experience
every man has within himfelf; and the phyfician can only know
it by the relation he receives. For I muft always tell the phyfician
how much I have eaten and drank, as he cannot know what is
proper for me, unlefs I tell him firft what ails me, what fits well
in my ftomach, what I digeft well. The emperor Tiberius
laughed at thofe, who confulted phyficians after they were thirty
years old; becaufe (he faid) at that age every one was able to tell
by experience, how to manage themfelves. And indeed he feems
to have been a ftriking proof of the truth of his own maxim; for
without being much concerned about his diet, or way of living, he
lived 78 years; and he probably had lived much longer, if Caligula had permitted him : for altho' he was very weak, his fucceffor would not truft his death to the ftrength of any difeafe :
hiftorians agreeing, that Caligula helped on his death, altho'
they differ in the manner of its being done. However, this maxim

xim of TIBERIUS, generally taken, is certainly true, at leaſt with
regard to eating and drinking.

THERE is no eatable, which one can ſay is abſolutely hurtful;
this is not my doctrine, but that of HIPPOCRATES, as he has
well proved it in his book *De veteri medicina :* for, as he ſays, if it
was hurtful to one, it would be ſo to all.   Cheeſe, for inſtance,
hurts not every one ; there are thoſe who eat of it without the
leaſt offence.   If cheeſe, which is ſo earthy, bad of digeſtion, and
hard, can be taken without hurt, what eatable can we ſay is abſolutely hurtful to all ?

QUAILS and goats feed upon poiſons, according to PLINY :
Venenis capreæ & cothurnices pinguescunt, lib. X. c. 72.   That
which kills other animals feeds them.   Will you ſay then, that
there is a greater diverſity of conſtitutions among the different ſpecies of animals, than among individuals of the ſame ſpecies ? For
my own part I think there is a much greater among the huma
ſpecies.   In the obſervations of SCHENKIUS, he tells us of a man,
that eat an ounce of ſcammony, which neither purged him little
or much.   And in other medicinal authors we read of ſome, who
were purged by the ſmell of róſes.   Is not this a ſufficient difference in conſtitutions ? It is true, that in general there is no great
difference between the conſtitutions of men.   But there is always
ſome, and that a very material one; habits of body vary like faces;
in all ſuch caſes as are obvious to our ſenſes we obſerve ſome diſſimi-
litude in all men.   What can be more ſimple, than the ſound of
the voice ? And yet there is none like that of another's. Nay,
among thoſe who have lived in the ſame houſe or community together for many years, it never happens but one can diſtinguiſh
the voices of them, tho' you do not ſee them.   If this is the caſe
in ſo ſimple a thing, how muſt it be in the conſtitution, which is
combined of ſuch a variety of materials.

IF our ſenſes were more acute, in caſes where ſome men appear
much alike, we ſhould find them very different.   There are ſome
brutes, which deceive us in the ſame manner.   We do not perceive by ſmell the effluvia of human bodies; or if we do, we do
                                                              not

not diftinguifh one from the other.   The dog perceives them, and
diftinguifhes them in all men : tho' he be at a great diftance, he
follows his mafter without feeing him, determining himfelf, tho'
he meets with many roads, by the fmell of the effluvia, which he
finds as he walks : he hunts and choofes out among many others
the glove of his mafter, tho' he never faw it before : and what is
more, he recovers a ftone thrown by his mafter among others
thrown at the fame time by other hands, that little touch fufficing,
by which with his fubtile fmell he perceives a different odour
from that of the reft.   This is a fufficient proof to convince you
of the *difference of conftitutions*, becaufe without a difference of
conftitutions there cannot be a difference in the *effluvia*.

NOT only the variety of conftitutions in men makes it impoffible to know what diet is proportionate to each ; but alfo the variety which there is between meats of the fame fpecies.   All wine
of grapes, for inftance, is of the fame fpecies.   Withal, one wine
is fweet, another is acid, another bitter ; one has one colour, another fmells differently ; one is thinner, another is thicker : It is
the fame in meats ; the fame in the fruits of all the plants, though
we do not perceive fo ftrongly in all this variety, upon account of
the imperfection of our fenfes.   By this means it may happen, and
does continually happen, that altho' it be the fame individual, one
wine may be wholefome, another noxious.   Meat fed in fome
lands is wholefome food, in others noxious.   Add to this a point
of no fmall confideration, that the fame food, without diftinction,
or perceivable difference, may be found, by the fame individual,
wholefome at one period, and noxious at another, either through
the different feafons of the year, the different temperature of the
air, the difference of country, or the difference of age.   In fine,
whatever change happens in the body, that fhould be a rule to
vary more or lefs the diet in quantity, as well as quality.

———

THUS I have given fome of the celebrated Father FEIJOO's
thoughts on phyfic, and could wifh out of humanity for the fake of
the Spanifh nation, that their phyficians were anfwerable to the
character and qualifications he requires.   It is obvious enough how
little he knows of that neceffary art.

IN

IN Poetry they have many writers; such as D. AL. DE ERCIL-LA, the PRINCIPE ESQUILACHE, ANT. LOFRASO, J. RUFO, PI-NEDA, FIGUEROA, ANT°. DE NEBRIXA, the two VEGA's, GAR-CILASSO, and LOPEZ; CALDERONI, BARRIOS, GONGORRA, and others. But as to a complete lift of them, I have never been able to find one; and am much lefs qualified to decide of their refpective merit. LOPEZ DE VEGA CARPIO, as VOLTAIRE tells us, comes the neareft to our SHAKESPEARE. He wrote the *Jerufalem Con-quiftada*, tragedies, comedies, &c. One thing may be faid of the lit-tle that I have feen of the Spanifh poetry; that there is a won-derful air of fimplicity in their common fongs, or *fequedillas*: That in fome pieces which I read in the *Caxon de Saftre*, or *The taylor's drawer of fhreds*, there was much fentiment, as well as dignity: vaft variety of meafure, all formed on the old Roman profody; and in fome of them a pleafing air of romance: but grave, majeftic, moral, penfive, like the people themfelves. Very few attempts to wit or humour, and, I believe, none of drollery or buffoonery. Many upon love, but all in the drapery of the chafte *Venus*; no *Erycina ridens*, no *Corinna*, no loofe or debauched *Eutape* among that collection of fongs of the *Spanifh Nine*.

As to fubjects and writers of humour in profe, I know of none among the old *Spaniards*, but CERVANTES and GUEVARA; the moft celebrated work of the latter is, the *El Diablo Coxuelo*, or as we fhould fay in Englifh, *The Devil upon two Sticks*, which Mr. LE SAGE modernized into a romance, that is very well known. It is much to be wifhed, that GUEVARA's original was well tranf-lated into Englifh, as we fhould find in it an infinity of old *Spa-nifh* manners and cuftoms; and the names of all the then nobility at full length; moft of which titles and families fubfift to this day.

K   LETTER

LETTER IV. PART III.

CATALOGUE of *SPANISH* AUTHORS.

Spanish Writers of HISTORY.

Cronica general de Espana, par Amb. Morales, 4 vol. 4to.
                                                                    Alcala 1577
This writer was the great antiquarian, the CAMBDEN of SPAIN; he has continued the work of FLORIO OCAMPO. SANDOVAL, by the particular command of PHILIP III. carried it down farther to ALPHONSO VII. MORALES wrote alfo,

Las Antiquidades de las Ciudades de Espana.
Compendio Hiftorial de las Cronicas de Espana, par Eftevan de Garibays, 4 vol. folio.   *Barcelona* 1628
    And *Don Juan de Mariana.*—— Thefe two copied MORALES and OCAMPO in great meafure. As *Mariana's Hiftory of Spain* feems to be fo much better known, than that of himfelf, indulge me in a few words about him. He was born at EBORA, now TALAVERA, in NEW CASTILE; educated at ALCALA DE HENARES, or the antient COMPLUTUM; he lived at TOLEDO, and publifhed the following works:

I. On the weights and meafures of the antients.
II. On the exchange of money.
III. A defence of the Vulgate.
IV. *De Rege, & Regis Inftitutione.*—— This piece was burnt at ROME and PARIS, and was quoted to authorize Dr. OATES's narrative in the Popifh plot.
V. On the ftage.
VI. His hiftory.

He

He was kept in prifon, by order from the Pope, twenty years, in which time he compofed his hiftory, as our Sir W. RALEIGH did in the Tower.   He wrote it firft in Latin, and afterwards in Spanifh.   But it went no lower than the end of FERDINAND and ISABELLA's reign, about 1516.   He wrote, however, a fupplement afterwards, down to 1621 ; and he has had fince *three* continuators, *Ferd. Camargo y Salcedo*, to 1649 ; *Bas. Varen de Soto*, to 1669 ; *Fr. J. M. de Miniana*, to 1699.   The firft Latin edition, *Toleti*, 1592, folio, is the beft, tho' it contains only twenty books. The laft ten are printed in the edition, *Moguntiæ* 1605, 4to.   The Spanifh editions are, *Madrid*, 1608, 2 vol. folio ; *Toledo*, folio, 1601 ; *Madrid*, 1668, and 1670.   There is alfo a new edition, printed at *Amberes* in 16 vol. 12mo. but very incorrect ; and one lately at *Madrid*, in 3 vol. folio.

Hiftoria General de Efpana, par Don Rodrigo Ximenes de Rada.

Hiftoria del Rey d'Efpana Don Phelippe II. par Luis Cabrera, folio.   *Madrid* 1619

Hiftoria del Rey Don Phelippe II. par Ant. de Herrera, 3 vol. folio.   *Valladolid* 1606

Hiftoria del Rey Don Phelippe III. par Gonzalez de Cefpedez, folio.   *Barcelona* 1634

Hiftoria de la Rebellion, y Caftigo de los Morifcos del Reyno de Granada, par Luis de Marmol, folio.   *Malaga* 1609

Guerra de Granada, becha por el Rey Don Felippe II. contra los Morifcos, par Mendofa, quarto.   *Lifboa* 1627

Hiftoria de la vida y bechos del Emperador Carlos V. par Prud. de Sandoval, folio.   *Pampelona* 1614

Commentarios de la Guerra de 1700, par el Marquez de San Felippe, 2 vol. quarto.

This book, which is extremely well wrote, has been tranflated into French, and was publifhed at Amfterdam in 1756, in 4 vols. 12mo. under the title of *Memoires pour fervir à l'Hiftoire d'Efpagne, fous le Regne de Philippe V.*

Hiftoria de Efpana par Rafis, an Arab, written at *Corduba* in 976.

Continuacion de la Hiſtoria General de Eſpana de ano 1516
(where MARIANA left off) *a 1700, par Medrano,* 3 vol.
folio.   *Madrid* 1741

Volume 1ſt, CHARLES V. Volume 2d, PHILIP III. Volume 3d,
PHILIP IV. and CHARLES II. This is a new work, but I do
not find that it bears a very great character. Some able men,
whom I conſulted, lamented much their not having any good
hiſtory of SPAIN carried down to the preſent times. This is ſur-
prizing, as it will plainly appear from the face of this liſt, that no
country in the world poſſeſſes better materials from whence to
compile ſuch a hiſtory. Their chroniclers are numerous : ſuch
as,

> The *Cronicon* of FLAVIUS DEXTER.
> > M. MAXIMUS.
> > ELECA.
> > BRAULION.
> > LUITPRANDO.
> > HUGO PORTA.
> > JULIAN.
> > ST. ATHANASIUS.
> > GR. BETICUS.
> > HUB[S.] HISPALIS.
> > LIBERATUS OF GIRONA.
> > ILLACII.
> > ABB[S.] VALCLARA.
> > L. RAMIREZ DE PRADO.
> > DE WULFILAS.

Cronica de Eſpana del Don Alonzo el Sabio, folio. *Valladolid* 1604.
Cronica de los Reyes Don Fernando y Iſabel, folio. *Saragoſſa* 1567,
Cronica Gotica de Saavedra.
Cronica de los Moros de Eſpana, par Juan de Bleda, folio.
                                                  Valentia

BESIDES theſe, they have the annaliſts of the ſeveral kingdoms
or provinces : thus,

Annales del Reyno de Eſpana, in ſeveral volumes in folio.
———— *de Catalonia,* 2 vol. folio.

                                                  Annales

Annales de Valentia.
———— de Arragon, par Hyeronymo Zurita.
This writer is very well known to the learned world for his other
works : thefe annals of Arragon are very finely wrote.

Arragonenfium Rerum Comimentarii, par Hyeron de Blancas,
   folio.   *Cæfar Augustæ* 1588

Geographica & hiftorica Defcriptio Cataloniæ, par Petro de
   Marca, folio.   *Paris* 1688
After thefe come the hiftories and antiquities of particular cities,
which are alfo very numerous : fuch as,

Las Antiquedades de Madrid, par Quintano.
               Sevilla, par Rod. Caro, folio.   *Sevilla* 1634
               Salamanca, par Gonfalvo de Avila.
               Granada, par Pedraza.
Defcription de la Ciudad de Toledo, par Fr. de Pifa, folio,
                                            Toledo 1605
———————————————— par Vergara, folio.
————————— de Madrid.
————————— del Monafterio de San Lorenzo del
   Efcorial, par Fr. de los Santos, folio.   *Madrid* 1681
This is the book which Mr. THOMPSON has tranflated into
Englifh, and made fo magnificent an edition of lately in quarto.
It is to be wifhed, that the infcriptions in this work had been more
correctly copied; they are often falfe Latin, imperfect, and make
a very unfcholar-like appearance.

Hiftoria de la Ciudad de Segovia, par Don Diego de Colme-
   narez, folio.   *Segovia* 1637
Las Antiquedades de Cordova, par Pedro Dias de Ribas, 4to.
                                          Cordova 1627

❁❁❁❁❁❁❁❁❁❁❁❁❁❁❁❁❁❁❁❁❁❁❁❁❁❁❁❁

Mifcellaneous Books and Writers.

L As Obras del Padre Feijo, 13 vol. quarto.
   This writer, who lives at BURGOS, has juftly acquired a very
high degree of reputation: He has done more towards rightly
                                            forming,

forming, and enlarging the minds of his countrymen, than any *Spaniard* before him.   He declares war againſt all their vulgar prejudices, and popular errors; has ſaid much freer things than thoſe, who write within the circle of the inquiſition, very prudently care to do; and, if the court had not protected him, he himſelf had felt the Dominican ſcourge long ago.

Deſcription Iglefiaſtica del Reyno de Eſpana, 3 vol. fol.
Obras de Don Bern. Aldreti, ſive Explicatio Characterum antiquorum, 2 vol. 4to.
Origines Rivorum Orbis, par Don Greg. Mayans y Siſcar, 2 vol. 4to.
Origines Litt. Ant. Hiſp. par Manuel de Sarramendi, 8vo.
Obras de Braganza de Ant. Rom. 5 vol. fol.
Concilia Max. Hiſpanica, 7 vol. fol.
Polygraphia Eſpagnola, par Rodriguez, fol.   Madrid 1738
Diario de los Literatos en Eſpana, 7 vol. 8vo.   Madrid 1748
Concilia Toletan, par Jorge Loyiſa.
La Lava de Coronicas, par Alph. Martinez.
Eſcritores del Reyno de Valentia, par Ximenes, 2 vol. fol.   *Valentia*
Enſayo ſobre las Medallas de Eſpana, par Don L. J. Velaſquez, 4to.   Madrid 1752
Annales de la Nacion Eſpagnol, par Don L. J. Velaſquez, 4to.   Malaga 1759
De las Medallas de los Reyes Gothicos, y Suecos en Eſpana, par Don L. J. Velaſquez: cum viginti tabulis æri inciſis, 4to.   Madrid 1752
Noticia de los mas principales Hiſtoriadores de Eſpana, par el Marquis de Mondecar, 4 vol. fol.

This is a very learned, uſeful, and judicious work.

Conquiſta de Mexico et Peru, par Don Ant. de Solis, fol.
There is a very handſome copy of this book in Spaniſh lately printed at Barcelona.

Yſtoria de los Incas de Peru, par Garcilaſſo de la Vega.
Herrera de Agricultura.
Iſtoria de las Indias, par Herrera, 6 vol. fol.
Obras de Palomino ſobre la Pintura, 2 vol. fol.

An

An Account of the Spanish Paintings, by Palamino Velasco, and Francisco de los Santos; reprinted in Spanish by H. Woodfall, London 1746

Uno Pedazo de Lapiz, para dibujar de mejor que se puede encontrar.

Historia Latina Hispaniæ, par Sanchez.

Impresas Politicas, par Miguel de Cervantes Saavedra.
This is a collection of political emblems; it is not written by the author of *Don Quixote*, but by a much older writer of the same name. His works are in 3 vol. folio.

El Diablo Coxuelo, or the Lame Devil, *par Ant. de Guevara.*
Mr. Le Sage's *Devil upon Two Sticks,* is taken from this work.

Coronista de los Reyes Catholicos, por 1500, par Gonzalo de Arcedondo.

Obras de Sepulvedo.
—— *de Villalpando.*
—— *de Bonaventura.*

Criticon de Lorenzo Graziano, 2 vol. 4to.
This celebrated writer was a native of CALATAJUD, or the antient *Bilbilis.* His writings are full of an abstruse and sublime policy; and have been translated into French by the famous Monst. AMELOT.

Historia del Famoso Predicador Frey Gerundio de Campazas, 4to. *Madrid* 1758
Or, *The history of the famous preacher.* This is a satire upon the monks, written with much spirit and wit. For a specimen of the high ridicule, and satirical drollery employed in this work, take the following extract. Chap. 8. book II. page 205. *Frey Gerundio* preaches the anniversary sermon in his convent, in the chapel dedicated to St. ANNE, on the festival of that saint: in which sermon there is the following paragraph: *Fuè Ana, como todos saben, madre de nuestra Senora, y afirman graves authores, que la tuvo veinte meses en su vientre:* Hic mensis sextus est illi; *y anaden otros, que illoro:* Plorans ploravit in noctem: *De donde infiero que fue Maria Zahorri:* et gratia ejus in me vacua non fuit. *Atienda,*
pues,

pues, el Rethorico al argumento: Santa Ana fue madre de Maria:
Maria fue madre de Chrifto: Luego Santa Ana es Abuela de la fan-
tiffima Trinidad: Et trinitatem in unitatem veneremur.   Por effo
fe celebra en efta fu Cafa, Hæc requies mea in fæculum fæculi. . . .
Which is in Englifh: " We all know, that Anne was the mother
" of our Lady, and grave authors affirm, that fhe was twenty
" months in geftation of her: others add, that fhe wept: from
" whence I infer, that fhe was Mary Zahorri.   Attend, logician,
" to the argument: Saint Anne was the mother of Mary; Mary
" was the mother of Chrift: therefore Saint Anne was the grand-
" mother of the moft holy Trinity.   And therefore fhe is cele-
" brated by this feftival in this her chapel."

THERE is no doubt but Dr. ISLA, that *Spanifh Swift,* who
wrote this fatire, had copied this from the real fermon of fome
Spanifh monk: the Latin citations are very much in their manner.   They were fo galled and irritated by the feverity and propriety of this fine ridicule, that they foon got the inquifition to
forbid the fale of the book: It occafioned fome pamphlets at Madrid in anfwer to it   The author intended a fecond part; but
the perfecution becoming too ferious, he dropped his defign.

IN page 214. and the following, the provincial calls *Frey Ge-*
rundio to an account for this fermon: " Don't you fee, Sir," fays
the provincial, " that by faying, that Saint Anne is the grand-
" mother of the moft holy Trinity, you advance one of the
" moft formal, herefies poffible: Becaufe the Trinity is uncreate,
" unproducible, eternal, and confequently can have neither mo-
" ther nor grand-mother.   By this you fee how neceffary it is to
" ftudy theology, in order to be a preacher; for, had you pro-
" perly ftudied it, you had not advanced fuch herefies as this.
" If you had put no more in your *fumula* than you ought, you had
" never drawn fuch a confequence: but only this, *Therefore Saint*
" *Anne is the Grandmother of Chrift.*   For Chrift is not the Tri-
" ni y, but only the fecond perfon in it: thus *Frey Gerundio* is a
" monk of the convent, but not the convent.   It would be wretched
" reafoning to fay, *Cecilia Rebollo* was the mother of *Catanla Ce-*
" *bollon; Catanla Cebollon* was the mother of *Frey Gerundio de*

3   " *Zotes,*

" *Zotes*, monk of the convent of the lower *Colmenar*, therefore *Ce-*
" *cilia Rebollo* was the grandmother of the convent."

This fpecimen will fuffice to fhew the turn of that fatire.

El Itinerario del Obifpo de Santo Domingo.

Los Dialogos del Antonio Auguftino, Obifpo de Tarragona,
    fobre las Medallas, 4to.   *Madrid* 1744
This learned work is fufficiently known. The edition is a very
mean one, bad paper, full of errors, and the plates miferably en-
graved.

Hiftoria del Convento de San Auguftino de Salamanca, par
    Padre Emman. Vidal, 2 vol. fol.   *Salamanca* 1758

Hippocrates in Greek and Latin, with a Spanifh tranflation, by Dr. And. Piquer, Profeffor of Anatomy in Valentia.   *Madrid* 1758

Antient and Modern Phyfic, by the fame, 4to.   ib. 1758

A Treatife on Fevers, founded on Obfervation and Me-
chanifm, by the fame, 4to.   Va.Itia 1751

Moral Philofophy, for the ufe of the Spanifh Youth, by
the fame, 8vo.   *Madrid* 1757

Difcourfe on the Application of Philofophy to Matters
of Religion, by Dr. And. Piquer, 8vo.   *Madrid* 1757

Bibliographia Critica, by Father Miguel de San Jofeph,
Bifhop of Guadia.

Abridgment of Navigation, for the ufe of the Marine
Guards, by Don Jorge Juan, 4to.   Cales 1757

Retorica de Don Gregorio Mayans y Sifcar, 2 vol. 8vo.
                          Valentia

Moralis Philofophia, by the fame, 8vo.   Valentia

Relation of the War in Valentia, and the Entrance of the
Allies and Auftrians into that Kingdom, by Jof. Emm.
Miniana, 8vo.   Hague 1752

There are many tracts of Spanifh lawyers, collected by Don
Greg. Mayans y Sifcar, publifhed by Mr. Meerman,
the Syndic of Rotterdam, in his

Novus Thefaurus Juris Canonici, 7 vol. fol.
                L   *De*

De Ant. Canonum Cod. Ecclefiæ Hifp. Hift. Differtatio, per
  Don Lopez de Barrera, 4to.   Rome 1758

The Hiftory of John Cardinal Carvacallo, dedicated to the
  Prime Minifter in Portugal.   ibid. 1752

Elements of Arithmetic and Algebra, by Father Thomas
  La Cerda, 2 vol.   Barcelona 1758

Curious and learned Fragments of modern Authors, with
  Maxims of a general Critique, by Don Lewis Roche,
            Port St. Mary's 1758;

Efpana Sagrada : or, The Hiftory of the feveral Dioceses
  and Churches of Spain, by Father Henry Flores, an
  Auguftine Monk, 15 vol. 4to.   Madrid 1747

Hiftory of the Queens of Spain, 2 vol. 4to.   Madrid 1760:
A very poor performance.

A Compendium of Theology, by the fame, 5 vol. 4to.

The Miracles of Mother Mary of Ceo, tranflated from the
  Portuguefe, by the fame, 2 vol.   Madrid 1744:

Treatife of Virtue, by Father Francis, tranflated by the
  fame, 2 vol. 4to.   Madrid

Hiftorical Key, by the fame, 4to.   ibid. 1749

Medallas de las Colonias Romanas, y Municipios, &c. by the
  fame, 2 vol. 4to.   ibid. 1758

He has placed in this collection thofe which Vaillant, Mezzobar-
ba, and others have publifhed, but with the addition of many new
ones : he has added an explanation of each, 58 plates, and a map
of the fite of the colonies. This is a good book; it fhould have
been wrote in Latin; but that is a language with which Spanifh
monks are but little converfant.

Origin of the Caftilian Poetry, 4to.   Malaga 1754

Means of advancing the Belles Lettres, by Francis Xavier
  de Idiaquez, 8vo.   Villagarcia 1758
This writer is the eldeft fon of the late Duke of Granada, grandee
of Spain.

Differtatio de Deo Endovellico, par Miguel Perez Paftor,
  4to.   Madrid

          Phy-

Phyſico-Medical Diſſertations on Breathing, and of conveying Remedies into the Veins, by Ant. Joſ. Rodriguez, 4to.   Madrid 1760

A Critico-Medical Diſſertation to introduce true Phyſic, and baniſh the falſe, by the ſame, 6 vol. 4to.   Madrid 1754

Theological Reflections, Canonical and Medicinal, upon Faſting, 4to.   Madrid 1748

An Account of California, by Andrew Marc Burriel.

Palæographia Hiſpanica, by the ſame, 4to.   ibid. 1758

Of the Authority of the Laws of the *Fuero Juſgo*, or famous Gothic Code, by the ſame, 4to.   Madrid

This is a very learned, judicious, maſterly, and ingenious work. See the extract from it, concerning the Spaniſh meaſures.

Tratado de la Ortographia Eſpanola, par Juan Perez Caſtiel y Artigues, 8vo.   *Valencia* 1727

Memorias Hiſt. de la Fundacion de la Univerſidad de Valencia, 4to.   M~~adr~~id 1~~73~~~

Hiſtoria grande real, par Joſeph Gonzalez   *ibid.* 1746

Hiſtoria Civil de Eſpana, de 1700 a 1733, par Manuel Fernandez   *ibid.* 1740

De los Derechos Nacional y Romano en Eſpaña, par Don Thomas Ferrandis, 4to.   *ibid.* 1747

Sobre unos Monumentos Antiquos, 4to.   *Valencia* 1736

Ambaſſades du Marechal Baſſompiere en Eſpagne, 4 vol. 8vo.   *Cologne* 1668

Voyage en Eſpagne, fait en 1655, 4to.   *Paris*

The Lady's Travels is a tranſlation from this book, a ſpurious work.

Voyage en Eſpagne, par Madame la Comteſſe D'Aunois, 3 vol. 12mo.   *Paris* 1691

Voyages d'Eſpagne, par le Pere Labat.

L'Etat preſent d'Eſpagne, par l'Abbé Vayrac.

Lettres de Madame de Villars, Ambaſſadrice en Eſpagne, 12mo.   *Amſterdam* 1761

Annales d'Eſpagne & de Portugal, par Don Juan Alv. de Colmenar, 2 vol. 4to.   *ibid.* 1741

    L'Hiſ-

L'Histoire d'Espagne, par M. Desormeaux, 5 vol. 12mo.
                                                    Paris 1759.

Memoires sur le Commerce, & les Finances d'Espagne, 2 vol.
12mo.   *Amsterdam* 1761.

Tour through Spain and Portugal, by Udal ap Rhys,
8vo.   London 1760

Theory and Practice of Commerce, by Don Geronymo
de Uftariz, 2 vol. 8vo.   London 1761.

Dr. Geddes's Tracts, 4 vol. 8vo.   ib. 1709.

Memorable Expulsion de los Moriscos de Espana, 4to.
                                                Pampelona 1613.

*Inscriptiones Antiquæ in Hispaniâ repertæ, per Ad. Occo-
nem,* folio.   *Heidelb.* 1596.

*Compendio de la Vida del Card. Ximenes, y del officio, y Missa
Muzarabe, par Eugenio de Roblez,* 4to.   *Toledo* 1604.

This *Mosarabic Mass* is one of the greatest curiosities in all SPAIN;
it is celebrated at TOLEDO. The present King of SPAIN heard
fo much said of it, that he affisted at it in person.

De Regis Hispaniæ Regnis & Opibus, par De Laet; 8vo.
                                           Lugduni Batavorum 1619.

L. And. Requesendii Antiquitates Lusitanicæ, 8vo.
                                           Coloniæ Agripp. 1613.

I have set down the titles of most of the new books in English,
for the sake of the English reader.

SPANISH POETS.

QUEVEDO. The same author who wrote those *Visions,*
which we have translated into English.

LOPEZ DE VEGA CARPIO, who wrote the *Jerusalem Conqui-
stada,* tragedies, comedies, &c.

CALDERONI, the celebrated comic Poet. The great favourite of
the Spanish nation: they relish little else upon the stage, but
what he has wrote. See the article *Stage.* His works are in eight
or nine volumes 4to.

                                                           Don

Don ALONZO DE ERCILLA.
GIL POLO, PRINCIPE DE ESQUILACHE.
ANTONIO LOFRASO.
JUAN RUFO.
PINEDA.
FIGUEROA.
ANTONIO DE NEBRIXA.
GARCILASSO DE LA VEGA.
DON MIGUEL DE BARRIOS.
GONGORRA, &c.

A LIST of Modern *Spanish* LITERATI,

(Most of them, I believe, now living.)

FATHER FEIJOO of BURGOS.

Father BURRIEL, a great antiquarian, in the imperial college of Jesuits at MADRID.

Father HENRY FLORES, of the Augustine order, historian, and medallist.

—— FLORES, his brother, antiquarian.

—— SARMIENTO, a Benedictine, has studied natural history, botany, and the languages.

—— PONCE, a Franciscan, master of the oriental languages.

—— ISLA, the author of *Frey Gerundio*.

—— MIGUEL PEREZ PASTOR, antiquary and medallist.

—— VELASQUEZ, antiquary and medallist.

SAN FELIPPE (Marquis of) an officer, an envoy from the court of SPAIN to Genoa.

Don GREGORIO MAYANS Y SISCAR, a gentleman who lives at Oliva near Valentia, and tho' 63 years old, pursues his former studies with a vigour beyond his years. He was born at Oliva in 1699, and made library keeper to PHILIP V. at Madrid, in 1733, which place he he threw up in difguft, in 1740. He has the *Teftimonia Erudito-rum* of the greateft fcholars in moft parts of Europe in his favour. He is commended by Luis Antonio Muratori, in his *Supplement to Grævius and Gronovius*, publifhed at Venice in 1740: by John Burcard Menkenius, prefident of the univerfity of Leipfic, in the *Acta Lipfiaca :* By Chrift. Aug. Heumannus, in his *Via ad Hifto-riam Literariam :* By Marc. Aug. Beyer, in his *Memoriæ Hiftori-co-criticæ Librorum Rariorum, Lipfiæ* 1734: By Fred. Otto Men-kenius, in his *Notes* to his father's life : By Gottofrid Mafcou, au-lic counfellor to his late Majefty King GEORGE II. and profeffor of law in the univerfity of Gottingen, in his *Preface to Gravina's Works :* By J. Gott. Heineccius, counfellor to the King of Pruffia, who publifhed *Corn. Van Bynkerfhoek :* By Peter Wefieling, in his *Preface to the Epiftles of Don Man. Marti, Dean of Alicant*, printed at Amfterdam in quarto, 1738 : By the prefent Earl of Granville, who prefixed the life of Don Quixote, wrote by Don Gregorio Mayans y Sifcar, to the noble impreffion he publifhed of that ro-mance in 1738, in 4to, and which he dedicated to the countefs of Montijo, the Spanifh ambaffadrefs in London.——His brother, Don Antonio, lives with him, and purfues the fame ftudies. As I was much obliged to this gentleman for the favour of his cor-refpondence, I could not refufe this little acknowledgement.

Don PEREZ BAYER, canon and treafurer of the metropolitan church of Toledo; an univerfal fcholar, a great mafter of Hebrew and the oriental languages. He was fent, in the late reign, by or-der of the court, into Italy, to pick up MSS. and medals : he has a very fine cabinet of Roman medals in his own poffeffion, and fe-ven Hebrew MSS. which he has promifed to collate for the ufe of Dr. Kennicott. He has publifhed a very learned work, intitul-ed, *Damafus & Laurentius Hifpanis vindicati, Romæ,* 4to. He has written befides, *Differtatio de Antiquiffimo Hebræorum Templo, To-leti reperto;* and, *De Nummis Samaritanis, & qui vocantur Medallas Defconnocidas.* Thefe two are not yet publifhed, but I believe the latter will foon be printed. This gentleman is of the order of the Jefuits, and very much efteemed by the court. As I have received feveral very obliging letters and civilities from him, this juftice is at leaft due to his merit.

Padre TERREROS.

Don LOPEZ DE BURRERA.

4   Don

Don LEWIS ROCHE.——FRANCIS XAVIER IDIAQUEZ, eldest
son of the late Duke of GRANADA.——ANTONY JOSEPH RO-
DRIGUEZ.——Pere EMMANUEL VIDAL.—Dr. ANDREW PIC-
QUER, professor of anatomy in VALENTIA.——ANTONIO CAP-
DEVILA, professor of physic in VALENTIA.——Bishop of GUA-
DIA.——Don VICENTIO XIMENES.——Jos. EMMANUEL MI-
NIANA, continuator of Mariana's history.——JUAN PEREZ CAS-
TIEL Y ARTIGUES, Valentian.—JOSEPH GONZALEZ, historian.
MANUEL FERNANDEZ, or BELLANDO, historian.——Don THO-
MAS FERRANDIO, historian.——Don JORGE JUAN, Don ANT.
DE ULLOA, mathematicians.

The Count GAZOLA, a very learned and skilful judge of architecture, painting, and the elegant arts. He intends publishing
the ruins of the antient *Poestum* in ITALY, so famous for its
roses. He is a lieutenant-general, chief engineer, and intendant of
his majesty's fabrics and buildings.

MICHAEL SYRI, a Syro-Maronite, perfect master of the East-
earn languages, and chief librarian to his majesty at MADRID. He
has published the first volume of the catalogue of the Arabic MSS.
in the Escurial. It is a very fine work in folio, well printed, and
contains large specimens of each MS. and an accurate account in
Latin.

THE other librarian, whose name I forgot, intends likewise to
publish the catalogue of the Greek MSS. but it will be some time
before it will come out.

Of the UNIVERSITIES in SPAIN.

THE Universities in Spain are very numerous; but it may
be easily seen, from the preceding account, that the state of
learning in them must be at a very low ebb. I believe, among
them, that of SALAMANCA claims the precedence. There is very
little of the learned languages, the belles lettres, or indeed, of
true and found learning studied in them. To say the truth, a good
political reason might be assigned for this; the study of true and
found learning, if well pursued and cultivated, would let in too
much light: and how far that might be prejudicial to the inte-

rests of their religion, I cannot say. The university of VALEN-
TIA seems, at present, to have the fairest claim to precedence in
point of learning; but that is owing solely to the example, directions, and instructions of that eminent scholar Don GREGORIO
MAYANS Y SISCAR. They are twenty-three in number.

One in LEON.

1. SALAMANCA,   founded in 1200, by ALFONSUS IX.

Six in the CASTILLES.

2. PALENCIA,   founded in 1200.
3. VALLADOLID,   ——— in 1346.
4. SIGUENSA,   ——— in 1471, by C. XIMENES.
5. TOLEDO,   ——— in 1475.
6. AVILA,   ——— in 1445.
7. ALCALA DE HENARES,   { ——— in 1498, by C. XIMENES ; next in rank to SA-
                            LAMANCA.

Four in ANDALUSIA.

8. SEVILLE,   founded in 1503.
9. GRANADA,   ——— in 1531.
10. BAESA,   ——— in 1533.
11. OSSUNA,   ——— in 1549.

Two in ARAGON.

12. HUESCA,   founded in 1354.
13. SARAGOSSA,   ——— in 1474.

Three in VALENTIA.

14. VALENTIA,   founded in 1470.
15. GANDIA,   ——— in 1549.
16. ORIHUELA,   ——— in 1555.

Three in CATALONIA.

17. LERIDA,   founded in 1300.
18. TORTOSA,   ——— in 1540.
19. TARRAGONA,   ———   by PHILIP II.

    N. B. PHILIP V. in 1717, deprived these in CATALONIA of their charters, and gave
them to CERBERA, a town in the same province, which had declared for him.

One in GALLICIA.

20. SAN JAGO DE COMPOSTELLA,   founded in 1532.

One in GUIPUSCOA.

21. ONATE,   founded in 1543.

One in ASTURIAS.

22. OVIEDO,   founded in 1580.

One in NAVARRE.

23. PAMPELUNA,   founded in 1608.

    The rank of them are as follows.—SALAMANCA, ALCALA, VALLADOLID, SEVILLE,
SARAGOSSA, VALENTIA, LERIDA.——The rest are of no moment.

    3   There

There are, however, in thefe univerfities, fome valuable books and MSS. which the poffeffors themfelves make no great ufe of: fuch as manufcripts of PRISCIAN and DONATUS, in Gothic charac-ters, with Arabic notes; MSS. of SALLUST, SENECA, and OVID; two Gothic Bibles, written before the invafion of the MOORS, and a very old Hebrew manufcript of the Bible: all at the city of TOLEDO. A Gothic Bible at ALCALA DE HENARES, where there are the fineft MSS. of the Hebrew Bible in the world. In the Royal Library at MADRID there are of firft editions, PLAU-TUS, *Venetiis* 1472; LIVIUS, *ad tertium librum tertii decadis,* 1485; VIRGILIUS, *Venetiis* 1475; ODYSSEA HOMERI, *per Bern. Deme-trium Milanenfem, Florentiæ* 1488; HESYCHIUS, *Florentiæ,* 1520; Idem, *Aldi.* 1514.

[As the two following *Latin Epiftles* contain feveral particulars relating to the Prefent State of Literature in SPAIN, efpecially the latter, in which are fo many curious facts and obfervations, together with a lift of the works of his own countrymen, the VA-LENTIAN Writers, from the beginning of this century, I have thought proper to infert them in this place. The literary hif-tory of the two gentlemen, who wrote them, has been already given to the reader. He will meet with fome uncommon words and phrafes in them, but they are *Plautinæ Dictiones,* a book which the *Spaniards* much delight in.]

✝

FRANCISCUS PEREZIUS BAYERIUS
EDVARDO CLARKE,

S. P.

QUANQUAM mane a prandio, fummum perendie matritum co-gitem, qua in urbe ut te præfentem præfens alloquar fperare mihi fas fit: nolui tamen perbrevem hanc temporis ufuram negli-gere, aut tecum interea parum officiofus videri, qui me tuis huma-

M   niffimisniſſimis literis provocaſti.   In iis quod me nihil tale meritum effuſis laudibus cumulas, perbenignè mecum agere videris, qui fundi mei fines anguſtiaſque probè intelligo.   Totum igitur muneris eſt tui, a quo nihilominus laudari, pergratum mihi eſt ac perjucundum.

DISSERTATIUNCULAM de Toletano Hebræorum Templo ſummis olim precibus extorquere à me voluit vir cl. Blaſius Ugolinus, antiquitatum Hebraïcarum collector atque illuſtrator, ut eam theſauro ſuo inſereret, nec tamen obtinuit; nolui enim committere ut vix exaſciatum ac planè tumultuarium opus publici juris fieret, id quod nunc etiam in cauſa eſt quo minus de eodem Hiſpanis aut exteris typis edendo ulterius cogitem: ſaltem donec eidem ſupremam manum impoſuero.

IN DAMASO & LAURENTIO Hiſpaniæ aſſerendis, non ego pro arbitrio, neque ut ingenium periclitarer, argumentum mihi ſelegi, ſed coactus aliorum importunitate.   Cum enim nihil ego minus quam ea de re cogitarem, ac ne noſſem quidem de utriuſque patria litem Hiſpanis intentari, bonâque eoſdem fide in ephemeridibus noſtris inter divos patrios retuliſſem, cum riſu & cachinnis exceptus ſum a nonnullis Romanorum hypercriticis, quaſi Romanam illorum patriam, rem ſcilicet lippis atque tonſoribus notam, unus ego omnium ignorarem.   Itaque coactus eam provinciam ſuſcepi; quod tamen nolim ita intelligas, quaſi me locatæ in eo argumento operæ uſpiam pœnituerit, aut pœniteat.   Quamvis enim alia deſint omnia in opuſculo illo (quod ego non diffiteor) ſunt nihilominus aliqua per occaſionem explicata quibus, ſi me mea non fallunt, rei *liturgicæ*, atque hiſtoriæ *eccleſiaſticæ* non parum lucis affulgere poteſt; præterea univerſum opus pietatem in patriam ubique ſpirat, deque ea benemerendi ſtudium, quod nemo unquam bonus reprehendit. In eo autem an *Uſſerium* alicubi nominaverim, non ſatis memini: tantum abeſt ut ipſum, qua de re mihi ſubiraſceris, parvi fecerim. (Pearſonum & Dodwellum, p. 19.) Dodwellum merito ſuo carpo, quod & multi ante me præſtitere, alii quidem alio nomine, ego quòd miſerè ſeſe excruciet, totuſque in eo ſit, ut cœlites ipſos e ſedibus deturbet ſuis, et ſi quem denique e ſanctorum martyrum albo expungendum pro lubidine ſibi perſuadet, geſtit, erumpit

2   præ

præ gaudio, triumphumque putat palmarium. Egregiam vero lau-
dem! Itaque ut verbo absolvam, Dodwelli in hac parte judicium
odi ac detestor, doctrinæ nihil detractum volo. Menagium ibidem
dum genio ad facetias atque hilaritatem composito nimis obscun-
dat, sæpissime scurram agit. Nihil est in Cœlo sordium. Valeat
Lucianus! Sed de his plus satis.

Hebraicos Veteris Testamenti Codices, qui scilicet aut totum
illud, aut Pentateuchum, aliosque sacri Fœderis libros continent
penes me habeo circiter *viginti quinque*. Erunt forsan nonnulli
sæculo duodecimo exarati, aut eo non multo recentiores; unus
certe omnium ante ejusdem sæculi dimidium scriptus est: habet
enim in fine numeralem notam anni ab orbe condito 4904, quem
salutis anno 1144 respondere optime nosti. De collatione ac va-
riantibus, quod ais, Toleti res est supra quam dici potest impedi-
ta; pauci enim ea in urbe sunt, qui Hebraicas litteras norint, nec
sine duorum minimum interventu negotium istud peragi tuto potest.

Domino Pitt, quanquam paullo quam oportuerat serius fidem
tamen meam liberabo. Sustineat me interea quæso & aliis impli-
citum, & summa quoque adumbratorum inopia ibidem in hac urbe laborantem. De nummis plura coram Deo Optimo Maximo
desuper largiente, a quo tibi felicia omnia comprecor & fausta.

Toleti, *postridie Idus Junias,* M.DCC.LXI.

+

EPISTOLA

Domini GREGORII MAJANJSII,
GENEROSI VALENTINI,

EDVARDO CLARKE
AMANDATA.

MEUM ingenium ad amicorum obsequium paratissimum facit, ut illi de me multo præclarius & sentiant, & loquantur, quàm ipse mereor. Itaque si fidem adhibueris eorum testimoniis, senties nimis magnifice de meo studio literarum. Tu, vir prudentissime, si decipi non vis, voluntatem meam pluris facito, quàm facultatem satisfaciendi desideriis tuis. Illa sponte sua fœcundissima est; hæc, invito me, sterilis: prout nunc experior sane perdolenter. Vellem enim Sacrorum Bibliorum omnes *Hebraicos codices*, qui latent in Hispaniæ Bibliothecis, in potestate mea habere, & publicè exhibere, ut a viris doctissimis cum aliis codicibus conferrantur, in commune Christianæ Reipublicæ bonum, & incrementum. Mihi enim in mentem venit illud Isaiæ a Michea repetitum : * *Ibunt populi multi, & dicent, Venite & descendamus ad montem Domini, & ad domum Dei Jacob, & docebit nos vias suas, & ambulabimus in semitis ejus : quia de Sion exibit lex, & verbum Domini de Ierusalem.* Gloriorque ejus discipulum esse, qui cum sit Verbum Æternum, de se professus est : *Ego palam locutus sum mundo : ego semper docui in synagoga, & in templo, quò omnes Judæi conveniunt, & in occulto locutus sum nihil.* Quare *Vetus* illud Testamentum, quod ille coram omnibus revolvere & legere solitus fuit ; itemque *Novum*, quod ipse jussit scribi, & omnibus gentibus annuntiari; existimo minime occultari debere; sed ibi proponendum, unde de plano recte legi possit. Sed cum libri sacri Hebraica lingua scripti, in Hispania legi desierint ob ejus linguæ inusum, atque hic

---

* Micah iv. 2.

inu-

inufus ortum habuerit a metu, & poftea ab ignorantia confirmatus
fit; inde factum eft, ut in privatis bibliothecis non fuperfint, & in
publicis religiofe cuftodiantur. Cum autem Hifpani habemus
regem, qui fuperftitiofus non eft; credo eum, modo petentis adfit
auctoritas, & prudentes cautiones adhibeantur, minime denegatu-
rum facrorum codicum lectionem, collationem, defcriptionem, &
quidquid neceffe fit ad divini verbi fententiam intelligendam.
Quod fi Rex Catholicus voluerit, crede mihi, impedimenta omnia
quæ enumeras, nihil obftabunt. Verum, quod omittis, non eft le-
vis momenti, difficultas inveniendi Hifpanos Hebraicæ linguæ bene
peritos. Et, ut exiftimo, hæc eft cauffa difficilis aditus ad facros
codices ea lingua fcriptos.

Placuisse tibi epiftolam illam, quam in gratiam excellentif-
fimi viri Benjamini Keene fcripfi, vehementer gaudeo. Vir fuit
ingenii dulciffimi, quique facile confequebatur quæ volebat ob ftudium & perfpicaciam morum hominum, humanitatem facile fefe
infinuantem, & liberalitatem. Frequentiffime ille mecum de rebus
literariis agebat; nam, ut erat rerum omnium curiofiffimus inda-
gator, optimos Hifpaniæ fcriptores nofcere fatagebat, & ftudiofe in
otiofis intervallis lectitabat.

Miraris Henricum Florezium de Nummis antiquis Hifpani- *Henricus*
cis Hifpana lingua fcripfiffe. Ego mirarer multo magis, fi Latina *Florezius.*
fcripfiffet. Tunc enim neque exteris, neque popularibus fuis
placeret. Laudanda in eo viro diligentia, quâ tot numifmata edidit: quod perfacile fuit promittenti famam perpetuam commu-
nicantibus fecum antiqua numifmata. Antonius Auguftinus dili- *Antonio Au-*
genter hoc ftudium inter noftrates coluit: clarus Vincentius Jo- *guftinus.*
hannes Laftanofa, adamavit, oftentavitque: Nobiliffimus vir Pe- *Johannes La-* *ftanofa.*
trus Valerus Diazius, juftitia Arragonum, adeo præclare calluit, ut *Petrus Vale-* *rus Diazius.*
eximias laudes confecutus fuerit a peritiffimo hujus literaturæ cen-
fore, Ezechiele Spanhemio prope finem differtationis nonæ de præ-
ftantia & ufu numifmatum antiquorum. Ex illius magni viri lo-
cupletiffimo thefauro plufquàm tria millia numifmatum obtinuit, *300 numif-*
& hodie cuftodit clarus vir Ferdinandus de Velafco in auditorio *mata.*
duodecemvirorum Stlitibus judicandis in domo & urbe regia (Hifpani dicimus *Alcaldes de Cafa y Corte*) patronus fifcalis: idemque
vir

plusquam 100vir doctiffimus nactus eft ex ejufdem Diazii bibliotheca plufquam
libri de re centum libros de re nummaria agentes.   Nonnulli alii in fuis ga-
nummaria.
Emmanuel zophilaciis magnos habuerunt thefauros, fed abfconditos.   Edidi
Martinus. ego Emmanuelis Martini, Decani Lucentini, Epiftolas ad hoc ar-
Decanus Lu-
centinus. gumentum fpectantes : noftratium animos excitavi ad hoc ftudium
Gonzalecius excolendum.   Clarus vir Andreas Gonzalezius Barcia recudi juffit
Barcia. Antonii Auguftini immortale opus numifmatum, infcriptionum, &
aliarum antiquitatum.   Eo vita functo, agnatus illius, ejufdem nominis, prætorii Granatenfis fenator, me adhortante illud edidit : &
ftatim innumeri oculi aperti, & incredibilis multitudo eft inquiren-
tium antiqua numifmata, atque inde orta difficultas inveniendi ea.
Ego ibi fum, ubi rariffime reperiuntur : & ubi nemo verfatur in
hoc erudito ftudio.   Perfæpe inter amicos divifi nummos antiquos,
quos obtinere potui.   Romani, qui apud me manent, tui erint.

SCIRE cupis, qui libri manufcripti Græci, aut Latini, vel hif-
toricorum, vel poëtarum ; qui vetufti auctores inediti in Hifpania
fuperfint? Catalogum Græcorum Latinorumque fcriptorum, qui
extant in regia Madridienfi bibliotheca diligenter confecit, & edere
Johannes cogitat clarus vir *Johannes Iriarte*, bibliothecarius regius.   Biblio-
Iriarte. thecæ Scorialenfis varii indices evulgati.   Sed quia rari funt, faci-
Bibliotheca lius eft ipfam bibliothecam adire, & in ea ipfos libros confulere,
Scorialenfis. fi comes adjungaris alicui viro, qui auctoritate vigeat apud biblio-
thecarium, aut illi monafterio præfectum.   An vero poffint fuppleri lacunæ aliquæ, Livii, Taciti, Diodori Siculi, Dionis Caffii,
aliorumque fimilium, res eft, quæ fciri nequit, nifi ipfi codices in-
fpiciantur.   Crediderim vero multa poffe fuppleri, & quamplari-
ma alia melius legi : nam thefauri Hifpanici nondum funt effoffi.
Quanti vero fint, facile colligere poteris, fi confideraveris, quàm felectæ bibliothecæ Scorialenfem formaverint. Magnus ille Alphon-
*Alphonfus V.*fus V. Aragonum Rex, qui literas ita amavit, ut non dubitaverit
dicere, *Malle fe omnium regnorum fuorum* (feptem autem potiebatur)
jacturam facere, quàm minimam doctrinæ, adeoque doctos adamavit,
fovitque, uti Laurentiam Vallam, Antonium Panormitam, Bartho-
lomæum Faccium, Georgium Trapezuntium, Johannem Aurif-
pam, Jovianum Pontanum : & *librum apertum* pro infigni habuit,
fignificans ftudium fuum erga libros, quibus fuorum regnorum bibliothecas implevit, ornavitque ; præcipue fuam inftruxit raris,
& antiquiffimis libris Græcis, Latinifque, qui poftea beneficio Ferdinandi

dinandi ducis Calabriæ ex teſtamento pervenerunt ad Gundizalvum Perezium, Carolo V. a manu, Homeri Odyſſeæ interpretem Hiſpanum celeberrimum. Illi autem libri teſte Antonio Perezio ejus filio tranſlati etiam fuerunt in *Bibliothecam Scorialenſem*, quam locupletarunt aliæ bibliothecæ ſelectiſſimæ eruditiſſimorum virorum: veluti *Didaci Furtati de Mendoza*, linguæ Latinæ, Græcæ, & Arabicæ peritiſſimi; *Antonii Auguſtini*, ad miraculum eruditi; *Benedicti Ariæ Montani* in eruditis linguis verſatiſſimi; aliorumque eximiorum virorum, quorum longa ſeries referri poſſet. Diligentia itaque oculari opus eſt ad ſecretas illas opes inſpiciendas. Atque hoc velim conſideres. Libri manu exarati, pluriſque faciendi in *Bibliotheca Scorialenſi*, aut ſunt Hiſpani, aut Arabici, aut Latini, aut Græci. Hiſpani nondum in uſum publicum derivati ſunt; Arabici nunc incipiunt orbi literario innoteſcere per *Michaëlem Caſiri*. Conjectare igitur quantum ſperari poſſit de Latinis, Græciſque.

Didaci Furtati. Anton. Auguſtini. Ariæ Montani.

PRÆTEREA in Hiſpania fuiſſe homines Latinæ Græcæque linguæ peritiſſimos, optimiſque & exquiſitiſſimis libris inſtructos, nemo negaverit, ſi meminerit Ferdinandi Nonnii Pintiani, Petri Johannis Nunneſii, aliorumque ſimilium: quorum omnium libros ab Hiſpania exportatos ad exteras bibliothecas, & plures in ea non manſiſſe, difficulter crediderim. Remanent igitur adhuc plurimi eorum, & ſuperſunt alii in paucis, ſed numeroſiſſimis, & antiquis bibliothecis, quæ adhuc conſervantur, & a gryphibus cuſtodiuntur.

QUANTUS vir ſit clariſſimus JOHANNES TAYLORUS, fama prædicat, & abunde didici ab amico ejus ampliſſimo *Meermano*. Quamobrem licet linguam Anglicam non intelligam, libenter a te accipiam *Elementa Juris Civilis* ab illo edita, ut meam inſtruant bibliothecam.

SCIRE cupis præcipua opera literaria, quæ ab Hiſpanis publica luce donata ſunt ab anno MDCC.? Vaſtam provinciam mihi mandaſti. Eam breviter percurram.

VALENTINI habemus duas bibliothecas, quarum auctores, videlicet Joſephus Rodriguezius, monachus ſodalicii Sanctiſſimæ Triadis, & Vincentius Ximenes, preſbyter & doctor theologus, liberaliſſimi ſunt in conterraneorum laudibus. Præcipue vero Valentini regni ſcriptores, qui hoc noſtro ſæculo floruerunt, ſunt hi.

Valentini Scriptores.

THO-

THOMAS Vincentius Tofca, prefbyter congregationis B. Philippi Nevii, qui in Hifpanorum gratiam edidit *Compendium Mathematicum*; itemque *Philofophicum*, fed hoc Latinè fcriptum, cui ego adjunxi inftitutiones morales.

JOHANNES Baptifta Corachàn, cujus eft *Arithmetica Démonftrata*, fæculo elapfo edita, & *Mathefis Sacra* a me evulgata.

JOSEPHUS Emmanuel Miniana, monachus fodalicii Sanctiffimæ Triadis, celebratiffimus ob *Continuationem Hiftoriæ Johannis Marianæ*, & *Bellum Rufticum Valentinum.*

EMMANUEL Martinus, decanus Lucentinus, cujus elegantiffimas *Epiftolas* proculdubio legifti.

HIACYNTHUS Segura, monachus Dominicanus, cujus eft *Norte Critico*, id eft, *Polus Criticus.*

PASCHASIUS Sala, præpofitus Valentinus, poft cujus mortem in lucem prodiit *Sacrum Veterum Hebræorum Kalendarium.*

NOBILISSIMUS vir, Georgius Johannes, qui fcripfit *Narrationem Hiftoricam Itineris fui in Americam Meridionalem.*

AUGUSTINUS Salefius, hujus regni hiftoricus, qui præter alia multa edidit *Differtationem de Turiæ Marmore nuper effoffo.*

INTER fcriptores Cathalanos numerandi funt, clarus vir Narciffus Felix, qui evulgavit *Annales Cathaloniæ, definentes in rebus Anni* MDCCIX.

EMMANUEL Marianus Ribera, monachus fodalicii B. Mariæ Virginis de Mercede, qui præter *Regium Sacellum Barcinonenfe*, editum anno 1698, evulgavit hoc fæculo librum de *Regum Hifpaniæ Patronatu in Regale & Militare Sodalicium Dominæ Mercedis Redemptionis Captivorum, & Centuriam primam ejufdem Sodalicii*, in quibus libris quamplurima leguntur ex Barcinonenfi antiquiffimo archio depromta.

CLARUS vir Antonius Baftero Romæ fecit publici juris *Crufcam Provincialem*, opus eximium.

CELEBERRIMUS vir Jofephus Fineftrefius edidit *Jurifprudentiam Antejuftinianeam, Prælectiones Cervarienfes, de Jure Dotium libros.*

3   *quin-*

quinque, & Commentarium in Hermogenianum, eruditiſſima opera le-
galia. Idem brevi exhibebit *Syllogen Inſcriptionum Romanarum,
quæ in Principatu Cathalauniæ, vel extant, vel aliquando extiterunt.*

EJUS frater, Jacobus Fineſtreſius, monachus Ciſtertienſis, edidit *Hiſtoriam Monaſterii Populeti,* e cujus tabulario produxit multa
ſcitu digniſſima.ɩ

MATTHÆUS Aymerich ſocietatis Jeſu nuper in lucem publi-
cam emiſit *Nomina & Acta Epiſcoporum Barcinonenſium ;* in cujus
operis fine legitur *Syllabus Chronologico-Hiſtoricus,* ab eruditiſſimo
Joſepho Fineſtreſio compoſitus.

EX reliquis Hiſpaniæ provinciis, regniſque, multi viri hoc noſtro ſæculo ſcriptis ſuis nobilitati ſunt, ut clarus *Ludovicus Sala-
zarius,* ob innumera genealogica ſcripta celeberrimus.

JOHANNES Ferreras regiæ bibliothecæ Madridienſi præfectus ob *Johannes
Annales Hiſtoricos* valde notus, in quibus illud utile eſt, quod ſcrip- *Ferreras.*
tores, quos ſequitur, allegat.

FRANCISCUS de Berganza, monachus Benedictinus, qui in fine *Franciſcus de
Antiquitatum Hiſpaniæ,* varia chronica vetera edidit, et in *Ferreras Berganza.*
convicto, Iſidori Pacenſis Chronicon.*

JOHANNES Interian de Ayala, monachus ſodalicii B. Mariæ de *J. I. de
Mercede,* vulgavit *Humaniores atque amœniores ad Muſas Excurſus, Ayala.*
itemque *Pictorem Chriſtianum eruditum.*

CLARUS vir Andreas Gonzalez de Barcia *Antonii Leonis Pineli Andreas
Bibliothecam Orientalem & Occidentalem* mirifice auxit, multos li- *Gonzalez.*
bros ad hiſtoriam Indiarum pertinentes recudi juſſit, & *Antonii Auguſtini Dialogos de Numiſmatis, Inſcriptionibus, & Antiquitatibus,* a
me jam commemoratos.

CLARUS vir Joſephus Bermudez, *de Jure Regii Hoſpicii* ſcripſit. *J. Bermudez.*

CHRISTOPHORUS Rodriguez de *Palæographia Hiſpana.* *Rodriguez.*

JOHANNES Gomez Bravo *Catalogum Epiſcoporum Cordubenſium Gomez*
edidit. *Bravo.*

PRODIIT etiam in lucem *Benedicti Ariæ Montani Lectio Chri-B. A. Mon-
ſtiana,* interprete Petro de Valentia, eximius liber ad ediſcendam *tanus.*
linguam Hiſpanam, ſi conferatur cum *Dictato Chriſtiano* ejuſdem
auctoris.

N. Antonii.   LUCE publica fruitur Nicolai Antonii *Cenfura Hiftoriarum fabu-*
lofarum.

Marchio   PLENA funt bonæ frugis Marchionis Mondexarenfis *Opera Chro-*
Mondexar.   *nologica : Differtationes Ecclefiafticæ* repetitæ editionis, ab auctore
ipfo emendatæ & auctæ; & *Animadverfiones in Hiftoriam Johannis*
Marianæ.

Laurentius   EQUES Mediolanenfis, Laurentius Bonivini, evulgavit *Ideam No-*
Bonivini.   *væ Hiftoriæ Generalis Americæ Septentrionalis,* in cujus fine leguntur præclariffima opera hiftorica, quæ auctor poffidebat.

Bernardus de   EMMANUEL Bernardus de Ribera fodalicii Sanctiffimæ Triados,
Ribera.   duo volumina edidit *Inftitutionum Philofophicarum,* & promifit duo-
decim.

Stephanus   STEPHANUS Terreros, Societatis Jefu, evulgavit *Palæographiam*
Terreros.   *Hifpanam,* cujus verus auctor eft *Andreas Marcus Burriel,* ejufdem
A. M. Bur-   focietatis, qui præter *Hiftoriam de Rebus Caliphornicis,* edidit erudi-
riel.   tiffimum librum de *Æquatione Ponderum & Menfurarum,* nomine
urbis Toleti.

POSTREMO *Valentiæ* renovantur varia opufcula, quibus Latinæ
linguæ cognitio fit facilior per interpretationes Hifpanas, cujuf-
modi funt tranflationes Hifpanicæ aliquorum auctorum ex *clafficis,*
ut felectæ Ciceronis Epiftolæ, interprete Petro Simone Aprili, &
alia opera fimilia, quæ ego dedi imprimenda. Omitto alios fcriptores tibi notos, quorum judicium malo effe tuum, quam meum.

HABES epiftolam plenam feftinationis. Diligentior ero, cum
tua intererit, Vir humaniffime. Vale.

OLIVÆ, *Pridie Calendas Septembres, Anno* MDCCLXI.

[Thofe readers, who do not underftand the Latin tongue, will
have no reafon to regret, that there is no tranflation of thefe
epiftles annexed to them; fince the literary hiftory they contain,
and the lift of authors, would afford them but very dry entertainment.]

LETTER

LETTER V.

STATE of MEASURES and WEIGHTS.

THERE is no part of the *Spanish* cuftoms, of which it is fo difficult to give any clear account, as thofe which relate to their *Meafures and Weights:* for they retain in ufage to this day, all the meafures and weights, which their feveral conquerors or invaders have introduced at different periods.

NOTHING can give one a ftronger proof of the uncommercial genius of this people, and of the little attention which they have ever given to trade, than their miniftry's having permitted this matter to reft upon the prefent footing. There is fcarce any thing which is more ferviceable to the exigencies of commerce, or which facilitates its courfe more, than an univerfal conformity between the meafures and weights of the fame country. The ROMANS, tho' far from being the moft trading nation in the world, yet perhaps for fome ages the wifeft, paid always the moft minute attention to this point, and even eftablifhed a *commercial pound*, for the greater convenience of their trade.

THE confufion, which refults from this ftrange variety, may be eafily conceived. In one province you will find *Moorifh* meafures and weights, in another *Roman*, in a third *Gothic*. The inquifition hath had little influence in this matter, for of thefe they have made an *olio*, and mixed Pagan, Mahometan, Jewifh and Chriftian meafures and pounds all together. Thus, in SEVILLE you meet with

N 2   the

the *Laſt*, the *Caby*, and the *Ancyra*; in CADIZ, the *Fanegue*, or corh-meaſure of two buſhels Engliſh; which are plainly *Mooriſh* by the barbarity of their names.   In CASTILE you will find one pound; in ANDALUSIA another.   In this city you will fee a pound of 16 ounces, in that one of 32, in another of 40, which is the butchers pound in SEGOVIA, or the *libra carnicera*, as LIVY calls it: that is to ſay, theſe different cities make uſe of one pound, two pounds, and two pounds and a half.   But this is not the worſt view of this matter; for in meaſures of the *ſame name*, you will find a moſt unſyſtematical variation in different places: Thus, for inſtance, the moſt common meaſure of length in SPAIN is the *vara*, or *bar*; this wants three inches of our Engliſh yard, being exactly two feet nine, or 33 inches long, if it be after the ſtandard of BUR-GOS, which was fixed by PHILIP II. in 1568: and FERDINAND VI. by an edict of February 14, 1751, ordered, that in all things relating to war and the marine they ſhould uſe the *bar* of CASTILE.   For till theſe later injunctions, SPAIN followed in this matter the regulations of ALPHONSUS *the Wiſe*, who fixed the ſtandard himſelf, and gave it to the City of TOLEDO; that is to ſay, he very politically endeavoured at ſome uniformity in this point, by reducing all the meaſures and weights in his dominions to the Roman ſtandard.   Such is the ſtate of this matter in CA-STILE; but when you leave thoſe kingdoms, and get into the other provinces, you will find the variations of this *vara* very con-ſiderable; nay, even in CASTILE itſelf; for the *bars* of BURGOS, TOLEDO, AVILA, and MADRID are all different.   The propor-tion, however, between this meaſure of BURGOS and our Engliſh yard, is always as 100 Engliſh yards = to 109 and 3 inches of the *Spaniſh vara*.

OUR modern calculators have made the *Roman foot* much leſs than our *Engliſh foot*; that is to ſay, the *pes Romanus*, according to them, is, in Engliſh meaſure, 11 inches, and 604 decimal parts of an inch, or almoſt half an inch leſs: but I am ſtrongly inclined to believe, that the Engliſh and Roman foot were the ſame thing.   For whoever will peruſe the following account of the Spaniſh *vara* and *league*, extracted from a work of the learned Father BURRIEL, of the Imperial College of Jeſuits at MADRID, will

will perhaps find reaſon to alter his ſentiments in this point, and will perceive this truth eſtabliſhed by his accurate reaſonings upon the *Roman Eſtadal* ſtill preſerved at TOLEDO. For there being exactly the ſame difference between the *bar* of TOLEDO, and that of BURGOS, as there is between the *bar* of BURGOS, and the Engliſh yard: conſequently, if the *bar* of TOLEDO was taken from the *Roman* foot, the Engliſh yard muſt come from the ſame ſource. The *bar* of BURGOS was, as I ſaid, 33 inches, the *bar* of TOLEDO 36, the Engliſh yard 36, conſequently theſe two laſt meaſures are *the ſame*.

THAT the antient foot of TOLEDO was the exact Roman foot, there can be no doubt; the Spaniſh and Roman meaſures, as well as weights being, for many ages, even after the diviſion of the empire, the ſame thing. The GOTHS, tho' they pulled down that vaſt fabric, had an amazing reverence for the wiſdom of its builders; they preſerved with a religious care, not the names only, but the exact uniformity and correſpondence, which ſubſiſted between the Roman weights, moneys, and meaſures of all kinds, as CURRIEL hath proved from the authority of thoſe two biſhops IDACIUS and ISIDORE. And the MOORS did in great meaſure the ſame thing. You may ſee, by one trivial inſtance, how much the Roman weights and meaſures prevailed in SPAIN in after times: the ſtyle-yard, which is much in uſe among them at preſent, is called *Uno Romana* to this day, and by no other name.

FOR liquid meaſures the CASTILIANS uſe the *Açumbre*, which, as appears by the name, is an Arabic meaſure, and perhaps originally taken from the *Omer* of the Hebrews. The *Açumbre* contains two quarts Engliſh, or half a gallon. And the table of their liquid meaſure may ſtand thus:

Dos Açumbres	——	4 quarts	——	1 gallon.
Un Açumbre	——	2 quarts	——	½ gallon.
Medio Açumbre	—	1 quart	——	¼ gallon.
Uno Quartillo	——	1 pint	——	⅛ gallon.

IF

IF the quantity be greater, you then reckon by the *Arroba*, which is likewife another Arabic meafure, and is exactly the quarter of the hundred, or 25 pounds Englifh weight: for four *Arrobes* make the *Quintal*, or 100 pounds weight. But here again the *Arroba* is not the fame throughout all SPAIN; for the pound of CADIZ and SEVILLE, and confequently the *Arrobe*, are much larger than thofe of CASTILE. In SPAIN almoft every thing, whether dry or liquid, is fold by the pound, by the avoirdupois pound of 16 ounces, and confequently by the *Arrobe:* Thus wine, oil, wood, coals, corn, bread, falt, &c. are fold by the pound, and as many of thefe are ufually purchafed in large quantities, they are generally fold by the *Arrobe*. I make no doubt, but the ufage of the old Roman pound of 12 ounces avoirdupois, or 10 troy, prevails ftill in fome parts of SPAIN, tho' I am not able to prove it: As the ftandard of the *bar* has been kept at BURGOS, fo the ftandard of the *Arroba* has been preferved at TOLEDO; and corn hath been regulated by the *Fanegue* of AVILA.

THE gold and filver-fmiths weights are,

The *Quilate*, or *Carat*, 4 grains.
A *Tomin* = to 3 carats, 12 grains.
A *Caftillan* = to 8 tomins.
The *Ounce* = to 6 caftillans and two tomins.
The *Caftillan* is the gold weight of SPAIN, and is = to 14 rials and 16 peniques.
The *Mark* = to 8 ounces.

The ftandard of the *mark* for filver has been kept at BURGOS; but the ftandard of the gold *mark* at TOLEDO.

THIS may fuffice for a fhort view of the *Caftilian* meafures and weights; for he who would give an accurate account of all which prevail in the feveral provinces of SPAIN, had need write a *folio*, and not a *letter*. Thofe who would wifh to know with the greateft precifion the exact length of the *Caftilian bar* and *league* may find it in the following extract taken from Father BURRIEL's book *Upon the Authority of the Laws of the Fuero Jufgo*.

5

Of

Of *Spanish* Measures and Distances.

WE will now endeavour to fix the value of *The Bar of Castile*, to determine the length of *The Spanish League*, and consequently to discuss a very important point of modern geography.

THE *bar* is that *Spanish* measure from whence are derived all those which serve as measures of distance : and as long as its value is not fixed, it will be very difficult to ascertain justly the *Castilian League*. But this is only a part of the difficulty : it is not sufficient to know what is the number of *feet* that go to make a *bar :* it is necessary to search still farther, and find out what kind of *feet* they are, that is to say, whether they are *Spanish*, or *Roman* feet. Such is the question now before us. We have already said, That ALPHONSUS *the Wise* ordered all the cities and states to make their weights and measures after the standard of those which he had himself given to the city of TOLEDO. PHILIP II. found it convenient to annul in part so wise a decree, by ordering, in a declaration made 1568, that the *bar of Burgos* should be the universal bar of his monarchy. TOLEDO sacrificed, without difficulty, her pretensions to the public good, which ought to result from such uniformity; and conformed at first to the will of the prince, in sending to BURGOS for a copy of her bar ; a copy, which TOLEDO has always preserved, and preserves to this day, with the greatest care. If all the cities of CASTILE had shewed the same vigilance as TOLEDO in the preservation of their bar, it is certain, that one should not see that vast difference between them, which is so visible at present. It was natural, that this change in the bar should have an influence in the ascertainment of distances, which it has been applied to measure ; and this perhaps is the source of so many opinions which clash among those who have wrote upon the *Length of the Spanish League*, which of all the measures is the most important, and that which we have most frequently a necessity of knowing its real value.

THE

The Spanish writers make mention of *three* forts of leagues, *common, legal,* and *geographical.* Philip II. ordained by a decree of 1587, that the legal leagues fhould be common leagues, and not legal leagues: it is difficult to comprehend the fenfe of this decree. For if the *common* league is an arbitrary diftance, it would not ferve as a rule in points where the property of individuals is concerned, where it is neceffary to have a conftant and determined meafure.

Ambrosius Morales and Esquivel eftablifhed it as a maxim, that by a *common league* we ought to underftand a diftance of 4000 paces, 20,000 feet, or 6666½ bars. And this fuppofing after the refearches of Esquivel, that the antient Spanifh foot was the third of the *bar of Caftile*, which was without doubt the *bar of Burgos:* But thofe refearches are pofterior to the decree of 1587; and the authority of thefe two writers cannot ferve to the interpretation of a law of Philip II. By the confeffion of all thofe who have come after them, there exifts no fuch thing in Spain as *common leagues* of 4000 paces; nor can they any more take for a *common league*, thofe which the inhabitants of a province fix by their eye, or travellers and couriers by the watch: Becaufe this league might ferve at moft to fix the fpace of ground to a traveller, but not to the furveyor, when it is neceffary to meafure the ground without roads, and in the moft exact manner.

The uncertainty is no lefs great as to the extent of the *legal league:* Morales, who fpoke of it before the decree of 1587, makes it 5000 bars, 3000 paces, 15,000 feet. Moya gives it the fame extent in his *Theoretical and Practical Geometry*, printed in 1563, and their eftimations have been adopted by Cespedes in the treatife of *Hydrography*, which he publifhed in 1606, by order of Philip III. Pere Mariaux, and Don Garcia Gabelloro are of a different opinion; they make the legal league 5000 paces, or 25,000 feet.

By *geometrical leagues* we underftand thofe, feventeen of which make a degree; but the exiftence of *equal* leagues has no foundation in theory, nor obfervation; and ftrangers have adopted

them

them without examination, upon the credit of fome Spanifh authors, devoid of that inftruction, which is neceffary in a matter fo important as this.

FROM what we have faid, there refults a new problem, namely to know, if it is poffible, how to fix the number of Spanifh *leagues*, which compofe a *degree*. They cannot give a pofitive anfwer to this queftion, without having firft a fundamental point from whence to deduce it. It is certain that we can know exactly the value, or length of the Spanifh league, if one knew the number neceffary to a degree : and alfo one fhould know how many of thefe leagues the degree contains, before one can be certain of the value of each of them.

IT is this laft method which Don JORGE JUAN employed, when he was reducing the number of French toifes into bars of CASTILE which a meridional degree contained, contiguous to the equator, meafured by Meffrs. GODIN, BOUGUERE, and LⷭCONDAMINE, to whom was affociated, by order of the Spanifh court, Don ANTONIO DE ULLOA. The Spanifh geometrician, fupported by the authority of many laws of the *Partida*, which he cites in his work, fuppofes with MOYA and CESPEDES, that the Spanifh league contains 3000 paces, 15,000 feet : and this fuppofition becomes a principle in his hands, to proceed to the reduction propofed.

MR. GODIN, before he fat out for PERU, had the attention to provide himfelf with a copy of the toife of the *Chatelet* at PARIS, which he drew with the greateft exactnefs, in order to make ufe of it in the meafures which were the object of his voyage.

WHEN JORGE JUAN returned into SPAIN, he carried with him a copy of Mr. GODIN's toife, which he took with all thofe phyfico-mathematical precautions, which the defire of accuracy prefcribed to him, and the importance of the work which he meditated. After having compared this copy of the French toife, at MADRID, with the bar which the council of CASTILE fent him, he found, that the bar of MADRID contained 371 lines of

O

the

the French toife, and that the foot of the French toife was to the
bar of MADRID, as 144 to 371. The obfervations made upon
the equator gave 56,767 toifes to a meridional degree, and it was
eafy to Don JORGE JUAN to reduce this number of toifes to
132,203 bars: in dividing the relation which he had fixed between the foot of the toife, and the bar of MADRID; or in dividing 132,203 bars, which the degree contains, by 500, which
is the number of bars that make a league, he found, that the
degree contained 26 Spanifh leagues and a half.

IT appeared, however, that it was not till after this reduction
by Don JORGE JUAN, that they thought more ferioufly in SPAIN
of the difference which there is between the bars of BURGOS,
AVILA, and that of MADRID, upon which this geometrician had
made his experiments. It was for this reafon the late King FER-
DINAND VI. ordered, in 1750, feveral mathematicians to proceed to a geometrical comparifon of thefe three bars. Don
JORGE JUAN, who was one of thefe commiffaries, determined
with his colleagues, that fix Paris feet made feven Caftilian; that
is to fay, that the French toife was exactly $2\frac{1}{3}$ bars Spanifh. His
majefty ordered that for the future, they fhould abide by this
decifion in all affairs relating to war, and the marine.

YOU fee then the number of bars contained in a Spanifh *league*,
the number of Caftilian leagues which form *a degree*, and the
number of feet of which the degree is compofed, determined and
fixed in adopting the calculation of Don JORGE JUAN. It now
remains to determine the nature of thefe *feet*.

DON JORGE JUAN thought, that the feet, of which mention is made in the laws of the *Partidas*, were Caftilian feet, and
fuch is, as far as appears, the fentiment of CESPEDES, MORA-
LES, MOYA, and the council of CASTILE itfelf.

HOWEVER refpectable thefe authorities may feem, Pere BUR-
RIEL thought he ought not to ftop there: he pretends, on the
contrary, that the feet mentioned in the laws of the *Partidas*,
and 15,000 of which make a Spanifh league, are ROMAN FEET.
The

STATE OF MEASURES, &c. 99

The method by which he came to the demonſtration of this pro-
poſition, for we look upon it as demonſtrated, is equally ſolid and
ingenious, and gives a new proof of his ſagacity.

We will now enter into the diſcuſſion of his proofs, undertaking
with him things a little higher.

It is evident, that if we could know the length of the bar
which ALPHONSUS X. gave to TOLEDO, we ſhould immediately
know the kind of foot, which He uſed, and which iṣ ſpoke of in
the laws of the *Partidas*, ſince from one unanimous conſent the
foot hath always been the third of the bar. Then we ſhould obſerve, that when the repreſentatives of the ſtates, held at TOLEDO
in 1436, wanted to take away from the meaſures of that city the
prerogative of being univerſal models, they alledged, among other
reaſons, that the bar of TOLEDO exceeded by an eighth that of BUR-
GOS. The animoſity of the deputies of BURGOS was ſo great, as
they were the leaders of the cabal, it might make us believe, that
this exceſs was exaggerated, and that the bar of TOLE did not
ſurpaſs that of BURGOS but by a twelfth, and not an eighth. If
the ſtates fixed this exceſs at an eighth, it was, without doubt, becauſe in the diviſions of the bar, one ſees parts marked as eighths,
but no twelfths. By conſequence, the bar of TOLEDO ſurpaſſed
that of BURGOS by three inches: and the foot of the bar given to
TOLEDO by ALPHONSUS X. was greater than that of BURGOS by
one inch, which is the twelfth part. Beſides, all the authors, who
have compared the Roman foot to the Spaniſh foot, aſſure us, that
the Roman foot of the capital is one twelfth more in length, than
the foot of CASTILE. Therefore the antient foot of TOLEDO,
or that of the bar of ALPHONSUS X. was equal to the Roman
foot.

If TOLEDO ſtill preſerved its antient bar, it would be eaſy to
bring experience to the ſupport of this reaſoning; by confronting
this bar with that of BURGOS: but ſince this bar exiſts no longer,
we will make uſe of a meaſure which was taken from it. The
meaſure I mean is the antient *Eſtadal* which one ſtill ſees in the
archives of TOLEDO.

The

THE *Eſtadal* paſſes commonly in SPAIN for a meaſure of eleven feet; the antient *Eſtadal* which we ſee at TOLEDO is exactly ten feet ten inches: now I cannot be perſuaded, that the old *Spaniards*, whoſe attention was ſo extreme for every thing that regarded œconomical government, ſhould give to the *Eſtadal*, to a meaſure which is ſo frequently in uſe, the unequal number of eleven feet, or the fractionary one of ten inches. It is much more probable that they gave it the equal length of 8, 10, or 12 feet.

As the antient *Eſtadal* of TOLEDO, which, as we have ſaid, was taken from the bar of ALPHONSUS X. contains 10 feet, 10 inches, then, if the *Eſtadal* ought to be a meaſure of 10 feet, the antient exceeds the modern preciſely one 12th; each foot of the ancient *Eſtadal* ſurpaſſes alſo, by one twelfth, each foot of the modern: in fine, the bar of ALPHONSUS X. was one twelfth greater than that of CASTILE. From whence we muſt conclude, that the foot of that bar had the ſame proportionate exceſs beyond the Caſtian foot, that the Roman foot had; conſequently the laws of the *Partidas* ſpeak of Roman feet, when they fix the paces and the feet of which a league is compoſed. Therefore in following theſe laws, the Spaniſh league, which contains 3000 paces of five feet each, contains 15,000 Roman feet, or 3250 Caſtilian paces, or 16,250 feet of the bar of BURGOS, meaſured by the copy of that bar, which TOLEDO keeps in its archives.

THESE reaſons are without doubt very ſtrong; but the following reflections give them ſtill a new degree of force. We cannot doubt, but that the foot, which was in uſe in SPAIN during the Roman government, was the common Roman foot: by conſequence, if by the antient Spaniſh foot they underſtand that which the Spaniards uſed during the firſt ages of the Chriſtian æra, it is certain it was the ſame as the Roman. How could the Romans, who took as much care of SPAIN as if they would make it a ſecond ITALY, how would they have permitted, that the Spaniards ſhould be diſtinct from the reſt of the world (which it had conquered, and policed) in ſo eſſential a point, as that of weights and meaſures. The uniformity between the meaſures of the Spaniards

*

niards

niards and thofe of the Romans fubfifted after the divifion of the
Empire, which never faw any change in that article in its provinces.   This uniformity fuftained itfelf even againft the invafion of
the barbarians, as appears from the authority of the Bifhop IDA-
CIUS, who was witnefs and hiftorian of thefe invafions.   This author always reckons diftances by *milliaria*, which without doubt
he could never have done; if it had not been the ufage of the
fifteenth century, in which he wrote.   The writings of St. ISI-
DORE make us believe, that the GOTHS never touched the meafures which the Spaniards had received from the Romans : becaufe one may prefume, from the known accuracy of that faint,
that he could not have paffed over in filence alterations of this
nature, in the works which we have of his *De Ponderibus & Men-*
furis: fo far from it, he marks always the diftances by the fame
names which the Romans gave them, and which they had introduced
into SPAIN, with the meafures which ferved to determine them.
Thefe reflections are fupported in the work of Father BURRIEL,
concerning *The Authority of the Laws of the Fuero Jufgo,* which
he cites in great numbers, but always with a view to prove, that
almoft to the time of ALPHONSUS X. the weights and meafures of
the Romans continued to be ufed in Spain; and that they ftill
reckoned the diftances conformably to the manner which thefe
conquerors had introduced: Could then this learned prince, who
was an able and complete legiflator, could he be ignorant, of
this continuation of the Roman weights and meafures?   And if
he knew it, as we ought to believe, confidering the extent of his
knowledge, and the lights he had, which fhine much more in
thofe of his works which exift in the obfcurity of our archives,
than in thofe which are printed: Could fuch a prince have recourfe to foreign meafures, when he determined and fettled thofe
which were to be ufed in his dominions, and of which he gave
the originals to the city of TOLEDO ?

LETTER.

LETTER VI.

VIEW OF THE STAGE.

Incolumi gravitate jocum tentavit; eò quòd
Illecebris erat, & gratâ novitate morandus
Spectator, functusque sacris. —— HORAT. ART. POET.

I AM induced to believe, that there is a resemblance between the stage of MADRID at this time, and that of ROME, when my author was describing it: that is, at a period after its infancy, and before it had arrived at its full perfection in propriety of action, sentiment, and taste. For I cannot well compare CALDERONI's productions to those of TERENCE; nor look upon any of the present Spanish actors, as equal in merit and genius to the Roman ROSCIUS, an ÆSOP, or an English GARRICK. And tho' I venture to give this opinion, it is the opinion of one, who is only an *eye*, and not an *ear*-censor: For I pretend not to understand enough of the language to be able to judge as decisively as a *French* critic, of the dramatic merit of CALDERONI, or any of his poetical countrymen. But there certainly is a way of forming some judgement, tho' by other means; facts often speak as clearly as words; and actions and gestures, though silent, are by no means dumb: And I dare affirm, that General JOHNSON often understood *the little Carpenter*, a *Cherokee*, or *the bloody Bear*, though he was not a great master of the elegancies and purity of the *In-*
dian

dian language. But farther; when a play has any degree of unity in action, time, and place; when the feveral fcenes, the characters lead on to, and terminate in one grand defign, or event; I will venture to fay, if it be tolerably well acted that a *foreigner*, tho' he does not underftand the language, will be able to tell you what the general drift and defign of the play was: Let a Spaniard, or Frenchman, who is ignorant of the Englifh tongue, be prefent at the reprefentation of *Othello, Lear, Richard, The Journey to London*, or *The Bold Stroke for a Wife*, and I am certain he will give a juft account of all he faw: he will tell you, that *one* murdered his wife for jealoufy; that the *other* went mad for the ingratitude of his daughters; that confcious guilt filled the *third*, though no coward fpirit, with all the horrors of remorfe.

WHEN I went firft to the Spanifh comedy, it was the feafon for acting the *Autos*, that is to fay, plays in fupport of the Catholic faith; for *Auto de Fe* is in their language *an act of faith*. I found at my firft entrance a good theatre, as to fize and fhape, but rather dirty, and ill lighted; and what made it worfe was an equal mixture of day-light and candles. The *prompter*'s head appeared thro' a little trap-door above the level of the ftage, and I firft took him for a ghoft, or devil, juft ready to afcend to thefe upper regions: But I was foon undeceived, when he began to read the play loud enough for the actors and the boxes too, who were near him. The *pit* was an odd fight, and made a motley, comical appearance; many ftanding in their night-caps and cloaks; officers and foldiers interfperfed among the dirtieft mob, feemed rather ftrange. That which anfwered to our *two-fhilling-gallery*, was filled with women only, all in the fame uniform, a dark petticoat, and a white woollen veil. The fide and front-boxes were occupied by people well dreffed, and fome of the firft fafhion.

WHEN the play began, the actors appeared much better attired, that is, in richer clothes, than thofe in England; and thefe they change perpetually, in order to let you fee the expenfive variety of their wardrobe. After fome fcenes had paffed, which were tedious and infipid, there came on an interlude of humour and drollery, defigned, I fuppofe, for the entertainment of the pit. One

2   of

of thefe comedians appeared tempting, with a bag of money, a lady
who fung to him very prettily, and did not feem altogether averfe
to grant him fome favours: in the mean while to my great furprize
a man brought in three *barbers blocks* upon the ftage: after thefe
three faid barbers blocks were placed upon the ftage, the fame
man returned and dreffed them firft in *mens clothes*, and undreffed
them again, and then dreffed them once more in *womens clothes*.
Now, Sir, to tell you the truth, it was for the fake of fuch fcenes
as thefe that I placed thofe lines of HORACE at the head of this
account; becaufe I am perfuaded the author attempted this excellent piece of humour, for the reafon there given, for the fake of
his friends in the pit, and this without violating the decorum due
to the national gravity of his countrymen.

However, I fhould not forget to tell you, that when thefe
block ladies were properly attired, there came in three men, who
had a fancy to tempt thefe three ladies likewife; but they were
inflexibly coy, and I think it was not long before their gallants difcovered the miftake. But to quit this interlude, and return to the
play again: In procefs of time, and after fome fcenes had paffed,
which were long, tirefome, uninterefting, and full of fuftian and
bombaft; the grand fcene approached; an actor, dreffed in a
long purple robe, appeared in the character of JESUS CHRIST,
or the *Nueftro Senor*, as they call him; immediately he was blind-
folded, buffeted, fpit upon, bound, fcourged, crowned with thorns,
and compelled to bear his crofs, when he knelt down and cried,
Padre mi! Padre mi! " My Father! my Father! why haft thou for-
" faken me?" After this he placed himfelf againft the wall, with his
hands extended, as if on the crofs, and there imitated the expiring
agonies of his dying Lord. And what think you, my friend, was the
conclufion of this awful and folemn fcene? why, really, one every
way fuitable to the dignity and ferioufnefs of the occafion: one of
the actreffes immediately unbound Chrift, divefted him of his crown
and fcarlet robes; and when he had put on his wig and coat again,
he immediately joined the reft of the actors, and danced a *fegue-
dillas*.

   Spectatum admiffi, rifum teneatis, amici?

As

As to the *fequedillas*, or dance, it is little better upon the Spanish stage, than gently walking round one another; tho' when danced in its true spirit, in private houses, it much resembles the *English Hay*. After this one of the actresses, in a very long speech, explained the nature, end, and design of the *facraments*; you must know also, that the Spaniards admit a great number of soliloquies, full of tiresome, and uninteresting declamation, into their plays. In the last scene, Christ appeared in a ship triumphant; and thus the play concluded. I forgot to tell you, that Christ, before his passion, preached to the four quarters of the world, in their proper dresses, upon the stage: *Europe* and *America* heard him gladly, and received the faith; but *Asia* and *Africa* remained incorrigible.

SOME time after I had seen this *Auto* (for, to say the truth, my curiosity was a little abated with regard to the Spanish stage, from this specimen of it) I went to see a regular comedy; there were two English gentlemen in the box with me at the same time. We understood very little of the design of the first act; we saw a king, queen, an enchantress, and many other pretty, delightful sights: but the *interlude*, with which that act concluded, is, I think, not to be equalled either by ROME or GREECE; neither FARQUHAR, CIBBER, or any of our lowest farce-writers, have ever produced any thing comparable to it. The scene was intended for the inside of a *Spanish Pofada* (or *inn*) in the night; there were three feather-beds, and as many blankets brought upon the stage; the queen and her maids of honour personated the mistress of the *Pofada* and her maids; and accordingly fell to making the beds. After this there came in six men to lie there, who paid three quarts a piece; one of them being a miser, had rolled up his money in twenty or thirty pieces of paper. Then they undressed before the ladies, by pulling off six or seven pair of breeches, and as many coats and waistcoats, and got into bed two by two: When behold, the jest was, to see them all kick the clothes off one another, and then fight, as the spectator is to suppose, in the dark. The absurdity of this scene, and the incomprehensible ridiculousness of it, made us laugh immoderately. The fight of the feather-beds, the men kicking and sprawling, the peals of applause, that echoed through the house, were truly inconceivable; tho', I believe, our

P   neigh-

neighbours in the next box thought we laughed at the wit and humour of the author. It was a scene that beggars all possible description, and I defy any theatre in EUROPE, but that of MADRID, to produce such another. SHUTER's favourite *Beggars Bush*, with all its low ribaldry, is by no means a match for it. But to return once more to the play: When this *interlude* was finished, there succeeded some other scenes, between the king, queen, enchantress, and the rest of the actors; such as five or six of them drawing their swords upon the enchantress all at once, who parries them with her wand, and retires into her cell unhurt. They are surprised to find that their swords made no impression, and so put them up into their scabbards for a better occasion, crying, *Muy grande maravilla!* that is, " It is a very great wonder !" At other times the enchantress kills with one look, and makes alive with a second. Once she came in, fell down upon the stage, broke her nose, got up again, went out, and returned with a black patch. Then we had another *interlude,* in which some husbands pursued their wives in great anger, and with clubs something like Goliah's staff, or a weaver's beam, in order to beat their brains out; but, by the friendly interposition of some kind neighbours, they were prevented from that rude species of divorce. In revenge for this insult, the wives in the *interlude* that followed at the end of the next act, dressed themselves up like amazons, with arms and armour, and pursued their husbands, who in their turn now submitted to the conquerors. I remember nothing very remarkable that passed after this, excepting that the enchantress renounces the devil, and all his works, and in conclusion embraces the catholic faith, and declares she will adhere to that only.

THIS, I hope, will serve at present for a short sketch of the *Spanish Stage.* Indeed, I had almost forgot to tell you, that TERESA, one of the actresses, was this winter imprisoned by the King's order, for being too free of her charms to some of the grandees; it was said she would be condemned to the workhouse for life. However that be, she remains in prison still, and, as far as I can learn, is like to remain so for some time longer.

CALDERONI is at present, and has been the favourite author upon their stage for some years.

6   L E T-

LETTER VII. PART I.

Defcription of the BULL-FEAST, exhibited in the *Plaça Mayor* at *Madrid*, upon occafion of His Catholic Majefty's Public Entry into his Capital, on *July* 15, 1760.

WE arrived at the balcony of the Englifh Ambaffador in the *Plaça Mayor* about half an hour after three in the afternoon, and were at once ftruck with the chearfulleft, gayeft fight imaginable. The *fquare*, which is large, was thronged with people; the *balconies* all ornamented with different coloured filks, and crouded from the top to the bottom of the houfes; the avenues to the fquare were built up into balconies, and a fort of floping fcaffolding was placed round for the common people, elevated above the ground, or pit, if I may fo call it, about eight or nine feet, with openings in proper places, and wooden doors.

FIRST came in the coaches of the *cavaliers*, four in number, of an antique and fingular make, with glaffes at the ends, and quite open at the fides: The cavaliers were placed at the doors of their coaches, from whence they bowed to the people, and the balconies, as they paffed round the fquare; and they were accompanied by their fponfors, the Dukes of OSSUNA, of BANOS, of ARCOS,

and

and MEDINA CÆLI. Before the royal family came a company
of *halberdiers*, after which the king's coaches in great state, I
believe about seven or eight in number, preceding his *Caroſſe- de
Reſpeƈt*, which was extremely rich, with red and gold ornaments,
and beautiful painted pannels: Then a coach with some of the
great officers, who go always immediately before the king; next
came the KING and QUEEN in a very sumptuous coach of blue,
with all the ornaments of maſſive silver, and the crown at the top;
the trappings of the horses were likewise silver, with large white
plumes. These were followed by the coaches of the Prince of
ASTURIAS, the two infanta's, and Don LUIS, with their attendants.

THEIR Majesties were placed oppoſite to us, in a gilt balcony, with a canopy and curtains of scarlet and gold; the queen on
that occaſion taking the right hand. On the right hand of the
king's balcony were placed the reſt of the royal family: and on
the left were ranged the gentlemen of the bed-chamber in a row;
all dreſſed in a very fine uniform of blue and red, richly embroidered with gold. The *halberdiers* marched from the king's balcony, which was in the center on one ſide, and forming themſelves
into two lines, fronting different ways, inſtantly cleared the square
of the croud, who retired into the scaffolding, ereƈted for them round
it. Next the halberdiers formed themſelves in a line before the
scaffold, under the king's balcony. Then appeared *two companies
of boys*, dreſſed in an uniform with caps, and red taffeta jackets,
ranged againſt the right and left hand ſide of the square, who carrying buckets of water in their hands, watered the ſtage as they
croſſed over to the ſide oppoſite to them. This being performed,
the six chief *Alguazils* of the town, mounted upon fine horſes,
covered with trappings, and dreſſed in the old Spaniſh habits,
black with flaſhed ſleeves, great white flowing wigs, and hats with
plumes of different-coloured feathers, advanced towards the king's
balcony, under which they were obliged to ſtay the whole time,
to receive his orders; except when they were frightened away by
the bulls, when they were obliged to ride for it, being abſolutely
unarmed and defenceleſs.

HAVING

HAVING obtained the king's permiſſion for the *bull-feaſt*, the troops belonging to the *knights* entered upon the ſtage in four large companies, dreſſed in liveries of *Mooriſh habits* of ſilk, richly and elegantly ornamented with lace and embroidery : Theſe marched firſt to make their bow to the king's balcony, and then in proceſſion round the ſquare : and from the elegance, ſingularity, and variety of their uniforms, made one of the moſt delightful ſcenes that can be conceived. After them came the *four knights*, habited in the old Spaniſh dreſs, with plumes in their hats, and mounted upon the moſt beautiful horſes : each carried in his hand a ſlender lance, and was attended by two men on foot, dreſſed in light ſilk, of the colour of his livery, with a ſort of cloaks or mantles of the ſame ; theſe never forſake his ſide, and are indeed his principal defence. After the *cavaliers* had done their homage to the King, their companies retired, and there remained with them only, beſides thoſe who walked by their ſide, a few dreſſed with mantles in the ſame manner, who diſperſt themſelves over the ſtage. The cavaliers then diſpoſed themſelves for the encounter; the firſt placing himſelf oppoſite to the door of the place where the bulls are kept, the other at ſome diſtance behind him, and ſo on.

THE KING then making the *ſignal* for the doors to be opened, the bull appeared, to the ſound of martial muſic, and the loud acclamations of the people : and ſeeing one of the attendants of the firſt cavalier ſpreading his cloak before him, aimed directly at him; but the man eaſily evaded him, and gave his maſter an opportunity of breaking his ſpear in the bull's neck. In the ſame manner the bull was tempted to engage the other cavaliers, and always with the ſame ſucceſs: till having received the honourable wounds from their lances, he was encountered by the other men on foot : who, after playing with him, with an incredible agility, as long as they think proper, eaſily put an end to him, by thruſting a ſword either into his neck or ſide, which brings him to the ground; and then they finiſh him at once, *by ſtriking a dagger, or the point of a ſword, behind his horns into the ſpine, which is always immediate death* *. After this the bull is inſtantly hurried off by mules, finely adorned, and decked with trappings for the occaſion.

* This was the way the *Numidians* uſed to kill the elephants, when they became unruly ; ſee LIVY, lib. xxvii. cap. 49. The words are, *Rectores eorum ſcalprum cum malleo habebant*;

My

My apprehensions were at first principally for the men *on foot*; but I soon perceived they were in no sort of danger: their cloaks are a certain security to them, as the bull always aims at it, and they can therefore easily evade the blow. Besides this, there are so many to assist each other, that they can always lead the bull which way they please, and even in the worst case they can preserve themselves by leaping into the scaffold, as they frequently did.

The *knights* are in much more danger; their horses being too full of fire to be exactly directed; they cannot therefore so well evade the aim, and are liable every moment to be overthrown with their horses, if the attendants by their side did not assist them. Two beautiful horses nevertheless we saw gored; one of which was overthrown with his rider, but fortunately the man escaped any mischief from his fall. The courage of these horses is so great, that they have been often known to advance towards the bull, when their bowels were trailing upon the ground.

'After the knights had sufficiently tired themselves with these exploits, the king gave them leave to retire and repose. We had then bulls let out (one at a time always) from another door, of a more furious nature; these were encountered entirely by the men on foot, who were so far from fearing their rage, that the whole business was to irritate them more, by throwing upon their necks, and other parts, little barbed darts, ornamented with bunches of paper, like the *Bacchanalian Thyasus*, some of which were filled with gunpowder, and burst in the manner of a squib or serpent, as soon as they were fastened to the bull. Nothing can be imagined more tormenting than these darts, which stick about him, and never lose their hold. But the courage and amazing dexterity, with which they are thrown, takes off your attention from the cruelty of it. Another method they have of diverting themselves with the fury of the bull, is by dressing up *goat-skins*, blown up with wind, into figures, and placing them before him, which makes a very ridiculous part of the entertainment. Many

---

id, ubi sævire belluæ, & ruere in suos cœpe ant, magister inter aures positum, ipso in articulo, quo jungitur capiti cervix (in the spine) quanto maximo p terat ictu adigebat. Ea celerrima via mortis in tantæ molis belluâ inventa erat, ubi regendi spem vicissent. Primusque id Asdrubal instituerat.

ef

of the bulls, however, would not attack them, and one of the
moſt furious that did, ſhewed more fear than in encountering his
moſt ſturdy antagoniſts : ſo great is their apprehenſion from an object that ſtands firm, and ſeems not to be diſmayed at their approach.   There is likewiſe another kind of a larger ſpear, which
is held by a man obliquely, with the end in the ground, and the
point towards the door, where the bull comes out, who never fails to
run at it, with great danger to the man, as he is always thrown
down; but greater to the bull, who commonly receives the point
in his head or neck, and with ſuch force, that we ſaw a ſpear
broke ſhort, that was much thicker than my arm.   They alſo
baited one bull with dogs, which ſhewed as much courage and
obſtinate perſeverance as any of that breed in ENGLAND.   As
to the *laws* of this ſpectacle, and other circumſtances relative to
the *punctilios* of the bull-feaſt, I cannot pretend to explain them,
and imagine others, who have attempted it, have been obliged to
take it moſtly upon truſt, nor do I think it very material.

THIS ſpectacle is certainly one of the fineſt in the world, whether it is conſidered merely as a *coup d'œil*, or as an exertion of the
bravery and infinite agility of the performers.   The Spaniards are
ſo devoted to it, that even the women would pawn their laſt rag
to ſee it; and we were aſſured, that ſome of the balconies did
not coſt leſs than a hundred piſtoles for that afternoon.   Nothing can be imagined more crowded than the houſes, even to the
tops of their tiles; and dearly enough they paid for their pleaſure,
pent together in the hotteſt ſun, and with the moſt ſuffocating
heat that can be endured.   Nor do I greatly wonder at them,
when I conſider how much my own country, that is certainly as
humane as any nation, is bigotted to its cuſtoms of bull-baiting,
cock-fighting, &c.——I do not deny, that this is a remnant of
Moorish, or perhaps *Roman* barbarity; and that it will not bear
the ſpeculations of the cloſet, or the compaſſionate feelings of a
tender heart.   But, after all, we muſt not ſpeculate too nicely,
left we ſhould loſe the hardneſs of manhood in the ſofter ſentiments of philoſophy.   There is a certain degree of ferocity requi-
ſite in our natures; and which, as on the one hand it ſhould be re-
ſtrained within proper bounds, that it may not degenerate into
cru-

cruelty; fo, on the other, we muſt not refine too much upon it, for fear of ſinking into effeminacy. This cuſtom is far from having cruelty for its objeĉt; bravery and intrepidity, joined with ability and ſkill, are what obtain the loudeſt acclamations from the people : it has all the good effeĉts of *chivalry*, in exciting the minds of the ſpeĉtators to great aĉtions, without the horror that prevailed in former times, of diſtinguiſhing bravery to the prejudice of our own ſpecies. It teaches to deſpiſe danger; and that the ſureſt way to overcome it, is to look it calmly and ſtedfaſtly in the face ; to afford a faithful and generous aſſiſtance to thoſe engaged with us in enterprizes of difficulty : And in ſhort, tho' it may not be ſtriĉtly conſonant to the laws of humanity and good nature, it may yet be produĉtive of great and glorious effeĉts; and is certainly the mark of qualities, that do honour to any nation.

This ceremony of the *bull-feaſt* in the *Plaça Mayor* is never exhibited, but upon the greateſt occaſions, ſuch as the acceſſion of a new age of their kings, and is attended with a very great expence both to the king, as well as the city. There is a theatre built juſt without the walls, on purpoſe, where there are bull-feaſts every fortnight; and theſe to connoiſſeurs in the art are infinitely preferable to the others; the bulls being more furious, and the danger greater to the cavaliers. But that which I have deſcribed, would, I think, very ſufficiently ſatisfy my curioſity.

I have ſince ſeen a bull-feaſt in that amphitheatre, and found little material difference in the manner of fighting, except that the cavaliers, who rode better, and ſeemed more adroit, were not ſo cloſely attended by the men on foot : and that they ſometimes uſed a long lance of ſtrait, tough wood, with a ſhort point, and a knob of twiſted cord, which hinders it from entering deep into the wound. This they held tight to their ſide, paſſing under their arm-pit, and direĉted it with their hand. In this manner they wait the bull's approach, and generally have ſtrength enough to keep him off from themſelves and their horſes, when he runs upon it : tho' it is dangerous, the bull ſometimes bearing down both man and horſe. This was one of the ordinary ſpeĉtacles, and therefore attended with little of the pomp which I had ſeen in the

Plaça

Plaça Mayor. The building is erected on the ancient plan, round, with rows of feats raifed above the area, for the common people ; and two rows of boxes, or large balconies, above them. It is not only admirably contrived for the purpofe which it is built for, but has a very ftriking appearance, from its fize and regularity. One could not, however, help obferving ladies of the firft quality in the balconies, feafting, with thefe bloody fcenes, thofe eyes, which were intended only to be exercifed in fofter cruelties. And among the common people we even faw numbers of women with children at their breafts.

I SHALL now take the liberty, as many are divided in their opinions, whether the *Spanifh bull-feaft* be of *Roman* or *Moorifh* origin, to give my fentiments upon that fubject. I remember fomewhere, that CICERO, when he was obliged for the fake of the argument, to declare whether he thought thofe bloody and favage *exhibitions,* fo much coveted by his countrymen, were really *cruel and inhuman, or not:* in order to avoid fixing, by his opinion, any reproach upon them, dextroufly eludes the queftion, and with the addrefs of a cafuift gives this remarkable anfwer, *Crudele gladiatorum fpectaculum—haud fcio, en ita fit.* A ftrange fentiment for a civilized writer! A diverfion, at the expence of humanity, muft be *cruel;* the practice was fit only for barbarians. But to the point: to fay, that the *Spanifh Fiefta de los Toros* is plainly an imitation of the *Romans,* becaufe they exhibited wild beafts in their amphitheatres, is fpeaking very generally, and not with any precifion: One might as well affert, that they copied it from the *Afiatics,* for St. PAUL fays, ἐθηριομάχησα ἐν Ἐφέσῳ. And perhaps the Spaniards might as well own, as he did, that *it profits them nothing.* But if I can find this very *Fiefta de los Toros,* the *Spanifh bull-feaft,* among the *Roman* cuftoms, I fuppofe nobody will doubt from whence the Spaniards took it.

LIVY tells us, *per eos dies, quibus hæc ex Hifpaniâ nunciata funt, ludi* TAURILIA *per biduum facti, religionis caufâ.*

FESTUS has very luckily preferved the firft inftitution of this feaft. The *Taurilia,* according to him, were inftituted to the infer-

Q   fer-

fernal gods, for this reason; in the reign of TARQUINIUS SUPER-
BUS, when a moft violent plague had feized all the women big
with child, they procured abortions by eating fome bulls fleſh,
that was fold at the ſhambles: upon this account thefe *ludi* were
inſtituted, and were called *taurilia*, and they are celebrated in the
Flaminian Circus, that the infernal gods might not be called *within
their walls*.

PURSUANT to their fuperſtitious ritual, fo favage an inſtitution
was rightly dedicated to the infernal gods : from this account of
it, it is proper that the *Spaniſh* women ſhould bring their children
at the breaft, and thofe in the womb, as we fee they do, to this
fpectacle.   But they commit a great impropriety in celebrating it
in the *Plaça Mayor*. It ſhould be without the walls. LIVY fays,
that the *ludi*, which FULVIUS gave juft after, were much more
fplendid, that is, I fuppofe, much more bloody and barbarous, for
he exhibited lions and panthers.

BUT the refemblance between the *Roman*, and the *Spaniſh
Taurilia* appears ſtill ſtronger from other circumſtances now remaining; it is a cuſtom for the *Spaniſh* nobility themfelves to engage the bulls, and none are permitted to fight as cavaliers, unlefs
they can prove their defcent to be noble.   The true *Spaniards* are
all fond of the diverfion ; it is accounted honourable and heroic : it
recommends them to the fair, to their prince, and to their country;
and it is a ſtanding theme of honour among the people.

IT was juft the fame at ROME; the nobility, the patricians,
voluntarily undertook a part in thefe encounters :

> *Luſtravitque fugâ mediam gladiator arenam,
> Et Capitolinis generofior & Marcellis——*

And even the ladies were ambitious of appearing in the fame lifts.
MÆVIA was a lady of quality, and yet we find ſhe could ſtep out
of her fex, and enter the *arena*.

> ——*Tufcum
> Figat aprum, & nudâ teneat venabula mammâ.*

I   I do

I do not find, that the *Spanish* ladies had ever any of this martial, or rather masculine spirit. It is amazing how desirous the *Romans* were of being killed, even in jest; senators, patricians, and knights, were at last not ashamed to appear on these occasions.—I think I have done some honour to the *Spanish* nobility in thus placing them on a footing with *Roman* senators; but still be it remembered, that these were not senators of ROME, when ROME *survived*, as CATO calls it, but when she was enslaved, and dishonoured by the worst of emperors, I might indeed say, by the worst of men.

I AM surprized to find these *taurilia* omitted by Mr. KENNETT.

LETTER VII. PART II.

BURIAL——GRANDEES——KING's
PUBLIC ENTRY.

THE funeral rites of the rich in SPAIN are ſplendid, as well as decent; they are ſolemnly interred with their beſt ſuit of clothes, with hat, cloak, and ſword.

> *Nam vivis quis amor gladii, quæ cura togæve*
> *Manſit, & hæc eadem remanet tellure repoſtis.*

And I am firmly perſuaded, that the old knights, condes, and grandees of this kingdom were antiently buried, juſt as we ſee their *ſculptured figures* upon their tombs; armed *cap-à-pee*, and at all points; juſt as if they had been harneſſed out for battle, with their beaver, coat, cuiraſs, the target, lance, ſword, ſpurs, and jack-boots. And this ſhews the great propriety of that famous joke of old SCARRON, who, when he was receiving extreme unction, told the anointer, " Pray, ſir, take care to greaſe my boots well, for I " am going a very long journey."

THEY commonly put a great deal of lime into the grave, in order to haſten the corruption of the body; at NAPLES I am told they have a great hole, half filled with lime, into which they throw all their dead, naked.

THE late Queen of SPAIN, conſort of the preſent King CHARLES III. died September 27th, 1760, aged 35, after ſhe
had

had reigned only one year and fourteen days. She was a daughter of the prefent King of POLAND, and had fuffered greatly for the diftreffes of her father, who has been driven from his electorate by the King of PRUSSIA : She had lived twenty years with his prefent Majefty. She was in a bad ftate of health when he came firft into SPAIN, catched the meazles at SARAGOÇA, then a cold : and afterwards was taken ill with a fever and flux at St. ILDEFONSO, in September, and upon its increafe returned to MADRID; when both thofe diforders ftill kept harraffing and weakening her, till they at laft ended in a delirium and mortification. Every art of phyfic was ufed to fave her, and every *Spanifh* faint invoked, but all in vain. They brought the *image* of ST. ISIDRO to her, and fome were fetched even from TOLEDO and ALCALA DE HENARES : But neither the interpofition of faints or fubjects could avail any thing; tho' all the churches of MADRID were crowded with people, offering up prayers for her recovery, fate was inexorable, and death relentlefs. The *nuncio* came and gave her the laft papal benediction, and by that means conveyed to her the firft notice of her approaching diffolution ; fhe received the fhock with fome furprize, but with much piety, refignation, and refolution. Upon her obferving to the nuncio the infignificance and emptinefs of all human grandeur; and that it was now of no advantage to her, that fhe ever was a Queen—He replied, " Your Majefty has certainly had much greater opportu-
" nities of doing good, and which have not been neglected."
She lingered a day or two after this, till the delirium came on, attended with convulfions, and at length expired on the twenty-feventh of September, about three o'clock in the afternoon.

CEREMONIES of a ROYAL FUNERAL.

ON the twenty-eighth, fhe was laid in ftate in the *caffon*, or great-hall of the BUEN RETIRO ; fhe lay upon a fpond covered with gold tiffue, under a canopy of ftate : She was dreffed in a plain cap, tied with a broad white fattin ribband, and with a
                                    fmall

fmall black egret over her forehead : On each fide the fpond were fix large *girandoles*, of *Mexican* filver, about four feet high, with large tapers burning, and round the room were feveral altars with gold and filver candlefticks. On the right hand fide of the fpond, at the feet, knelt the dutchefs of MEDINA SIDONIA, behind her another lady of diftinction, and then an exempt, and on each fide ftood two *purfuivants* bearing the crown and fceptre. The ladies were relieved every hour by others, fuch as the dutchefs of BUR-NOMBILF, the dutchefs of ARCOS, &c. but the purfuivants were obliged to remain the whole twenty-four hours—Thus lay the Queen all that day and night ; on the twenty-ninth, fhe was carried to the ESCURIAL in this manner: About feven o'clock in the evening the proceffion began from the gate of the BUEN RETIRO in this order : Firft came forty *Carmelite*-monks on horfe-back, each with a torch in one hand, and the bridle in the other ; then as many *Cordeliers*, and laft of all the *Dominicans*, all with torches in their hands : Then a body of the guards on horfeback, without tapers, headed by the duke of VERAGUEZ, or duke of BER-WICK. Thefe were followed by the facrift in his cope, bearing a gold crucifix, at the head of the curates. Then the ftate-coach with the Queen's body, followed by two *caroffes de refpect* ; then the duke of ALVA ; behind him the inquifitor-general, with fome other people of diftinction, fuch as the duke of ARCOS, &c. then followed another body of the guards, and laft of all a fuite of coaches. Thefe were obliged to travel in this manner all the night, with their torches burning, which muft be a vaft expence ; it being eight leagues to the ESCURIAL, and they propofed burying her Majefty about eight o'clock the next morning. The monks are paid for this journey, and they commonly fhare the tiffue pall between them. And thus ended the folemnities of this funeral, which I fhall conclude with the moral of our Eng-lifh Poet :

.A heap of duft alone remains of Thee ;
'Tis all thou art, and all the Great fhall be.

GRAN-

GRANDEES.

IT is very difficult to make out a clear and exact lift of the grandees of SPAIN, the Spaniards themfelves have publifhed no good
one : and there are very few, who can give you any juft information. In the firft place, there is no fuperiority and gradation
of title here, as there is in ENGLAND. A duke is no more than
a marquis, a marquis no greater than an earl; in fhort, all titles
are equal. And you will often fee the father an earl, and the fon
a duke; juft the reverfe as with us. The great diftinction antiently confifted in being grandee of the firft, fecond, or third order: but thefe diftinctions are now dropped; the king making them
all grandees of the firft clafs. Thefe three claffes were, 1. Thofe who
came into his majefty's prefence with their heads covered before
they fpoke to the king : 2. Thofe who did not cover till they had
fpoke to his majefty, and the king had anfwered them : 3. Thofe
who did not cover, or put on the hat, 'till after they had withdrawn
to their place. If the king bids them be covered, without any
addition to the word *cubridos*, they are only grandees for life ; if
his majefty adds the title of any of their lands, the honour is hereditary. Indeed, with us in ENGLAND, it ufed formerly to be a
cuftom for the peers to fit *covered* when the king went to the
houfe of lords, till that polite parliament at queen ANNE's acceffion dropped it, out of compliment to her majefty, becaufe they
thought it ungenteel to fit covered before a queen. All the titles
in SPAIN are feudal to this day. The crown gives them in the
firft inftance free for the life of that perfon, or, as they call it, *Li-
bres des Lances*; but ever after, as feofs of the crown, they pay
a yearly fum of money in lieu of their knights, or feudal fervice.
Befides thefe grandees, there are a great number of good, antient families in this country, who from their antiquity have an
undoubted right to rank as grandees; but as the crown has not
thought proper to *cover* them, as fuch, they have no rank : Thefe
are called *Cafas aggraviadas*, or *injured houfes*. The mark of diftinction,

tinction, which thefe grandees conftantly keep up, and give to each other with the greateft exactnefs, is the always addreffing one another with the *TU:* whereas, when they fpeak to any other of inferior rank, they ufe the *Eccellencia, Vueftra Merced,* the *Vofia, Vofenoria,* &c.

The following is the moft correct lift of the Spanifh grandees, which I could meet with.

LIST *of the* SPANISH GRANDEES, *alphabetically, by their Titles, with their Family-Names, &c. &c.*

A.

Abrantes	Duke	Don M. Carvajal.
Aguilar	Earl	Vic. Offorio Mofcofo y Gufman.
Altamira	Earl	Ben. Mofcofo.
Alva	Duke	Fern. Sylva y Toledo (his eldeft fon is Duke of Huescar.)
Alcanizas	Marquis	Manuel Oforio.
Albuquerque	Duke	Pedro de la Cueba (eldeft fon Ledesma.)
Amarante	Earl	Fr. Gayofo.
Arco	Duke	Alp. Zayas.
Argete	Duke	L. Lafo de la Vega.
Arion	Duke	Ign. Pimentel.
Arissa	Marquis	Joackim de Palafox.
Arcos	Duke	Ponce de Leon.
Aranda	Earl	Po. Abarca.
Astorga	Marquis	Infantado.
Atares	Earl	St. Jago Funes

B.

Banos	Duke	Don A. Ponce de Leon.
Banos	Earl	J. de Mufcofq.

BALBACES	Marquis	Don J. de Efpinola (his eldeft fon is Duke of SEXTO.)
BEJAR	Duke	J. de Zuniga.
BENEVENTE	Earl	Fr. de Pimentel; or, Duke de MEDINA DEL RIO SECO.
BERAGUAS	Duke	Sn. Jago Eftuardo (pretended Duke of BERWICK.)
BOURNOMBILE	Duke	Fr. de Bournombile.

C.

CASTRO-PINIANO	Duke	Don Eboli.
CASCAHUELAS, commonly called the COUNT DE FUENTES.	Earl	Joackim Pignatelli (they married into the houfe of GUSMAN, and then took that title FUENTES Y GUSMAN. The eldeft fon MORA.)
CASTEL DE LOS RIOS	Marquis	
CASTELLAR	Marquis	Lucas Patinho.
CIFUENTES	Earl	Juan de Sylva.
CAMINA	Marquis	Pedro de Cordova, or Cogolludo.
CORDUBA		
CORUNNA	Earl	Manuel de Caftejon.

E.

ESTEPA	Marquis	Don Juan Centurion.

F.

FRIAS	Duke	Don B. de Velafco, conftable of Caftile.
FUENCLARA	Earl	Ant. de Sylva.
FERNAN-NUNEZ	Earl	Jof. de los Rios.

J.

JACCHI	Prince	Don Regio.
INFANTADO	Duke	This title at prefent in abeyance, but will come to the Duke of LERMA.

R   LER-

L.

LERMA	Duke	
LOSADA	Duke	Don Jof. de Miranda.

M.

MACEDA	Earl	Don Fr. Lanzos.
MALPICA	Marquis	Jof. Pimentel.
MANZERA	Marquis	Joack. Pimentel.
MASSERANO	Prince	Fil Frefco, Prince of CAMPO FLORIDA.
MEDINA COELI	Duke	Luis de Cordova (eldeft fon Cogolludo or Camina; the old family-name was LA CERDA.
MEDINA SIDONIA	Duke	Pedro de Gufman *El Bueno*. They had the name of EL BUENO, from that Gufman, who defended Tariffa fo bravely in the year 1292.
MINA	Marquis	Gufman.
MIRANDA	Earl	Antonio de Zuniga.
MONTIJO	Earl	Ch. Portocarero.
MONTELLANO	Duke	Jof. de Solis.
MONDECAR	Marquis	N. de Mendofa.
MONTE LEON	Duke	—— Pignatelli.

O.

ONATE	Earl	Don Jof. de Gufman.
OSSUNA	Duke	Pedro Giron.

P.

PAREDES	Earl	Don Diego de Gufman.
PARSEN	Earl	Joack. de la Cerda.
PERALADA	Earl	Fer. de Bujados.
PIO	Prince	Regio.
POPULI	Dutchefs	
PRIEGO	Earl	Juan de Croix.
PUNO EN ROSTRO	Earl	Fr. Xavier Arias.

R.

RICLA	Earl	Don Amb. de Funes.

SAN

S.

SAN ESTEVAN	Duke	Don A. de Benavides.
SAN JUAN	Marquis	Juan Pizarro.
SALVA TIERRA	Earl	Juan de Cordova.
SANTA CRUZ	Marquis	Jof. de Sylva.
SARRIA	Marquis	Nic. de Carvajal.
SERBELLONI	Earl	
SIRUELA	Earl	Fr. Balbi.
SOTO-MAYOR	Duke	F. S. M. Maffones y Lima.

T.

TENEBRON	Earl	Don Ger. de Montezuma. This gentleman is a lineal defcendant from the famous Prince MONTEZUMA, and enjoys a penfion from the court of Spain on that account.
TORRECUSO	Marquis	Carracciolo.

V and U.

VEDMAR	Marquis	Don Ph. Pacheco.
VILLA FRANCA	Marquis	Ant. de Toledo.
VILLA GARCIA	Marquis	Bart. de Mendoza.
UZEDA	Duke	Ant. Pacheco.
VILLADARIAS	Marquis	
VILLENA		*(In Abeyance)* Zuniga.

Some OFFICERS *about the* COURT *of* SPAIN.

King's Houfhold.

Duke of MEDINA COELI, Mafter of the Horfe.
Duke of ALVA, Steward of the Houfhold.*

R 2   Duke

* The Duke of ALVA, in December 1760, defired leave of his Majefty to refign his employments, and retire from court: He prayed the King to continue his *honours*; to which the King replied, that he would not only continue his honours, but his *appointments* too. The refignation of the chief great man in SPAIN made, as you will imagine,

Duke de LOZADA, Squire of the Body.
Don PEDRO STUART, firſt Equerry.

Infant's Houſhold.

Duke de MONTELLANO, Mayor Domo to Don LUIS.

Queen's Houſhold.

Marquis de MONTE ALLEGRE, Firſt Steward.
Marquis TRIPUZI, Second Steward.
Duke of MEDINA SIDONIA, Maſter of the Horſe.
Marquis de ANDIA, Gentleman of the Horſe.

Queen Dowager's Houſhold.

Don PEDRO DE VILLA REAL, Mayor Domo to the Q. Mother.
Conde de BANOS, Maſter of the Horſe to the Queen Mother.

Duke de BEJAR, Governor of the Prince and Infant.

Don LUIS DE CORDUBA, Card. and Archbiſhop of TOLEDO.
Grand Patriarch, Don BERT. DE CORDUBA, Son to the Duke of
MEDINA COELI.

LADIES *of the* BED-CHAMBER *to the late* QUEEN AMALIA.

Marchioneſs of AYTONA.
Princeſs JACCHI.
Marchioneſs of ARESA.
Counteſs of ABLITAS.
Dutcheſs of ST. ESTEVAN.
Marchioneſs of MINA.
Princeſs MASSERAN.
Dutcheſs of BOURNOMBILE.
Dutcheſs of CASTRO PINIANO.

imagine, much noiſe at MADRID. The Duke of ALVA has undoubtedly great parts
and abilities; there are few, if any, of a capacity equal to his. The Marquis of
MONT-ALLEGRE ſucceeded him. The Duke, to ſay the truth, having been the
firſt man, manager, and director during all the late reign, did not like to find himſelf leſs conſidered in this, and therefore choſe to retire. It was not apprehended, that
his retiring would at all affect Mr. WALL. The Duke is hereditary chancellor of the
Indies, dean of the council of ſtate, and director of the academy, &c.

Counteſs

PUBLIC ENTRY.

Countefs of BENÆVENTE.
Countefs of FUEN CLARA.
Princefs PIO.
Marchionefs of VALDERAVANO.
Countefs of FUENTÈS.
Countefs of CASTRO PINIANO.
Dutchefs of MEDINA SIDONIA.
Dutchefs of ARCOS.
Dutchefs of UZEDA.
Dutchefs of VERAGUA.

LADIES *of the* BED-CHAMBER *to the* QUEEN MOTHER.

Dutchefs-Dowager of MEDINA SIDONIA.
Countefs of SIRUELA.
Marchionefs of CASTEL RIOS.
Countefs of SERBELLONI.
Countefs of BANOS.
Marchionefs of BANEZA.
Countefs PRIEGO.
Dutchefs of POPULI.
Marchionefs of TORRECUSO.

Defcription of the King of *Spain*'s Public Entry into *Madrid, July* 13, 1760.

(Tranflated from the Spanifh Gazette.)

SUNDAY the 13th being the day fixed by his Catholic Ma--
jefty for his public entry, the requifite preparations having
been all finifhed, fuch as triumphal arches erected in different
parts of the city †, the fountains adorned, the fronts of the houfes

---

† Thefe triumphal arches, though they were very expenfive, yet few of them were
in a good tafte; the figures ill-grouped, and crouded; the allegory not very intelli-
gible, and moft of them rather heavy.

covered

covered with paintings, hangings, looking-glaſs, and furniture, in all the ſtreets, through which his majeſty intended to paſs; the ſilver-ſmiths, in particular, having ornamented their houſes in the nature of a long ſquare, with four towers at each corner, all ſet off with plate and ſome jewels §. Things being thus prepared, at four in the afternoon the two companies of Spaniſh and Walloon guards were placed with their officers and colours, and the regimental muſick, along the *Carrier*.

AT ſix o'clock, his Majeſty, with the Queen and royal family, came out of the back gate of the *Retiro*, in this order of proceſſion :

1. The companies of halberdiers, with muſick.
2. Three ſquadrons of horſe life-guards, Spaniſh, Italian, and Flemiſh, with trumpets and kettle-drums.
3. Four gilded coaches of the king's ſtables, with trumpets and kettle-drums, in which were the Mayor Domos DE SEMA-▰▰, who went before to St. MARY's Church.
4. Coach of the queen's officers, with the Marquis de MONTE ALLEGRE, her firſt ſteward, the Duke of MEDINA SIDONIA, her maſter of the horſe, and the Marquis de ANDIA, gentleman of the horſe.
5. The Mayor Domos de SEMANA, in another coach.
6. Nine of the ladies of the bed-chamber in other coaches.
7. Nine coaches with four horſes, in which were the gentlemen of the king's privy chamber.
8. A coach with eight horſes, richly harneſſed, with four footmen and eight grooms walking on each ſide.
9. A coach with eight horſes, equally rich, attended in the ſame manner, in which were the king's maſter of the horſe, the Duke of MEDINA COELI; the Duke of ALVA, ſteward of the houſhold; the Duke de LOSADA, *ſumilier de corps*, or

§ The ornaments of the houſes likewiſe were many of them immenſely expenſive; but in the worſt, moſt abſurd, and ridiculous taſte you can imagine: that of the Marquis DONIATI was, I think, the moſt expenſively ill-deſigned of any, with mottos and devices in plenty.

3

ſquire

fquire of the body; the Principe de MASSERANO, captain
of the Italian company of life-guards; and Don PEDRO
STUART, firft equerry.

10. Twenty four of the King and Queen's footmen, and the
Ecuyers de Campo.

11. The King's coach, of maffy filver, drawn by eight fine Neapolitan horfes richly harneffed, in which were the KING
and QUEEN, guarded by all the officers of the life-guard,
that were not otherwife ftationed, and twelve of the king's
pages in their liveries embroidered with gold, walking on
each fide.

12. A large body of life-guards, with their officer.

13. The Prince of ASTURIAS, and the Infant Don GABRIEL
in their coach, attended with guards.

14. The Infants Don ANTONIO PASQUAL, and Don FRAN-
CISCO XAVIER in theirs, with their guards.

15. The Princefs Donna MARIA JOSEPHA, and Donna MA-
RIA LUISA, in another coach, with their guards.

16. The Infant Don LUIS ANTONIO JAYME, in his coach,
with his guards *.

17. Ladies of honour in gilt coaches.

18. The *Mayor Domos de Semana* to his Majefty, in their coach.

19. Two battalions of foot, Spanifh and Walloon guards.

IN this order of proceffion their Majefties came up to the firft
triumphal arch, erected at the entrance of that fine ftreet *De Alcala*,
oppofite to which the QUEEN MOTHER was feated in a principal
balcony, belonging to the houfe of the Marquis de TRIPUZI her
firft fteward; the King and Queen made their refpects to her, as
they paffed, which fhe returned. Their majefties then went to St.
MARY's Church.

THE concourfe of people, both natives and foreigners, was immenfe in all the ftreets; and the balconies were lined with people
of fafhion, in great variety of dreffes, colours, and jewels.

* The *Viva Don Luis!* was by much the loudeft and moft hearty of the people's
acclamations.

THEIR

Their Majesties being come to St. Mary's Church, his Eminence the Cardinal-Archbishop of Toledo waited at the portico in company with the stewards and gentlemen of the month, and houshold, to present the royal family, and the rest with *holy-water:* after which they heard the *Te Deum* and *Salve* sung, with the band and music of the royal chapel: Then taking a different route, they found the houses, arches, and fountains all illuminated, it being now after sun-set.

After their return to the *Buen Retiro*, they saw the fire-works prepared by the town, from their own balcony, which were exhibited in the small *Plaça de Pelota* ‖.

On the 14th, in the afternoon, there was a comedy represented before their Majesties, named *the Triumph of Hercules*, after which the fire-works were the same as the night before.

On the 15th, their Majesties went to see the *bull-feast*, and were much pleased with the spectacle, as no fatal misfortune happened to the cavaliers *. During these three days, the houses of the gentry and others were illuminated.

On the Saturday the King attended at the *Jura*, and took the accustomed oath. In the evening the trades-people of the town having passed before their majesties in masquerade dresses, one of them made a speech, and so retired. This evening concluded also with fire-works and illuminations: and thus ended the solemnities celebrated on occasion of the Public Entry of Don Carlos III. King of Spain.

———

In my opinion, much the most pleasing part of the sight was the immense mob in the streets; which being composed of all reli-

‖ These fire-works were very poorly contrived, and went off extremely ill.
* It was no wonder that the cavaliers on this occasion came off so well; for the poor bulls had been kept almost fasting for four days before, in order to lower their courage: and this was done, lest the *Queen* and the *Court* should be shocked at the sight of any tragical event, that might otherwise have happened. But see the account of this article, p. 107, & seqq.

4   gious

gious orders, of all kinds of lay, civil, and ecclefiaftical habits; in fhort, of all dreffes in the world, and of both fexes, formed the moft motley fcene that fancy ever painted!   ·

THE theatre of the *Buen Retiro* is extremely pretty, and very finely ornamented: It will always remain as a ftriking proof of the genius, fancy, and invention of the celebrated FARINELLI; who had no reafon to regret the leaving ENGLAND, fince SPAIN has made him ample amends: his apartments were the beft in the whole palace of the *Retiro*, the fame that the Duke de LOSADA has now; and his levee was more crouded than the minifter's, or King's. He retired with an immenfe fortune on the death of Queen BARBARA.

THE *Venetian Ambaffador* made his public entry into MADRID, on the 23d of July, in his Venetian black habit, on horfeback. There were fome who preferred his entry to that of the King's; but his ftate-coaches were miferably tarnifhed and fhabby.

S   LETTER

LETTER VIII.

Defcription of the CONVENT of St. LAURENCE, commonly called the *ESCURIAL.*

THE ESCURIAL is a village in the kingdom of NEW-CAS-TILE, feven leagues to the north of MADRID, fo called from the word *efcoria*, which fignifies the drofs of the iron mines, which were there formerly, and therefore the proper name is Es-CORIAL.

THIS little village gives name to the palace of the ESCURIAL, which was built by GIOVANNI BAPTISTA, by order of PHILIP II. in the year 1563, as appears by this infcription:

D. O. M.
OPERI ADSPICIAT.
PHILIPPVS II.
HISPAN. REX.
A FUNDAMENTIS EREXIT
MDLXIII.
JOAN. BAPTISTA
ARCHITECTVS.
IX. KALEND. MAII.

THE motive which engaged that prince in this religious work, I fhall fpeak of hereafter; for, as he had fo little piety himfelf in mind or action, one cannot but be furprized at his conceiving

2 fuch

such a defign. Such as it was however, it gave a fresh occasion of disgust to the Spanish parliament, or the *Cortes*, as they call it, the general assembly of the states, or representatives of the several cities. For PHILIP having called a *Cortes*, to ask supplies for carrying on the war against *France*, the states very freely voted a large subsidy of some millions; which the artful monarch, as soon . as he had once secured in his own coffers, applied to the building of this convent. This misapplication of the public revenues so disgusted the *Cortes*, that they met less frequently, and with more reluctance, being unwilling to be cajoled out of their money by the tricks of defigning princes : and succeeding monarchs, having found out other ways of raising their supplies, have rarely called a *Cortes* since that time, for a very political reason, the fear of becoming *less absolute*.

THERE are two libraries in the ESCURIAL, one upon the first floor, and the other upon the second: that upon the first floor is a fine, long, arched room; the cieling and the walls all painted by PELLEGRIN Y PELLEGRINI, (a *Milanese*) a disciple of BUA-NOROTI, and BARTHOL. CARDUCHO, a *Florentine*. This library contains all the printed books, excepting some *first editions*, which are kept above, and paintings, and the usual baubles shewn to strangers : such as moneys, medals, and casts ; a Jewish shekel; an iman, or calamite stone, or, as I should call it, a *magnet*, weighing seven pounds, which supports an arrobe, or twenty-five pounds weight. Here they shew you an illuminated MS. of the Revelations, in a small folio, supposed to be written by St. AMADEUS : a MS. in gold letters, of the four gospels, in Latin, large folio, upon vellum, written in the time of the Emperor CONRAD, called *the Golden Book of Eusebius Reterodamus*. There are also some other curiosities, mentioned in the *History of this Convent, by Padre Frey Francisco de los Santos*, 4to. *Madrid* 1667, which I could not obtain a sight of; such as, their oldest MS. of St. AUSTIN *De Baptismo Parvulorum, litteris majusculis Longobardicis* ; a MS. of the Gospels, in the oldest Greek letter, a book of St. CHRYSOSTOM'S. These I asked for several times, but was always told, *No puede verle,* or, " You cannot see it :" But I believe they are behind the altar in the sacrifty, where I saw a very fine illuminated

Missal,

Miffal, and are made ufe of to decorate that altar, upon great folemnities, being finely bound.   I fucceeded no better with regard
to a Greek Bible of the Emperór CATACUZENUS, exactly agreeing
with the LXX.   I afked after the famous drawings of men, women, animals, plants, &c. in feveral volumes folio, by Don FRANC.
HERNANDEZ of TOLEDO, taken foon after their firft difcovery of
AMERICA; but the librarian told me, they were burnt in the fire
that made fo much havock in this library, on June 7, 1674, which
lafted 15 days.

BUT the other library, which is above ftairs, contains all the
manufcripts, except the few above-mentioned, and is, I believe,
one of the nobleft collections this day in the whole world. There
are 1824 volumes of Arabic MSS. only; Greek MSS. in profufion, in folio and quarto, of immenfe antiquity, yet fair and legible throughout.   There are no lefs than three MSS. of *Diofco-*
rides, when it has been thought, that only one MS. of it exifted,
and that at CONSTANTINOPLE, as BUSBEQUIUS tells us.   Here
are parts of *Livy, Dion Caffius, Diodorus Siculus,* and others never
yet publifhed.   If I remember right, I think there are 13 volumes
in folio MS. of *Livy* only.   Then as to MS. copies of the New
Teftament, they are in great numbers, either containing the whole
or part.   There are too fome new, unpublifhed claffical authors:
three *Olynthic Orations of Demofthenes;* four of the *Philippics;*
Oratio ad Epiftolas Philippi; Oratio de Republica ordinanda, Epif-
tola Philippi; Iliad in black ink, with a comment or fcholia by
TZETZES, in red ink, in the oppofite column. I found there
MSS. of *Terence, Juftin, Valerius Maximus;* of *Horace* and *Virgil*
many; fome of *Juvenal, Catullus, Tibullus,* and *Propertius, Sueto-*
nius, Salluft: but, what I regretted much, none of *Tacitus.*   The
Greek tragedians, &c. in abundance, remarkably finely written,
particularly *Ariftophanes* in folio: fome of the moderns, fuch as
Aretinus de Bello Punico Primo: Idem de Bello Gothico: Epiftolæ
ejufdem.

I COPIED a little Greek poem, at the head of which was written, *Cartophylacis Bulgariæ duo Carmina, quæ infcripta funt* Πόθος.
In priori defcribit Mala Mulieris malæ; in pofteriori bona bonæ.——

                                                                    N.

N. B. Quis autem noverit, quis Cartophylax hic fuerit; erat enim Nomen Officii, fæpeque inter Libros hofce MSS. occurrunt Opera Joannis Rediafeni, Cartophylacis Bulgarienfis. The poem itfelf is not worth inferting here.

WITH regard to the MSS. of the *New Teftament*; I was determined to collate two or three of the moft remarkable texts, to fee how they ftood. Having feen in England, how the famous text, *Johannis Epift.* I. cap. V. ver. 7, 8. ftood in our *Alexandrian* MS. I took down two of the oldeft MSS. of *the Epiftles* which I could find in the Efcurial, and having a fmall Greek Teftament in my pocket, I collated that text firft, in prefence of the auditor and fome other gentlemen. It is remarkable, that both the MSS. fhould concur word for word in this reading : Ὅτι τρεῖς εἰσιν οἱ μαρτυρᾶντες· τὸ πνεῦμα, καὶ τὸ ὕδωρ, καὶ τὸ ἇιμα· καὶ οἱ τρεῖς εἰς τὸ ἕν εἰσιν· ἐι τὴν μαρτυρίαν τῶν ἀνϑρώπων λαμβάνομεν, κ. τ. λ. One of them read ἐλάβομεν, which, I think, has more force. I do not enter into the controverfy whether this be the right, or the wrong reading ; I fhall only add, that fuch I found it in two MSS. of a different character, and age, and which did not appear to be copies of each other. But the curious reader, after having examined Dr. MILLS's long note on this verfe, and alfo the tedious comment of Mr. WETSTEIN, may fee more in *Une Differtation Critique fur le Verfet feptieme du Chapitre V. de la premiere Epitre de St: Jean, par M. Martin, à Utrecht,* 1717, 12mo.

As to the famous paffage, *ad Timotheum, Epift.* I. *c.* iii. *v.* 16. all the MSS. clearly read Θεὸς, or ΘΣ.

WITH regard to that in the beginning of St. JOHN, it is out of doubt Θεὸς ἦν ὁ Λογὸς, and not Θ., or Θεῦ, as fome would have it.

THERE is in this library all the collection of MSS. and printed books, formerly belonging to the famous Cardinal SIRLETUS, with the cardinal's notes in moft of them: the very catalogue itfelf of Cardinal SIRLETUS's collection is a vaft curiofity. The book contains, firft, the original letters of the Duke D'OLIVARES, and others, about fettling the purchafe of it. Then follows the

the catalogue of his Greek MSS. in Greek: the title runs thus, Κατάλογος τῶν Βιβλίων κα]αγραφέν]ων τῦ ἐνδοκιμοτά]ϰ Καρδινᾶλ☉ Σιρλήτϰ, &c. &c. After this follows a Latin catalogue of his Latin MSS. and printed books; at the end of which the cardinal's librarian tells us, " Take notice, that there is no book here, of what " kind foever, in which his eminence hath not wrote with his " own hand fome notes : *adeo ut omnes aucti & correcti ab ipfo verè* " *dici poterint.*"

In a very old Latin defcription of the iflands of EUROPE, with the maps, the writer, whofe name I could not find, mentions the following cities in GREAT BRITAIN, *Londinum, Neomagus, Peturia, Otuana, Callagum, Orria, Coria :* in SCOTLAND, *Trimontum, Uzellum, Rethigonum, Corda, Linopibia ;* which I leave for our antiquaries to decypher. In the library below, I found *Apthonii* Προγυνάσματα; *M. Bruti Epiftolæ Græco-Latinæ,* and *Phaleridis Epiftolæ,* all bound together. Thofe of Brutus contained only epiftles of his to the Pergamenians, with their anfwer; to the *Rhodiis Cois, Pataræis, Cauniis, Lyciis, Damiæ, Cyzicenis, Smyrnæis, Mytelenfibus, Mylefiis, Trallianis Bythyniis,* all Greek, *per A. Commelinum,* 1597. One in Latin, *Brutus Ciceroni fuo.* The epiftles of Phalaris were Περὶ τῦ Επιϛολικῦ Χαρακ]ήρ☉.. Not thofe which BOYLE publifhed.

BUT to return to the manufcript library above ftairs; it certainly abounds with ineftimable riches too numerous to be defcribed. But as to the *catalogues* of the principal Greek, Latin, and Hebrew MSS. I fhall give them at length at the end of this account.

ALL this wealth is depofited in the hands of a few illiterate monks, poor *Jeromites;* but they are full as jealous of thefe treafures, as if they underftood their true value. It was with great difficulty, and by the help of fome intereft, that I got any accefs at all to thefe MSS. and when I had got accefs, if I wrote down or collated any thing, it gave them fufpicions; becaufe, fay they, if you copy our MSS. the originals will then be worth nothing. That is as much as to fay, that the originals will be of no value, if they become of any ufe.

I DO

I DO not doubt but there are many very valuable things among the printed books, both below and above ſtairs; ſome I have ſeen, but few of them; ſuch as *Virgil*, in folio, whether a forgery, or not, I cannot ſay; date 1407. It appeared to me as a literary phænomenon; *Terence* 1482; another *Virgil*, large letter, with ſuperb illuminations. But the backs of the books below ſtairs are all turned from you, beſides being locked up, ſo that no one but the librarians themſelves can poſſibly tell you what they are; and as they are ſo wretchedly ignorant, their informations will avail you but very little. They have had no man of learning among them, ſince the times of ARIAS MONTANUS, who was indeed a truly great man. There is a copy of his Bible, in ſeven or eight volumes in folio, finely printed on vellum, with the Hebrew text, JEROM's verſion, the Vulgate, and the LXX.

IT is much to be lamented, that this library is not in other hands; for then the world might ſtand ſome chance of being be-nefited by it. MICHAEL SYRI, a Syro-Maronite, one of the King's librarians, has printed one volume of the *Arabic catalogue*; but why it is not permitted to be ſold, I cannot ſay; if it had, I had ſent it into England before now.

THE principal things in this convent are, firſt, the *Church*, which is a noble edifice in the inſide; its riches and paintings are ineſtimable; but of theſe *latter*, I ſhall give a ſeparate *catalogue* hereafter. The outſide, however, of this church, is the heavieſt building imaginable. The whole convent is truly a ſort of quarry above-ground. It has often put me in mind of thoſe lines of Mr. POPE:

Greatneſs with Timon dwells in ſuch a draught,
As brings all Brobdignag before your thought.

I can diſcover no ſtile of architecture in it, though it is moſt pro-bably of the Doric order. It is a large, confuſed ſtupendous pile, divided into a vaſt number of ſquare courts. The reaſon of which is owing to the following circumſtance.

PHILIP II. the founder of this convent, made a vow, when he gained the battle of St. QUINTIN, (againſt the French in the frontiers

tiers of Picardy, in 1557) fix years before, to build a convent at the Escurial for monks of the order of St. Jerom. This order is unknown in France, and was abolished in Italy, because one of them attempted the life of Charles Borromeo. He preferred this order, because he was obliged to cannonade a convent of *Jeromites* during the siege of St. Quintin. He said to his confessor during the battle, when the bullets flew about pretty thick, " And how do you like this music ?" " And it please " your Majesty," replied the monk, " I do not like it at all." " Nor I neither," said the King; " and do not you think *my fa-* " *ther* was a very strange man, who could find any diversion in " this kind of entertainment ?" The battle was gained on St. Lawrence's day, on the 10th of August, wherefore he called the convent after the name of that saint; and as the holy father was unhappily burnt upon a *gridiron*, this prince has immortalized the very manner of his martyrdom : for he has not only stuck gridirons, either of paint, wood, metal, or stone, all over the convent, but has built the very convent itself in the form of a gridiron. That part of the building, which is now the King's apartment, is the handle of the gridiron; and the rest being divided into a great number of square courts, in this form ;

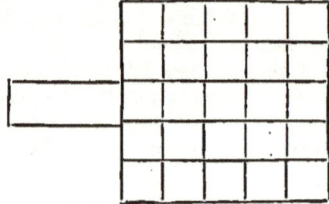

it doth not unaptly resemble a gridiron. Having now done with the gridiron, I must not forget another circumstance : As a proper compliment was necessary to be paid to St. Lawrence, another was full as necessary to be paid to St. Jerom: St. Jerom, it seems, lived among the mountains, and therefore, tho' from the lofty site of this convent you command one of the most extensive prospects, that you commonly meet with in Spain; yet so much respect was to be paid to the memory of this saint, as to turn

6

the

the great front of this convent and palace *directly from the pro-spect*; so that you should see nothing at all but mountains, as the saint himself had lived among them. They give another reason for this; and say, the chapel could not have stood due east and west without it. Why not? Was there any necessity to make the front of the convent and the church too, both to the same aspect?

But high as the names of these two saints stand here, the name of the founder, PHILIP II. is still higher; so that they respect, first, the *Fundador*, then St. LAWRENCE, and then St. JEROM. Their regard for their founder is indeed but a decent part of gratitude; for as he thought he should atone for all his sins by raising this fabric, so he spared no expence to make it complete. It cost PHILIP II. during his reign, 28,000,000 of ducats, which is about 3,360,000 l. sterling. He lived here chiefly the last fifteen years of his life; and when he died, he ordered himself to be brought out in his bed to the feet of the high altar, that he might die in sight of that, and thus he expired. The place where his bed was placed, is since railed off, as sacred; and the late Queen BARBARA was the first person who had courage enough to enter it, since it was shut up after his death.

However, some are still so superstitious, as to believe even now, that his unquiet and perturbed spirit still nightly visits his favourite mansion, and stalks horrid round the long arcades and corridores of the ESCURIAL: For a certain princess, to my know-ledge, gave orders, last October, that the guard should patrole in the night round the cloysters, to see if PHILIP II's ghost really walked there, or not.

There are in the lower library four very fine portraits of CHARLES V. PHILIP II. PHILIP III. and PHILIP IV. In CHARLES V. you see from his face and attitude, in his air and manner, the spirit of a prince, who was born to lead armies to the fields of conquest, and to aim at nothing less than universal monarchy. In PHILIP III. and IV. you discern rather a pacific mien, inclining somewhat to effeminacy. But in PHILIP II. the painter has been

T very

very happily expreſſive of his character; cruelty, pride, hypocriſy, malice, revenge, and a dark air of diſſimulation, are all well aſſembled in the lines and colours of his countenance.

But however fond he was of this convent, as I ſaid before, he did not live to finiſh it: The *Pantheon*, or the royal burial-chapel for the Kings of SPAIN, their conſorts, and their deſcendants, tho' begun by the founder, was not completed, but by PHILIP IV. This edifice is ſo ſingular, it is no eaſy matter to deſcribe it, without the help of drawing, ſo as to give a juſt idea of it.

INSCRIPTION *on the* PANTHEON.

D. O. M.
Locus Sacer Mortalitatis Exuviis
Catholicorum Regum,
A Reſtauratore Vitæ, Cujus Aræ Max.
Auſtriaca Adhuc Pietate Subjacent,
Optatam Diem Expectantium,
Quam Poſthumam Sedem Sibi Et Suis
Carolus Cæſarum Max. In Votis Habuit,
Philippus II. Regum Prudentiſſ. Elegit.
Philippus III. Vere Pius Inchoavit.
Philippus IIII.
Clementia, Conſtantia, Religione Magnus
Auxit, Ornavit, Abſolvit,
Anno Dom. MDCLIIII.

It is an octagon temple; the ſtaircaſe that deſcends to it, is all fine marble, the walls, cielings, &c. being wainſcotted; if I may ſo term it, with marble, and the inſide alſo of the temple is very richly ornamented in the ſame manner. As I was going down the ſtairs, my guide told me; "Here, Sir, is the *rotting-place* for the "late Queen AMALIA; and this, Sir, is the *rotting-place* for the "young princes:" and ſo indeed they were; for the bodies are depoſited here till ſuch time as the work of putrefaction is pretty well finiſhed, and the inoffenſive relicks are tranſported into the *Pantheon.*

WHEN

WHEN this vault was finished, PHILIP IV. gave the following directions for removing the bodies into it, by a mandate dated MADRID, March 1654: where he says, " You shall place in it " the Emperor CHARLES V. and Donna ISABELLA his wife; PHI-" LIP II. and his queen Donna ANNA; PHILIP III. and Donna " MARGARETA; and the queen Donna ISABELLA, my dear and " much-loved wife. The first urn shall be CHARLES V. the last " I design for myself, whenever it shall please God to take me " from this life."

IT is impossible you should understand these directions of PHI-LIP IV. without being told, that as this temple is in an octagon form, each side contains three or four niches from top to bottom, with two over the door-case, in all 26: and these are filled up with oblong urns, or *sarcophagi*: each having a brass plate in the center, with the name of the prince or princess which it contains. In this order :

Left-hand side.	*Right-hand side of the Altar, which takes up one eighth of the Room.*
Donna ISABELLA, Charles V's Queen.	
—— ANNA, Philip II's Qu.	CHARLES V.
—— MARGARETA, Philip III's Queen.	PHILIP II.
—— ISABELLA, Philip IV's Queen.	—— III.
	—— IV.
Second left-hand.	*. Second right-hand.*
MARIA ADELAIDE, Philip V's first Queen. *	CHARLES II.
AMALIA, Charles III's Queen.	LUIS I.

There is an urn designed for ISABELLA of PARMA; but she is determined not to lie there.

So that you see, as there are but 26 niches in all, it is just half-full. There are only six kings, and seven queens. The rea-

* Here is one Queen omitted; none are placed here, but what have children.

T 2

son

fon of this is, becaufe PHILIP V. is buried at SAN ILDEFONSO ;
as the queen-mother intends to be, whenever fhe dies; though
fhe fays, "She had much rather not die at all," having an utter
averfion to that operation. But, I fear, ELIZABETH of PARMA
and TUSCANY muft be contented to tread the fame gloomy paths
which all the ISABELS and KATHARINES of ARRAGON trod before her. FERDINAND VI. and his Queen BARBARA of POR-
TUGAL are buried at the new convent of the *Salefas* in MADRID,
which they founded.

I REMEMBER being told by an Englifh earl, who travelled
into SPAIN a few years fince, That when he came to fee the *Pantheon*, he afked the guide, who fhewed to him this vault, how it
came to pafs, that he faw there fo few princes of the houfe of
BOURBON ? "My lord," fays the man, "the reafon is, that they
"are all afraid of the man with the great whifkers ;" meaning
CHARLES V. "for," fays he, "if thofe princes of the houfe of
"BOURBON were to come here, they would never agree, and there
"would be fuch a dance of the dead, as would be heard as far. as
"MADRID."

BUT to be ferious, it is certainly a great pity, that the Spanifh
kings and queens are not now all placed together, as this certainly
is a *maufoleum* worthy of their reception, and in every refpect fuitable to the grandeur of the Spanifh monarchy. I confefs, were I
King of SPAIN, I fhould make no fcruple of ordering it fo, without ever thinking, that I in the leaft difquieted thereby the repofe
of their afhes.

⸺ *id credis cineres curare fepultos ?*

Or, as another fays,

⸺ *nec fentit damna fepulchri.*

BUT before I take my leave of the *Pantheon*, which fhews you
by its very name the great and majeftic ideas which the *Spaniards*
entertain of their fovereigns ; fince this is not the burial-place of
their *monarchs*, but their *Gods :* I muft not omit one very extraordinary anecdote, which is as follows.

WHEN

WHEN PHILIP IV. in 1654, as I said before, removed the bodies designed for this mausoleum from their antient sepulchres,
with all the funeral pomp and solemnity possible, nay, I might
add, conceivable: That they were re-buried with the most awful
services and functions of mass and burial imaginable, at. which
PHILIP IV. assisted in person: and, in conclusion, a monk of the
order of St. JEROM, spoke a funeral oration, with this remarkable
text, taken from the Prophet EZEKIEL, chap. xxxvii. verse 4.
O ye dry bones, hear the word of the Lord!

THIS oration, or funeral discourse, I had curiosity enough to
translate part of; and it is indeed the most extraordinary funeral
sermon I ever saw.

❖❖❖❖❖❖❖❖❖❖❖❖❖❖❖❖❖❖❖❖❖❖❖❖❖❖❖❖❖❖❖❖❖❖

Part of a FUNERAL ORATION, *spoken upon
removing the Bodies of the* KINGS *and* QUEENS *of*
SPAIN *into the Vault at the* ESCURIAL, *in*
1654.

O GREAT GOD! where shall the understanding go that is
not struck with admiration? What is this discourse, Sacred
Catholic, Royal, and August Majesty! that shall not be finished
in the time! What is this wonder that is found in the state of
men! What is this fear, that keeps pace with the revolution of
years? What is it? Can the world hope to see such a theatre of
Majesties? Seven crowns, which have not been joined together
in seventy ages; who would ever have thought, that they could
meet together to hear one sole orator? What imagination could
suggest this assemblage of dead Kings, hearing a sermon, as well
as if they were alive? Who has brought hither your *Cæsarean*
Majesties? Monarchs great of the earth, great Monarchs in
heaven!

heaven! Who has brought you hither! But what do I afk? That God is God, and cannot fail in that, which he has fpoken—Let us hear him with reverence.

"*Son of man, prophecy concerning thefe bones, and fay unto* "*them, Dry bones, hear the word of the Lord; Thus faith the* "*Lord: Behold I will open your tombs, and I will lead you out of* "*your fepulchres, and I will bring you into the land of Ifrael.*" EZEK. xxxvii. 4. Let us adore the fecrets of God; a function fo great, as this of to-day, requires that it fhould have been foretold by prophefy in this 37th chapter of EZEKIEL. *Offa arida*, "*Dry* "*bones*," this is the day to hear a fermon: *Audite verbum Domini* : "*Hear the word of the Lord:*" That is to hear? Perhaps the voice of the living fhall break the filence of the dead? Perhaps thofe who die are not deaf till the found of the laft trumpet? *In noviffima tuba.*

PERHAPS—but fuppofe I do not fay perhaps; there are dead, which in ending their lives do not enter into death; there are dead, which reft with a defire of life, and thefe hear as well as if they were alive, but if there were fuch, how fhould our princes die? Afk the moft eminent cardinal of BETHLEHEM, JEROM; which great *Palefine* doctor left in fome of his writings, language and fpirit fufficient to form this difcourfe to the glory of our moft potent SPANISH Monarchs: It is all his, great Sir, becaufe all St. JEROM, all his religion, all his fons, and all his fplendor, and all his exaltation is derived from your *Cæfarean* Majefty, and from the Cæfars your anceftors. Of what death did thofe die whom God made Potentates? Afk JEROM, and afk him upon occafion of feeing MOSES die. Of what grief? Of what accident? Of what infirmity? Who will fay thus, *Mortuus eft Moyfes jubente Domino*; "*Mofes died becaufe the Lord com-* "*manded him; He died obedient.*" The LXX tranflate it, *Mortuus eft Moyfes per verbum Domini*; "*God killed Mofes by his word.*" And here we may explain the firft Apocalypfe of St. JOHN the Evangelift. Admire and hear the Almighty, who fpeaks thus—*I am Alpha and Omega, the firft and the laft, the beginning and the ending;*

·4   but

but how sharp a word is the *ending!* And its force is to be sharp, because with that comes out of the mouth a two-edged sword. *De ore ejus gladius utraque parte acutus exibat.* What different things hath God said by that mouth! *He breatheth into his nostrils the breath of life.* With that breath and spirit in the breast of ADAM, the mouth said truly, *I am the beginning, I am the beginning of life.* And what a sword was that which said, *I am the end, I am the end, I cut the thread of life.* How powerful is God! What must those lips be, which speak life, and speak death at the same time.

DIE MOSES, die now, now, now; God kills thee with his word; expect it; a death which is caused by the word, death is hearing, because it is death to hear God much. *He it is, who lived by the word, and dies by the word,* says JEROM to FABIOLA. *For if he seems to have been governed by the spirit of the word, he could cease from that government by the word only.* Princes, who are made such by the hand of the Most High, shall die by the same means which they lived; they live by hearing God, and when they die, the voice rests them being heard, they die and hear. See here a sovereign auditory of dead bodies : O my most august auditory! Ye dry bones, hear the word of the Lord.

HEAR thou *Cæsarean Majesty,* GERMAN CHARLES, FRENCH CHARLES, ITALIAN CHARLES, AFRICAN CHARLES, INDIAN CHARLES, SPANISH CHARLES, CHARLES most gloriously the Fifth, hear, thou *Cæsarean* Majesty, the voice of a monk of the order of St. JEROM, who will not think it strange, because he expired hearing our voices, and our songs. *Thus saith the Lord.* This is what God says : *Ecce ego aperiam tumulos vestros;* " the " day shall come, in which I will open your tombs;" and is not this to-day? It is plain : *And I will lead you out of your sepulchres.* And is not this time come, in which from the obscurity of your sepulchres ye are taken out into the light of the living? Is it not now? Who doubts it? *Et inducam vos in terram Israel;* "And thence here " ye shall come into a land like Israel:" And is not this now? It is certain.

BUT

'BUT before we leave the subject, that ye lost life, what? Have
we not to give to the eternity of fame, a voice of praise, which
will fill the world. The text says, *Fili hominis vaticinare de ossibus
istis;* " *Man divine concerning those bones before thee.*" And JE-
ROM explains it, that the bones of the just were to be exalted and
praised, as it were with the spirit of prophets, and the fury of the
old sybils.   Men call those dead deities : What grief ! To be commanded to exalt those with the prophetical spirit, and to have only
mine own ?   *Quasi spiritu vatum.*   But let him use that which he
is able, and let it become fury, *quasi furore.*   Let it be fury, because it is boldness; it shall be boldness, and let us begin with the
greatest man of men.   There thou art, thou always conqueror,
and never conquered CHARLES! there thou art gone.   And God
leaves me to say, that it is the honour of his Divine Majesty,
which is much honoured there.

THE first angel grew proud; that action has always been won-
dered at; of what could Lucifer be proud ? Of being very handsome ? No; because it is easy to imagine, that God was hand-
somer. Of much understanding ? Much less; because he must own
that of God to be greater.   Of much valour ? Softly. *Ubi eras,
quando me laudabunt astra matutina?* said God to Job.   " *Come*
" *hither, where wast thou, when the morning stars sang praise to*
" *me? Astra matutina---*JEROM says in his commentary upon this
passage: " *The morning stars are the angels inseparable from God,*
" *because they were first called to sing his praise.*" Which orison of
that great world sweet and sonorous birds celebrated; the angels
of God dispraised themselves sounding his praises; and well. Do
we not know what they sung ? Isaiah tells us, Holy, holy, holy
Lord God of Hosts.   With those words broke forth the first
morning of heaven and earth, Holy, holy, &c. how well it sounds?
What is it to sound well ? Does Lucifer say, Lord God of the
Hosts of God ? And my valour ? and my spirit ? and my vivacity ?
Moreover I say, I will ascend into heaven, I will be like the Most
High.

ST. JEROM says in his *Hebrew* traditions, that Lucifer being
made præfect of the camps of God, was seized with such a mili-

*

tary

tary ardor, that he could not bear even God the Lord of Hosts. Lucifer grew proud of his valour; he was the first of the celestial hosts; he was general of them; O ill-gotten employment! He was lost by his much valour, which threw out many vain boasts against God, and that he could equal him in sounding the voice of war: *Lord God of Hosts.*

THAT best gift of valour, which God has given to his creatures, broke out into pride: *I will ascend into heaven.* The most heroic spirit of the warrior budded out into arrogance: *I will be like the Most High.* The most brave impulse of the warrior appeared in making a riotous war in all heaven—*Michael fought with the dragon.* O great Creator! what could make a boaster! and what could prompt the proud! O Lord God of Hosts, from that throne divine, let thy sovereign Majesty behold this human tomb, now redressed from the wrongs of old. This potent arm was in CHARLES: But what did it not do? It made him monarch of both worlds; it made him a firm pillar of the church; it made him a cutting sword against heresy; it made him a shining light to infidels; it made him the terror, and the admiration of rebels; it made him a general arbitrator of all empires; it made him feared by FRANCE, obeyed by GERMANY, acknowledged by ITALY, and revered by EUROPE; it made ASIA tremble; it humbled AFRICA; it conquered AMERICA; it caused his valour and fortune to obtain more trophies and victories, than all monarchies have counted; it made at length a man, than whom, from the first of men, the world hath not seen one more valiant, more fortunate, more a soldier, or more glorious.

Now ask Curiosity, This warrior, in whom God effected so much, how did he meet God? What must be the joy in heaven to see one man amend the fault of an angel?

PERMIT me here to paraphrase the second vision of PATHMOS: *Vidi & audivi vocem angelorum multorum;* " *There resounded the po-* " *pulous voice of many angels.*" How many? Millions of millions. It ought to be a great thing, that cannot be contained in so many breasts! Which was poured out by so many mouths; it ap-

pears

pears to be a novelty; it appears to be a myftery, if it is a myftery : God, who can clear it, does clear it; behold it plain, and given
to be feen; *Ecce oftium apertum in cœlo : A gate opens in heaven:
beautiful appearance!* St. JOHN the Evangelift looks at this, and
fays---There is a throne :·*Ecce fedes pofita in cœlo.* And well?
Have they not reafon to rejoice, that God holds his throne in
heaven? Who will fay fo? Stay---Behold the Lamb ftanding in
the middle of the throne : On that throne, where there is a lamb,
fhall be God, and he fhall reign for ever with patience; it is much
that there appears a lamb. Suppofe that a proceffion came from
the other part. I fay more. *Behold the lion of the tribe of Judah
has conquered.* That Lamb is alfo a Lion. Let it go; a novelty
appears; but God has both qualities, he is gentle, and he is valiant. But further : There do not come from thence the words. Do
not attempt it, becaufe it is great. There walked four and twenty
feniors, and laid down their crowns before the throne : There go
Kings, if they are Kings, and quit their crowns. God blefs me!
Kings crowned, and their crowns laid afide! yes, they lay them at
the feet of the Lion-Lamb; Jefus! what a novelty! and fo great,
fays JEROM, fo great, that it is only feen in heaven : but what
voices are thofe, which fpring from thence? It is true, ZACHA-
RIAS writes in the third chapter it is true; we read in the Revelations of feniors finging a new fong, new becaufe it was heard not
on earth, but in heaven; *That potentates defpifed the crown of
power.* One crown well altogether in right, and nature, it is little
to draw it from theirs and to let it fall at the feet of God? Is it
little? Since when once it is feen in heaven, heaven is filled with
applaufe and admiration.

MAY God preferve Auguft CHARLES in his glory!·thou haft
given to be feen among men that novelty, which the angels moft
celebrate. What front of the fons of ADAM was better girded
than thine? What crown was enriched with fuch refplendent
ftones? Catholic, magnanimous, potent, juft, pious, liberal,
amiable, feared, heroic, not to be withftood. Holy God! from
whence came the lights of that Imperial diadem? From whence?
And the world beheld them, and the world beheld him quit the
crown, and renounce the greateft of all human pomp, with thefe

words :

words: *Tu solus Dominus, tu solus Altissimus; Thou only art the Lord, thou only art the most High.* I say, that here broke forth the voices of all *Jerusalem* triumphant, the voices of many angels.

It might be a novelty in heaven, as well as earth, to see a majesty, which almost was not contained in the world, to see him contain himself in the narrow cell of a monk? without aspiring, but after death; without any more life, than what sufficed to meditate on a good death. This might be a spectacle of wonder to the most fortunate, to see the most triumphant Emperor celebrating the last triumph of his life, and at the same time the obsequies of his death. This appears only to be a child of the imagination, but it was real fact.

They erected a tomb in the church of St. Justus, but without apparatus, without pomp; that he, who when alive was above all, was willing to die no more than a mere man: The mass for his soul was celebrated with solemnity; and there were two sacrifices; one, that of the altar; the other, that of his breast: The time of the *Responso* came; the mourning of the body. He entered the church in mourning; while he lived there was no entrance so glorious as that: He placed himself (who yet had vigour) in the front of the tomb; he was the sole actor of that theatre; he was alive, and represented one dead, with so much propriety, that even he thought himself, that he was dying; and it is certain, that from that place he went and died: The monks sung, and wept; they esteemed him as their master, and even to think, that he was to die, was a grief. And to think that he really was to die became a torment. What a great thing was it to see, that majestic age of Charles all attentive, with a taper in his hand, as if with his light he was contemplating the dark glooms of death; he bathed in tears his venerable cheeks, as one who died with understanding, and knew what it was to die, and understood that there were faults to be bewailed. He prayed the Divine Majesty for his soul, never more happy; since, for this his supplication, God was giving him life at that time to enable him to make that prayer. The *requiescam in pace* was sung; and lifting up his crying eyes to heaven, he said aloud, *'Amen.* And he was in suspense long

enough

enough to remain in a lively faith, that the Lord of the living and the dead heard him. He turned himself to the priest, and prostrating himself before him, he offered into his hands the lighted taper, saying : *Into thy hands I commend my spirit.* Into those hands, which had compleated offering to the Eternal Father the unbloody sacrifice of his only Son, he placed his soul; and from thence he went to that bed, in which he died a natural death. &c. &c. &c.

The KING's other PALACES.

BUT before I go on to the paintings and manuscripts, give me leave to take this opportunity of describing briefly the rest of his Catholic Majesty's palaces, that I may dispatch for once this article all together.

THE BUEN RETIRO, or the old palace in MADRID, is not so good a royal mansion as St. JAMES's: a very indifferent quadrangle, with gardens, which no one would mention here, as being any thing extraordinary.

THE PALATIO NUEVO is indeed a very fine fabric in MADRID; but then it has cost two millions sterl. of our money already. It was begun in 1725, and is not finished, and has no gardens, or opening round it as yet.

THE palace of SAN ILDEFONSO is a very good one; the building not grand, nor in a good taste; but the gardens are magnificent, and the fountains the finest in Europe : The gardens are said to have cost five millions sterling. During the building and finishing of this palace, &c. in the years 1731, 32, 33, I have been told, that neither the army, navy, officers of the court, or the ambassadors abroad received any pay, tho' it was in time of war. The statuary who made the fountains was never paid; he died of poverty and a broken heart. The same thing, it is said, happened to the man, who made the iron rails at HAMPTON COURT for King WILLIAM; Queen ANNE did not choose to pay the debt. I mention this circumstance as a sort of apology for Queen ISABEL's not remembering an artist employed by PHILIP.

THIS

THIS palace is about fixty miles from MADRID. When the court goes thither, moft ambaffadors, except the family ones, refide at SEGOVIA, about ten miles diftant: tho' his late Majefty thought that too far off.

THE palace of the SARSUELO, a few miles out of MADRID, is nothing but a hunting-box.

THE palace of the PARDO, about eight miles out of MADRID, is likewife but an indifferent feat for an *Englifh* country-gentleman.

THE palace of ARANJUEZ, about thirty miles diftant from MADRID, is a very tolerable edifice; has one fine front; is agreeably fituated in a pleafant vale upon the confluence of two rivers, the *Xárama*, and the *Tagus*. The air becomes very unhealthy, when the heats begin. Though the gardens are only a dead flat, and the walks plantations of trees in ftrait rows, yet there is fomething chearful and refrefhing in fo cool and fhady a fpot. Here are rows of very fine elms, tho' raifed and watered at an incredible expence; particularly in the Queen's Walk, or the *Calle de la reyna*, which is as noble an avenue or vifta, as any to be found in England.

THE palace of the CASA DEL CAMPO is clofe to MADRID, but an indifferent box, now quite neglected, and ufed only by the king for fhooting.

THE palace of the RIO FRIO is a new building, not yet finifhed, within a few miles of SEGOVIA: It was begun by the prefent queen-dowager, about nine years ago, who never went to fee it till laft year. She will probably leave it to the Infant Don LUIS.

THERE are feveral other palaces, and royal manfions in different parts of SPAIN, but moft of them are ruinous, or forfaken. The *Alcaffar of Segovia*, I have defcribed in another place; and the palace at TOLEDO was burnt by the allies in the fuccefion-war. Since MADRID was made the capital, or rather fince (to go back to the true caufe) the kingdoms were united, thefe ftately edifices

mouldered away, and became almoſt as forgotten as the vain monarchs, who firſt raiſed them to ſooth their pride. They now form
a ſet of very fine remains, to gratify the curioſity or *virtú* of modern travellers, particularly at CORDUBA, SEVILLE, and GRA-
NADA.

LIST of PICTURES in the Convent of the ESCURIAL.

LIBRARY.

CIeling and walls painted by *Pellegrino* and *B. Carducho.*
    Painting of St. Ambroſe and St. Auguſtine diſputing. Mot-
to, *A logicâ Auguſtini libera nos, domine!*
Portraits of Charles V.
        Philip II.
        Philip III. par *J. Pantoja de la Cruz,* regiæ majeſtati
                Camerarius; Pictor.
        Philip III.
        Philip IV. por *Diego Velaſquez.*

CHURCH.

Painted Cielings by *Luca Giordano.*
                Juan. Fern. Mudo.
                Fred. Zucaro.
                Pellegrino y Pellegrini.

SACRISTY.

Over the door through which you enter.
Woman taken in adultery. *Van Dyke.*

Lower range on the right-hand ſide.
Chriſt in the garden (6 feet long, 5 broad) *Titian.*
Elizabeth and Mary. *Raphael.*

                                  Virgin

Virgin and child.	*Titian.*
Chrift wafhing the difciples feet. *This picture is 7 feet broad, and 19 feet long: bought by the Spanifh ambaffador out of Charles I's collection; as well as the next, which fold for 250 l.*	*Tintoret.*
Madona y Bambino.	*Andrea del Sarto.*
Chrift fcourged.	*Luca Cangiagio.*
Ecce Homo.	*Titian.*

Upper range on the right-hand fide.

Madona y Bambino.	*Guido Rheni.*
Noli me tangere (8 feet long, 3 broad)	*Corregio.*
Jofeph and the infant.	*Paul Veronefe.*
Chrift bearing the crofs.	*Sebaft. del Piombo.*
Magdalen.	*Titian.*
Pharifees with the tribute-money.	*Id.*
Affumption.	*Hannibal Caracci.*
Sacrifice of Ifaac.	*Paul Veronefe.*

Altar-Piece.

Hoft elevated to Charles II.	*Claudio Clelio.*

On the left-hand fide, beginning from the altar.

St. Margaret.	*Titian.*
St. Sebaftian.	*Id.*
Chrift taking the fathers out of limbo (8 feet high, 4 broad)	*Id.*
Holy family, after their flight into Egypt.	*Id.*
Magdalen (5 feet long, 3 broad)	*Tintoret.*
Holy family, *bought out of Charles I's collection, and fold for 2000l. This picture was called the pearl of Philip IV.*	*Raphaet.*
Chrift before Pilate.	*Titian.*
St. Jerom.	*Van Dyke.*
Chrift on the crofs.	*Titian.*
Mary Magdalen before her repentance.	*Paul Veronefe.*

In

In the SALAS CAPITULARES.

First Sala.

Holy family.	*Rubens.*
Converfion of St. Paul (10 feet long, 16 broad)	*Palma Vecchio.*
Centurion (9 feet long, 14 broad)	*Paul Veronefe.*
David's victory over Goliah (10 feet long, 16 broad)	*Palma Vecchio.*
Heads of two apoftles.	*Guido Rheni.*
St. Nicholas.	
Holy family.	*Rubens.*
Woman in adultery.	*Van Dyke.*
Virgin and child.	*Leonardo Vincio.*

Second Sala.

Dead Chrift.	*Raphael.*
Efther and Ahafuerus (10 feet high, 16 broad)	*Tintoret.*
Jacob feeing Jofeph's bloody coat (fame fize as the former)	*Don Diego Velafquez.*
Chrift giving the keys to St. Peter (fix feet high, 8 broad)	*Giorgione de Caftel Franco.*
Martyrdom of St. Sebaftian.	*Spagnolett.*

Before the entrance of the king's apartment.

St. John and the lamb.	*Spagnolett.*
St. Roque.	*Id.*
St. Sebaftian.	*Id.*
St. Thomas.	*Id.*
The heads of the Virgin and Child in baffo relievo, cut out of porphyry.	
Chrift dead.	*Spagnolett.*
Æfop.	*Id.*
A philofopher.	*Id.*
St. Andrew.	*Id.*
Heraclitus.	*Id.*
Democritus.	*Id.*
Chrift dead in his father's bofom.	*Id.*
Blind philofopher.	*Id.*

St.

St. Jerom penitent.	*Spagnolett.*
Nativity.	*Luca Giordano.*
St. Thomas convinced.	*Id.*

In the *Anti-Sacriftia.*

St. Peter and St. Paul.	*Spagnolett.*
St. John preaching.	*Paul Veronefe.*
Prefentation in the temple.	*Id.*
Flight into Egypt.	*Titian.*
Lord's fupper.	*Rubens.*
Apoftles heads.	{ *Almuda* and *Juan Fernandes.*

Over the door upon the ftair-cafe into the church.

Chrift, St. John, Virgin Mary, and St. Anne. *Raphael.*

In a fmall room near the King's apartment.

Holy family. *Raphael.*

This picture is called *Nueftra fenora del los pifcayo*, or, *Our lady of the fifh*. It is the fineft in the whole collection, and of immenfe value. The Virgin is feated with the infant in her lap; Jofeph ftands by, holding a book. A boy prefents fome fifh in his hand, behind whom ftands an angel. Ufari fays of it, in his life of Raphael, that it was painted for a church at Naples. See *The hiftory of the Efcurial*, page 224.

There are, in this convent, 51 ftatues, 1622 paintings in oil; 10 cielings by Luca Giordano, with the battle of St. Quintin, by the fame hand.

Marriage of Cana *Paul Veronefe.*

This picture was certainly bought out of Charles I's collection, but where placed, I cannot fay.

Whether the pictures that came from England, were bought by Don Lewis Mendez de Haro, as the Spaniards fay, or by Don Alonzo de Cardinas, as Lord Clarendon affirms, is a controverfy of no moment. The fact is certain that we have loft

X the

the pictures; and the fale of them in CROMWELL was mean and infamous.   Lord CLARENDON and Lord COTTINGTON were fent away from the Spanifh court, left they fhould fee them. This fufficiently fhows, that that court itfelf thought it to be a bafe tranfaction.

THERE are many fine collections of paintings in SPAIN befides this; the churches and convents abound with them.   There is a moft magnificent one at the palace of SAN ILDEFONSO; where there is likewife an amazing collection of antique ftatues, of the *Mufes, Cleopatra, Venus Medici,* and of *Ægyptian* and *Roman Deities* and *River-gods:* fome at the BUEN-RETIRO, fome at ARANJUEZ. Many pictures in the poffeffion of the Marquis DONIATI, at *Madrid:* Great numbers in the king's new palace in that city, which the famous painter MINX is juft come from ROME to decorate.   Their great painters, befides SPAGNOLETT, have been MURILLO, Don DIEGO VELASQUEZ, and Don FERNANDES MUDO. The moft numerous works of the firft are at SEVILLE, where he died. The fecond was a moft aftonifhing mafter of the art, great in defign and expreffion, as may be feen in that picture of his in the ESCURIAL, where JOSEPH's bloody coat is brought to JACOB. The third was chiefly a ceiling-painter, and worked in frefco. It feems to me to be a great error, in imagining ITALY to be the only fchool for painters: SPAIN, if vifited by fome of our artifts, would, I am perfuaded, open new, aftonifhing, and unexamined treafures to their view. The fculptor would return back with improved models, and the painter with a fancy enriched from the works of great mafters, that have been little ftudied. And I recommend it to the gentlemen patrons of *the arts and fciences,* as an object worthy their attention, to fend fome perfon thither for that purpofe.

LETTER

LETTER VIII. PART II.

Catalogus MANUSCRIPTORUM LIBRORUM in Bibliothecâ SCORIALENSI Cœnobii Sancti LAU-RENTII in *Hispaniâ.*

A.

ACronis Comm. in Horatiùm
A Acta Apost. & Epist. Can. cum Gloffis

Æmilianus Codex

Æmilii Probi (five Corn. Nepotis) excellentium Ducum Vitæ, fol.

Idem, & ex Libro Cornelii de Latinis Historicis Vitæ

Annæus Seneca

Æneæ Sylvii, five Pii II. Vita

Æfopi Vita & Fabulæ

Alberti Medici, de Medicinâ

Albi Tibulli Carmina & Vita, 4to.

Quintus Curtius

Arrianæ Historiæ

Alphonsi Arr. Regis Historia, cum Privilegiis Regni

Alphonsi Regis Epistolæ

Apocalypfis Fr. Amadæi, mire illuminata & depicta

Ambrofiii Moralis Mifcellanea

And. Alciati Lect. Var.

Annotationes in Horatium & alios auctores

Constitutionum Græcarum Codicis Collectio, & Interpretatio, cum Epitome Novell. Julian. per Ant. Augustinum

Idem de Notis

Idem de Notis Antiq. Cod. Decretal.

Apocalypfis St. Johannis, cum Expositione & pulchris Figuris

Apocalypfis Fr. Amadæi

Apollonii Conica

Elementa, lib. 4.

Arrag. Regni Legitima Succeffio

Archimedis Liber Secundus

Arriani Historia

Auli Gellii de Noctibus Atticis

Aufonii Poemata

Ambrofii Moralis Annotationes

Excerpta quædam de Concil. Tolet.

B.

Barcelonæ Regni Confuetudines

Jura Cataloniæ

Privilegia & Foedera

Constit. Synod. Aragon.

Bi-

Biblia vulg. edit.
　　vulg. cum Interpret. & Gloſſ.
　　vulg.
　　vulg. diverſâ ordine diſpoſita
　　fol.
　　fol.
　　a Geneſi uſque ad Sancti Jo-
hannis Evangelium
　　a Proverbiis uſque ad Apocal.
　　Pſalt. Proverb. Eccleſ. Cant.
Literis Longobardicis
　　Pſal. cum Offic. Defunctorum
　　Pſalt. Literis Gothicis
　　Iterum
　　Iterum
　　Eccleſiaſticus
　　Proph. Minor. cum Comment.
　　Novum Teſtamentum.
　　Evangelicæ Liber Vitæ, litte-
ris aureis, juſſu Henrici Conradi
Ihp. f.
　　Pauli Ep. cum Comment.
　　Act. & Ep. Canon. cum Gloſ.
　　Acta, Ep. & Apocalypſis
　　Apocalypſis, cum Comment.
& figuris, literis perantiquis
　　Apocalypſis cum Comment.
　　Apocalypſis, literis Gothicis
Blondi & Columellæ Fragm. quæd.
Boëtii Hiſt. Eccleſ. Belgarum, Teu-
tonumque
Bruti Epiſt. per Renutium, Latinè
　　　　C.
Canones Apoſt. Literis Gothicis
Caſſiodori Opera
Catonis Diſtica, & alia quædam
　　ad Legem, Siquis pro eo, &c.
Catulli Poemata.
Conſtitut. & Leges, per Petrum, Ar-
ragonum Regem
Ciceronis Officia
Ciceronis Officia, cum Epitaph. a
XII viris compos.

Offic. de Amicitia, Senec-
tute, Paradox. & Somn. Scipionis
　　Iterum, cum Comment.
　　de Officiis Liber
　　Iterum, Liber III.
　　de Officio ad Q. Fratrem
　　Epiſtolæ Familiares
　　Iterum, Lib. XXI.
　　Iterum
　　Iterum, Lib. XV.
　　Epiſtolæ ad Atticum
　　Iterum
　　pro M. Marcello, Oratio
　　Oratio pro M. Marcello,
Dejotaro, Ligario, & Philippica-
rum, Lib. IV.
　　Orationes pro Pompeio,
Marcello, Ligario, Milone, Planco, Sylla, Licinio, Archia, Dejotaro, Q. Flacco, Cluentio, Sextio,
Murena, M. Cælio, L. Cornelio,
in Vatinium, de Aruſpicum Re-
ſponſis, de Provinciis Conſulari-
bus, pro L. Flacco, de Petitione
Conſulatus, pro Roſcio, in L. Pi-
ſonem, in Rullum, pro Leg. Ag-
rar. in Rutilium, pro C. Rabirio
duæ, & pro Cecina
　　pro Pompeio, Milone,
Planco, Sulla, Archia, Marcello,
Ligario, Dejotaro, de Reditu, &
alia ad Populum, in P. Clodium,
pro M. Cælio, in Vatinium, &c.
ut ſupra.
　　pro Pompeio, Marcello,
Ligario, Dejotaro, Archia, Planco, alia pridie quam iret in exi-
lium, pro Milone, in Vatinium,
pro ſuo reditu, & Philippicarum
libri XIII.
　　pro Marcello, in Catalin.
& Catalinæ in Ciceronem
　　　　　　　　　　　　　　Cice-

Ciceronis Orationes in L. Pifonem, pro Milone, Planco, Ligario Sulla, Flacco, Rofcio, Marcello, de Reditu ad Senatum, & alia ad Populum, pro Dejotaro, Archia, Seftii in Saluftium, & Saluftii in Ciceronem

      pro variis, ut fupra
      Philippica

Ciceronis Partitiones Oratoricæ, ad M. Brutum

      de Partitione Artis Rhetoricæ

      Rhetorica ad Herennium, & de Inventione

      ad Heren. liber, & ad Q. Fratrem

      Academ. Quæft. & ad Herenn. Rhetor.

      Philippicarum Quæft. lib. XIV, & Fragmenta quædam
      Orationes Verrinæ
      De Inventione Rhetor.
      In Catalinam
      In Saluftium
      Rhetorica
      De Oratore
      Ad Brutum
      De Oratore Perfecto libri III. ad Q. F.
      Iterum
      Iterum
      De Oratore, cod. antiq.
      Iterum; ad Brutum; Topica De Fato; Acad. Quæft. ad Herennium; Rhetorica
      De claris Oratoribus
      De Inventione
      De Orat. gen. ad Brutum de Oratione ad Qu. Frat.
      De Oratoris Officio
      Rhetoricorum lib. II. ad

Herennium, de Natura Deorum VI. de Divinatione de Fato; de Officiis III.

Ciceronis Rhetoricorum IV.
      Ad Herennium Rhetorica
      Tufculanæ Queftiones IV.
      Iterum
      Iterum
      Iterum
      Iterum
      De Divinatione
      Tufculanæ Quæftiones
      Philippicæ
      Caufa ad RR. ante exilium
ad Verrem
      De Legibus
      Iterum, & Academica
      De Partitione Orationis.
      Fragmenta
      Catalin. Orat.
      Liber Hortenfius
      De Natura Deorum
      De Finibus
      De Divinatione
      De Fato
      In Catalinam
      Som. Scipionis
      De Amicitia & Senectute
      De Divinatione, lib. II.
      Iterum
      De Amicitia & Senectute
      Som. Scipionis
      De Finibus
      De Natura Deorum
      Divinatione
      Topica
      De Fato
      Acad. Quæft.
      De Senectute
      De Amicitia
      Paradoxa
      Som. Scipionis
      Paradoxa

Cicero

Cicero de Natura Deorum
Divinatione
De Fato
De Re Militari
Som. Scipionis
De Amicitia
Som. Scipionis
Senectute
Paradoxa
Cindafiunthi & aliorum Regum Liber Judiciorum, fol. Literis Gothicis, compactus cum Æmiliano Codice
Claudiani Opera, 4to. in Memb.
Ejufdem Opera aliquot
Conftitutiones & Canon. Apoftol.
Codex Æmilianus, & Codex Confiliorum Virgilianus, Literis Gothicis in Memb. fol. Tom. duo j. d. 1. 2.
Columellæ, Catonis, & Varronis de Re Ruftica
Ingens Conciliorum Collectio, quam non defcripfi
Concordantiæ Bibl. fol. in Memb.
Cratis Cynici Epiftolæ, per J. Andream traductæ, 4to. in Memb.
Crifpi Saluftii Opera
Dares Phrygius, fol. in Memb.
S. Cypriani Epiftolæ
Ingens Collectio Juris Pontificii, & Canonici, quam non defcripfi
D.
Demofthenis Oratio ad Alexandrum 4to. in Memb.
Orat. pro Ctefiphone, L. Valla Interprete, fol. in Memb.
Ejus Vita per Aretin. ex Plutarcho
Digefti Veteris Tituli, 8vo. in Mem.
Diogenes Laertius, fol. in Memb.
Martialis cum D. Calderini Comm. In Ibim. Ovidii, & aliquot Ciceronis Epiftolas

Æl. Donat. Grammatica in Terent.
Hegefippi Hift. lib. V. fol. in Memb.
E.
Epiftolæ & Ingens earum Farrago, quas prudens præterii
Eufebii Cæfarienfis Hiftoria Ecclef. in Memb.
Eutropii Hift. Rom. 4to. in Memb.
F.
Frederici Imperatoris Teftamentum et Epiftolæ, fol. in Memb.
Feftus Pompeius de Re Latinâ
Flavii Jofephi Opera
F. Vegetii Opera
Rogeri Baconis Tractatus Varii
Forum Judicum (hodie *Fuero Juſgo*) Codex Gothicus, in Memb. ij. Z2.
F. Aretini in Phalaridis Epiftolas
F. Petrarchæ de Regibus Romanis, Codex Ant. in Memb.
De Rem. utriufq; Fortunæ
G.
G. Acoftæ Comm. in Threnos, Jeremiæ, in Ruth. & in 3ᵐ. Johannis Epiftolam
Galeni in Hippocratis Aphorifmos, ex Græco Verfus, Codex aut. in Memb.
Galli Poetæ Carmina
Gennadius de Viris illuftribus, Literis Gothicis
G. Fulginas in Avicennam
Gothicæ Leges, fol.
Ij. V. 15. De Gothorum & Vandalorum in Hifpania Ingreffu. Vide Ifidorum
Ingens Patrum Coll. quos præterii
H.
Hypocratis Epiftolæ, per R. Aretinum, Latine
Aphorifmat. & Progm. Libri IV. in Memb.
Horatii Flacci Opera, Codex aut in Memb.   Horatii

7

Horatii, cum Comm. Acronis
    Iterum, 4to. in Memb.
    Iterum, fol.
    Iterum, cum Gloffis
Horatii Flacci Odarum, Lib. IV. in
    Memb.
        Serm. & Ep. 4to. in Memb.
        Annotationes in Horatium
    & alios, 8vo.
Homeri Iliados Lib. 4to. in Memb.
        J.
Imperatorum R. R. Imagines
Indices Antiqui Manufcriptorum
    Lat. Hifp. Græc. Arab. Heb. &c.
    in Bibliothecâ Scorialenfi, ex qui-
    bus multi igne perierunt.) ‡. 16,
    17, 18, 19.
Index perantiquus Bib. Scorialenfis,
    Fol.) N. 9, 10. | ij. K. 10.
Index Antiquus Græco-Latinus Bib.
    Vaticanæ, fol. j, Ω. 2.
Index Bibliothecæ Card. Sirleti Græ-
    co-Latinæ, fol.) ‡. 15.
Flavii Jofephi Opera in Memb.
Ifidori Hifpalenfis Opera omnia
Ifidori Junioris Chronicon
Chronica Varia
Ifocrates L. Lippio Interprete, 4to.
    in Memb.
Cicero de Nat. Deor. 4to. Memb.
J. Cæfaris Comm. 4to. in Memb.
        de Bello Gallico, 4to. in
    Memb.
J. Firmici M. Aftronom. 4to. Mem.
Lucii Flori Hiftoria
S. Julii Frontini Stratagem. 4to. &
    fol. in Memb.
        De Aquæduct. Urbis, 4to.
J. Solini de Situ Orbis, 4to. in Memb.
    Iterum
    Iterum
    de Origine & Nomine Ur-
    bis Romæ, fol. in Memb.

Juftini Epitome Trogi Pompeis, in
    4to. & folio
    Iterum
    Iterum
Juftiniani Codex fol. Memb.
    Iterum
Juftiniani Partes
    Partes
Juvenalis Satyræ, 4to. in Memb.
J. Cœlii Hiftoria Attilæ, Hunno-
    rum Regis
    Carmina
Lactantii Opera
Lactantii Plinii Commentariis in
    Statium Poetam
L. Valla de Elegantiâ Linguæ La-
    tinæ
L. Aretini de Bello Gothico
        de Bello Punico
        Hiftoria Florentiæ
Lucania Pharfalia, cum Notulis
Lucianus de Longœvis
Lucii Flori Epitome Hiftoriæ Titi
    Livii, 4to. in Memb.
        De Bello Romanorum
Lucilii Libri 26 in 4to. periit in
    Igne
Macrobii Saturnalia, 4to. in Memb.
Catonis, Columellæ, & Varronis de
    Re Ruftica
M. Tullii Ciceronis Opera
V. Martialis Epigrammata
    Iterum
    Iterum
Ficini Liber de Voluptate.
Martianus Capella
Martialis Opera
Matt. Siculi contra Quintilianum
    Impreffus eft
Mahometi Hiftoria
Nenius Marcellus

                  Oro-

Orofander de Re Militari, 4to. in Memb.

    Idem de optimo Imper.

Onuphrius Panvinius—de Bib. Vaticana

Orofius de Situ Orbis

Ovidii Metamorphofis, 4to. & fol. in Memb.

    Idem, 4to. Memb.

    Epiftolæ, 4to. Memb.

    De Arte Amandi, cum Com.

    De Arte Amandi

    De Remedio Amoris

    Elegiæ, 8vo. Memb.

Palladii de Agricolturâ

    Iterùm

Sancti Pauli Epiftolæ ad Senecam, & Senecæ ad Paulum, 4to. in Memb.

    Refponfio de Chrifto ad Claudium Cæfarem

A. Perfii Satyræ

P. Criniti de Poetis Latinis, impreffus eft

P. Pomponatii de Incarnationibus

Phalaridis Epiftolæ

P. Cluverii Sicilia, 4to. Memb.

Phocæ Grammatica

Platonis Epiftolæ quædam

Plinii Sen. Hiftoria, Memb.

    Inn. Epiftolæ

Plutarchi Vitæ, L. Aretino Interprete

    Iterum

    Iterum

    Iterum

Poggii Difputatiunculæ

Pomponius Lætus

Porphyrius de Nymph. Antro.

    Grammatica Prifciani

        De Arte Gram.

        De Conftitutione

Prifciani Majoris Opéra

Propertii Carmina

Profperi Aquitani Sententia de D. Auguftino

Prudentii Carmina

Fab. Quintiliani Opera omnia, 4to. in Memb.

Q. Curtii Hift. 4to. Memb.

Renutii Aretini Verfio Epiftolarum Hypocratis & Bruti, è Græco Latina

Repertorium Legum ij. d. 1.

Caii Saluftii Invectiva in Ciceronem, 4to.

    Catalinarum ἀκέφαλον

    De Bello Jugurthino, Memb.

    Iterum, in Memb. 4to.

    Iterum & Catalina, 4to.

    De Bello Catalinæ & Invectiva in Ciceronem, fol.

    In Ciceronem, & Cicero in Salluftium, fol.

    De Conjuratione Catalinæ, & Bello Jugurthino

    Iterum, cum Invect.

    Jugurthinorum

    Conj. Catalinæ

Sapphus Epiftola ad Phaonem

Senecæ Tragœdiæ, cum Comm.

    Iterum

    Iterum

Omnia utriufque Senecæ Opera

Servius in Virgilium, fol.

Frontini Stratagemata

Card. Sirleti Bibliotheca

Solini Polytriftor.

Statii Thebais & Achilleis

    Comm. in Statium

Strabonis Geographica, ex Verfione Guarini, fol.

Suetonii Fr. Vitæ 12 Cæfarum

    Iterum, fol.

Sulpitii Severi Hiftoria

P. Terentii Comœdiæ, 4to. M.

    Cum Comm. Donati

                Varro

Varro de Lingua Latinâ
Alb. Tibulli Carmina, 4to,
    Iterum
Titi Livii Decas, 1ma fol. M.
    Libri a XXXI. ufque ad
XL.
        Decas II. fol. Memb.
        Hift. Rom. & de Bello
    Macedonico, fol. Memb.
        Ejufd. Libri, X fol.
        Hift. Rom. fol. Memb.
        A Lib. XXI. ufque XXX.
perfeƈtum, fol. in Memb.
        Primi X. Libri, fol. Memb
        A Lib. I. ufque ad XL.
caret 30. Pag. fol. Memb.
        A Lib. I. ufque ad XII.
cum Additione infra 12. Memb.
fol.
        Epitome
    Iterum, cum Lucio Floro
Trogi Pomp. Hiftoria, 4to.
Juftini Hiftoria, fol. Memb.
Epitome Hift. Juftini
Martialis Opera
Val. Maximus, 4to. Memb.
        Iterum
        Iterum

        Iterum excerpta
Varro de Re Ruftica, folio
    Iterum
Vaticanæ Bibl. Index Græco Lat.
    folio
Fl. Vegetii Epitome
Virgilii Maronis Opera, folio in
    Memb.
    Iterum
    Iterum
Virgilii Bucol. Georg. & Æneid.
    Bucolica
    Opera, cum Servio, fol. in
Memb.
    Opera, cum Fig. fol. Memb.
    Opera aliquot
    Bucolica, & Vita Virgilii
    Opera, fol. in Memb.
    Æneis, & Vita, fol. in
Memb.
Vitruvii Architeƈtura
Xenophontis Dialogus de Tyranno-
    rum Vita, Aretino Interpretè
        Cyri ad Milites Oratio
Pancirolli Opera
Leges Wifogothorum, fol. Memb.
    III. L. 12.

An Alphabetical Catalogue of GREEK MANU-
SCRIPTS, now exifting in the Library of the
Convent of the ESCURIAL.

        A.

A Bamonis Refp. ad Ep. Porphyrii
Aƈtuarii Methodi medendi
Æliani, Rhetoris, de Re Militari,
  cum Figuris in Membranâ

Æliani de inftruendis aciebus
    De Var. Hift. Libris XIV.
    De Animalibus
Ælii Alexamerii de Partibus, cum
  Tralliano
Æfchyli ικετύοντες cum χολιοις

Y   Ælii

Ælii Amydeni Medicinæ τιτραϛίϛλος
De Arte Medendi
Alcinoi de Doctrinâ Platonis Liber
Alexandri Aphrodisæi in Analytica
Aristotelis
    In Aristotelem de Repre-
hendendis Sophistis
      Nat. Problemata
      Fragmenta ex iisdem
      De Temperamento & In-
cremento.
      Tralliani, de Affectibus
      De Diebus Criticis
      De Auribus
Canonum & Conciliorum Collectio,
facta jussu Imperatoris Joannis
Comneni, 1 Volumen deest. ij.
ψ 3.
Alysii Isagoge in Musicam
Ammonii, Herm, in Porphyrium
   De Interpretatione
     In ejusdem Metaphysica
     Methodus construendi As-
trolabia
Anastasii, Episcopi Antiochensis,
Collectio Divinorum Decretorum
Andreæ, Arch Episcopi Cretensis
de XXX Argenteis, & venditio-
ne Christi. Sanctæ Liturgiæ In-
terpret.
Andronici contra Platonem ad Besa-
rionem
Andronici, Peripatetici, de Anima,
De Miris Aurificiis.
Aphthonius Sophista de Arte Rhe-
toricâ
Apollodori, Atheniensis Grammat.
de obsidendis Civitatibus
Apollonii Pergæi Comicorum Libri
tres
Apollonii Rhodii Alexand. Argo-
nauticorum, Liber Primus, cum
χολίοις incerti.

Apollonii Rhodii de Dictionum Pas-
sionibus, IV. ψ 23.
      Grammatici Li-
bri Tres, iij. V. 9.
      De Constructione
Partium Libri, IV. iv. ψ A.
Appiani Alex. Romanæ Hist. Li-
bri V.
Apsini de Proæmiis
Arati Φαινόμενα, σὺν χολίοις, ϗ τῦ αὐ-
τῦ βίος
Archetaii, Philosophi, de Divina
Chemiâ Versibus Iambicis
Archimedis Opp. cum Commenta-
riis Eutochii
Aretæi Cappadocis de Morbis
Aristarchi de Sole & Luna
Aristeæ ad Philocratem de LXX
Interp. Vide in Bibliothecæ prin-
cipio, iij. A. 6.
Aristidis Quintiliani de Musicâ, Li-
bri tres
      RhetorisSermones varii, XX.
      Παναθηναικος ϗ Μονῳδία ἐπὶ
      Σμυρνῆς καῖαβεβλημένης.
      De Urbano & Simplici
Sermone
Aristophanis Πλατ᷏. ϗ Νεφίλαι, ϗ
Βατραχοί, σὺν χολίοις.
      Βατραχοί iterum
Aristotelis Stagiritæ Opera omnia,
cum uberrimo eorum numero ;
Quæ, cum ista Philosophia diu
exoleverit, non descripsi
Aristoxeni Harmonic. Lib. III.
Asclepii, Phil. Tralliani
      In Arithmetica Nicoma-
chi
      In Aristotelis Metaphysica
Divi Athanasii, Archiepiscopi, A-
lexandrini Opera
Athenæus de Machinis Bellicis
Avicenæ de Urinis Tractatus opt.
               Au-

Aurolyci Sphærica
Acta Conciliorum, Vide infra Jus
   Canonicum, fol. 130.

B.

Barlaam & Joasaph Hist. per Joan.
   Monachum, vide Nomen
Divi Basilii Archiepiscopi Cæsareæ,
   seu magni Opera
        Monachi Opera
        Patritii ναυμάχια
Besarionis, Niceni Episc. Card. Opera

B I B L I A.

A I. Cap. Γενεσεῶς, ad XXII. Cap.
   Βασιλεῶν.
Βασ. Παραλιπ. Εσδρας. Εσθρ. Τωβίας.
   Ιεδίθ. Μακκ. Codex Imp. Catacuze-
   ni in Membrana
Psalterium ἀκέφαλον.
Psalmi Linguâ Armenicâ
Fragmentum Ezechielis, Danielis,
   & Maccabæorum
Evangelia cum Can. Eusebii, & Pic-
   turis, cum Actis Apostolorum &
   Epistolis Pauli
       cum iisd. Can. & Epist.
       cum iisdem
       cum Textu solo
       Litteris Majusculis, ἀκέ-
   φαλ⊚, κ᾽ ἀτέλει⊚, in Membranis
       per Annum, notâ antiquâ,
in Membrana
Acta Apostolorum, cum Glossis ano-
   nymi, in Membr.
       Et Epistolæ, in Memb.
       Et Apocalypsis, cum Scho-
liis marg. in Memb.
Acta Apost. & cum Argumentis
Epistolæ Paulli in Membr.
       omnes, exceptis ad Roma-
nos, Cor. I. Codex mutilus
Epistolæ aliquot Pauli, & Apocalypsis, cum Glossis in Membr.

Epistolæ distributæ per Sabbata to-
   tius Anni, in Membr.
Apocalypsis in Membr.
Bitonis Fabricæ Bellicæ, alter similis
Boethii Sev. Consolat. lib. V. cum
   Versione Græcâ Max. Mon. Pla-
   nudis, & Præfatione

C.

Q. Calabri Paralipomena Homeri,
   Lib. XIV.
Cl. Ptol. Constr. Math. Lib. XIII.
   Geog. Enarr. Lib. VIII.
       Apotelesmatum ad Syrum,
Lib. IV.
       Harmonicorum, Lib. I.
       idem, cum Comm. Porph.
τετράβιβλ⊚, aliaque nullius mo-
menti
Clementis Romani Præcepta
Constantini Imp. Porphyro-Ganne-
   tæ, & aliorum Impp. Novellæ
       M. Imp. Vita
       de eâdem Eusebius
       Epistolæ ad Plebem C.
Ecclesiæ Alexandrinæ cum Atha-
nasio
       Explicatio Literarum quæ
in ejusdem Sepulcro Marmoreo
inventæ sunt, per Genadium Scho-
larium. Vide Nomen.
       Lascaris de Verbis, Lib. II.
Cosmæ Ind. Pleusti in Proph. Dav.
Cyrilli Archiep. Alexomeniæ Coll.
   Dictionum, SS. iij. Ψ. 16.
       Lexicon ejusdem per Anton.
Philosophum, iij. V. 8.
       Ejusdem in Genesin
       De Retributione Judæorum
       Expositio in Amos, Joelem,
Malachiam, Sophoniam, Abdiam,
Jonam, & Aggeum
       In IV. Proph. maj. in Memb.

In

Aurolyci Sphærica
Acta Conciliorum, Vide infra Jus
 Canonicum, fol. 130.

B.

Barlaam & Joasaph Hist. per Joan.
 Monachum, vide Nomen
Divi Basilii Archiepiscopi Cæsareæ,
 seu magni Opera
          Monachi Opera
          Patritii ναυμάχια
Besarionis, Niceni Episc.Card.Opera

B I B L I A.
A I. Cap. Γενεσεῶς, ad XXII. Cap.
 Βασιλιῶν.
Βασ. Παραλιπ. Εσδρας. Εσθρ. Τωβιας.
 Ιυδιθ. Μακκ. Codex Imp. Catacuze-
 ni in Membrana
Psalterium ακίφαλον.
Psalmi Linguâ Armenicâ
Fragmentum Ezechielis, Danielis,
 & Maccabæorum
Evangelia cum Can. Eusebii, & Pic-
 turis, cum Actis Apostolorum &
 Epistolis Pauli
          cum iisd. Can. & Epist:
          cum iisdem
          cum Textu solo
          Litteris Majusculis, ακί-
φαλ©, κ, ατίλι©, in Membranis
          per Annum, notâ antiquâ,
in Membrana
Acta Apostolorum, cum Glossis ano-
 nymi, in Membr.
          Et Epistolæ, in Memb.
          EtApocalypsis, cumScho-
liis marg. in Memb.
Acta Apost. & cum Argumentis
Epistolæ Paulli in Membr.
          omnes, exceptis ad Roma-
nos, Cor. I. Codex mutilus
Epistolæ aliquot Pauli, & Apocalypsis, cum Glossis in Membr.

Epistolæ distributæ per Sabbata to-
 tius Anni, in Membr.
Apocalypsis in Membr.
Bitonis Fabricæ Bellicæ, alter similis
Boethii Sev. Consolat. lib. V. cum
 Versione Græcâ Max. Mon. Pla-
 nudis, & Præfatione

C.

Q. Calabri Paralipomena Homeri,
 Lib. XIV.
Cl. Ptol. Constr. Math. Lib. XIII.
 Geog. Enarr. Lib. VIII.
          Apotelesmatum ad Syrum,
Lib. IV.
          Harmonicorum, Lib. I.
          idem, cum Comm. Porph.
τιτραδιζλ©, aliaque nullius mo-
 menti
Clementis Romani Præcepta
Constantini Imp. Porphyro-Gynne-
 tæ, & aliorum Impp. Novellæ
          M. Imp. Vita
          de eâdem Eusebius
          Epistolæ ad Plebem C:
Ecclesiæ Alexandrinæ cum Atha-
nasio
          ExplicatioLiterarum quæ
 in ejusdem Sepulcro Marmoreo
 inventæ sunt,per Genadium Scho-
 larium. Vide Nomen.
          Lascaris de Verbis, Lib. II:
Cosmæ Ind. Pleusti in Proph. Dav.
Cyrilli Archiep. Alexomeniæ Coll.
 Dictionum, SS. iij. V. 16.
          Lexicon ejusdem per Anton:
 Philosophum, iij. V. 8.
          Ejusdem in Genesin
          De Retributione Judæorum
          Expositio in Amos, Joelem,
Malachiam, Sophoniam, Abdiam,
Jonam, & Aggeum
          In IV. Proph. maj. in Memb.

In Esaiam
Acclamatio ad Imp. Theodofium

Cyrilli, Archiepiscopi Hierosol. Catecheses
Epistola ad Regem Constantium, de Cruce in Cœlo visâ
Controversia adversus Julianum & Theodosium

Constantini Manassis Synopsis chronica a Româ conditâ ad Nicephorum Botoniatum

D.

Demetrii Phalerei de Interpretatione
Avicenii Epirroema, sive Consecratio

Democriti Physica & Mystica

Demosthenis Ath. Rhet. Oratio
de Fœdere Alexandrino.
de Rhodiorum Libertate
Fragmentum
Adversus Timochratem, cum Argumento
Orationes
Orationes X. cum Argum.
Orationes XIX, cum Argum. Libanii, & quorund. Schol.

Didymi Alexandrini de Marmoribus & omni genere Lignorum

Diodori Siculi Hist. Bibliothecæ Libri XV; demptis VI, VII, VIII, IX, X

Dionis Cassii, Nic. Epitome Rom. Hist. quam in comp. redegit Joannes Xiphilinus, Imperia XXV. Cæsarum, a Pomp. M. usque ad Alexandrum Mameæ filium complectens
Hist. Rom. de Capite 37 usque ad 58, hiatus est
Prusii Chrysostomi Rhetoricæ Exercitationes
7.

Dionysii Afri Alexandri in Lycophronem. Vide Nomen.

Dionysii Halicarnassei Methodus Panegyricorum
Orbis Descriptio
Problemata Rhetorica
De V. Dialectis Tractatus
De Thucydidis Proprietat.

Dionysii Areopag. de divinis Nominibus
De cœlesti & ecclesiasticâ Theologiâ

Dionysii Epistolæ Variæ, cum χολιοῖς in Membr.

B. Dionysii, Archiepisc. Alexandr. ad Basilidem Episcopum, de diversis Capitibus, &c.

Dionysiii Cerinthii Afr. Orbis Descriptio, & de XII. ventis cum Alexandrino
Eadem

Dionysii Thr. exotemata Grammat.

Diophantis Alexandri Arithmeticæ, Lib. VIII.
Iidem cum Exp. Maximi Planudis

Dioscoridis Opera 'ακιφάλαια

E.

Emm. Bryenii Harmonicorum, Libri III.

Emm. Calecæ de Fide Catholicâ

Emm. Heleboli Carmina, cum Moschopulo

Emm. Imp. Palæologi Oratio funebris pro Fratre suo Theodoro Porphyrogenneta

Emm. Moschopuli Dictiones Atticæ, cum Addit. Marg.
Schædia, iv. Ω. 5.
Comment. in Inventionem quadratorum numerorum

Emm. Philos. Ephesini Carmina var.
Emm.

Emm. Raulii Epiſtolæ tres, ad Ang. Colothetam, Emm. Metrochitam, Imp. Joannem Cantacuzenum

Epheſius in Cenſur. Ariſtotelicas Sophiſtarum, & in eaſdem Proleg.

Ephraim Syri Vita

Herodiani de Regno Marci, Libri XIX

    De Figuris

Erotiani Lexicon Hippocratis. ad Andromachum

Evagrii Hiſtoria Eccleſiaſtica

Ex Evagrio capita varia

    De Sermonis Diſcrimine capita LIV

Euclidis Geomet. Elementorum Lib. XIII. in Memb.

    Liber primus

        Sectio regulæ de Muſicâ & Iſagoge harmonica

        Catoptica, Phænomena, Dæomena

Eunapii Sophiſt. & Philoſoph. Vitæ

Euphraſini Magiri Narratio

Euripidis Hecuba, Andromache, Medea, Oreſtes, Phæniſſæ, & Hyppolitus

        Hecuba, cum Gloſſis

Euſebii Pamphylii Expoſitio in Iſaiam Prophetam

De Eccleſiaſtica Hiſtoria Libri duo, acta ſub Conſtantino Imp. XXX ann. complectens. De ejuſdem Conſtantini Vita Libri V.

De Martyribus, qui Cæſareæ Paleſtinæ ſub Diocletiano & Maximiano paſſi ſunt, Græce & Latine, Vincentio Marinerio Interprete

Euſtathii Parembolita Iſmenio

Euthymii Monachi Zigabeni Carmina

    in Prophetam Davidem

Euthymii Panoplia Orthodoxæ Fidei in Memb.

Eutochii Aſcalonitæ Comm. in Archimedem de Sphæra, &c.

G.

Galeni Opera

Gaudentii Harmonica Introductio

Gennadii Expoſitio Literarum, quæ inventæ ſunt in Sepulcro Marmoreo Conſtantini M. in queis agitur de principio & fine Imperii Iſmaelis, & de Famigerato & electo Imperatore.

Georgii Choniatis ἐξελληνισμῷ, ceu Græca Explicatio Antidotorum ex Perſiâ importatorum. Et Synopſis accuratiſſima de Urinis expoſita ex Perſarum medendi Arte

Georgii Codini de Palatio Conſtantinopolitano

Georgii Monachi Byzantinæ Eccleſiæ Chronicon in Membr.

Georgii Pachinreræ Romanæ Hiſt. Libri XII.

Georgii Preſb. Ceſ. Hiſt. Concilii Niceni, & quas Partes egerit Conſtantinus Imperator

Georgii Trapezuntii Iſagoge in Ptolomæum

    in Platonem

    contra Græcos ad Joan.

Greg. Nazianzeni Opera omnia

Greg. Thaumaturgi Opera

Greg. Nyſſeni Opera

Greg. Papæ Epiſt. ad Leonem Iſauricum

Greg. Mon. Comp. Philoſophiæ

Greg. Palaman Arch. Theſſ. Apologia adverſus Impios

Greg. Epiſcopi Tauromeniæ Siciliæ Homiliæ

Germani Patr. Conſt. de V. S.

H.

H.

Heliodori Phil. ad Imp. Theodosium
Heracliti Eph Pont. Defensio Hom.
Hermiæ Ph. in Platonis Φαιδων χόλια & Philos. Irrisio
Hermogenis Rhetorica cum χολιοις & ejus Vita in Membr.
Heronis Alexandrini
    de Re Militari
    Varia de Geometria
    de Mensuris
    Definitiones vocum
    Χιιροβαλιςης Constructio & Proportio
    πνευμάτικα, 'αυ]οματα, πο-λιορκέτικα
Hesiodi Opera & Dies, cum χολιοις Procli Platonici Diadochi
    Θεογόνια ζυν χολιοις, κ. τ. λ.
Hesychii Presb. Hierosol. Sermo
Hieroclis Phil. Comm. in Pythag. Dicta
Hierothei Philos. Carmina Iambica
Hippocratis Cei Physicorum Prin. αφορίζμων Sect. VI.
    'Αφορίζμαι η Προγνωςικα
    Πέρι αυπνία
    De Victûs Ratione
    De Ptisanâ cum Expositione Galeni
Hippolyti Thebani Cronicon
Hippolyti Episcopi Rom. de Consummatione Sæculi
Homeri Ilias cum χολιοις in Memb.
    Ilias, cum Paraphrasi Tzetzis
    Ilias iterum
    Odysseia
    Βατραχομυομαχεία, Γαλλομαχεία
Honorii Imp. Epist. ad Arcadium
Herm. Sozomeni Ecclesiast. Hist. Lib. IX.

I.

Jamblici Chalcedonensis de Pythagoreorum Sectâ, Liber 4tus.
    Idem, & Introductio Arithmetica Nicomachi
Ichnilatis Fabulæ & Sententiæ
J. Archi. Thess. de Resurrectione Christi
J. Argyropoli Solutiones dubiorum
J. Bechii Patr. Const. de Unione Ecclesiarum
J. Cantacuzeni Imp. Byz. Paraph. in Ethica Aristot.
J. Cantacuzeni Imp. Byz. Paraphrasis
    In Ethica Aristotelis
J. Cantacuzeni adversus Legem Saracenorum Apolog. 4.
    Adversus Mahumedam, Libri IV.
D. J. Chrysostomi Opera
D. J. Climaci Liber Asceticus in Memb.
    Idem, cum χολιοις
D. J. Damasceni Opera
J. Damasceni Medici Remedia in Memb.
    Idem, de Vacuis Medicamentorum
J. Diaconi Epistolæ Duæ
J. Geometræ Carmina
J: Gram. Alex. Philoponi Com. in Aristot. &c. &c. &c.
J. Metropolitæ Expositio in Tabulas magnas Festorum, cum pulchris Figuris
    Encomia.
Joannis Monachi Sermo
Joannis Moschi occursus
Joannis Pediaseni, Varia
Joannis Ph. Itali Synopsis Vocum Porphyrii

                Joannis

. Joannis Siculi Doropatris dicti Expositio in Hermogenem de Inven-
tione

    In Aphthonii προγυμ-
νάσματα
Joannis Stobæi ἐκλογαὶ, ᾗ ἀποφθίγ-
ματα κ. τ. λ.

    Libri duo in Mem-
branâ
Joannis Tzetzis Paraphrasis in Ilia-
da

    In Hesiodum
     σχόλια εἰς Ὀππίανον·
     ποικίλαὶ ἱστορίαι·
    In Lycophronem
J. Xiphilini Epitome Dionis
J. Zonaræ Chronicon a Sullâ usque
ad Alexium

    Exp. Canonum Anastasi-
orum
Argyni Monachi Chronicon ab An-
no 6976 Creationis Mundi
Is Tzetzæ Exp. in Lycophronem.
Isidori Epistolæ
Isocratis Oratio ad Demonicum
Fl. Josephi Judaicæ Antt. cum ejus-
dem Vitâ
Justiniani Imp. Novellæ
Juliani Cæsaris de Ælio Imp. ad Sal-
lustinum

    Orationes duæ
    Orationes & Epistolæ
Nic. Chalcocondyli Hist. Turc. usque ad Mahomet, Libri X.

    L.
Leonis Imp. Constitutiones Bellicæ
    Ecclogæ Digestorum & No-
vellarum
Libanii Soph. μονωδία, pro Imp.
    Juliano, &c.
    Epistolæ
Libanii Epistola ad Proconsulem
Montium, qui ab ipso postulaverat

ut scriberet Demosthenis Vitam,
et omnium Orationum ejus Ar-
gumenta
    Epistolæ ad Basilium
    Orationes
    Tractatus & Epistolæ
    Iidem
    Epistolæ
Luciani Philop. Opuscula
Lycophronis Alexandra, cum Scho-
liis Tzetzis
Libanius & Aristides ad Achillam.
    M.
Macrobius in Somnium Scipionis
Marcellinus in Genesim
M. Planudis exp.
Max. Tyrii Soph. Serm. XL.
Michaelis Italiotæ Procon. Chron.
Mich. Psilli in Platonem de animâ
    N.
Nemesius de Hom. Naturâ   ●
Nicandri Θηρίακα & ἀλλεξιφάρμακα·
Nicephori. Imp. Novellæ : potius.
    Phocæ
Nicolai Damasceni Historia.
Joannes Antiochenus
Georgius Monachus
Diodorus Siculus
Dionysius Halicarnasseus, &c.
Nonni Dionysiaca, Lib. XXIV.
    Inscriptiones, ex iisdem, Lib.
    XLVIII.
    O.
Olympiadori Philos. Alex. σχόλια in
    Platonis Gorgiam, Alcibiadem,
    & Phædonem
    Iterum in Phedonem
Orresandri Platonici de Re Militari
Oppiani Libri de Aucupio, forte
    Κυνηγίτικα
Hor. Apollinis Hieroglyph. Ægyp-
    tiaca ex Linguâ, Ægyptiaca Gre-
    ca versa per quendam Philippum
              Orphei

Orphei Argonautica
Ovidii Epiſtolæ Græcæ Verſæ, per
Max. Monachum

P.

Palladii Epi ex Brackmanum
        Hiſtoriâ de Indiæ Gentibus
Palladii Sophiſtæ Scholiæ in Hippo-
        cratem
Palchi ἀποτελέσματα
Pantaleonis Narratio Miraculorum
Pantaleonis Preſb. Byz. Oratio
Pappi Alex. Collectanea Geome-
        trica
Patritii Sacerdotis Homerocentra ab
        Eudoxia Imp. diſpoſita
Pauli Æginetæ de Menſuris & pon-
        deribus Pharmacorum
        Medicinæ Artis Libri
        Signa Medicinalia in Scripturis
        In Materiam Medicam
    " De ſuccedaneis Galeni
        De Febribus
P. Alexandrini de Domûs Domi-
        nio
Pelagii Philoſophi de Chemia
Petri & Paulli Apoſtolorum πράξεις
Petri Epiſcopi Alexandri Canones
Petri Patriarch. Antioch. præſcrip-
        tum
Phalaridis Epiſtolæ, cxxxix. ad di-
        verſos
Philonis Judæi Opera
Fl. Philoſtrati in Apollonium Ty-
        aneum, Sermones VIII.
        Vitæ Sophiſtarum
Phocyllidis παραινίσεις
Photii Bibliotheca
        Eadem
Nomocanon in Titulis XIV. cum
        exp. Zonaræ
Selecta quædam ex Photii Bibliothe-
        câ de Grammatica ex Proclo cum
        Nonio

Acta Synodi Conſt.
Epiſtolæ XLVIII. ad diverſos
Platonis Euryphron.
        Alcibiades cum Proclo
        Idem & Cratylus
        Phædon, cum χολιαῖς Olym-
piadori
        Idem, & Philebus, & Gor-
gias, cum XXVIII. Dialogis
        Phædon & Gorgias
        Gorgias, Alcibiades, & Phæ-
don
        Cratylus
        Timæus
        Parmenides
        Platonis Theologia
        Opera fere omnia, præter
Libros de Legibus, & aliquot
Dialogos
Plotini Ph. ἐννεάδες mutilæ
Plutarchi Vitæ Parallelæ
        Alexander
        Sertonius
        Eumenes, &c. &c.
        Parallelæ iterum
        De Animæ Generat.
        Opuſcula aliquot
Polyæni Stratagemata, Lib. VIII.
        Idem Opus, & Fontes, Stag-
na, &c. &c.
Polybii de Rebus Publicis, & Po-
tentatibus
Porphyrii Quinque Voces
        Iſagoge
        De Virtutibus
        De Abſtinentiâ ab ani-
mantibus
        In Harmonica Ptolomæi
        Vita Platonis
Procli Patriæ Conſt. de Traditione
        Divinæ Liturgiæ
Procli, Litii Ph. χόλια in Opera &
        Dies Heſiodi

                                        Procli

Procli in Platonis Alcibiadem, &
  Cratylum
Procli in Alcibiadem
    Timæum
    Parmenidem
    Theologiam
    In eandem IV. Exemplaria
Procopii Belli Gothici Libri duo
        Ejufdem Libri IV. Epiſto-
læ V.
Pyndari Olympia, cum χολιοῖς
        R.
Rhodionis Lex Nautica
        S.
Somnium Scipionis, cum Macrobii
  Expoſitione, & Max. Planudis
  Verſione Græcâ
S. Harmenopuli de Verborum con-
  ſtruct. & Lexicon, cum Add.
  Marg. IV. Ω 5.
Sexti Empirici adverſus Mathema-
  ticos
        Idem
Sybillina Oracula
Simplicius in Ariſtotelem
Cardinalis Sirleti Index ſuæ Biblio-
  thecæ Græcæ, cum variis diver-
  ſorum Epiſtolis
Socratis Ecclef. Hiſtoria Lib. VII.
        de apparentibus differentiis
  quarundam Obſerv. Eccleſiaſt.
Sophoclis Ἀιας Μαςιγόφοϱ@·
        Ἐλίκἰρα
        Ὀιδίπυς Τύϱαν@·
        Ἀνἰιγόνη
        Ὀιδίπυς Κολώνευς
        Τραχινίαι
        Φιλοκτήτης
        Ejus Vita
        Ἀιας Μαςιγόφοϱ@·
Sophoclis Ἐλίκἰρα cum χολιοῖς
        eadem
        Ὀιδίπυς Τύϱαν@· cum χο-
λιοῖς

Stephani Byzantini de urbibus & Po-
  pulis
Strabonis Geogr. Lib. XVII.
Suidæ Lexicon, Semiuſt. tamen le-
  gibile, Characteribus nitidiſſimis
Syneſii Epiſtolæ CXLVI. cum
  Gloſſis
        Epiſtolæ XIV.
        Ad Dioſcourum in Lib. De-
  mocriti
        Oratio ad Andronicum
        T.
Themiſtii Explorator, ſive Philo-
  ſophus
Theocryti Idyllia, cum Scholiis
Theodoreti Opera
Theodori Abucaræ Opuſcula
Theodori Gazæ Grammaticæ, Li-
  bri IV.
        Idem   ●
        De Proſodiis
Theodori Prodromus in Moſchopu-
  li Grammat.
        τιτϱάςικα
        ἰἀμβικα
        ἠϱωικα
Theodoſii Grammatica
Theonis Alex. Grammat. Spec.
Theonis Smyrnæi Mathematica
Theonis Soph. πϱογυμνάσματα ϱητό-
  ϱικα
Theophanes contra Judæos
Theophylacti Opera
Theophyli de Medicâ Arte varia
Theophraſti Characteres
Thomæ Aquinatis Opera
Xenophontis Λακεδαιμαίων Πολιτεία
        Κύϱμ Παιδία
Uxoris ſuæ & Filiorum Vitæ
Ypſicles Arraphoricus
Theoricus Smyrnæo
Zozymi Commentaria
        De Aquis Lib. III.
Z   Zozymi

Zozymi Thebani, Liber Mysticus
Ἐπιγράμματα in Ariftotelem
　　　　Platonem
　　　　Agathonem
　　　　Euripidem
　　　　Ariftophanem
Variæ Epiftolæ
Poematæ Varia
Epiftolæ XV.
Vitæ Imp. a Gallieno ufque ad Theo-
　philum
　　　　Conftantini Maximi
　　　　Conftantii
　　　　Hermogenis
De Legatis Romanorum ad Genti-
　les, Tomi duo
De Menfuris & Ponderibus in Mem-
　branâ
Catalogus Herbarum, cum variis de
　Re Medicâ
Collectanea ex Hippocrate
　　　　Galeno
　　　　Oribafio
　　　　Ruffo
　　　　Paullo
　　　　Alexandro
　　　　Philomeno
　　　　Archigene
　　　　Afclepiade
　　　　Ætio
　　　　Ifaac, & aliis
　　　　Diofcoride

Jus Civile.

Lexicon Legis, & de Menfuris et
　Pond.
　　　　Rom. Dict. in Lege
Synopfis Bafilicorum
　　　　Novellarum Leonis
De Legibus ufeq. ad C. Annos
Bafilicor. Lib. VIII.

Leges Juftiniani collectæ
　　　　Per Leonem
　　　　Conftantinum
　　　　Bafilium
Hexabiblos
Collectio Conftitutionum
　　　　Novellarum, cum Paratit-
　lis, & novellis
Selecta ex IX. Libris Imp.
Novell. Fragmenta

Jus Canonicum.

Acta Synodi Œcumeniani
　　　　eadem
　　　　Ferrarienfis
　　　　Sextæ Conftant.
Acta Octav. Synod. Conftant.
　　　　Non. Syn. Conft.
Conftitut. variæ Conc. Conft.
Acta Synodi Nicæni
　　　　III. Ephefini contra Neftorium
　　　　IV. Chalcedonen.

Collectio Paræmiarum, ex Suidâ &
　aliis, per Tarrhæum, & Didymum
Poemata
Pythagorica Dicta

Sacra Biblia, cum ejus Par-tibus.

A 1mo Genefeos ad 20 Cap. Libri
　II. Regum
Regum Libri Quatuor Paralyp.
　Efdras, Efther, Tobias, Judith,
　Maccab.
Pfalterium ἀκέφαλον
　　　　Armeniacum
Fragg Ezeck. Dan. & Maccab.
Evang. IV. cum Can. Eufeb. & Pic-
　turis
Epiftolæ Pauli & Acta App.
Evangelia κατ' ἐνιαυτὸν, cum Pictu-
　ris　　　　　　　　　　　IV.

IV. Evangel. fine Principio, cum Picturis

IV. Evangel. fine Principio, aut Fine, fed Litteris Majufculis ·
    In Membr. iij. ψ. 5. 6. 7.
    iv. X. 21. fcripta an. 522

Paulli Epiftola in Memb.
    Omnes duntaxat ad Rom.
    & Corinth.
      Aliquot & Apocalypfis
    παρ ἰβδομάδας κατ' ἰνιαυτὸν,
antiquâ Notâ in Membrana

Acta & Epiftolæ in Memb.
    cum Gloffis in Memb.
      Et Apocalyp. cum Scholiis Marg. in Memb. cum Argum. caret Fine
    Paulli, cum Arg.

Apocalypfis, in Memb.

Nov. Teftament. fine Apocalyp.

Efdras, Efther, Tobias, Judith Maccab.

Quædam Traditiones SS. ex Hebraico in Græcum Verfæ, monftrantes Quinam fuerint SS. Interpretes, & quo tempore

Hebrew Manufcripts in the Efcurial.

R. D. Kimchi in Pfalterium
    Threnos
    Ecclefiaften
    Efther
    Efdras
    Daniel
    Nehemiah
    In Ifaiam
    Offeam
    Johelem
    Amos
    Abdiam
    Mickeam
    Habacuck, & alios Prophetas minores

In xxvi priora Capita Efaiæ Fr. de Zamora Verfore iij. R. 8.

Dictionarium Arab. Charact. Hebraicis, ij. R. 7.

Abenzohar Liber Medicinæ

Avicenæ Canon.

Biblia Sacra, cum Notis & punctis, tom. 3. in Memb.
      cum Punctis in Memb.
      Pars cum Punctis

Genefis cum Latina interlineali Petro Ciruelo Interprete. (There is another copy of this book in the church-library at SEGOVIA.)

Liber Radicum in Memb. I. Σ. S.

Comment. in Leviticum
      in Deuteronomium
      in Pfalmos, curâ B. Ariæ Montani, ex antiquo Romano Codice defcriptum

De obfervandis X. Præceptis

M. Gerundenfis Gloffæ in Job

Hymni pro Diebus Feftis

Comm. in Job, cum Salomone

Liber contra Judæos

Liber dictus, Secunda Domus Orationis

Liber IX. Fundamentorum Religionis Chriftianæ, Opus Filii Arthur, Difcipuli S. Jacobi Apoftoli Sermone Syro impreffus

Pfalterium ⎤
Job ⎥
Proverbia ⎥
Ruth ⎥
Cant. Canticorum ⎥
Ecclefiaftes ⎬ In eodem
Threni ⎥ Codice.
Efther ⎥
Daniel ⎥
Efdras ⎥
Paralipomena ⎦
Expofitio Hebdom. Danielis, &c.

Hift. Imperii Nabucodonofor Regis & fequentium Regum

Galenus de Medicam. fimplicibus

J. Forali Expofitio Parabolarum Evangelicarum

R. Jonæ Portæ Pœnitentium
Opus Impreffus cum Salomone

R. Ifaiæ Matrani in Jofuam
Judices
Ifaiam
Ezekielem
Pfalmos, Proph.

De Jure Civili Opus, de Damno, Nocumento, & de Reftitutione, fol. in Memb.

Matthiæ Nifchari Expofitio Alphabetica Pfalmorum

De Medicâ Materia ex Galeno, & Diçfcoride excerpta quædam, Opus Anonymi

De eâdem Liber

R. Moyfis Chimchy Liber Gram. Hebraicæ

On Kelos, 4to. in Memb.

R. Salamonis Filii, Moyfis, Malgurii, Domus Dei, Liber fic appellatus, in quo tractatur de Caufâ, ob quam Moyfes tegebat fuam faciem Velo : Et quare Tabulæ Legis fcriptæ erant in utroque Latere ; & alia fecreta Legis Rabinorum, & aliorum his fimilium in Fol. in Membr.

Commentaria in Danielem, Proverbia, Cantica, Ruth, & Threnos.
in Pentateuchum
in Leviticum
in Numeros

R. Salmonis Liber de Medicamentis, fol.

Targum Onkelos, 4to. in Memb.

LETTER

LETTER IX.

Defcription of the City of TOLEDO.

WE arrived at the city of TOLEDO, from ARANJUEZ, where the court then was, May 12, 1761. We travelled in a coach drawn by fix mules, and were conducted by the *Arrieros*, or carriers, as is ufual: For you muft know, that the nobility and gentry of SPAIN only ufe poftilions, or drivers, in the cities and great towns; and when they take a journey, tho' they go in their own coaches, they generally have hired mules, and two drivers, one fitting between the two fore-wheels, upon the bed of the carriage, and the other generally running along-fide of the mules: which, as the two laft only are reined, or rather roped, run on with the coach with their heads pointing four or five different ways. This is but a trifling circumftance, yet even the mereft trifles may fometimes ferve to fhew the turn and genius of a people. We found the road to TOLEDO good for travellers, the country about it but indifferent, tolerably tilled, and planted with *olive-trees*: We paffed almoft the whole way upon the banks of the TAGUS, which are not by any means fuch as would furnifh a poet with fine landfkips, or beautiful images. But the river runs through a rude and wild wafte: the windings of it near the city of TOLEDO are beautiful; and where the river paffes between the rocks on which the city is built, and thofe adjoining, with the bridge and gate of the city, all together form fuch a view, as the wild imagination of the extravagant SALVATOR ROSA would have delighted in.

THE

THE Cathedral is certainly equal in riches to the grandeur of
the fee, but not in fabric; which is of the modern Gothic, not
remarkably large, rich in carving, but the building neither light,
nor of a good taste: the cieling of the facrifty is painted by LUCA
GIORDANO, and is indeed fine, entire, and well-preferved. There
are fome valuable pictures, one particularly of TITIAN: the cuftodia, jewels, pearls, and precious ftones, are inconceivable, as well
as ineftimable: altars with fteps to them of maffy filver, gilt; the
figures of the four quarters of the world, each dreffed with the
precious ftones peculiar to its own quarter, and fitting on globes
of two feet diameter, the globe refting on a pedeftal, and that
on a bafe; the figure, globe, pedeftal, and bafe being all together about ten feet high: all thefe, of maffy filver, were the gift
of CHARLES II's Queen, who furvived him; not to mention a
filagree brazier, fome chefts, and a multitude of veffels, candlefticks, lamps, fhrines, &c. &c. of filver likewife. Marble and
granite in profufion. What plunder NEBUCHADNEZZAR took
away firft, or TITUS at the laft, from the temple at JERUSA-
LEM, I know not; but I am fure there is enough here. The revenues of this archbifhopric are well known to be the greateft of
the ecclefiaftical fort in SPAIN, and are, as well as I can learn,
above 30,000 pounds a year. But the prefent archbifhop has not
himfelf the whole revenue; for fince the refignation of the Infant
Don LUIS, the Infant has referved to himfelf the yearly appoint-
ment of 60,000 ducats, or about 7400 l. fterling. This prelate
likewife ranks very high as a civil or ftate-officer, being primate,
chancellor of CASTILE, and privy-counfellor. Mr. AP-RICE,
I remember, mentions there being 10,000 weavers in filk and cloth
in that city only: but, to fay the truth, that gentleman's accounts,
with regard to this country, are very erroneous; and as to the manufactures of SPAIN in general, they are all now in a declining
condition.—But give me leave here to make one remark upon the
wealth that is fo ufelefly locked up in the feveral churches of
thefe kingdoms; thofe dormant riches, which a miftaken piety
has fo abfurdly fet apart forever; which anfwer no rational purpofe, and which neither ferve to the glory of God, nor the good
of man: Mr. MACANAS, who had been Plenipotentiary at BRE-
DA, propofed to PHILIP V's minifters fome plans for making this

3   ftag-

ftagnate wealth circulate a little, and become of fome ufe; but the propofals were not accepted by the court; and this man had the fate fo common to genius in this country : His parts raifed him envy and enemies at court, and in the end he was banifhed entirely, and confined to CORUNNA, where he died. His *Political Teftament* is a great curiofity; but I could never get fight of it. And fince his time another gentleman defigns laying fome propofals of the fame fort and tendency before the prefent minifters. Thefe may poffibly meet with a more favourable reception : for as the prefent King has juft now had fpirit enough to confine the inqui-fitor-general, and banifh him to a great diftance; a bolder ftroke than any of his predeceffors ever dared to attempt! he certainly need not fear to put any meafures in execution, which he judges to be expedient.——But to return to TOLEDO.

THE *Alcaffar*, or Palace, built by CHARLES V. as fome fay, or, as others, by the Archduke CHARLES, is a noble building; though it is now almoft a ruin, being burnt by the Allies, and Auftrian party, in the partition or fucceffion-war, left it fhould fall into the hands of PHILIP V. Who would ever conceive, that this very PHILIP fhould have afterwards defired an alliance with the burner of his own palace, and the competitor for his throne? It was fuch a counfel as no one but a RIPPERDA could fuggeft, or indeed execute : yet fuch was the VIENNA-*Treaty!* But I forget TOLEDO. The manufactory for *fwords* is juft revived there, and their goodnefs is folely owing to the confluence of the XA-RAMA and the TAGUS: for thofe two rivers have been tried fepa-rately, by way of experiment, by the King's order, and their dif-united waters will not give that *trempe*. This manufactory is all worked by Englifh tools, which came into the hands of the Spa-niards very oddly: The ftory, as I was told it, runs thus;—About twenty years ago, a fet of Englifh workmen came upon contract to TOLEDO, to make fuch works, or engines, as were neceffary for throwing the water of the river up the rock into the town; for at prefent it is brought by affes, each afs carrying fix earthen pitchers burthen, as indeed is the general cuftom throughout SPAIN: Thefe Englifh contractors brought with them all forts of Englifh inftruments and tools neceffary for fuch a work, and fome very

large

large iron pipes. The undertaking certainly was difficult; but foreigners profeffing and endeavouring to execute fuch a work, as the *Spaniards* owned themfelves unequal to; and then thefe being *Englifh Heretics*, all thefe circumftances foon raifed the envy and jealoufy of the people: In fhort, from their oppofition, and their endeavours to counteract every ftep the Englifh undertook, the whole project and defign came to nothing. But here my ftory begins to grow dark; for the conclufion is, that thefe Englifh all died, and as there was no heir to claim their effects, they were kept *as goods without an owner;* and what remains of thefe tools and effects are now in the hands of the King of SPAIN, and employed in the old, but juft-revived *Sword-Fabric* of TOLEDO.

BUT give me leave here to make one or two remarks.——— The effects and goods of thefe unfortunate contractors amounted at leaft to above 1000l. What! were they and their fervants all fo abfolutely fwept away, that no one fhould remain as heir, claimer, or inheritor of thefe effects? Had they no friends, or even relations left in ENGLAND? Was there no refident, or ambaffador then in SPAIN, to apply to for the removal of thefe goods, or at leaft for the fale of them? All thefe circumftances feem to me fo improbable, that I am at a lofs what to fay, or what to conjecture: And the whole, I think, that can be faid, is, that it is really a very blind ftory.

BUT to return to TOLEDO; the city, like that of SEGOVIA, is built upon a rocky mountain; but you muft remember at the fame time that it was built by the Goths or the Moors. I take particular notice of this circumftance for two reafons; firft, becaufe it is evident, that a principle of fear, and felf-defence, drove thofe people into fuch marvellous fituations: And fecondly, Becaufe a Spaniard would never have been induftrious enough to have carried fo much weighty and bulky materials up fo high, and into fuch impregnable and almoft inacceffible ftrongholds. For you can neither get in or out of thofe cities, without paffing a defcent or afcent of immenfe length, and all in zigzags, juft like lines of circumvallation. The gates and portcullis's, like fome of the *Saxon*

I have

I have feen in ENGLAND, or *Norman*, never face the ftreet, but are all in oblique pofitions. The ftreets of TOLEDO are remark-ably narrow, but thofe of SEGOVIA much broader, and the walls of immenfe height, with turrets all round.

THERE is indeed one very great curiofity at TOLEDO, not yet mentioned, which is an *original Hebrew Temple*, and it certainly is a fine remain; but here, to my forrow, the piety of the Spaniard in converting this temple from Judaifm to Chriftianity, or rather to Popery, has taken away much matter of entertainment to the antiquarians. The antient divifions, or *cancellæ*, were all taken down; the *fanctum fanctorum*, and even the *tabernacle* itfelf was here literally done away. There was likewife above a feparate *tribune* for the women, as I remember there had been at St. CROSS at WINCHESTER; and the walls, which are covered with the fineft Hebrew characters in the world, I believe; written all over with the *Pfalms in Hebrew*; thefe the good Spaniard had very zealoufly plaiftered over with untempered mortar. (Whether or no this temple will furnifh arguments for or againft Bifhop HARE or Dr. LOWTH; whether it will determine any thing relating to the metre, the points, the vowels; or whether it will fupport any *Hutchinfonian* nonfenfe; all thefe things muft be left to another time, and in the interim I fhall go on with my tale.)

THERE were now no longer any traces or appearance of aught that ever had been *Jewifh*, as much as if TITUS, or the Inquifitor-General had been vifitors; and fo this temple ftood for many years: There was nothing but a vague and vulgar tradition remaining, to prove that it ever had been Jewifh, and was now wearing the *San-Benito*. But fortunately for the antiquarians, a canon and trea-furer of the church of TOLEDO, whofe name is Don PEREZ BA-YER, being a man of parts and learning, and having a particular turn for Hebrew, as one would think indeed from his name: This gentleman, I fay, happily obferving, that in fome places where the plaifter had fallen off, *Hebrew letters* might be traced, he had fpirit enough inftantly to fet about the difplaiftering the infide of the temple, and has fince very accurately and carefully copied the whole into a book, taken drawings and a fection of the

build-

building, and explained all with a learned and elegant differtation: This book, you muſt know, he cannot well publiſh in SPAIN; Spaniſh writers lie under diſagreeable reſtraints in that particular. UGOLINUS, the great collector of Hebrew antiquities, would fain have begged it of him, but he refuſed: I offered to publiſh it in ENGLAND for him, if he would let me; but he ſaid he had not finiſhed it, and would at leaſt put the laſt hand to it, before he ever thought of printing.

THERE are, I am told, near the city of TOLEDO, ſome remains of a *Circus* and *Amphitheatre*, which are *Roman*, but at preſent one may almoſt ſay,

—— *etiam hæ periêre ruinæ.*

As I had but an indifferent *Ciceroni*, theſe I did not ſee. Nor, which I am ſorry for, the very curious *library* which belongs to the *cathedral*, replete with invaluable treaſures. But as one frankly owned to me, they do not much care to ſhew their library, and leſs to print a catalogue of what it contains; left they ſhould diſcloſe' how rich they are: politically apprehending, perhaps not without reaſon, that if others were let into the ſecret, they might poſſibly like to have a greater ſhare in thoſe treaſures, than would be agreeable.

THERE is alſo an hoſpital for the *French diſeaſe* only, which will eaſily tell you the prevalence and malignance of that diſtemper in this country. This is more owing to their want of neatneſs, and their ignorance in phyſic and chirurgery, than to any other cauſe. I remember the King's phyſician told me, that it had been obſerved, that patients infected with this diſeaſe, if they came from a colder climate, were eaſily cured here; but if they went from hence infected into a colder climate, that they ſeldom or ever could be cured. There is an hoſpital alſo for *foundlings*, where the children ſeem to be well taken care of.

I DO not remember any thing more worth obſerving with regard to TOLEDO, than that they had hung on the wall of one of their convents a vaſt number of fetters, which were taken when they releaſed ſome chriſtian captives from the MOORS. The fetters are indeed monſtrouſly large, and of inhuman weight: ſuch is Eaſtern cruelty! They were taken at the conqueſt of GRANADA.

LETTER

LETTER X.

Defcription of the City of SEGOVIA.

HAVING juft given a defcription of TOLEDO, I fhall now give an account of SEGOVIA, for though the two cities are a: fuch a diftance from each other, they have fome refemblance in common, and may ferve as companions, like two pictures, to each other.

THE fite of the city has fomething of a very martial air, built upon a high rude rock; by which means moft of the entrances to it are fteep, and difagreeable, efpecially as you are obliged to make feveral zigzag-windings before you can gain the fummit : It is entirely furrounded with a lofty old Moorifh wall, with battle-ments and turrets, in the ftile of the fortifications of thofe days; which indeed were almoft impregnable. There are feveral *Roman infcriptions* in the walls; fome too high ever to be read, others turned wrong fide upwards, others defaced, and fome with the infcription turned inwards: For as the MOORS confidered thefe only as meer ftones to build with, it is no wonder to find them in fuch ftrange pofitions. I copied one or two of them of no moment, but however they ferve me as proofs to make out one point, which I fhall fpeak to hereafter. On the *caftle* or palace-fide of the town is a deep, natural fofs, formed by two contiguous ridges of mountain; on the northern fide a fmall river runs at the foot of the rock; which ferves to little other ufe, but to turn a large paper-mill, where they make great quantities of an ordinary

coarfe

coarfe paper. The next advantage they draw from this river, is the wafhing themfelves and their linen; which laft is performed in SPAIN in the following manner, however it may furprize a good ENGLISH houfewife. The women carry all their linen down in great bundles, to the fide of this river; and having chofe a good fmooth ftone, or fometimes a piece of wood, they kneel down, wet the linen, and then wring it and foap it; and then beat it upon the ftone or wood, till they have got the dirt out of it. And this is all the operation; the chief inconvenience of which is, that the linen is apt to be beat to pieces, otherwife it is clean enough. *Ironing* is, I believe, but little ufed in this country; plaiting never; and the folding or fmoothing the linen is moft commonly done by the hand, or what we call the mangle, or calendar. In FRANCE, I am told, the linen is wafhed in the fame manner, as may be feen on the banks of their rivers, and on thofe of the SEINE at PARIS, where the water is fo muddy and yellow, as to leave a bad tinge upon the linen. I am informed by a friend, that at St. MALO and other fea-ports in BRITANNY and NORMANDY, the women take the opportunity of the tide's going out, to wafh their linen in the fea-water left in the cavities or bafons in the rocks; when having foaked, foaped and wafhed it, they lay it on the rock, and beat it with a kind of wooden battledore, which commonly pinks it full of holes.

BUT as to the river's being of much ufe to the city, by fupplying it with water for all the domeftic purpofes of life: This you will eafily imagine could not be the cafe, from the extreme height of the mountain; and, becaufe they muft conftantly have brought it up with affes, as they do at TOLEDO. It was this inconvenience, and the defire of fupplying the city more effectually, that gave rife to one of the nobleft works, to one of the moft magnificent fabrics of that fort poffibly in the whole world: You will naturally guefs, I mean, THE AQUEDUCT.

THE extent of this *Aqueduct* is faid to be about three miles; at the eaftern entrance of the town it begins with fmall arches
gradually

gradually encreafing, and rifing, till it expands into a double row of arches and pillars, and has then the nobleft effect you can pof-fibly conceive : Some of the firft arches are a little more *pointed* than the reft (which are fairly circular) tho' not enough, I think, to be really called pointed arches. The people have built fo many houfes round this *Aqueduct*, it would grieve any true Antiqua-rian to the heart; fince you are hindered from having fo full and complete a view of it, as a whole, which every curious fpectator would wifh : The ftone-pipes too, or ducts of water, fixed to the fides of it in fome places, deface it much, and look rather like props; but they are certainly of the fame age with the reft. With regard to the height, and other meafures of this fabric, I was forced to take them myfelf : for as to the people, they nei-ther know nor care how high it is, or how broad. Thus it fares with objects, which we fee every day. Let them be ever fo noble, or excellent, when they become familiar, they are neglected : It is the novelty that ftrikes, and not the excellence. This is not peculiar to thefe people, but is the cafe of all : let an Englifhman never have feen the fea before, and I will warrant for his admira-tion and furprize; though if you afk a peafant about it near BRIGHTHELMSTONE, he will tell you, " He don't fee any thing " very extraordinary in it."—Upon enquiring about the *Aqueduct*, fome faid it was 108 feet high, and that the number of arches was 150; others 144 feet, and 177 arches. The reafon of this difference is, that as the arches muft be of unequal heights, to maintain *a level*, they have meafured from different ftations : This indeed ac-counts for the difference of the meafures, but not for the number of the arches : How that happened I cannot fay. The following meafures I can anfwer for, fince I took them upon the fpot with my own hands. Its greateft height is exactly 101 *feet, and* 1 *inch*; for I took the meafure from the higheft trace of ftone.

The breadth of the front of the pillars, 6 feet, 2 inches;
The depth of them, 11 feet, 3 inches;
The width of the arches, 12 feet, 7 inches, and one quarter.

As to the number of the arches, we counted them, and we could reckon only 118 to the city-wall from the firft vifible arch;
and

and feven more arches within the walls; in all 125: But then, where the arches were double, that is, placed one over another, we did not count thofe, as two arches, but as fingle: Becaufe in conveying an idea of this *Aqueduct* to one who had never feen it, we judged, that a ftranger would always form his notion of the length of this *Aqueduct* by the number of arches continued in length. Again, as to the meafures, except that of the height, they are only true with regard to that particular part, arch, or pillar, which I meafured at that time: For I meafured feveral others fince, and find their dimenfions differ widely from one another, fo that there is no one general proportion, which runs through the whole ftructure. The reafon of which I take to be, that where they were obliged to make the *Aqueduct* higher, in order to preferve the level; that there they were obliged to enlarge the proportions, and increafed the bafe in proportion to the height of the pillar; and confequently contracted the arches, in order to make the building more ftable. It feems to be built without any *cement*, and the ftones are about *three feet* long, and *two feet* thick; all roughly hewn, and with the edges rounded, not fharp. Why the SPANISH writers chufe to call this *the Bridge of* SEGOVIA, and not *the Aqueduct*, is a folecifm I cannot account for: But this is the language of MARIANA, PINEDA, and many others. A Spaniard being afked, why he called it The PUENTE DE SEGOVIA, anfwered, *becaufe it was a bridge*; for though it was not indeed a bridge for people to walk over, yet it was a bridge for water to go over. And perhaps this may be their reafon, though it certainly is a very odd one. Old Spanifh writers call it PUENTE SECA, which is ftranger ftill; for fure no one can fay with any propriety, that an Aqueduct is a *Dry Bridge*.

HAVING now given a defcription of this truly magnificent ftructure; the next enquiry is, *who* was the author? and *when* it was built? I think, there are but three or four opinions about it. MARIANA, according to his ufual modefty, is in fufpenfe; and doubts whether it is to be attributed to the Emperor TRAJAN, or to LICINIUS LARIUS, who was prætor in SPAIN, under VESPASIAN, and a friend of PLINY the elder. Father HENRY
                                                                FLORES,

*F*LORES, who is vain enough himself, and willing in all things to gratify the vanity of his countrymen, attributes it to the GOTHS, who, as they lived here once, were for that time a sort of SPANI-ARDS: COLMENARES, the writer of the history of SEGOVIA, goes many lengths indeed ; and in order to make his native city, SEGOVIA, as old as possible, tells us at once, that the aqueduct was built by HERCULES. HERCULES certainly did great wonders ; but I believe built few aqueducts: and if it must be the work of some strong man, he might as well have called in SAMPSON. As to the GOTHS, tho' it is certain they raised very noble fabrics wherever they went, and, as it were, built themselves into fame ; yet I cannot give them this aqueduct, for many reasons. The *Go-thic structures* in general appear to me to have this character; that though they are for the most part noble by their being so very large, yet they are generally clumsy and heavy, and the *old Gothic* particularly so: You seldom see any thing light, elegant, or of a good taste, except in the *modern Gothic*; all which circumstances are remarkably conspicuous in *this Aqueduct.* The *Gothic* indeed will last for ages, and so will the *Roman,* without one half of their hea-vy stability. I am therefore, upon the whole, inclined to think this aqueduct undoubtedly *Roman**. For though I grant to COLMENA-RES, that there is nothing now visible upon the aqueduct itself, no remains of *an inscription,* no traces left to decide this question ; let the order too, if he will have it so, be either Doric, Ionic, Co-rinthian, or Composite: And tho' it be true, that the *Romans,* when they executed such great works as these, generally took sufficient care to secure their *title* to it, and their *name* upon it : Yet all these arguments and objections do not weigh with me: I am where I was; I think it *Roman.* There is something in the grandeur of the *Roman* works, that still *speaks* for them, though their usual witnesses should happen to be lost : a greatness, that no other na-tion has attempted, or ever been able to equal. There is no in-scription remaining now, nor is there much appearance, that there

---

* The first 13 arches are certainly Roman; the 36 next in sequence are clearly of another stile, of a much inferior workmanship, and have been repaired by the *Spa-niards* or *Goths:* for the stile will agree with either. But at the 49th arch the *Roman master-hand* appears again ; the same form of stone, large, round-edged, and exactly in the same taste with the 13 first arches.

ever

*

ever was one: What then ? is this negative a fufficient proof that there never was one? The Roman infcriptions fo frequent about the walls of this town fufficiently fhew their footfteps at SEGOVIA, to this day: there might have been an infcription, but now defaced or deftroyed by ignorance, fuperftition, time, and the turbulence of the age, when SPAIN fucceffively received fo many mafters. Thefe infcriptions are ftill legible to this day: SEXTO· LIC· MIL· near the gate of St. JUAN. Another is

```
M· IVN Æ· FI
   ETIS CAES
N Q̣F     AṆN
LV· S· T· · T· L·
```

Another near the gate of SAN ANDRES, thus:

PVBLICIO
IVVENALI
IVVENALIS

COLMENARES upon this fays, that JUVENAL was not born at AQUINUM, but SEGOVIA; for how could MARTIAL, who was a *Spaniard*, otherwife call him *Juvenali meo* ?

AFTER having given fome account why I think it a Roman work, I fhall now fearch after the *Author*. The reafon why it has been afcribed to the Emperor TRAJAN, is, becaufe that prince has left fo many noble monuments of his own erecting in SPAIN, particularly in ESTREMADURA and ANDALUSIA; that, forfooth, every Roman work that the Spaniards find any where, muft immediately be afcribed to TRAJAN ! This, indeed, is natural; for the Spaniards ftill revere his memory, and they have a very remarkable proverb, which fays, *Felicidad de Augufto, y Bondad de Trajano:* that is, *The happinefs of Auguftus, and the goodnefs of Trajan.* But I have one objection to its being the work of that great emperor: that

9

he was a native of *Italica*, or OLD SEVILLE, by birth an Andalusian : and I cannot help thinking, that if he had intended a
work of so much expence and magnificence in SPAIN, he would
never have given the benefit of it to the inhabitants of OLD CAS-
TILE. But here I am sensible, that I am unawares drawn into
a controversy, and shall presently raise all the Castilians to a man
against me. For it seems these gentlemen will have it, that the
Emperor TRAJAN was an *Estremaduran* by birth, and not an
Andalusian. Well then, let us weigh the authorities on both sides,
and see how that matter stands. XIMENES, and other compilers
of the *Historia general de Espana*, MARINEUS SICULUS, PEDRO
DE MEDINA, JUAN SEDENO, and others say, that TRAJAN was
born at PEDRAÇA DE ESTREMADURA, or PEDRAÇA DE LA SI-
ERRA, so called, because it joined to the mountains, and to distin-
guish it from that in the plains, which was likewise called ITA-
LICA. To this they add the constant tradition of this Estremadurian village, which says to this day, that TRAJAN was born there,
and they shew travellers the site of the house he was born in : and
they give this as another proof, that the villagers say, his mother
was OREJANA, or OREJANILLA, which was romanized afterwards
into AURELIANA. To all this they join the blunders of the par-
tial ZOZIMUS, ἔλεξε τὸν ἴσον ἑαυτῷ ἐν τῇ ἀρχῇ Θεοδόσιον, τῇ γενέσει
ἘσπᾶνΘ· ἐν πόλει Κόκα τῆς Γαλικίας. and the dreams of some Spanish bishop. This is one side of the question, and is at the same
time a specimen of Spanish learning. Now on the other side. DION
CASSIUS, AMMIANUS MARCELLINUS, AURELIUS VICTOR, and
EUTROPIUS all affirm, that the Emperor TRAJAN was a native
of the *Andalusian Italica*, or OLD SEVILLE. *Amm. Marc. Theodosius Hispanus* Italicæ *Divi Trajani Civitatis*. The words of VIC-
TOR are to much the same purpose. It is clear, however, I think,
that THEODOSIUS was no Estremadurian, whatever TRAJAN
might be ; and as to ZOZIMUS, he makes him a poor Gallician.
All the remark I shall make upon this controversy is, that TRA-
JAN's being an Estremadurian would suit well enough with the
public works he raised in that province, but it will not bring him
so far as SEGOVIA into OLD CASTILE.

UPON the whole, then, I am induced to think, that this aqueduct was the work of LICINIUS LARIUS, the Prætor under VESPA-

B b

SIAN :

sian : for TRAJAN had need have been a master-builder all his life-time, if we ascribe every thing to him. But then it is said, that if LICINIUS LARIUS built the aqueduct, that his friend PLINY would certainly have mentioned it. I do not think this a certain objection; a probable one, I own, it is. But be that as it will, it is as certain, that there is an *Inscription* extant in AMBROSIUS MORALES, the famous old Spanish antiquarian, which is published by ADOLPHUS OCCO, and shews, *That Licinius Larius really did build the Aqueduct of Segovia*. They may say, perhaps, that this inscription is a false one: It may be so, for ought I know to the contrary, as I have never been able to see MORALES, or Occo's book, or to copy the inscription *. I shall now take my leave of the aqueduct, adding only, that I am told the cement is lead, and that the key-stones are tied with iron; and that between the two highest arches, or the *Açoguejo*, as they call it, there are two niches remaining, which plainly contained formerly the statues of the emperor and the lieutenant, or prætor, under whom this aqueduct was erected: but now they are very piously filled up with the statues of those, who might possibly work miracles, but I am sure never brought water in so noble a manner to any city in this world; I mean two saints.

---

* You will find it in Don. G. MAYANS's Latin Epistle, annexed to this account.

Aa

Ad Cl. Patrem

HENRICUM FLOREZIUM,

HISPANIÆ SANCTÆ SCRIPTOREM,

Ab Opinione fuâ & Judicio de Aquæductu Segovienfi diffentiens Poeta.

*PYramidum moles ceffêre; Segovia pontem
Ducendis veteri numine jactat aquis:
Trajanus fuerit, fueritve Licinius autor,
Haud fua Lucifero lympha jubente fluit:
Nec tamen Alcidi dederim, Maurove, Getifve,
Hoc tantum Hifpano vix licet effe decus:
Macte animi FLOREZE! fed hæc monimenta per orbem
Non nifi Cæfareæ fic pofuêre manus.*

Tranflation of Father HENRY FLOREZ's Account of the AQUEDUCT of SEGOVIA.

(Taken from his Efpana Sagrada, *Vol. VIII.)*

' SEGOVIA is one of the moft antient cities of SPAIN, not
' fo much as appears by the name, and the mention which
' hiftorians and geographers make of it, as by the remarkable mo-
' nument of the *Aqueduct,* which fhews fuch notable antiquity,
' that it is not eafy to determine its origin precifely. Some afcribe
' it to HERCULES, others to the Emperor TRAJAN, and ftill no
' inconfiderable part of the common people judge it to have been
' built by the DEVIL.

' THIS very variety of opinions is a proof, that we know no-
' thing certain about it. As for afcribing it to HERCULES, we

Bb 2 ' do

' do not difcover any other foundation, than the knowledge, that
' a ftatue of HERCULES was formerly placed in the niche, where
' now is the image of St. SEBASTIAN: no ftrefs ought to be laid
' upon this fact, which only proves, that in the times of paganifm
' the antient Spaniards might dedicate that work to the memory
' of HERCULES.

   ' As to what relates to TRAJAN, it is very difficult to acknow-
' ledge him for the author, becaufe there is no trace left of a Ro-
' man infcription on it, and that in a work of fuch great length,
' and fo well preferved; we knowing, on the other hand, the tafte
' which prevailed in the works of that emperor, viz. to leave his
' name perpetuated upon them. Confequently one called them
' *yerba parietaria* ||. And on the bridge of ALCANTARA in SPAIN,
' confifting of fix arches, they placed divers infcriptions, in which
' his name is repeated in each. Befides, not having any account of
' the Romans being concerned in the aqueduct of SEGOVIA, we
' have no grounds to afcribe it to TRAJAN, or to any other em-
' peror, unlefs it be thought fufficient to produce other works of the
' fame age, which have a fimilar ftile. But they differ either in the
' manner of joining the ftones together; or it will be difficult to
' contradict that which the Romans have faid of thefe, and other
' very antient works, fuch as the Pyramids of ÆGYPT; concern-
' ing which COLMENARES writes, c. i. § 11. of *The hiftory of Se-*
' *govia*, that they very much refembled the fabric of this aqueduct,
' according to the defcriptions which they have given of the work-
' manfhip of them, of the greatnefs of the hewn ftones, and un-
' hewn ftones. COLMENARES too adds no bad remark, that the
' ftile or order of architecture of the Segovian aqueduct is different
' from that ufed by the Romans, fince it is neither of the Doric,
' Ionic, Corinthian, Tufcan, or Compofite orders, but of fome other
' not known; infomuch that we have fome grounds not to ac-
' knowledge it for a Roman work, but of a much older date.

   ' OF this argument drawn from the ftile of the architecture, the
' public has not been able to judge, infomuch as no one has been
' bold enough to engrave it. COLMENARES was deterred by the

|| It fhould be *verba parietaria*; that is, *palabras paredanas*, or *wall-words*.

           ' greatnefs

' greatnefs of the attempt, as he expreffes it in the place I have
' quoted. The celebrated Father MONTFAUCON in the IV.
' Tome, P. ii. Ch. 10. of his *Antiquité expliquée*, complained, that
' he was not able to procure a defign of it : But afterwards in the
' IV. Tome of the *Supplement*, page 102, he fays that M. LE GEN-
' DRE, furgeon to his Catholic Majefty, fent it him, with a defcrip-
' tion of it in Spanifh, of which that father availed himfelf. But
' the *defign* which was fent to Father MONTFAUCON confifted on-
' ly of ten arches, without any meafure or fcale, without the due
' proportion between the arches, omitting the under-cornifhes of
' the pillars, and failing in the proportion of the upper arches with
' the lower, without regulating it to the form of the dye of the
' pedeftal, nor to the lower line, which is not right in more than
' the three central arches : and he adds, in the upper part of the
' pillar, which is in the middle of the greateft height, an head of a
' woman between two flowers, with this infcription at the bottom,
' * CABEZA DE ESTREMADVRA ; which is not fo, becaufe
' upon the canal, through which the water runs, that figure is not
' to be feen.

' WE here give the whole delineation of it with exactnefs, by
' means of Don JUAN SAENZ DE BURUAGA, an ALCALA DE HE-
' NARES Doctor, of the greater college of SAN ILDEFONSO, Ma-
' giftrate of the holy church of SEGOVIA ; of whom I availed my-
' felf, by reafon of the friendfhip we contracted at the univerfity of
' ALCALA, and he took that bufinefs fo much to his own account,
' that in a little time after I had applied to him, he favoured me
' with the utmoft difpatch ; having affociated to himfelf, for this
' end, a perfon very able and knowing, who is architect of that holy
' church, and is called Don DOMINGO GAMONES, whofe name is
' worthy to be perpetuated, for having given us that which no other
' has done, without feeking any other intereft, but that of ferving
' the public : and although we know not the name of the firft ar-
' chitect, we know that of the firft who ever attempted to draw
' this fabric.

' THIS great aqueduct is called a *bridge* vulgarly, its intention
' being contrary to the ufe of fuch like fabrics : for whereas they

* Or, *The Head of Eftremadura.*

' are

' are defigned to give paffage to people over the waters, this is
' to conduct the waters over the people, leaving free paffage below:
' The water comes by means of fome arches of ftone, which fuftain
' a canal formed of the fame ftones in conformity to its paffage.
' That as in all other bridges, people walk upon a pavement laid
' upon the fuperficies of the convex part of the arches; and as in
' thofe the ground and the parapet walls ferve for the cover and
' fecurity of the paffengers: In this, both the one and the other are
' defigned for the courfe only, and the direction of the waters.

' THE motive for fo great an undertaking was, that feeing on
' one hand, that in the fite of the city, nature afforded a foil very
' well difpofed to build a town, and very fuitable to the genius of
' the antient inhabitants: That it had the due elevation which
' they wanted, for the ventilation of the air; and alfo that it was
' able to refift any invafion. They reduced the fite to a great rock,
' or mountain fufficiently fcarped, and able to contain a city not
' very large, but fortified by nature, which raifed the ground above
' fome plains, watered by different ftreams, which flow from the
' *Cumbræ Capitanæ* (the name which PLINY gives to fome bran-
' ches of the IDUBEDA, called to this day *Puerto de la Fon-fria,**
' *y de Guadarrama.)* Towards the north runs the river ERESMA,
' which fprings from fome fountains on the other fide of the faid
' pafs in the mountains, and goes by COCA to fall into the DUERO.

' SOME will have it, that the ERESMA is the *Areva,* of which
' PLINY affirms, that the name came from the region of the *Are-*
' *vaci.* But we have nothing to add to the propofal againft what
' is faid of the *Arevaci* in tom. V. The Marquis of MONDEJAR,
' concerned in fome things very ftrange about SEGOVIA, in the II.
' tome of his *Differtations,* p. 218, thinks, that *Areva* is a little
' river, which falls into the DUERO near the antient *Numantia,*
' called at prefent *Tera.* But that cannot be the cafe, confidering
' that the fpring of the DUERO, and the fame *Numantia* were the
' *Pelendones* of PLINY. And for the fame reafon, the river that

---

* Or, *The Port of Fon-Fria, and of Guadarama.*—This is a pafs in the mountains;
all fuch *Paffes* being called by the Spaniards *Ports.*

' waters

‘ waters *Numantia* muft be of the fame country. Befides which,
‘ it is fo very fhort in its courfe, and fo little known, that it could
‘ not give a name to fo famous a people.

‘ By the plain to the fouth of Segovia there runs another
‘ fhort ftream, called by the peafants *Clamores*, which joins the
‘ Eresma at the Weft point of the city, where the Alçassar
‘ ftands.

‘ Notwithstanding the ftreams which run by the vallies
‘ of the city, the ancients defired, that there fhould be no want
‘ of water to the inhabitants within the walls, neverthelefs that the
‘ earth was not commodious for fountains, on account of its height
‘ and drynefs: With this view, they undertook the giant-like work,
‘ to convey a river within the city, conquering by art the impedi-
‘ ments which nature had oppofed to it, by reafon of the height
‘ and depth of the ground: although the architect plainly fhewed,
‘ that he was mafter of a greater height, if it had been neceffary,
‘ fince he made the water pafs above the walls and roofs of
‘ the houfes.

‘ The fource of this aqueduct is a little river, called Rio Frio,
‘ which rifes at the fkirts of the pafs in the mountains, and is that
‘ which comes to the city, taking from its ftock as much water,
‘ as would fill a duct that would contain a human body: It is re-
‘ ceived in an arch of ftone at the diftance of 500 paces from the
‘ city: and from thence it begins to run in the channel of the
‘ aqueduct, which does not require more elevation than 5¼ bars,
‘ that is, 17 feet. By little and little the height increafes, as it
‘ comes to deeper ground, but without requiring more than one
‘ range of arches, until the water has paffed over 65 arches, where
‘ the arches have a height of 39 feet, clofe to the convent of San
‘ Franciso. There they begin to wind from the eaft to the weft,
‘ requiring two ranges of arches, one arch being put upon the other.
‘ That being the loweft part of the valley which is the little fquare,
‘ now called Azoguejo.

‘ In that part the aqueduct is 102 feet high, the channel en-
‘ tering by the battlements of the walls, with an extreme elevation
‘ from

' from the ground to the top of the arch. The aqueduct goes
' through the middle of the city, from the eaſt to the weſt, with
' an arched duct ſo large, that a man might walk in it : And from
' thence it goes dividing itſelf into the public fountains, and the
' ciſterns of convents and private houſes.

' THIS fabric conſiſts of 161 arches. The materials are hewn
' ſtones of a bluiſh granate, placed one upon the other, without
' any coherence of bitumen, lime, or mortar, which equals the
' joints, becauſe the ſtones unite one with another, faſtening them-
' ſelves in their ſquare form ; ſo that the whole number of the
' ſtones of which this aqueduct conſiſts, might be counted, accord-
' ing to the art and correſpondence with which they are placed.
' Look at them, ſays COLMENARES, and they ſeem to be cemented
' by lead, and that the key-ſtones of the arches were barred by iron,
' as they tell us of the temple of SERAPIS in ALEXANDRIA.
' The pillars are eight feet in front, and eleven broad. It being
' moſt aſtoniſhing, that this fabric ſhould laſt to the end of ſo
' many ages, ſuch as we ſee it, without giving way to the weight
' of the water upon it, or to the rains, the floods, the wars : for
' it not only appears, that nations have revered it, but even time,
' which does not uſe to reſpect other wonders of the world.

' UPON the top of the three pillars of the greateſt height there
' is a baſe common to the three uppermoſt. And in that of the
' middlemoſt there are on each ſide two niches, where were the
' ſtatues of HERCULES, as COLMENARES ſays he found in manu-
' ſcripts, which in his time were above 200 years old, that is be-
' fore the middle of the XVth century, in which then exiſted theſe
' monuments. At preſent they are the images of our Lady of SAN
' SEBASTIAN, becauſe that part belongs to the diſtrict of the pa-
' riſh of that ſaint, and they were placed there March 21, 1520,
' by the care of a citizen, an aſſayer of the mint, as COLMENA-
' RES tells us, in his hiſtory of that year.

' BESIDES this teſtimony, which is the moſt authentic of the an-
' tiquity of the city, there is mention made of it in LUCIUS FLORUS,
' where he is relating the war of SERTORIUS, lib. 3. ch. 22. where
' he ſays, *that the Herculean lieutenants of Sertorius were defeated*
'   ' near

5

‘ *near Segovia*, without adding any more interefting particulars.
‘ *His apud Segoviam oppreffis*, &c. This was about the year 675
‘ of the foundation of ROME, in which POMPEY came againſt
‘ SERTORIUS, following *Grævius's chronology upon Florus*, which
‘ anſwers in our way of reckoning to the 79th year before Chriſt,
‘ taking the vulgar æra for an epoch.

   ‘ PLINY, in telling us who the ſeveral people were, who form-
‘ ed the aſſembly of CLUNIA, ſays, that one were the people of
‘ SEGOVIA among the *Arevaci*. HARDUIN, in the notes to c.
‘ iii. lib. 3. of that author, will not have it to be the SEGOVIA
‘ ſituated between VALLADOLID and MADRID (of which we are
‘ now ſpeaking) but another ſmall town, placed by PTOLEMY in the
‘ ſame ſite with NUMANTIA : *Non ea eſt, quæ inter Valliſoletum &*
‘ *Madritum nobis* Segovia *dicitur : ſed altera ejuſdem nominis urbecula,*
‘ *quæ ſub eâdem fere cæli parte atque ipſa Numantia, eodemque ſitu a*
‘ *Ptolomeo collocatur*. But if one denies this, it would be very
‘ difficult for any one to prove it : for we may juſt as well ſay,
‘ that PLINY means the city of which we are ſpeaking, and not
‘ that deſigned by HARDOUIN, for he owns that to be an *urbecula*.
‘ And it is more natural, that PLINY ſhould mention that which
‘ was the moſt great and famous (in caſe there were two of the
‘ ſame name among the *Arevaci)* and not the leaſt illuſtrious, to-
‘ tally omitting the greateſt.

   ‘ I SAID *in caſe* there were *two in the Arevaci* ; becauſe neither
‘ PLINY, PTOLEMY, or ANTONINE mention more than *one* in
‘ that territory : And as there were no more than one, we ought
‘ not to ſay, that PLINY and PTOLEMY mentioned the leaſt illu-
‘ ſtrious, and omitted the moſt famous mentioned by ANTO-
‘ NINE. It is clear that PTOLEMY places SEGUBIA in a ſite that
‘ does not ſquare with SEGOVIA, about 42 degrees of latitude,
‘ and 13¼ of longitude. But it is as certain, that if you take his ſite
‘ in reference to the direct diſtance, which there is between that
‘ and NUMANTIA, it will be one of the many errors of his tables ;
‘ becauſe they place SEGUBIA and NUMANTIA in 13¼ degrees of
‘ longitude.’

THE

The Alcaçar, or Royal Palace, is the next object here of note; it is plain by the AL in the first syllable of this word, that it is an *Arabic* appellation; for it is the *Arabic* article, which they call *Solar*: And the tradition of the town says, it was a place of residence for some of the *Moorish* princes. I know not what truth there may be in it, but I cannot help attempting an etymology, especially when the occasion seems so fair. Thus Cæsar, Καισαρ, Moorish Cayzar, Alcaçar. The front of this building is about fifty feet long; there are two conic, or sugar loaf-turrets, at each wing; and the façade is adorned with several diminutive turrets in the same taste and style: Above the skilling or span-roof of this first front there rises another skilling roof adorned with turrets in the same style: And between the wings, in the middle rises a lofty square, brick tower, surrounded with small circular turrets ending in a console. Along the front of the first building runs a neat, small open gallery, just under the cornish. The whole of the fabric appears clearly to be in *the old Moorish style*; the governor told me the middle tower was *Roman*, but I should doubt it much; it seems to be of the same age and building with the rest of the fabric; the windows of the same form and taste; and there is a trace of small beads, that girts it, just as in the front and the wings: It is certainly all *Moorish*, and is indeed extremely pretty, and light, and pleases me more than almost any building I ever saw. The whole, except the middle tower, is covered with a blue slate, or shingles, I cannot say which. You go to it from a sort of court; or place, over a small bridge; for there is a deep foss, that surrounds one part of it, and the other sides are defended by steep precipices, as it stands upon a rock. Having passed the bridge you enter a cloyster, where there is a court within, and a fountain. From the cloyster you enter a large room prettily cieled, a sort of servant's hall. After that you come into a state-room, with a rich gilt cieling, carving of stucco upon the walls, and *Dutch* tiling round the room at the bottom. This brings you to a second apartment of much the same taste, but a much richer cieling; then you enter a magnificent room called the *Sala de los Reyes*, or, *The hall of their Kings*; and with reason, for it really is full of Kings. The wooden or waxen images of nineteen Kings of Castile, six of Leon, two

of

of ASTURIAS, and sixteen of OVIEDO, are all placed over your head, about the middle of the wall, round the room, with their Queens, and four counts, or dukes placed under them. Among them is the famous CID, or Don ROD. DIAZ de BIVAR, of whom such wonders have been recorded: CID, in *Arabic*, is *commander*, or general; he lived about 1055, in the reign of FERDINAND of LEON. This room is indeed an odd sight, and if one was to be there late at night, with a single taper, it would afford matter for a warm imagination to be very busy. From thence you pass into a small chapel, where there is a single painting over the altar with this inscription, BARTOLOME CARDUCCIO *Florent.* faciebat, 1600. Beyond this is a small room with odd pieces of sculpture of dogs and hares, and other animals, and pretty carving in Fresco, or Stucco. Round this room, as well as the rest, runs an inscription in very old *Gothic* characters; but I am sure of no moment; for in the next room, where the letters were likewise *Gothic*, but not quite so old fashioned, I could read them with no great difficulty: And they proved to be nothing else, but prayers, and pious sentences: Thus, LAUDAM TE IN SECOLA SE- COLORUM. MAYERDE MEMENTO ME. ORA PRO NOBIS. UDAL AP RHYS has given a very false account of this place: He says there are sixteen rooms hung with fine tapestry, and that there are many pictures, with other circumstances, which have not one word of truth in them.—PHILIP II. in 1590, caused those dates and accounts, which are affixed to the feet of each prince in the *Sala de los Reyes*, to be put up; it is the best chronology they have of them.

HAVING now given some account of this singular fabric; indulge me in a word or two about the age of it. The governor said the rooms we saw were five hundred years old; this is nothing; it would only throw the date of this building as far back as the 13th century, or about 1260. I have seen a grant of ALPHONSO in the year 1160, which mentions this ALCAÇAR. Is it not very strange, that the writer of *the History of* SEGOVIA should take no particular notice of this remarkable structure: He only says, that when in 755 the MOORS attacked SEGOVIA, and took it, the SEGOVIANS put *the* ALCAÇAR, the house

of

of HERCULES, and the tower of St. JUAN in a good posture of defence. · This period of the eighth century seems to me to suit better with the name and appearance of the building, and to place it in a much more *Moorish* age; though it may possibly be still older.   There is one *pointed arch* of a door-way in this build-ing, which is now stopped up; it seems of the same age with the rest; but as it may have been an after-work, as it is not an essen-tial part, what stress is to be laid upon it, I cannot say.   Here are two strange old cannon, or pipes, *canones* they call them.   And the doors of the offices are marked thus: *Bodeca, Postgo*; that is, *the cellar, the passage.*

THIS is the famous *Tower or Castle of* SEGOVIA, so celebrated in Monsieur *Le Sage's Gil Blas*, and other romances; the antient receptacle of state-prisoners: It was here that political QUIXOTE the duke of RIPPERDA was confined; and it was from hence he escaped.   There is another large prison in the middle of the city, but that is only for the reception of common felons, and is a mo-dern building. The very same man that was governor, when RIP-PERDA was confined there, is still alive, and the present governor: By his account it was the maid, not the daughter, that gave the duke his liberty; for his daughter is married to an ANDALUSIAN gentleman, and lives there: He says, that the room in which RIPPERDA was confined had but one door to it, and had two centinels placed at it; at the door of the next room two centinels more; and without the guard du corps. How he escaped, he says he cannot guess; but that the Duke's servant said his master was very ill; that another servant took his master's place in bed, and counterfeited a sick person; that he the governor knew nothing of his escape, *till nine days after he was gone*, and then they dis-covered the fraud.   It is plain from all this relation, that the court had a mind to let RIPPERDA escape; that the governor had or-ders to connive at it; though the means and contrivance were probably the duke's invention: that the court did not care for the expence of keeping him in prison, and had no inclination to take away his life.   When he found, that orders were given for seizing him in the year 1726, he fled to the house of Mr. STAN-HOPE, the then *English* ambassador. His lordship was at that
time

time not at home ; and it is inconceivable what difficulty he had at his return, to get RIPPERDA out of the houſe : He was at laſt taken out by force by the King of SPAIN's order. This, how-ever, trifling as it was, occaſioned a miſunderſtanding between the courts of SPAIN and GREAT BRITAIN. Mr. STANHOPE cer-tainly did right; he withdrew from MADRID, to ſhew his reſent-ment, and to aſſert the juſt rights and privileges of his CHARAC-TER: for otherwiſe no prudent ambaſſador would have riſked the embroiling himſelf with his court for the ſake of protecting ſuch a ſcoundrel. He was originally an envoy from the ſtates of HOL-LAND, afterwards miniſter to the court of SPAIN, being a crea-ture of Cardinal ALBERONI's, and was ſent to negotiate the fa-mous VIENNA treaty. To conclude, he betrayed his truſt, made the grand tour of all religions; fled from one court, could obtain protection from no other, could find no aſylum in EUROPE : And after having been ſucceſſively Proteſtant, Papiſt, Pagan, Jew, Turk, Infidel, and Heretic, weary of apoſtacies, he died at laſt a Mahometan among the ſtates of BARBARY.

THE next object of note here is the CATHEDRAL, which is indeed a noble ſtructure; it is of the *Gothic* ſtyle of architec-ture, and rather of the beſt kind of it; there are two quires, as it were ſurrounded by a moſt ample *Baſilica*, which is lined on the wall-ſide with a vaſt variety of fine altars, and rich ſhrines : The painted glaſs is good, and gives the dim, religious light. They told me it was built 1525, ſee *The Hiſt. of Segovia*, ch. 39. The ſacriſty is a fine room, and contains ſome pictures. The ar-ches of this building are all round. There is an old cloyſter ad-joining to the cathedral, where there is a monument of a biſhop of this ſee, and his epitaph in good Latin, well-cut. There are ſome hundreds of veſtments hung up here; the badges of ſo many unhappy *Jews*, who had the misfortune to be burnt, be-cauſe they did not believe all that the inquiſitor did: This tribunal, or the Holy Office as they call it, was at SEGOVIA at that time, but has been ſince removed. There are too in this cloyſter, the remains of ſad ſuperſtitious paintings on the wall. In the chap-ter-room is a fine picture of a MADONNA and BAMBINO, by SPAGNOLET; alſo the ſtory of AURÉLIAN and ZENOBIA, in
good

good tapeſtry. In the library is a MS. verſion of the PENTA-
TEUCH, from the *Hebrew, Chaldee,* and *Greek* into Latin, dated
1600. It is intitled *Verſio Pentateuchi per Ciruelum Darocenſem.*

THERE is a grant of Queen URRACA's in this cathedral in 1661,
which mentions the *Alcazar,* and the *Pons Caſtellanus,* or bridge
of the *Alcazar.* It concludes thus—" *Whoſoever ſhall violate this*
" *grant, let them be ever baniſhed from God's threſhold, and be eter-*
" *nally tormented with* DATHAM *and* ABIRAM, *whom the earth*
" *ſwallowed, be damned with the traitor* JUDAS, *and pay a thouſand*
" *pounds of unallayed gold* (auri obryzi) *to the biſhop.*"

THERE are ſeveral fine churches here beſides the cathedral;
that of ST. MILANO is very old; built by GONZALO FELIZ in
923. See *Hiſtory of Segovia,* p. 83. I found an inſcription on the
wall: L : DCCC : AI : XXX : X : HQI. Я . ↓ : Ꮒ . Q . AR.
ROI : S. K. Ꮯ . 2. There is another inſcription on the other wall,
on which there was MIL. I. CCC. XL. I. which I read 1341.
The arches of this church are all round and large; the columns
large and lofty, with carved capitals, containing many figures both
of men and animals. Some with beautiful foliage; the ſhafts were
round and plain ; and placed upon ſquare baſes, extremely large:
At the entrance is a ſort of *Arcade* with beautiful, ſmall columns
of black marble, and the pillars joined one to another, with a
ſort of ſpiral or ſerpentine line, what the heralds, I think, call
wavy.

THE church of ST. SEBASTIAN is a good room, not very
large, the roof modern, built in 1699. There is a ſmall nave ad-
joining, ſeparated by three elliptical arches, the moſt ugly, diſpro-
portioned things you can imagine. What date they are of I know
not; but certainly they are *Gothic.* There are two pillars remaining at the portal, as old as the *Mooriſh* times.

THE church of ST. FRANCIS is a fine large room, with a moſt
beautiful organ ; large and lofty arches, moſt of them round,
but one or two *pointed;* the roof modern. On the left-hand
is a ſmall chapel with the oldeſt *Gothic,* or *Saxon* carved work ;

4   the

the roof of it contains large beads, or mouldings: they projected 7 or 8 inches from the roof, and the arch over the door-way was composed of beads or tracery of stone in the same massy taste.

THE church of ST. MARTINI is a very old fabric, built before 1140. See *Hist. of Segovia.* At the west-end of it is the most lofty, round *Moorish* arch I ever saw, with a multitude of decreasing mouldings one within another; there is a pretty large arcade with very neat small columns of black marble.

THE church of ST. AUGUSTIN is a modern building, but a fine room, the arches round; some few good pictures, and a handsome sacristy.

THE church of ST. DOMINIC is a noble *Gothic* structure; built about 1406; beneath the cornish under the roof of the outside, all round the church, are cut in stone these words, in old characters, of what age I know not, but in this form **T**. I shall write it for the sake of dispatch in the common characters TANTO·MONTA. The meaning of which is—When by the marriage of FERDINAND and ISABELLA the kingdoms were united, they made this old *Spanish* proverb---*Tanto monta, monta tanto Isabella como Fernando*---That is to say, *Isabel is as good as Ferdinand, and Ferdinand as Isabel.* The only remark I shall make is, that hence comes our *English* word *tantamount.* The inside is now modernized, the arches are round, a little more than 300 years old.

THE church of ST. JOHN THE BAPTIST is said here to be the *oldest* in the city, built in 923. See *Hist. of Seg.* p. 83. It consists of three naves, all large round arches of the oldest *Gothic*; and may be considered as one long room. Here is the tomb of the knights, who took MADRID in 932; and here the archives of the city are kept in a handsome chest; the date of which is 1686. The chief knight was FERNAN GARCIA *de la* TORRE; his tomb still remains in this church, which was formerly called from thence *the church of the knights.* The statues of both these knights are placed over a gate in MADRID, the print of which is in the history
tory

tory of SEGOVIA. It is a pretty church, as well as a very old one; there are feveral pictures, but I believe none valuable; fome good *Spanifh* carving. Since the date of the taking MADRID by the knights, buried here, is 932; confequently *the pointed arch* at the weft-end of this church; the odd cornifh compofed of heads of animals; the capitals of the pillars carved with animal, and human figures; and the fmall, long, narrow lights, or windows, of this church, are all older than the tenth century: And confequently the *pointed arch* was ufed in this country, long before we had it in ENGLAND, which was not till 1216.

THE little church of ST. PAUL contains fome remains of an extreme old building on the outfide, but is quite modern within. Over an old *pointed arch* I found this date, the infcription of a tomb I. μ. CCC. LXXII. that is, 1372; for the *Spaniards* always write their cypher to exprefs *a thoufand* in that way, why I know not. At the great altar is a picture of St. PAUL falling from his horfe in his way to DAMASCUS. No traces of any other old arch here, but the roof is vaulted.

A CHURCH near the PLAÇA MAYOR, date found in it 1569. The *Hift. of Segovia* mentions the churches of St. COLOMA and St. MEMES, or St. LUCIA, built in 923; but I know nothing of them. It is remarkable that there are more churches, convents, and parifhes here, than at MADRID.

THE town, upon the whole, has a ftrange appearance; the buildings look wild, and odd, raifed fometimes upon the uneven and craggy parts of the rock without levelling it. Here are all forts and ftyles of architecture; *Roman, Gothic, Moorifh, Saxon,* and *Spanifh.*

THE PLAÇA MAYOR is a very tolerable, irregular fquare; but the buildings round it are in the old *Spanifh* ftyle, and look miferably. Though wood here is very dear, and fcarce, and cracks with the force of the fun; yet the fronts of moft of them are all wood, all fir, and fuch miferable, thin, ruinous, paper-buildings, you would be furprized at.

THE

THE town-houſe is a good modern building. The *Mint* here, or *Ingenium,* as they call it, was founded by PHILIP II. in 1583.

SEGOVIA has produced ſome writers of note ; among theſe the names of VILLALPANDO, SEPULVEDA, BONAVENTURA, and COVARRUVIAS are the moſt eminent.

THERE is a large *Cloth-Manufacture* here ; they ſold, in the year 1759, 7,400 pieces of cloth of 30, 60, and 80 bars in length. They have likewiſe a *Linen* and a *Paper* manufacture. The *Blankets* of this city are perhaps the fineſt in the world : But they are dear.

THE FOLLOWING IS

An EPISTLE ſrom Don GREGORIO MAYANS,

Containing his Sentiments about the AQUEDUCT.

QUIDQUID ego ad te ſcripſero, a benevolentiſſimo animo pro-ficiſci exiſtimare debes. Ego vero poſteaquam tuum conſi-lium aperuiſti mihi explicatius, laudo illud, & in nobiliſſimo argu-mento vellete exercere ingenii tui facultates, vehementer probo.

LIBENTER legi epigramma tuum de Aquæductu Segovienſi, ad Henricum Florezium. Et, ſi meam ſententiam ſcire cupis, ab illo ego valde diſſentio. Incipit *Tractatum vigeſimum ſecundum,* aiens, *Segoviam eſſe unam ex antiquiſſimis Hiſpaniæ urbibus ; non ob id ſolum quod nomen ejus indicat, & commemorationes hiſtoricorum, & geo-graphorum, verum etiam ob inſigne monumentum Aquæductus, qui an-tiquitatem adeo notabilem deſignat, ut non facile ſit ejus originem aſſerere.* Quibus verbis falſa veris permiſcentur, rerum ideis confuſis, quas breviter diſtinguam.

D d   IN

In eo quod ait de nominis indicio, fubobfcure alludit ad ridicu-
lam Ruderici Ximenii, Archiepifcopi Toletani, notationem, qui
Lib. I. *cap* 7. de Hifpano loquens, ita fcripfit. *Civitatem juxta*
jugum Dorii ædificavit in loco fubjecto promontorio, quod Cobia dicitur,
& quia fecus Cobiam fita, Secobia nuncupatur : quæ nominis notatio
fupponit in Hifpania Latinæ. linguæ ufum, antequam aliquis Romanus in eam adveniffet; immo antequam effet ipfa lingua. Segoviæ mentio apud hiftoricos & geographos, adeo recens eft, ut
ex illorum teftimoniis ejus antiquitas deduci nequeat. Antiquiora
enim hiftoricorum teftimonia funt A. Hirtii, & L. Flori, quorum
hic *Lib.* II. *cap.* 22. Segoviæ, ut puto, *Arevacorum,* meminit
agens de bello Sertoriano: ille libro *De bello Alexandrino,* *cap.* 57.
mentionem fecit Segoviæ fitæ ad Silicenfe flumen. Ex geographis
autem nemo antiquior Ptolemæo Segoviæ meminit. Eum vide *Lib.*
II. *cap.* 6. Quod fi mentionem apud nummos addere vis, cum poft
extinctum Caligulam nulli nummi imperiales in Hifpaniarum co-
loniis & municipiis percuffi fuerint, ut rei nummariæ peritiffimus
Emmanuel Martinus Vaillantium fecutus docuit, *Epift.* *Lib.* III.
epift 11. nulla probatio antiquitatis deduci poteft, nifi ex nummo
illo fingulari, quem Rudericus Carus affirmavit fe poffidere, *Antiq.*
Hifpal. Lib. III. *cap.* 50. & præterea nummus ille ad Segoviam
Arevacorum non pertinet : utpote in eo pons defignatur, non aquæductus: pons fcilicet ad tranfeundum Silicenfe flumen, quod eft
in Bætica, etfi quale fit, ignoretur. Fortius igitur antiquitatis urbis Segoviæ argumentum ab aquæductus fabrica vult ducere Florezius, nulla vero ratione allegata: nam in eo quod *art.* 3. ejufdem capitis ait, architecturam non effe Romanam, adverfarios habet oculatos teftes anonymum auctorem Dialogi Linguarum; quem
ego edidi in *Originibus linguæ Hifpanicæ,* *Tom.* II. *pag.* 165, atque
clariffimos viros Laurentium Padillam in *Antiquit. Hifpan. cap.* 3.
& Marchionem Mondexarenfem, *Differtat. Ecclefiaft. Tomo* I. *diff.*
2. *cap.* 3. §. 7. & in *Noticiis Genealogicis Gentis Segoviæ,* editis nomine Johannis Roman & Cardenas, *cap.* 4. *pag.* 20.

VIDEAMUS tamen inter quas opiniones fluctuet Florezius. Ejus
verba de aquæductu loquentis, funt hæc : *Aliqui* (ejus originem)
referunt ad Herculem; alii ad Imperatorem Trajanum; & non exigua
vulgi pars judicat fuiffe Diaboli fabricam. Et continuo fubjungit, *ip-*
fam

fam opinionum varietatem probare, nihil esse certum. Si nihil igitur
certum est, cur Segoviæ antiquitatem ab aquæductus fabrica colligit,
atque hanc probationem cæteris omnibus anteponit ?

OPINIO vulgi asserentis diabolum fuisse structorem aquæductus, omnino despicienda est. Prior illa tribuens Herculi illud
opus, ridicula: ejusque originem detexit Didacus Colmenares in
Historia Segoviæ, cap. 1, §. 2. subjunxitque multos alios hi-
storicos, quos ibi recenset, secutos fuisse Rudericum Ximenium,
qui *Lib.* I. *cap.* 7, scripsit, Hispanum ab Hercule Hispaniæ præfectum aquæductum illum construxisse. Quæ opinio æque falsa
est ac præcedens. Verum hoc obiter noto, nomen hoc, *Hispanum*, idem esse atque *Hispalum :* nam *n* facile convertitur in *l*. Sic
Messalæ dicti a Messana devicta, & qui in Cornelia gente dicuntur
Hispali, syllaba penultima producta, Hispani dicti a Diodoro Sicu-
lo in *Excerptis*, sicut etiam ab Appiano in Libyco, adnotante Hen-
rico Valesio, *pag.* 59. Re vera autem Hispanus fuit amnis, ut
egregie probatur eleganti Trogi Pompeii testimonio, quod apud
Justinum legitur, *Lib.* XLIV. *cap.* 1. sic se habens : *Hanc veteres
ab Hibero amne primum Hiberiam, postea ad Hispano Hispaniam cog-
nominaverunt*, quod testimonium præ oculis habebat B. Isidorus,
cum *Etymol. Lib.* IX. *cap.* 2. dixit : *Hispani ab Hibero amne primum Hiberi, postea ab Hispalo Hispani cognominati sunt.* Ex quibus
constat Hispanum amnem eundem esse ac Hispalum, a quo urbs
Hispal nomen accepit, aut vice versa.

SED primum illud verisimilius est, cum flumina soleant esse antiquiora urbibus juxta ea sitis. Novum autem non est amnium
nomina confictis regibus applicari solere, uti factum videmus in
Præfatione assuta B. Isidori *Chronico Mundi, in Hispania illustrata,
Tomo* IV. *pag.* 41. Variis igitur Bætis nominibus hoc adjunge cæteris illustrius, quia & urbi celeberrimæ, & universæ Hispaniæ nomen dedit.

Ex tribus igitur opinionibus a Florezio commemoratis, una super-
est, quæ in examen adduci debet, an aquæductus scilicet ab Imperatore
Trajano ædificari jussus sit, aut ejus tempore constructus, quod ad
ejus antiquitatem comprobandam idem est. Quæ opinio dignissima

est,

eft, ut in eam inquiramus, quoniam pro fe habet infcriptionem : quæ fi vera fit, lis eft finita ; fin conficta, fictio ejus probari debet, ne aliud afferentibus obftet. Verum Florezius, qui eodem *Tract.* XXII. *cap.* 1. *num.* 13. allegavit nonnullas infcriptiones, fciens prudenfque infcriptionem, de qua loquor, filentio præteriit, ne fi eam probaret, opinionem immodicæ antiquitatis, quam ipfe tenet, abjicere cogeretur; aut, fi improbaret, rationes fictionis reddere deberet, quas hiftorici, præcedentes eum, omiferunt. Videamus autem quid fentiendum fit. Valdefius apud auctorem *Dialogi de Linguis* ait, in Segovienfi aquæductu fuo tempore fupereffe nonnullas literas, ex quibus conftabat Romanos illum ftruxiffe. Paullo poftea nullam infcriptionem invenire potuit clarus vir Laurentius Padilla, ut ipfe memorat in *Antiquit. Hifpan.* fol. 13. *pag.* 2. Ambrofius Morales, *Lib.* IX. *cap.* 22. *fol.* 273. *pag.* 2. confirmat in fuperiore parte illius ædificii fuo tempore fupereffe indicia litterarum, nullas vero extare. Refert autem dictitari fuiffe lapidem infcriptum hoc modo :

    1.

        LARTIUS. LICI
        NIVS. CVM. GV
        BERNASSET. HIS
        PANIAM. HVNC
        AQVAEDVCTVM
        IVSSIT. AEDIFI
        CARI.

Defcripfit hunc titulum Occo, *pag.* 29. *n.* 5. & ex eo, ut folet, licet e Morali dicat, Gruterus, *pag.* 180. *n.* 4. Subjungit autem Morales, *neminem memoria tenere, fe vidiffe illas litteras, neque audiviffe fuiffe. Et ego* (inquit) *pro certo habeo, titulum, qui ibi fuit, non fuiffe eum, quem hic pofui : nam neque ftilum, neque ullum faporem habet infcriptionis Romanæ. Alii dicunt, litteras, quæ ibi fuerunt, indicaffe ædificium illud factum fuiffe impenfa multorum populorum, inter quos nominabantur Carpetani, & Vaccæi. Hoc fictio eft, & valde inconfiderata; nam cum effet ædificium in utilitatem fingularem unius urbis, non debebant contribuere alii populi, uti faciebant in pontibus ad tranfeundos amnes, qui pontes toti provinciæ erant utilet.* Huc ufque Morales, judiciofe, uti folet.

5   QUOD

Quod vero attinet ad infcriptionem, ea proculdubio conficta
eft. Nam, fi vera effet, Lartius Licinius praenomen fuum non omififfet. Et cum *Prætor* primum tefte Plinio, *Lib.* XIX. *cap.* 2.
ac deinde *Legatus*, in quo munere obiit, fuerit, ut idem refert,
Lib. 31. *cap.* 2. nullo modo omififfet munus, quo ipfe funge-
batur, fi vivens aquæductum ædificari juffiffet : & fi ex ejus tefta-
mento factus fuiffet, Plinius, qui fcripfit poft ejus mortem proculdubio id commemoraffet : Plinius, inquam, *fenior*, qui poft Lar-
tii Licinii mortem fcripfit : de quo duas res memorabiles refert,
nimirum, *Lib.* XIX. *cap.* hanc. *Lartio Licinio, prætore viro, jura
reddenti in Hifpania Carthagine, paucis hinc annis fcimus accidiffe, ut
mordenti tuber, undeprehenfus intus denarius primos dentes inflecteret :*
alteram *Lib.* XXXI. *cap.* 2. quæ inter varias obfervationes referri
debet. *In Cantabria* (inquit) *fontes Tamaraci in augurio habentur.
Tres funt, octonis pedibus diftantes. In unum alveum coëunt vafto
amne. Singulis ficcantur duo decies diebus aliquando vicies, citra fuf-
picionem ullam aquæ, cum fit vicinus illis fons fine intermiffione largus.
Mirum eft, non profluere eos aufpicari volentibus, ficut proxime Lartio
Licinio legato poft præturam poft feptem dies accidit.* Quis igitur du-
bitabit, Plinium, qui *Lib.* III. *cap.* 2. mentionem fecit Segoviæ,
nullo modo filentio præteriturum adeo magnificum opus amici fui,
qui tanti faciebat, fua electa, ut de iis loquens Plinius junior, *Lib.*
III. *epift.* 5. ita fcripferit. *Referebat ipfe* (Plinius fenior) *potuiffe
fe, cum procuraret in Hifpania, vendere hos commentarios Lartio Licinio, quadringentis millibus nummum: & tunc aliquanto pauciores
erant.* Præterea locutio illa, CVM GVBERNASSET HISPANIAM,
infolens eft, & inaudita in hujufmodi titulis: & minime conveni-
ens prætori aut legato : & multo minus ei, qui uti admonui, in
ipfo legationis tempore obiit. Ex falfa igitur infcriptione nullum
argumentum defumi poteft.

Nunc vellem fcire, quo vultu legeris, quod ipfe Florezius fentit, *num.* 3. *difficile fore impugnare dicentem Romanos architecturam
didiciffe ab hujufmodi operibus.* Nimirum fupponit, aquæductus architecturam antiquiorem effe Romana. Si hoc verum effet, qua
fronte Vitruvius, C. Cæfaris & Augufti architectus, *Lib.* II. *cap.* 1.
ita fcripfit. *Ad hunc diem nationibus exteris ex his rebus ædificia
conftituuntur, ut in Gallia, Hifpania, Lufitania, Aquitania, fcandu-
lis robufteis, aut ftramentis.* Plinius, *Lib.* XXXV. *cap.* 14. refe-
rens

rens Hifpanorum ædificia, fic ait; *Quid! non in Africa, Hifpania-*
que ex terra parietes, quos appellant formaceos, (quoniam in forma cir-
cumdatis utrinque duabus tabulis, inferciuntur verius, quàm inftruun-
tur,) **ævis durant, incorrupti imbribus, ventis, ignibus, omnique ce-*
mento firmiores? Specta etiam nunc fpeculas Hannibalis Hifpania,
terrenafque turres, jugis montium impofitas. Adde B. Ifidorum, *Lib.*
XV. *cap.* 9. Plinii verba defcribentem, & Palladium, *Lib.* I. *cap.*
34. Vides quomodo ædificaretur in Hifpania, Pœnis dominanti-
bus. Vidifti jam & oculis tuis confirmafti, aquæductus Segovien-
fis architecturam effe Romanam. Ergo cum videatur non fuiffe
Plinii hiftoria antiquior, non multo pofteriorem ea fuiffe creden-
dum eft. Fulcit hanc conjecturam, Plinium, & fcriptores eo anti-
quiores, non meminiffe Segoviæ, ut urbis ampliffimæ. Oportet
autem magnam urbem fuiffe, quæ fumptus fufficeret ad ædifican-
dum aquæductum longiffimum & fumtuofiffimum in fuorum civium
ufum, ita firmum atque magnificum, ut duratione, integritate, atque magnificentia vincat omnia antiquitatis monumenta, quæ hodie fuperfunt, infervitque ufui, cui deftinatus fuit: quod permi-
rum eft.

Si verò a me fcire cupis, quid exiftimem de ipfius urbis antiqui-
tate, ego ita judico. Antiquæ civitates, quæ originem fuam non
debent Romanis, ut Emerita Augufta: ne que Græcis, ut Rhoda,
Emporiæ, Arthemifium aut Dianium, Alone (hodie *Guardamar)*;
neque Pœnis, ut Carthago Nova; neque Phœnicibus, ut Cartalias,
Cartima, Carteja, Gaddir; eam debent prifcis Hifpanis, inter quas
Segovia numerari debet: nam exteri, qui ante Romanos in Hif-
paniam venerunt, negotiatores erant, ideoque colonias fuas fta-
biliebant in ora maritima, a qua longe diftat Segovia, quæ cum inter Arevacorum urbes nominetur a Plinio & aliis, inter Hifpanas an-
tiquiores civitates adnumerari debet. Cupio ut judicio tuo meam
fententiam confirmes, aut meliora me doceas. Deus Optimus Maximus Tibi propitius fit, ut enixe oro.

OLIVÆ, *quinto Idus Novembres, Anno* MDCCLXI.

---

* As odd as this paffage of PLINY may appear to the Reader, it is right: and
he defcribes their manner of building in SPAIN to this very day:—they place two
planks on each fide, and then throw in their mortar and bricks all together, which
the fun afterwards hardens to a wall.

LETTER

LETTER XI.

Some Account of the Antiquities at CORDUBA, SE-
VILLE, CADIZ, GRANADA, SAGUNTUM, TAR-
RAGONA, and BARCELONA.

THE city of CORDUBA is finely fituated on the banks of
the GUADALQUIVIR, in a wide plain. The ftreets are narrow, not unlike thofe of TOLEDO. The MOSQUE is a large,
fquare building, nineteen naves running from north to fouth,
feparated by fmall beautiful columns of black marble, jafper, ala-
bafter &c. fome with fine Corinthian capitals, taken out of the
old temple of JANUS AUGUSTUS, as appears by the following *Infcription*, on a pillar of green marble, which in MARIANA's time
ftood in the Francifcan convent there.

IMP. CAESAR. DIVI.
F. AVGUSTVS. COS.
VIII. TRIB. POTEST.
XXI. PONT. MAX. A.
BAETE. ET. IANO.
AVGVSTO. AD.
OCEANVM.
CXXI.
CONSTANTIAE.
AETERNITATI
QVE. AVGVST.

(Vide Marianam, *L.* III. *C.* xxiv. *P.* 129.*)*

Thi_s

This muſt have been a noble Roman road, for it reached from SALAMANCA to CADIZ, paſſing through MERIDA and SEVILLE, to the diſtance of above three hundred miles. The latter part of it, from CORDUBA through EZIJA to the ſea, was finiſhed in the eleventh conſulate of AUGUSTUS, as appears by another *in-ſcription*, relating to the ſame road, which I ſhall now give you. See MARIANA, p. 49. UDAL AP RHYS, p. 122.

IMP. CAES. DIVI. F. AVGVSTVS. PONT.
MAX.
COS. XI. TRIBVNIC. POTEST. X.
IMP. VIII.
ORBE. MARI. ET. TERRA. PACATO.
TEMPLO.
IANI. CLVSO. ET. REP. P. R. OPTIMIS.
LEGIBVS.
ET. SANCTISSIMIS. INSTITVTIS.
REFORMATA.
VIAM. SVPERIOREM. COS. TEMPORE.
INCHOATAM.
ET. MULTIS. LOCIS. INTERMISSAM. PRO.
DIGNITATE.
IMPERII. P. R. LATIOREM. LONGIOREM
QVE.
GADEIS. USQ. PERDUXIT.

This road was afterwards repaired by the Emperor HADRIAN, as is plain from a third *inſcription* found in its neighbourhood.

IMP. CAESAR.
DIVI. TRAIANI. PAR-
THICI. F. DIVI. NER.
VAE. NEPOS. TRAIA-
NUS. HADRIANVS.
AUG. PONTIF. MAX.
TRIB. POT. V. COS.
III. RESTITVIT.

But to return to the MOSQUE; the columns in the church would have a beautiful effect, if they were not interrupted with croſs-walls,

walls, altars, and the choir, and the prefbytery, which is built in the middle. The arches round and re-entering; the coving and roof modern. The re-entering arch was probably firft taken from the *crefcent*, or *Mahometan-device*.

THERE are many Roman infcriptions at CORDUBA, in the pof-feffion of a private perfon; chiefly *fepulchral*, but no names of note in them; tho' there are fome of families, that had received their freedom. The whole will be foon fully explained by PA-DRE RUANO, a Jefuit, who intends publifhing the antiquities of this church and city. From CORDUBA the road leads you to the city of SEVILLE.

SEVILLE ftands in an immenfe plain, on the GUADALQUIVIR, having a bridge of boats acrofs the river; it is a city of great ex-tent, and I am not fure whether it does not contain as many in-habitants as MADRID. The ftreets are worfe than thofe of TO-LEDO, but the houfes are clean, built round a fquare-court, with green *lattices*, and fhaded from the fun by a *canvafs* on the top.

THE *cathedral* of SEVILLE is an extreme fine *Gothic* ftructure, raifed on noble *pointed* arches, and adorned with good painted glafs-windows. It confifts of *five naves*, but the whole is fpoilt by the fcreen of the choir, which intercepts your view to a magnificent altar, and a miraculous virgin at the eaft end. Be-fore that altar is a *farcophagus* of filver, within which lies the body of FERNANDO SANTO. There is much plate belonging to this church; one whole altar and frontifpiece of plate, and a moft beautiful filver *cuftodia*. They have a pleafing oval room for a *chapter-houfe*; befides there is a *tower* about 44 feet fquare, and upwards of 130 feet high, built by the Moors in the year 1000, with turrets, and a cupola added by the Chriftians, which makes it altogether about 300 feet to the top of the image upon the cupola. The afcent of the tower is fo eafy, that there are no fteps, and an horfe might eafily afcend to the top. In the convents are many capital *pictures* by MURILLO. In a convent of *Jeromites*, upon the river, is a glorious ftatue of *St. Jerom*, in clay; and from the turrets one has a lovely profpect of the plain,

E e   the

the river, and the city. SEVILLE is watered by a *Roman aque-duct*, extending from CARMONA to the city, the diftance of twenty Englifh miles. There are two fine, large *Corinthian pillars,* taken from a temple of DIANA, on which they have placed the ftatues of JULIUS CÆSAR and HERCULES. In the houfe of the Duke of MEDINA CÆLI, are fome *Roman* pillars, ftatues, and infcriptions. The walls of SEVILLE are all *Roman.*

AT CADIZ there are fome fine pictures of MURILLO, particularly an altar-piece, from whence he fell, and loft his life. There are great *Roman* remains and *infcriptions* in the high church, and bits of columns every where ferving as threfhholds and pofts. In the corner of one houfe they have ftuck into the wall, the remains of a confular toga, and have added to it an head, painted red and white, and a green laurel crown. In one convent there is a *farcophagus*, with curious marble bas-reliefs : it is now a ciftern, and the good fathers have ftruck two brafs-cocks into the bellies of two water-nymphs, who are henceforward 'condemned to a perpetual diabetes. They difcovered lately a beautiful column, which to prevent trouble and expence, they buried carefully again. The place is plainly a mount, made up of ruins, fo that they can hardly ftir the ground, but the rub-bifh turns up fomething curious.

THERE are fome *Roman infcriptions* at MEDINA SIDONIA ; but you would be moft delighted with the city of GRANADA : it ftands at the foot of a moft noble ridge of barren mountains and rocks, which ftretch round on each fide, in fuch a manner as to embrace a lovely plain, which is varied with plantations, gardens, and villages : had it but a river, like the GUADALQUIVIR, nothing could exceed it, unlefs it were an Englifh profpect of the THAMES from CLIFFDEN, or the TRENT from CLIFTON.

THE AL-HAMBRA, at GRANADA, is built on a high hill, which overlooks the city and the valley, containing many grand apartments, all in the MOORISH ftyle, with alcoves, domes, fountains, *Arabic infcriptions,* &c. &c. befides which there is a part built by CHARLES V. but not finifhed. The front is hand-

2 . fome

fome for this country, and the apartments are built round a very beautiful, circular court, with 32 fine marble columns below, and as many in a gallery above. Not far from it, there is a delicious garden of the MOORISH KINGS, called the GNIHALA-RIFFEE, with all kinds of trees, flourifhing upon a fteep hanging rock, and as much water as fupplies numberlefs *jette-d'eaux's*, and fountains. The rides round the city are charming.

THERE is at SAGUNTUM a fquare teffelated *pavement*, with Bacchus upon a tyger in the middle; a border on the fides, and flowers iffuing in fcrolls from the four corners. There are alfo the almoft entire remains of a *Roman amphitheatre*, built under the caftle, upon the fide of a rocky mountain, and commanding a view of a moft fertile country, bounded by the fea.—This *theatre*, together with fome *infcriptions*, are defcribed in MARTI, *the dean of Alicant's* epiftles, lately publifhed in 4to. by Mr. WESSELING, and, if I miftake not, the building is fuppofed to have contained 14,000 people. It is certainly a moft noble fpecimen.

AT TARRAGONA there are a multitude of *Roman infcriptions*, moft of them to be found in *the Annals of Catalonia*. Not far from thence, in the road to BARCELONA, you pafs under a very handfome *triumphal arch*, erected by the family of the LICINII, adorned with fluted Corinthian pillars, and a pediment, with dentiles, like the Ionic order. The *infcription* on the frieze, on one fide, is quite effaced; on the other the letters are more vifible, and contain the following :—EX TESTAMENTO L. LICINII. On the other fide was F. SERG. SVRAE CONSECRATVM. (See Anto. Auguft. dialog. IV. p. 142.—a dos Leguas de Tarragona, &c. &c.)

A LITTLE way on one fide the road, fomewhat farther on, is the TORRE DE LOS SCIPIONES, or more properly, *the tomb of the Scipios:* being the bafe of an obelifk, or pyramid, erected to their memory, with a figure on each fide in the Roman habit; thefe are by fome judged to exprefs the two SCIPIOS, by others two weeping flaves.

IN BARCELONA there is hardly any thing curious, except an old *mezzo-relcivo* of a lion hunting, with different figures, men, horfes, dogs, &c. This is now converted into a ciftern, and ftands in the court of one of the canons. Upon a wall by it are two beautiful heads in *profile*, very well preferved; one reprefenting JULIUS CÆSAR with the laurel crown; the other with an ornamented helmet. There are fome few *family infcriptions*. The city is large, but the ftreets are dark and narrow, with as much induftry in them, as if the people were not Spaniards. The fortifications, tho' expenfive, are injudicious.

I CANNOT conclude this account without prefenting my reader, now I am upon the fubject of *Roman antiquities* remaining in SPAIN, with the moft remarkable genuine *Roman infcription* written in *verfe*, and ftill to be feen in a temple near the bridge of ALCANTARA in ESTREMADURA: the architect LACER, who built both the bridge and the temple, was a good *poet*, as well as builder, tho' his affurance in both arts is fcarce to be equalled.——

>Imp. Nervae Trajano Cæfari
>   Augufto, Germanico, Dacico facrum.
>
>Templum in rupe Tagi Superis et Cæfare plenum,
>   Ars ubi materiâ vincitur ipfa fuâ;
>Quis, quali dederit voto, fortaffe requiret
>   Cunque viatorum, quos nova fama juvat;
>Pontem perpetui manfurum in fæcula mundi
>   Fecit divinâ nobilis arte LACER;
>Ingentem vaftâ pontem qui mole peregit,
>   Sacra litaturo fecit honore LACER;
>Qui pontem fecit *Lacer*, et nova templa dicavit,
>   Scilicet et Superis munera fola libant;
>Idem Romuleis templum cum Cæfare Divis
>   Conftituit: Felix utraque caufa facri.
>
>   C. Julius Lacer H. S. F. et
>   Dedicavit amico Curio Luconi
>   Igæditano.

See Bleau's Atlas, and Mr. Ap-Rice, p. 116.

I

LETTER

LETTER XII.

A LIST of the LAND FORCES of His Most CATHOLIC MAJESTY, CHARLES III. King of SPAIN, in the year 1760.

Regiments of Infantry.	Years.	Uniform.	Bn.	Men.
Spaniards.				
The Spanish Guards	1703	Blue and Red	6	3180
The Walloon Guards	1703	Blue and Red	6	3180
The Queen's Regiment	1735	Blue and Red	2	1166
The Regiment of Castile		White and Yellow	2	1166
of Lombardy	1537	White and Red	2	1166
of Galicia	1537	White and Red	2	1166
of Savoy	1537	White and Blue	2	1166
of the Crown	1537	White and Blue	2	1166
of Africa	1553	White and Blue	2	1166
of Zamora	1580	White and Red	2	1166
of Soria	1531	White and Red	2	1166
of Cordova	1650	White and Red	2	1166
of Portugal	1657	White and Red	2	1166
of Guadalajara	1657	White and Red	2	1166
of Seville	1657	White and Blue	2	1166
of Granada	1657	White and Green	2	1166
of Victoria	1658	White and Red	2	1166
of Lisbon	1660	White and Red	2	1166
of Spain	1660	White and Green	2	1166
of Toledo	1661	White and Blue	2	1166
of Majorca	1662	White and Red	2	1166
of Burgos	1634	White and Red	2	1166
of Murcia	1634	White and Blue	2	1166
of Leon	1634	White and Red	2	1166
of Cantabria	1703	White and Blue	2	1166
of Asturias	1703	White and Red	2	1166
of Ceuta, stationed	1703	White and Red	2	1380
of Navarre	1705	White and Red	2	1166
of Artillery	1710	Blue and Red	2	1380
of Arragon	1711	White and Red	2	1166
of Marines	1711	Blue and Red	8	6060
of Oran, stationed	1733	White and Green	2	1380
Total of the Spaniards	—	—	78	46,876
				Regiments

Regiments of Infantry.	Years.	Uniform.	Bs.	Men.
Italians.				
A Regiment of Neapolitans	1552	White and Red	2	1060
of Milan	1704	White and Blue	2	1060
Total of Italians	—	—	4	2120
Short Walloons.				
Regiment of Flanders	1536	White and Blue	2	1060
of Brabant	1713	White and Blue	2	1060
of Bruffels	1734	White and Blue	2	1060
Total of the Walloons	—	—	6	3180
Irifh.				
The Regiment of Ireland	1638	White and Blue	2	1060
of Ibernia	1703	Red and Green	2	1060
of Ulfter	1703	Red and Blue	2	1060
Total of Irifh	—	—	6	3180
Swifs.				
The Regiment of Buch		Red and Blue	2	1480
of Senballar		Blue and Red	2	1480
of Young Reding		Blue and Yellow	2	1480
Total of the Swifs	—	—	6	4440
Regiments of Militia.				
The Regiment of Jaen		White and Blue	1	700
of Badajos		White and Red	1	700
of Seville		White and Red	1	700
of Burgos		White and Red	1	700
of Lugo		White and Yellow	1	700
of Granada		White and Green	1	700
of Leon		White and Green	1	700
of Oviedo		White and Blue	1	700
of Cordova		White and Green	1	700
of Murcia		White and Red	1	700
of Trujillo		White and Blue	1	700
of Xerez		White and Red	1	700
of Carmona		White and Green	1	700
of Niebla		White and Yellow	1	700
of Ezija		White and Blue	1	700
of Ciudad Rodrigo		White and Blue	1	700
of Placentia		White and Red	1	700
of Logrogne		White and Green	1	700
of Siguenza		White and Green	1	700
of Toro		White and Yellow	1	700 .
		Carried over	20	14000
			Regiments	

Regiments of Militia.	Years.	Uniform.	Bts.	Men.
		Brought over	20	14,000
The Regiment of Soria		White and Blue	1	700
of Santandero		White and Blue	1	700
of Orense		White and Yellow	1	700
of St. Jago		White and Red	1	700
of Pontevedra		White and Blue	1	700
of Tuy		White and Red	1	700
of Baranzos		White and Green	1	700
of Antequera		White and Red	1	700
of Malaga		White and Green	1	700
of Guadiz		White and Yellow	1	700
of Ronda		White and Yellow	1	700
of Alpujarras		White and Blue	1	700
of Bujalance		White and Yellow	1	700
Total of the Militia	—	—	33	23,100
Regiments of Invalids.				
The Regiment of Castile		White and Red	2	1200
of Andalusia		White and Blue	2	1200
of Galicia		White and Yellow	2	1200
of Valencia		White and Green	2	1200
Total of the Invalids	—	—	8	4800
Regiments of Horse.				
The Queens Regiment	1703	Red and Blue	2	245
The Regiment of the Prince	1703	Blue and Red	2	245
of Milan	1538	White and Red	2	245
of Bourbon	1640	White and Red	2	245
of the Orders	1640	Blue and Red	2	245
of Farnese	1634	Blue and Red	2	245
of Alcantara	1656	White and Red	2	245
of Estremadura	1656	White and Red	2	245
of Barcelona	1653	White and Blue	2	245
of Malta	1670	White and Blue	2	245
of Brabant	1683	White and Blue	2	245
of Flandres	1635	White and Blue	2	245
of Algarve	1701	White and Blue	2	245
of Andalusia	1703	White and Blue	2	245
of Calatrava	1703	White and Red	2	245
of Granada	1703	White and Red	2	245
of Seville	1703	White and Blue	2	245
of St. Jago	1703	Blue and Red	2	245
of Montesa	1706	White and Blue	2	245
of the Coast of Granada	1735	Blue and Yellow	2	600
of Carabiniers	1732	Blue and Red	3	460
of Body Guards	1703	Blue and Red	3	399
Total of the Horse	—	—	46	6114
				Regiments

Regiments of Dragoons.	Years.	Uniform.	Bs.	Men.
The Queen's Regiment	1735	Red and Blue	2	256
The Regiment of Belgia	1674	Yellow and Red	2	256
of Battavia	1684	Yellow and Red	2	256
of Pavia	1683	Yellow and Red	2	256
of Frifa	1703	Yellow and Red	2	256
of Saguntum	1703	Yellow and Green	2	256
of Edinburgh	1707	Yellow and Blue	2	256
of Numantia	1707	Yellow and Blue	2	256
of Lufitania	1703	Yellow and Blue	2	256
of Merida	1735	Yellow and Blue	2	256
Total of the Dragoons			20	2560

Independant Companies.		Uniform	Bs.	Men.
The Crofs Bow-men of Baeza		White and Green	1	200
The Citizens of Ceuta		Blue and Red -	1	150
The Fufileers of Jetares		Blue and Red	1	80
The Garrifons of Ceuta		Blue and Red	1	200
—— of Melille, Pegnon, Aluzemas, Penifcola		Blue and Red	2	400
—— of Oran		Blue and Red	1	400
The Gunners of Eftramadura		Blue and Red	1	100
Ditto of Oran and Ceuta		Blue and Red	2	200
The Miners and Workmen of Oran and Ceuta		Blue and Red	2	145
Ditto of Lanifa		Blue and Red	1	30
Madrid, Bon Ventura		Blue and Red	1	50
Oran, Mogataces		In the Turkifh manner	1	50
Total of the Independant Companies	——	——	15	2005

Sum total, 98,375 Men.

By an ordonnance of his Majefty, dated 1741, which was the refult of a grand council of the Sword, the order and rank of the regiments of Infantry, Horfe and Dragoons, was declared to be the fame that is obferved in this Table, referving always to each of them their right in fo far as they can offer new proofs.

Befides the above troops, his Catholic Majefty has for the guard of his Royal Perfon, a body of 150 Halberdiers, who are alfo employed to fupply vacant offices.

An

An eſtimate of the annual expence of the LAND FORCES *in the ſer-
vice of his* CATHOLIC MAJESTY.

The General Eſtabliſhment of the Army.

	l.	*s.*	*d.*
TO 6 Captains-General, 1000 crowns vellon per month each, is annually –	8,000		
16 Lieutenant-Generals employed, 750 crowns vellon per month each, is annually	16,000		
25 other Lieutenant-Generals, not employed, 375 crowns per month each, is annually	17,500		
21 Major-generals, employed, 500 crowns per month each, is per annum –	14,000		
20 other Major-Generals, not employed, 250 crowns per month each, is annually –	6,666	13	4
30 Brigadiers, 200 crowns per month each, is annually –	8,000		
61 Brigadiers, not employed, 137½ crowns per month each, is per annum –	11,183	6	8
11 Majors of Brigade, 100 crowns per month each, is annually – –	1,466	13	4
a Quarter-Maſter-General, annually –	266	13	4
a Quarter-Maſter-General of the Cavalry, annually – – –	266	13	4
a Major-General of Dragoons, annually –	266	13	4
a Controler, or Intendant, – –	200		
16 Commiſſaries of War, 150 crowns each per month, is per annum – –	3,200		
a Quarter-Maſter-General, annually –	100		
his two aſſiſtants, 35 crowns per month each, is annually – –	93	6	8
a Captain of the Guides, annually –	100		
his Lieutenant, annually – –	66	13	4
carried over	87,376	13	4

F f   brought

	l.	*s.*	*d.*
brought over	87,376	13	4
To 20 Guides on horseback, annually -	200		
the Prevot of the army, annually -	200		
his two Lieutenants, 75 crowns per month each, annually - -	200		
2 Exempts, 50 crowns each, per month, is annually - -	133	6	8
30 Archers, annually - -	332	4	
a Clerk, annually - -	53	6	8
the Chaplain-Major, annually -.	133	6	8
the first Physician, annually -	266	13	4
the Surgeon-Major, annually -	200		
the Apothecary, annually - -	133	6	8
	89,228	17	4

An estimate of the expence of the INFANTRY, *exclusive of the Body Guards, the Walloon Guards, the Swiss, the Regiment of Artillery, and Invalids.*

	l.	*s.*	*d.*
To 38 Colonels of 38 regiments of Infantry, 132¼ Vellon crowns per month each, is annually	6713	6	8
38 Lieutenant-Colonels, 80 crowns per month each, is annually -	4053	6	8
38 Majors, 65 crowns per month each, is annually - -	3293	6	8
38 Aids or Assistants, 30 crowns per month each, per annum - -	1520		
38 Chaplains, 17¼ crowns per month each, is per annum - -	886	13	4
38 Surgeons, 15 crowns per month each, is annually - -	760		
38 Drum-Majors, 5 crowns per month each, is annually - -	253	6	8
carried over	17,480	0	0

I

brought

	l.	s.	d.
brought over	17,480	0	0
38 Commandants of second battalions, 57 crowns per month each, is per annum -	2888		
38 Aids of second battalions, 30 crowns per month each, is per annum -	1520		
38 Chaplains of second battalions, 17¼ crowns per month each, is annually -	886	13	
38 Surgeons of second battalions, 15 crowns per month each, is per annum -	760		
456 Captains of Infantry, 57 crowns per month each, is annually -	34,656		
456 Lieutenants, 22¼ crowns per month each, is per annum - -	13,680		
456 Ensigns, 15 crowns per month each, is per annum - -	9120		
912 serjeants, annually -	6091	18	3
912 First Corporals, annually -	4351	6	8
1368 Second Corporals, per annum -	5221	13	
380 Drummers, per annum -	1266	13	6
17,784 soldiers, annually -	50,911	1	
2964 Grenadeers, annually -	11,313	11	11
152 Carabineers, per annum -	652	13	10
25,460 pairs of shoes, annually, at 2s. 8d. per pair, is - -	3394	13	4
25,460 pairs of stockings, at 13¼d. per pair, is - - -	1410		
25,460 hats, at 1s. 6¾d. each, is -	1980	4	5
25,460 shirts, with 50,920 rollers, at 3s. each, is - - -	3819		
11,400 coats, waistcoats, and breeches, at 1l. 11s. 1¼d. each suit, is -	17,705	12	2
5472 muskets, with their bayonets, at 1l. 8s. each, is - -	7650	16	
5472 belts, with their swords, is -	2221	8	8
5472 cartridge-boxes, is - -	1337	13	
carried over	200,318	18	9

F f 2   brought

	l.	*s*	*d.*
brought over	200,318	1	9
To 5472 Drums, with their braces, is -	1824		
25,460 rations, which the King pays every day to this body of Infantry, at three farthings each ration - -	29,200		
Sum total	231,342	18	9

As it would be too tedious to fpecify the particular articles of the other corps, I fhall only give the total expence of each of them; and after that fhall fum up the whole expence of the land army in 1760.

The expence of the body of Horfe Guards, confifting of 480 men . - -	26,535	13	6
expence of the regiment of Spanifh Foot Guards, of 5856 men - -	99,528	6	
regiment of Walloon Guards, of 5856 men - - -	97,939	6	
expence of 20 regiments of cavalry	220,349		
expence of ten regiments of Dragoons -	116,354	10	
expence of a regiment of Carabineers -	59,563	18	
expence of the three Swifs regiments -	66,240		
regiment of Artillery, and offices belonging to that department -	35,736		
four regiments of Invalids - -	12,670	10	
The firft article of the General Eftablifhment	89,228	17	4
The fecond article of the main body of Infantry - -	231,342	18	9
The total expence of the Land Army of 1760	1,035,488	19	7

R E M A R K S.

REMARKS.

The expence of the 23,000 militia is here not reckoned, as that corps receives no pay but when it is upon duty, in which cafe it is paid in the fame manner as the other regiments.

THE independant companies in the Catholic King's fervice are paid at the expence of the cities which they garrifon; and on that confideration the inhabitants enjoy certain privileges and exemptions: but a royal edict of the year 1752 ordains, that as oft as thofe companies fhall take the field, or march to any other place, in the King's fervice, they fhall be entertained at his expence.

A LIST of the NAVAL FORCES of his CATHOLIC MAJESTY CHARLES III. King of SPAIN, in the year 1760.

SHIPS of the LINE, 47.	Guns.	Years.	Gunners.	Marines.	Crews.
El Phenix	70	1749	12	120	750
El Atronador	70	1743	12	120	750
El St. Philipe	70	1745	12	120	750
* La Reyna	70	1744	12	120	750
El Conftante	70	1755	12	120	750
* El Tigre	70	1747	12	120	750
** La Afia	70	1751	12	120	750
El Fernando	70	1751	12	120	750
La Galicia	70	1751	12	120	750
* El Infante	70	1750	12	110	750
La Princefa	70	1751	12	120	750
El Septrention	70	1751	12	120	750
La Africa	70	1752	12	120	750
El Oriente	70	1753	12	110	750
El Eolo	70	1753	12	120	750
* El Aquilon	70	1754	12	120	750
El Soberbio	70	1754	12	120	750
El Serio	70	1754	12	120	750
** El Neptuno	70	1754	12	120	750
El Brilliante	70	1753	12	120	750
El Magnanimo	70	1754	12	120	750
La Galiarda	70	1754	12	120	750
* El Vincedor	70	1755	12	120	750
Carried over,	1610		276	2760	17250

El Guerrero

SHIPS of the LINE, 47.	Guns.	Years.	Gunners.	Marines.	Crews.
Brought over	1610		276	2760	17250
El Guerrero	70	1759	12	120	750
* El Soberano	70	1755	12	120	750
El Gloriofo	70	1755	12	120	750
El Hector	70	1755	12	120	750
El Firmo	70	1754	12	120	750
El Achilles	70	1754	12	120	750
El Terrible	70	1755	12	120	750
La Athalanta	70	1754	12	120	750
El Poderofo	70	1754	12	120	750
El Arrogante	70	1754	12	120	750
El Hercules	70	1755	12	120	750
El Dichofo	70	1756	12	120	750
El Triumphante	70	1756	12	120	750
El Monarcha	70	1756	12	120	750
El Diligente	70	1756	12	120	750
El Fuerte	60	1727	10	100	600
* * La Europa	60	1734	10	100	600
* La America	60	1736	10	100	600
El Dragon	60	1739	10	100	600
El Tridente	60	1748	10	100	600
El Nueva Efpana	60	1754	10	100	600
La Caftelia	60	1753	10	100	600
* El San Genaro	60	1762	10	100	600
* El San Antonio	60	1762	10	100	600
The total,	3200		546	5460	33900

PACKET-BOATS, 4.					
* El Marte	16	1753	4	30	250
El Diligente	16	1753	4	30	250
El Jupiter	16	1751	4	30	230
El Mercurio	16	1747	4	30	200
The total,	64		16	120	930

BOMB VESSELS, 7.					
El Vulcano	8	1728	2	20	150
El Sterope	8	1743	2	20	150
El Bronto	8	1733	2	20	150
El Piracmon	8	1743	2	20	150
El Rey	8	1721	2	20	150
El Bueno	8	1730	2	20	150
El Relampago	8	1743	2	20	150
The total,	56		14	140	1050

XEBECS,

XEBECS, 14.

	Guns.	Years.	Gunners.	Marines.	Crews.
El Aventurara	30	1758	6	50	400
El Cazador	18	1750	4	30	240
El Volante	18	1750	4	30	240
El Garcota	18	1750	4	30	240
El Galgo	16	1750	4	30	240
El Liebre	16	1750	4	30	240
El Gavilan	16	1753	4	30	240
El Majorquino	16	1744	4	30	240
El Gitano	14	1753	4	30	240
El Valenciano	14	1754	4	30	240
El Catalano	22	1754	6	40	300
El Ivifenco	22	1754	6	40	300
Another	22	1754	6	40	300
Another	22	1754	6	40	300
The total,	264		66	480	3760

FRIGATES, 21.

	Guns.	Years.	Gunners.	Marines.	Crews.
La Efparanza	50	1736	8	60	460
El Bizarro	50	1737	8	60	460
El Flor	30	1747	6	50	400
La Emeralda	30	1753	6	50	400
* El Venganza	30	1755	6	50	400
El Liebre	26	1755	4	40	360
La Induftria	26	1755	4	40	360
La Ventura	26	1755	4	40	360
La Venus	26	1755	4	40	360
La Pallas	26	1755	4	40	360
La Junon	26	1755	4	40	360
La Aftrea	26	1753	4	40	360
La Hermoza	24	1754	4	40	360
La Vitoria	24	1751	4	40	360
La Galga	22	1752	4	40	360
La Dorada	22	1753	4	40	360
La Perla	22	1753	4	40	360
La Aquila	22	1753	4	40	360
La Flecha	22	1753	4	40	360
La Reyna	22	1755	4	40	360
* La Thetis					
The total,	552		94	870	7520

A

A GENERAL SUMMARY of the NAVAL FORCES.

Ships of the Line	47
Frigates	21
Xebecs	14
Packet-boats	4
Bomb Veffels	7
Guns	4016
Gunners	712
Marines	6870
Crew	45,960

NOTE.

At CADIZ there is eftablifhed an academy of marine guards, who are maintained there, to the number of 150, at the expence of the finances of his Catholic Majefty.

The marines who are embarked on board the whole navy are drawn from the marine regiment, comprehended in the lift of the land forces in the Royal fervice of his Catholic Majefty. For this reafon, they ought not to be reckoned to belong to this general fummary. The fame ought to be remarked in regard to the marine gunners, who are drawn from the regiment of artillery, likewife included in the fame lift of land forces.

In the docks of GUARNIZO, FERROL, and CARTHAGENA, they are building four other fhips of the line, five frigates, and fome other fhips of war, which may be ready for the fea the enfuing year 1761.

N. B. The fhips marked * were taken by us at the HAVANNA, befides two others on the flocks, not finifhed. Thofe with this mark * * were funk in the mouth of the harbour.

3   An

An ESTIMATE of the EXPENCE of the NAVAL FORCES.

The Particulars of the Expence of 47 SHIPS of the LINE.

	L.	s.	d.
TO the Governor-general of the navy annually, - - - - -	2000	0	0
7 Lieutenant-generals of marine, 450 crowns vellon each, per month, is per annum -	4200	0	0
6 Admirals, 225 crowns per month, each, is annually - - - -	1800	0	0
5 of them, when embarked, by way of gratification, during the campaign, - -	666	13	4
47 Captains of ships, 100 crowns per month each, is annually - - -	6450	0	0
32 who are cruising, as a gratification, -	4000	0	0
47 Lieutenants of ships, 75 crowns per month each, is annually - - -	4837	10	0
32 who are cruising, as a gratification, -	768	0	0
47 Ensigns of ships, 30 crowns per month each, annually - - - -	1935	0	0
32 who serve on a cruise, as a gratification,	768	0	0
140 Marine-guards officers, annually, -	2240	0	0
The same, by way of gratification, - -	1803	8	9
5 Intendants of the marine, 60 crowns per month each, is per annum, - -	400	0	0
The same, by way of gratification, - -	146	13	4
32 Clerks of ships, 40 crowns per month each, is annually - - - -	1506	13	4
The same, by way of gratification, - -	188	17	6
47 Masters of the rigging, 30 crowns per month each, is per annum - -	1935	0	0
3 Chaplains majors, 50 crowns per month each, is annually - - -	200	0	0
47 other Chaplains, 30 crowns per month each, is per annum - -	1935	0	0
Carried over,	37,780	16	3

G g To

	l.	*s.*	*d.*
Brought over,	37,780	16	3
To 47 firſt Surgeons, 30 crowns per month each, annually - - - - -	1935	0	0
47 other Surgeons, 25 crowns per month each, is annually - - - -	1612	10	0
47 firſt Pilots, 30 crowns per month each, is annually - - -	1935	0	0
47 ſecond Pilots, 25 crowns per month each, annually ` - - -	1612	10	0
47 third Pilots, 15 crowns per month each, is per annum - - -	967	10	0
47 firſt Maſter-gunners, 25 crowns per month each, is annually - -	1612	10	0
47 other Maſter-gunners, 15 crowns per month, is per annum, - -	967	10	0
47 firſt Mates, 30 crowns per month each, is per annum - - -	1935	0	0
47 ſecond Mates, 25 crowns per month each, is annually - -	1612	10	0
45 other Maſter-gunners, 20 crowns per month each, is per annum - -	1260	0	0
270 Gunners, 9 crowns each per month, is per annum - - -	3233	6	8
7000 Sailors, 4½ *piaſtres*, or 15 ſhillings per month each, is annually - -	68,250	0	0
8250 Boys, 4½ vellon crowns each, per month, is annually - - -	49,500	0	0
7150 Swobbers, 3 crowns each per month, is per annum - - -	28,600	0	0
70 Sergeants, 9 crowns per month each, is annually - - - -	833	0	0
3770 Marines of the ſame fleet, annually,	18,303	0	0
The Purſer-general, for 9,577,600 rations, which they furniſh every year for the ſub-ſiſtence of 26,240 men, of which the ma-			

Carried over,	221,950	2	11

rines

	l.	s.	d.
Brought over,	221,950	2	11
rines and crew of the faid fleet are com- pofed,	225,355	4	6
To 47 Carpenters of fhips, 30 crowns per month each, is annually	1,887	15	0
An annual expence of 173 fhort cwt. of gun- powder, 53 ditto of balls, and 31 ditto of match, at the rate of 3 l. 6 s. 8 d. the cwt. of powder, 10 s. 6 d. the balls, and 1 l. 3 s. the match,	633	6	8
For extraordinary careenings and repairs,	11,189	0	0
The whole expence of 47 Ships of the Line,	461,015	9	1
The expence of 21 frigates,	117,851	0	0
The expence of 14 xebecs,	75,093	4	6
Of 7 bomb veffels,	22,483	13	0
Of 4 packet boats,	18,992	0	0
The whole expence of the fleet,	695,435	6	7

The Expence of the MARINE DEPARTMENTS.

	l.	s.	d.
To 3 Intendants of the 3 departments of the marine, 450 crowns each per month, per annum,	1800	0	0
6 Commiffaries, 150 crowns vellon per month each, annually	1200	0	0
3 Great Treafurers, 180 crowns per month each, is per annum	720	0	0
3 Treafurers, 200 crowns per month each, is annually	800	0	0
30 Major, or firft officers, 60 crowns per month each, per annum	2800	0	0
Carried over,	7320	0	0

	l.	*s.*	*d.*
Brought over,	7320	0	0
To 40 fecond Officers, 40 crowns per month each, annually, - - -	3133	6	8
43 Supernumeraries, 18 crowns per month each, is per annum - - -	1511	0	0
92 Clerks, employed at the arfenals, 21 crowns per month each, is per annum -	633	6	8
Others, maintained at the boards, according to their pay, annually - -	622	4	5
The Officers who enrol on the books, or Clerks of the check, by way of gratification, - - -	918	0	0
46 Clerks of the book office, 50 crowns per month each, per annum, -	1115	11	0
3 Chiefs of ditto, 60 crowns per month each, annually ' - -	400	0	0
3 Porters of the chamber of accounts, 18 crowns per month each, is per annum, -	72	0	0
The Mafter-builder at CADIZ, annually	304	3	0
The Mafter-builder at FERROL, annually	304	3	0
The Mafter-builder at CARTHAGENA, annually - - -	608	6	8
16 Draughtfmen, defigned as Affiftants to the Builders, 20 Crowns per Month each, is annually - -	426	13	4
3 naval Store-keepers, 60 crowns per month each, is annually -	671	0	0

The Tribunals of the MARINE.

To 3 Marine Auditors of war, 100 vellon crowns a-month each, per annum -	400	0	0
3 Secretaries of the marine, 60 crowns per month each, annually -	240	0	0
12 Alguazils of the marine, 15 crowns per month each, per annum, - -	192	0	0
Carried over,	18,871	14	9

	l.	s.	d.
Brought over,	18,871	14	9
To 3 Porters, 25 crowns per month each, is	100	0	0
For Extraordinaries, annually - -	154	13	4
The sum of the marine department and tribunals,	19,126	8	1
The whole expence of the fleet, - .	695,435	6	7
The expence of the whole marine, - -	714,561	14	8

The salaries of the members of the great offices, and tribunals, are as follows.

The COUNCIL of STATE.

	l.	s.	d.
To the Dean of the council annually -	1466	13	4
3 other Ministers, ditto, -	4400	0	0
The Secretary, per annum, -	444	9	0
The first Porter, - -	40	0	0
The second Porter, - -	22	4	5
For extraordinaries annually, that is, paper, ink, pens, refreshments, and for furnishing the apartments in summer and winter,	488	17	10

SECRETARIES of STATE, and of universal dispatches.

	l.	s.	d.
To the Secretary of State, and of universal dispatch, - -	1333	6	8
The Secretary of State, and of the dispatch of Favour, - -	1333	6	8
The Secretary of State, and of the dispatch of Favour and Justice, - -	1333	6	8
The Secretary of State, and of the dispatch of the marine, - -	1333	6	8
The Secretary of State, and of the dispatch of the Finances, - -	1333	6	8
Carried over,	13,528	17	11

To

	l.	*s.*	*d.*
Brought over,	13,528	17	11

To 5 firſt Officers, 202 vellon ducats per month
  each, is annually   -   -   **1481 0 0**

—5 ſecond Officers, 150 ducats per month
  each, is annually   -   -   **1100 0 0**

30 other Officers, 60 ducats per month each,
  per annum,   -   -   **2640 0 0**

20 Supernumeraries, 30 ducats per month
  each, is per annum   -   -   **880 0 0**

5 firſt Porters, 30 ducats per month each, is
  annually   -   -   **293 6 0**

5 ſecond Porters, 25 ducats per month each,
  is per annum   -   -   **183 6 0**

For extraordinaries annually,   -   **1294 9 0**

Royal and Supreme Council of his Majeſty.

The firſt HALL of GOVERNMENT.

To the Preſident annually,   -   -   **1333 6 ●**

7 other Commiſſioners, 200 ducats per
  month each, is per annum,   -   **2053 6 8**

The Fiſcal, annually   -   -   **333 6 8**

The Secretary, annually   -   -   **244 9 0**

The firſt Porter,   -   -   **66 13 4**

The ſecond Porter,   -   -   **44 9 4**

For extraordinaries,   -   -   **266 13 4**

The Second HALL of GOVERNMENT.

This Hall conſiſts of 4 Commiſſioners, a Secretary, 2 Porters; and the whole expences of
it, extraordinaries included,   -   **1951 0 0**

The HALL of MIL Y QUINIENTAS.

This Hall conſiſts of 5 Commiſſioners, a Secre-

Carried over,	27,694	3	11

tary,

	l.	*s.*	*d.*
Brought over,	27,694	3	11
tary, and other officers; and the whole expences of it, extraordinaries included, are	2133	6	8

The HALL of the PROVINCE.

This Hall confifts of 4 Commiffioners, a Governor, the Judges of the feveral Provinces, a Fifcal, three Secretaries, and other officers; and the expence of the whole is   -   6826 13 4

The HALL of the GRAND PREVOTS of the Houfe and Court.

This confifts of a Governor, two other Commiffioners, a Fifcal, Secretary, and other officers; the expence of the whole being   -   2283 6 8

The HALL of JUSTICE

Confifts of 3 Commiffioners, a Fifcal, a Secretary, and Porter; the expence is   -   1411 11 0

The GRAND COUNCIL of WAR

Confifts of 6 Commiffioners, a Fifcal, an Affeffor, a Secretary, &c. the expence is   4115 11 0

The GRAND COUNCIL of the INQUISITION.

To the Inquifitor-general, annually, -	489	0	0
7 other Inquifitors, annually, -	2566	13	4
The Fifcal - -	333	6	8
The Secretary of the chamber, -	333	6	8
The Alguazil major, - -	166	13	4

Carried over,   48,353 12 7
To

4

	l.	*s.*	*d.*
Brought over,	48,353	12	7
To 2 Inquisitors of the council, 200 ducats per month each, is per annum -	533	6	8
The first Porter, - -	66	13	4
The Porter of the Tribunal, -	122	4	5
For extraordinaries, - -	477	17	0

The GRAND COUNCIL of the INDIES.

To the great Chancellor of the INDIES, -	489	0	0
17 other Commissioners, 200 ducats per month each, is per annum, -	4986	13	4
The Fiscal respecting PERU, -	333	6	8
The Fiscal respecting NEW SPAIN, -	333	6	8
The Secretary respecting PERU, -	333	6	8
The Secretary respecting NEW SPAIN,	333	6	8
The Lieutenant of the Chancellor, -	400	0	0
2 Porters, - -	111	0	0
Extraordinaries, - -	888	17	10

The GRAND COUNCIL of MILITARY ORDERS

Consists of a President, 8 other Commissioners, a Fiscal, a Secretary, a great Treasurer, Treasurer, Alguazil, Procurator-general of the order of St. JAMES, several other officers of that order, and two Porters; the expence of the whole, with extraordinaries, being

5910	0	0

The COUNCILS of the FINANCES.

1. The HALL of GOVERNMENT.

To 15 Commissioners, 200 ducats each per month, is per annum, -	4400	0	0
Carried over,	68,072	11	10
	To		

	l.	*s.*	*d.*
Brought over,	68,072	11	10
To the grand Treasurer-general of the Chamber of Valuations, - -	333	6	8
To the grand Treasurer-general of the Distribution, - -	333	6	8
A Fiscal, Secretary, two Porters, and extraordinaries, are - -	1064	9	0

The HALL of the MILLONES

Consists of 8 Commissioners, a Secretary, Fiscal, 2 Porters; the expence of the whole, including extraordinaries, is - -	2771	0	0

The HALL of JUSTICE

Consists of 6 Commissioners, and officers as above; the expence, with extraordinaries, is	2066	13	4

The TRIBUNAL of the GREATER CHAMBER of ACCOMPTS.

14 Commissioners, and officers as above; the expence, including extraordinaries,	4468	6	1

The General Commission of CRUSADE.

A Commissary, 2 Assessors, a great Treasurer, and other officers, as above; the expence of the whole, including extraordinaries,	1866	13	4

The BOARD of WORKS and FORESTS.

7 Commissioners, a Judge of the Wood by Commission, and other officers, as above; the expence of which, with extraordinaries, is	1999	0	0

Carried over,	82,975	6	11

H h

The

S A L A R I E S of the

The COUNCIL of COMMERCE, MONEY, and MINES

Confifts of a Prefident, 12 other Commiffioners, and officers as above; the expence of the whole, including extraordinaries, being — 2771 0 0

The ROYAL JUNTA de FACULTADES.

3 Commiffioners, a Secretary, and 2 Porters; the expence, with extraordinaries, — 949 0 0

The ROYAL APOSTOLIC ASSEMBLY.

6 Commiffioners, and officers as above; the expence, with extraordinaries, being — 1413 6 8

The ROYAL JUNTA of TOBACO.

A Prefident, 7 Commiffioners, 4 Fifcals, a Secretary, and two Porters; the expence, including extraordinaries, — 2969 0 0

The ROYAL JUNTA of PROVISIONS.

7 Commiffioners, and officers as above; the expence, with extraordinaries, — 1621 0 0

The ROYAL ASSEMBLY of the SINGLE CONTRIBUTION.

5 Commiffioners, and officers as above; the expence, including extraordinaries, — 1444 6 8

Carried over, 94,143 0 3

The

	l.	s.	d.
Brought over,	94,143	0	3

The TRIBUNAL of PHYSIC.

A Prefident, Vice-prefident, firft Phyfician, Affeffor, Fifcal, Secretary, and 2 Porters; the
expence, including extraordinaries,　　-　　1001　0　0

COMMISSIONERS, and others employed in the PROVINCIAL TRIBUNALS.

The ROYAL CHANCERY of VALLADOLID

Confifts of a Prefident, 16 Commiffioners, 4
Prevots, a Judge, 4 other Prevots, 2 Fifcals,
a Secretary, 2 Porters; and the expences, with
extraordinaries, are　　　　-　　5262　5　5

The ROYAL CHANCERY of GRENADA

Confifts of a Prefident, 16 other Commiffioners,
8 Prevots, 2 Fifcals, an Alguazil major, and
2 Porters; and, with the extraordinaries, is　　4851　0　0

The GRAND COUNCIL of NAVARRE

Is compofed of a Viceroy, and Captain-general
of NAVARRE, of a Regent, 6 other Commiffioners, and a Fifcal,　　　　-　　2420　0　0

The HALL of GRAND PREVOTS

Confifts of 4 Prevots,　　　　-　　533　6　8

	l.	s.	d.
Carried over,	108,210	12	4

H h 2

The

	l.	*s.*	*d.*
Brought over,	108,210	12	4

The TRIBUNAL of the CHAMBER of ACCOMPTS

Confifts of 5 Commiffioners, a Patrimonial of the Kingdom, a Treafurer, 3 Secretaries, and 4 Porters; and, with extraordinaries, is — 1887 11 0

The AUDIENCES.

The ROYAL AUDIENCE of CORUNNA.

A Governor, a Regent, 7 other Commiffioners, a Fifcal, Secretary, and two Porters; the expence, including extraordinaries, is — 3121 0 0

The ROYAL AUDIENCE of SEVILLE.

A Regent, 8 Commiffioners, 4 Prevots, and other officers, as above; the expences, with the extraordinaries, are — 2733 6 8

The ROYAL AUDIENCE of OVIEDO.

A Regent, 4 grand Prevots, an Alguazil major, and other officers, as above; the expence, including extraordinaries, — — 1755 11 0

The ROYAL AUDIENCE of the CANARIES.

A Governor, or Commandant-general, a Regent, 3 other Commiffioners, and other officers, as above; the expence, with extraordinaries, is — — 2571 0 0

| Carried over, | 120,279 | 1 | 0 |

The

	l.	*s.*	*d.*
Brought over,	120,279	1	0

The ROYAL AUDIENCE of COMMERCE to the INDIES, at CADIZ.

A Prefident, 4 Commiffioners, a Fifcal, Great Treafurer, a Depofitary, a Comptroller, a Secretary, and 2 Porters; the expence, with extraordinaries,   —   —   3301 0 0

The ROYAL AUDIENCE of ARRAGON.

A Governor, or Captain-general, a General-commandant, a Regent, 8 other Commiffioners, 4 Judges, two Fifcals, an Alguazil major, a Secretary, and two Porters; the expence, with extraordinaries, being   —   4446 13 5

The ROYAL AUDIENCE of VALENCIA.

A Governor, or Captain-general, a Regent, 8 other Commiffioners, 4 Criminal Commiffioners, 2 Fifcals, an Alguazil, Secretary, and 2 Porters; the expences, including the extraordinaries, are   —   —   4024 9 0

The ROYAL AUDIENCE of CATALONIA.

A Governor, or Captain-general, a Regent, 10 other Commiffioners, 6 Criminal Judges, 2 Fifcals, a Secretary, 2 Porters; the expences, including extraordinaries, are   —   4817 16 0

The ROYAL AUDIENCE of MAJORCA.

A Governor, or Captain-general, a Regent, 5 other Commiffioners, a Secretary, Fifcal, and 2 Porters; the expences, with extraordinaries   2796 13 4

Carried over,	139,665	12	9

The

	l.	*s.*	*d.*
Brought over,	139,665	12	9

The GOVERNORS, SENESCHALS, and INTEN-
DANTS of the Kingdom, are 139 in number.

| The amount of all their salaries is | 30,327 | 6 | 8 |

The PRESIDIO's, or GARRISON'D FORTS.

	l.	*s.*	*d.*
First of ORAN, confifting of a General Com-mandant, a Governor, Lieutenant-Governor, Major, two Aid Majors, Captains Intendant, Secretary, and other Officers	2,825	0	0
The expence of the Convents there	410	13	4
The expence of the Hofpital	921	0	0
The Caftle of SANTA CRUZ	366	13	4
Caftle of ST. PHILIP	366	13	4
Caftle of ST. GREGORY	366	13	4
Caftle of ST. ANDERO	366	13	4
ROZALCAZAR	394	9	0
ALMARZAQUIVIR	14,954	9	0
CEUTA	3,211	3	0
The Hofpital	11,879	4	0
PEGNON	5,920	0	0
To the above muft be added MELILLA, ALU-ZEINAS, and the Arfenals of CARTHAGENA	124,428	0	0
	336,403	11	1

PENSIONS paid out of the FINANCES of his CATHOLIC
MAJESTY.

	l.	*s.*	*d.*
To the Queen Mother	100,000	0	0
Carried over,	100,000	0	0

3

To

	l.	*s.*	*d.*
Brought over,	100,000	0	0
To the Infant Don PHILIP (probably now difcontinued.) - - -	33,333	6	8
the Infant Don LEWIS - -	50,000	0	0
two Minifters of State, retired -	2,666	13	4
two Widows of General Officers -	266	13	4
feveral Perfons employed in the Royal Service, by way of gratification during their life -	5,666	13	4
other Widows - - -	844	9	0
two fuperannuated Confeffors -	266	13	4
Alms fixed by his Majefty annually -	1000	0	0
To the Great Treafurer of the Chamber of Penfions - - -	244	9	0
the Officer Major - -	166	13	4
the fecond Officer - -	89	0	0
the Officer of the Books - -	66	13	4
other Officers - - -	333	6	8
four Officers charged with the correfpondence of the Kingdom - -	400	0	0
ten Clerks board-wages - -	166	13	4
a Treafurer, annually - -	139	0	0
an Intendant - - -	222	5	5
a Porter of the Chamber - -	44	9	0
Extraordinaries annually - -	222	4	5
An annual payment of three per cent. of arrears of the Finances - -	6,889	0	0

The King's LIBRARY.

An annual affignment made by his Majefty for literary affemblies - -	1,555	11	0
To the firft Librarian - -	333	6	8
four fecond Librarians -	311	2	2
an Interpreter of Oriental Languages -	111	2	2
fix Clerks annually - -	133	6	8
Carried over,	205,472	12	2

To

	l.	*s.*	*d.*
Brought over,	205,472	12	2
To three Porters - -	83	6	8
Extraordinaries - -	18	17	11

The ACADEMIES of the King.

	l.	*s.*	*d.*
To the fupport of the Academy of the Spanifh Language - - -	444	9	0
Do. of Hiftory - -	666	13	4
Do. of Painting, Sculpture, and Architecture	1,333	6	8
Do. of Mathematics at CADIZ -	1,888	17	10
Do. of Mathematics at BARCELONA	1,444	9	0

The PALACE and ROYAL FAMILY.

	l.	*s.*	*d.*
To the Squire of the Body - -	333	6	8
the Majordomo Major -	333	6	8
the firft Equerry - -	333	6	8
the fecond Equerry - -	167	0	0
the firft Equerry of the Camp -	167	0	0
the fecond Equerry of the Camp -	111	2	2
the firft Equerry of the Queen -	167	0	0
the fecond - -	111	0	0
four Gentlemen of the Chamber of his Majefty peculiarly - -	444	9	0
fix others of the Table -	666	13	0
four Wardrobe Keepers -	444	9	0
four Fhyficians - -	1,778	0	0
two Surgeons - -	666	13	4
two Apothecaries - -	333	6	8
the Houfehold of the Pages -	2,100	0	0
the Patriarch - -	1,111	2	2
two Confeffors - -	889	0	0
Carried over,	221,509	7	11

2

To

	l.	*s.*	*d.*
Brought over,	221,509	7	11
To the Curate of the Palace -	1,033	6	8
thirty-two Honorary Priests -	3,555	11	0
the annual expence of the Sacrifty, and of the Fabrick of the Chapel -	3,666	13	4
For the subsistence of the Band of Musick for the Chapel -	1,089	0	0
Gratuities to Ambassadors and other Ministers residing at foreign Courts -	11,144	9	0
To the Camarera Major, or first Lady of the Bed-Chamber - -	333	6	8
four Camaristas - -	266	13	4
thirty-nine Ladies besides -	1,266	13	4
800 other Domestics -	39,111	2	2
The anual expence of the Kitchen by contract	4,444	9	0
The annual expence of the Pastery-Cook -	1,433	6	8
Ditto of the Side-Board -	333	6	8
Ditto of the Bake-House -	333	6	8
Ditto of the Wardrobe -	333	6	8
Ditto of the two Stables of the King and Queen	39,722	4	8
To small articles of House-keeping at the Palace	2,100	0	0
two Taylors - -	544	9	0
two Goldsmiths annually -	666	13	4
four Painters of the King's Chamber -	1,333	6	8
The annual expence of Counterpanes -	777	15	0
Ditto of Tapestry and Furniture -	555	11	0
The wages of the Grooms of the Stable -	14,655	11	0
To four Valets de Chambre, Perruquiers	666	13	4
Coal, oil, wax-lights, wood, &c. annually	3,366	13	4

The APOTHECARY'S OFFICE.

	l.	*s.*	*d.*
To the Apothecary - -	333	6	8
a second Apothecary -	111	2	2
different persons employed in that department	555	11	0
Carried over,	355,242	16	3

The

	l.	*s*	*d.*
Brought over,	355,242	16	3
The annual expence of the Shop -	2,444	9	0

The BOTANIC GARDENS of the King.

To the firſt Botaniſt annually -	200	0	0
the ſecond - -	66	13	4
the people employed in cultivating the ſame gardens - -	44	9	0

BUEN RETIRO.

To the firſt Gardener annually -	66	13	4
four other Gardeners -	44	9	0
extraordinaries for cultivation and planting	66	13	4
the firſt Gardener for flowers -	66	13	4
four other Gardeners -	44	9	0
extraordinaries - -	88	17	10
For the maintenance of the houſe where the Lion, Tygers, Eagle, and other animals are kept - -	88	17	10
To an Aſſiſtant - -	33	6	8
the ſubſiſtence of the ſaid animals -	644	9	0

ARANJUEZ.

To the Governor of ARANJUEZ -	366	13	4
the Keeper of the Magazine -	133	6	8
the Guard Major - -	100	0	0
fifty-four other Guards -	1,100	0	0
four Gardeners - -	533	6	8
ten ſupernumerary Gardeners -	333	6	8
ſix Keepers of the Palace -	200	0	0
extraordinaries - -	3,500	0	0

Carried over,	365,409	10	3

PARDO.

	l.	s.	d.
Brought over,	365,409	10	3

P a r d o.

For supporting the woods and gardens at the Pardo annually   -   2,100 0 0

San Ildephonso.

For supporting the Gardens of San Ildephonso annually   -   2,666 13 4

The Escurial.

For supporting the Gardens of the Escurial   889 0 0

Casa del Campo.

For the support of the Casa del Campo annually   14,622 4 8

385,687	8	3

The Annual Produce of Tobacco in each Province.

		l.	s.	d.
In the Canaries	-	17,386	13	4
Madrid	-	217,152	0	0
Burgos	-	82,222	4	9
Valladolid	-	137,666	13	4
Soria	-	13,505	11	0
Corunna	-	34,111	2	2
the Four Cities	-	12,222	4	5
Segovia	-	26,811	2	2
Avila	-	10,125	11	0
Toledo	-	12,127	15	7
Guadalaxara	-	19,777	15	4

Carried over,	483,108	13	1

I i 2   In

			l.	*s.*	*d.*
	Brought over,		483,108	13	1
In CUENÇA	-	-	12,388	17	10
TALAVERA	-	-	14,444	8	10
MANCHA	-	-	33,465	11	0
SALAMANCA	-	-	24,783	6	8
ESTREMADURA	-	-	87,666	13	4
GALICIA	-	-	51,111	2	2
ASTURIAS	-	-	39,333	6	8
SEVILLE	-	-	34,222	4	5
CORDOVA	-	-	25,222	4	5
JAEN	-	-	28,839	0	0
CADIZ	-	-	37,902	4	5
GRANADA	-	-	37,520	0	0
MALAGA, and the Garrisons		-	37,944	8	10
MURCIA	-	-	23,220	0	0
ARRAGON	-	-	37,445	11	0
CATALONIA	-	-	39,924	8	10
VALENCIA	-	-	36,444	8	10
MAJORCA	-	-	12,195	11	0
NAVARRE	-	-	24,640	0	0
			1,221,820	0	6

The Annual Produce of the POST-OFFICE in every Province.

			L	*s.*	*d.*
LA MANCHA	-	-	9,555	11	0
MADRID	-	-	140,077	15	7
GALICIA	-	-	8,494	8	10
ASTURIAS	-	-	10,088	17	10
VALLADOLID	-	-	5,917	15	7
ZAMORA	-	-	1,322	4	5
SEVILLE	-	-	10,666	13	4
GRANADA	-	-	9,766	13	4
	Carried over,		195,889	19	11

CORDOVA

			l.	*s.*	*d.*
Brought over,			195,889	19	11
CORDOVA	-	-	8,888	17	10
JAEN	-	-	4,777	15	7
SORIA	-	-	1,944	13	4
SEGOVIA	-	-	1,100	0	0
BISCAY	-	-	17,777	15	6
GUIPUSCOA	-	-	11,966	13	4
ALAVA	-	-	11,555	11	0
ARRAGON	-	-	12,348	17	10
VALENCIA	-	-	21,177	17	10
CATALONIA	-	-	16,700	0	0
MAJORCA	-	-	8,451	2	2
BURGOS	-	-	9,393	6	8
TOLEDO	-	-	10,314	8	10
LEON	-	-	961	2	2
SALAMANCA	-	-	10,333	6	8
AVILA	-	-	753	6	8
PALENCIA	-	-	555	11	0
TORO	-	-	411	2	3
CANARIES	-	-	9,638	17	10
BADAJOZ	-	-	4,488	17	10
MURCIA	-	-	7,777	15	0
GUADALAXARA	-	-	588	17	10
CUENZA	-	-	766	13	4
			368,562	10	5

The Annual Produce of the PROVINCIAL FARMS, or MIL-
LONES, by Provinces.

			l.	*s.*	*d.*
LA MANCHA	-	-	22,888	17	10
MADRID	-	-	45,500	0	0
GALICIA	-	-	45,222	4	5
ASTURIAS	-	-	22,822	4	5
Carried over,			136,433	6	8

VALLA-

		l.	*s.*	*d.*
Brought over,		136,433	6	8
VALLADOLID	-	45,377	15	5
ZAMORA	-	22,555	11	0
SEVILLE	-	34,588	17	10
GRANADA	-	24,657	15	5
CORDOVA	-	27,080	0	0
JAEN	-	33,555	11	0
SORIA	-	45,444	8	10
SEGOVIA	-	45,333	6	8
BISCAY	-	22,975	11	0
ALAVA	-	47,066	13	4
GUIPUSCOA	-	49,111	2	2
ARAGON	-	70,004	8	10
VALENCIA	-	68,890	0	0
CATALONIA	-	66,786	13	4
MAJORCA	-	35,343	6	8
BURGOS	-	23,777	15	5
TOLEDO	-	22,888	17	10
LEON	-	23,500	0	0
SALAMANCA	-	22,888	17	10
AVILA	-	23,477	15	7
PALENCIA	-	48,222	4	5
TORO	-	50,888	17	10
CANARIES	-	128,262	4	5
BADAJOZ	-	45,333	6	8
MURCIA	-	55,888	17	10
GUADALAXARA	-	56,333	6	8
CUENÇA	-	34,222	4	5
		1,310,888	17	2

The Annual Produce of the GENERAL FARMS in each Province.

		l.	*s.*	*d.*
MADRID	-	150,000	0	0
GALICIA	-	182,222	4	5
Carried over,		332,222	4	5

3   ASTURIAS

		l.	*s.*	*d.*
	Brought over,	332,222	4	5
ASTURIAS	–	108,888	17	10
VALLADOLID	–	110,000	0	0
ZAMORA	–	54,444	8	10
SEVILLE	–	57,777	15	6
GRANADA	–	91,111	2	2
CORDOVA	–	70,000	0	0
JAEN	–	52,222	4	5
SORIA	–	24,444	8	10
SEGOVIA	–	42,222	4	5
BISCAY	–	48,888	17	10
ALAVA	–	42,222	4	5
GUIPUSCOA	–	40,066	13	4
ARAGON	–	217,933	6	8
VALENCIA	–	230,262	4	5
CATALONIA	–	221,130	0	0
MAJORCA	–	54,222	4	5
BURGOS	–	38,288	17	10
TOLEDO	–	40,144	8	10
LEON	–	21,222	4	5
SALAMANCA	–	29,111	2	2
AVILA	–	15,888	17	10
PALENCIA	–	21,666	13	4
TORO	–	21,777	15	7
CANARIES	–	98,777	15	7
BADAJOZ	–	47,888	17	10
MURCIA	–	110,177	15	7
GUADALAJARA	–	32,435	11	0
CUENZA	–	19,377	15	7
LA MANCHA	–	235,811	2	2
		2,530,627	15	3

A GE-

A Gene͟ral Recapitulation *of the receiving and issuing of the* FINANCES.

The Annual Revenue.

	l.	*s.*	*d.*
BY the produce of Tobacco - -	1,221,820	0	6
Ditto of the Post-Office - -	368,562	10	5
Ditto of the Provincial Farms, under which are included all kind of taxes that are paid upon the following six kinds of vivres: bread, oil, wine, fat, flesh meat, soap; which taxes are renewed every six years; and under this head is also comprehended the Alcavalas, and other rights and taxes	1,310,888	17	2
Ditto of the General Farms, in which are included, besides the customs, the duties on wool, the admiralties, rights of sanity, cards, mercuries, brandy, lead, gun-powder, &c.	2,530,627	15	3
Total of the Revenue	5,431,899	3	4

The Annual Expence.

	l.	*s.*	*d.*
For the subsistence of the Land Army of 91,311 men, including the general officers of Artillery - -	1,035,488	19	7
Ditto of the Naval Forces, consisting of 45,810 men, in pay - -	714,561	6	7
Ditto of the Tribunals at MADRID, and through the whole kingdom, with the salaries of the Seneschals, Governors, and Intendants, in all 1800 men, in actual pay	169,992	19	5
Ditto of the Garrisons, 7158 men -	166,410	11	8
Carried over,	2,086,453	17	3

For

	l.	*s.*	*d.*
Brought over,	2,086,453	17	3
For the fubfiftence of 23,300 men, employed in the farms of Tobacco -	317,402	4	5
Ditto of 18,000 men, employed in the Poft-Office - - -	50,368	9	0
Ditto of 11,500 men, employed in the Provincial farms - -	53,240	0	0
Ditto of 19,000 men, employed in the General Farms - -	64,458	17	10
Penfions paid out of the Finances -	211,352	12	7
The expence of the Palace and Royal Family	174,334	5	8
Total of the Annual Expence,	2,957,610	6	9

The RECAPITULATION.

	l.	*s.*	*d.*
The Annual Revenue - -	5,431,899	3	4
The Annual Expence -	2,957,610	6	9
Remains free	2,474,288	16	7

R E M A R K S.

THE *General Farms* are the cuftoms, the fale of tobacco, falt, lead, and quick-filver; the poft office; licences to veffels which trade to AMERICA; ftamped paper; and fome other particulars, fpecified at full length in USTARITZ. The greateft number of the taxes called general, fuch as tobacco, falt, and the cuftoms, are under the management of a board for the King's behalf, and increafe daily fince they have been fo regulated. The revenue from tobacco in particular, has increafed annually a million of crowns vellon, or 111,111 l. fterling, fince 1739, that the management was regulated according to the plan drawn up by Don MARTIN DE LOYNAZ. That Adminiftrator-General gave fecurity for the augmentation, which he propofed, but was freed from all obligation at the end of one year, when he proved, that the fales had amounted to eleven millions of rials more than ufual. He increafed the tax upon the beft forts of tobacco ten rials, and in the fame degree leffened the tax upon the worft, which are purchafed by the common people. The clergy, as

K k   well

well as the other members of the state, are subject to the general taxes, because they are looked upon as rights of regality or sovereignty. They pay besides, the taxes of the Crusado, Subsidio, and Escusado, valued at 155,555 l. sterling.

The farm of the *Provincial Taxes* respects only the twenty-two provinces of the crown of CASTILLE, and includes several branches. 1st, The tax of Alcavala, established in 1341. This is ten *per cent.* upon every thing sold or exchanged, even upon land revenues, and all kinds of rents, with an augmentation of four additional taxes of one *per cent.* imposed each, successively in 1639, 1642, 1656, 1664.

Upon sales at first hand, the farmer of the Revenues requires only ten *per cent.* but upon sales in retail, fourteen *per cent.* is required. The regulation however does not appear to be uniform, since, according to USTARITZ, there is not more than between six or seven *per cent.* collected by this tax. Later writers nevertheless estimate this tax as I have done. After all, as the tax is repeated upon each sale, we may reasonably conclude, that every thing has at least paid the whole tax once, notwithstanding any abatement in the valuation. The clergy are not subject to this tax in their sales; on the contrary, they are allowed a discount in valuing the produce of their lands, or upon those things which are designed for their own consumption; and when they again sell that produce, they have the advantage of the rest of the King's subjects in the proportion of the whole tax. Those of the clergy, who have no lands, or who buy in retail, pay the tax, as it is included in the price of the commodity.

The second branch is the tax called Millones, with the additional taxes, known under the name of the new imposts. This tax began in 1590, when a service or subsidy of eight millions of ducats was granted to PHILIP II. by the States of CASTILE. In 1601 the same States granted an annual service of four millions of ducats during the course of six years. It was called the service of twenty-four millions, and the necessities of the monarchy have obliged it to be continued ever since. Of these

twenty-

twenty-four millions, four and one half were laid upon the price of falt, and the payment of the remainder was laid upon the price of wine, vinegar, oil, and butchers meat.   The liquid meafure called an *arrobe*, is compofed of eight parts, named *azumbres*.   One of thefe eights belongs to the King, and the proprietor is obliged to pay it according to the valuation of the feven remaining parts, including even the advance of price, by reafon of this excife; by which means the *arrobe* fold under the name of eight *azumbres*, really contains only feven, and its fub-divifions are in the fame proportion.   Thefe taxes are farmed at 892,888 l. fterling.

There are alfo other taxes that may be included under the general title of provincial taxes, fuch as the tax upon brandy, upon foap, upon fnow, upon cards, and other fmall articles.   Thefe taxes are farmed at 91,244 l. fterling.

Almost all the taxes of Spain, we may obferve, are laid upon things confumed by the people, in the manner of a general excife; and thofe included under the name of provincial taxes, in a more particular manner affect the neceffary and daily con-fumption of all ranks of men.   In Spain the general outcry, and the groans of the people, have been excited by thefe pro-vincial taxes.   At prefent the miniftry are labouring to make fome reformation upon them, and they are only continued till fomething better can be eftablifhed in their place.

Don Miguel de Zabala, in a memorial prefented to Philip V. in 1734, demonftrates, that though the provincial taxes, on the loweft computation, amount to *feventy-fix millions of rials vellon*, and though there is reafon to think that fum is raifed upon the people, yet only *feven* millions come into the King's ex-chequer.

The *Juros* are perpetual rights of propriety, or in other words, penfions which the King pays to his fubjects out of his own fi-nances, by a temporal favour, by the endowment of fome foun-dation, or for the reward of merit and fervices.   Sometimes the

K k 2   Juros

Juros mean a deduction of three *per cent.* from all the King's finances.

THE *Media Annata*, which is the fame as our *Firſt Fruits* is a tax of one half of the firſt years revenue, paid on every new fucceſſion to any eccleſiaſtical dignity or benefice. All lucrative or honourable employments, held from the King during life, are ſubject to this tax.

BESIDES the above-mentioned revenues, a general view of which (excluſive of the *Juros* and *Media Annata*) I have given in the *Recapitulation*; SPAIN likewiſe receives others that are very conſiderable from the *Indies.* The amount of theſe *per annum* is about 900,000 *l.* ſterling, conſequently there is ſaid to remain free annually in the royal treaſury, about 3,373,288 *l.* ſterling.

LETTER

LETTER XIII.

A short View of the *Commerce* and *Manufactures* of SPAIN, so far as they relate to GREAT BRITAIN.

I HAVE been informed from good authority, that our trade with Old and New SPAIN is full one third less than it was about forty years ago; and that the balance and exchange, between SPAIN and GREAT BRITAIN, are every day more and more turning against the later kingdom. The causes of this decrease are indeed not at all difficult to be discovered or accounted for. Part of it is owing to the extreme avarice and extortion of our own merchants, who, not contented with moderate profits, have kept up the prices of their goods beyond their just proportion, and thereby opened a door for the French and Dutch to undersell us at the Spanish markets. Another reason is, that the price of labour in those two countries, is considerably lower than in our own, which enables them likewise to afford their goods to the Spaniards at a much cheaper rate than we can do. A third reason is, the alteration introduced during the Spanish war in Queen ANNE's time, when the French crept into that trade, and deprived us of a greater share of it than we shall probably be ever able to recover. A fourth reason may be, the progress which the Spaniards themselves have made in some branches of manufacture; for the encouragement which the Kings of the House of BOURBON have given to manufactures and arts, has excited some few Spaniards to apply themselves to industry and trade. For several years past, the ministry in SPAIN have endeavoured, by means of foreign workmen, to set on foot various manufactures;

4

and

and the great attention they have given to that object, has not been altogether without effect. But at present, by a strange infatuation, the minister to whose department the care of the manufactures belongs, not only neglects, but discourages them; and they consequently decline very fast.

The state of trade between Great Britain and Spain, in the time of Joshua Gee, was as follows. Our *Exports* to Spain were, 1. Broad cloths. 2. Druggets. 3. Callimancoes. 4. Bays. 5. Stuffs. 6. Leather. 7. Baccalao, or salted fish. 8. Tin. 9. Lead. 10. Corn. Our returns from Spain were in, 1. Wines. 2. Oil. 3. Fruits. 4. Wool. 5. Indigo. 6. Logwood. 7. Cochineal. 8. Materials for dying. Mr. Gee has taken no notice of *silk* in this account, and for a good reason; for the exportation of it from Spain was not permitted till 1760, and then limited to the ports of Barcelona, Alicant, and Carthagena, from the 16th of November to the 16th of May every year, there being no exportation allowed during the other six months, that the manufacturers may have leisure to take care of their fabrics.

We used about that period to take off at least two thirds of all the produce of Spain, which made our manufactures an easy purchase to the Spaniards, who nevertheless paid us a very considerable balance in bullion.

Since the accession of the House of Bourbon, this balance in our favour has been daily declining. For many years past we have ceased to be considered as *the favoured nation*; and France now shares a great part of the gold and silver of the Spanish West-Indies, in return for her silk, her linen, and other manufactures introduced into Spain.

The infamous peace of Utrecht was hardly signed, when we began to feel the effects of a *predilection*, which the Spaniards discovered towards the French nation; so that a *Family Compact*, if things be justly considered, will appear no novelty. This will be evident enough from the following curious extracts from

8   the

the letters of feveral Englifh gentlemen, relating to that point:
——Mr. POULDON, the Englifh Conful at the CANARIES, in a
letter dated from TENERIFF, the 22d of March 1715, and addreffed to Sir PAUL METHUEN, then minifter at MADRID,
fays, " Since the fufpenfion of arms, the fubjects of his Britan-
" nic Majefty, in the CANARIES, have been continually oppref-
" fed. The bifhop of GERONDA had publifhed an order in the
" name of the King, in virtue of which order all Britifh veffels
" were to pay only the ordinary duties; but fince the arrival of
" the new General, this order is explained in a new manner.
" They exclude from being comprehended in it all kinds of mer-
" chandize, which, as they pretend, are not properly Englifh
" manufactures, although tranfported by and in Englifh veffels.
" In confequence of this explanation of the order, the fubjects
" of his Majefty have paid lately, upwards of 3000 pounds
" fterling."

THE following are the words of Mr. KEEN, our conful at
ALICANT, in a letter to Mr. STANHOPE at MADRID. " By
" an exprefs order of the court, publifhed here by the governor
" of VALENCIA, all foreigners are obliged in lieu of the Alca-
" valas and Millones, to pay a duty named *quartals*, which
" amounts to 14 *per cent.* and is to begin with the year 1714,
" for merchandize, on which the duties have already been paid,
" at the rate of 15 *per cent.* fo that we muft at prefent pay 29
" *per cent.* for the entry of all kinds of merchandize. Befides
" the exorbitancy of thefe duties, this proceeding is attended
" with another inconvenience; for the factors have already regu-
" lated their accounts with the merchants, on the footing of 15
" *per cent.* Moreover, thofe who refufe to pay thefe duties,
" are expofed to be quartered upon by foldiers, and to give them
" fo much *per* day till fuch time as the duties be paid. Thefe
" are unheard of demands, which were never before made upon
" any fubjects of GREAT BRITAIN, who never paid more than
" 7½ per cent. under the reign of CHARLES II. the laft prince
" of the Auftrian line."

SIR

Sir Martin Westcomb, and conful Russel, in a letter to Sir Paul Methuen, at Madrid, dated the 22d of May 1715, exprefs themfelves thus: "The alteration they have made in re-" gard to the duties which were paid in the reign of Charles " II. has interrupted our trade, and will infallibly ruin it. Don " Juan Antonio Zavalos has caufed an order to be pub-" lifhed, by which all the favours granted to our merchants, " and conftantly enjoyed by them, are revoked; fo that for the " future all merchandize muft pay all the duties of entry and ex-" port, according to the valuation of the tariffs, which in fome " kinds of merchandize will· amount to 25 per cent. and in " others even to 28."

The rigorous and oppreffive impofitions, complained of in thefe letters, were not only contrary to feveral treaties, made and concluded between Great Britain and Spain, but alfo to the engagements of Lewis XIV. who, in the name of Spain, and in quality of plenipotentiary of his Grandfon, previous to the fuf-penfion of arms, promifed to the Englifh,

" First, That all the advantages, rights, and privileges, which " the Spaniards had granted, or might in time to come grant to " the French, or to the *moft favoured nation*, fhould be granted " to the fubjects of Great Britain.

" Secondly, That all merchandize of the growth and· ma-" nufacture of Great Britain, that fhould be fent to the In-" dies from the ports of Spain, fhould be exempt from the " duties of entry and export in Spain, and from thofe of entry " in the Indies. And that thefe conditions and thefe promifes " fhould be extended in the treaty of peace, in the moft ample " and convenient manner."

Lewis and Philip had hardly gained their ends, by thefe promifes, than they took off the mafk, and interpreted them, as it beft fuited their own advantage; for even before the peace between the two Crowns was entirely fettled, Lord Lexington wrote home to the following purpofe: " Affairs are not here
" upon

" upon the fame footing on which they were before the fufpen-
" fion of arms; for the King has told me in exprefs terms, We
" know that peace is as neceffary to you as to us, and that you
" will not break with us for trifles."——

THE chief of the *Treaties*, mentioned above as infringed upon
by PHILIP, and which relates to the general ftate of commerce
between GREAT BRITAIN and SPAIN, is that of 1667 : for the
treaty of 1670 chiefly refpects AMERICA. It was regulated by
the treaty of 1667, that the trading fubjects of either crown
fhould reciprocally pay no higher impofts and duties, than the
inhabitants of the places themfelves, where the goods were bought
or freighted, ufually paid; that they fhould enjoy the fame privileges as the natural fubjects of each country enjoyed; that it
fhould not be lawful in either kingdom, under any pretence whatever, to detain the traders in the ports or harbours, or after their
departure to fue at law their factors or merchants, on account of
any merchandize put on board their veffels; that Englifh veffels
arriving in the ports of SPAIN, or others, fubject to the dominion of that crown, fhould be exempted from all vifit or fearch of
officers of contraband merchandize; that any fhips belonging
either to SPAIN or ENGLAND, might, if it fuited their convenience, land part of their cargo, in any road, and proceed to fea
with the remainder, without giving any account to the cuftom-
houfe; and that, in return for merchandize fold, the payments
fhould not be made *in copper money*, or in any other fpecie, but
what the merchants fhould actually agree for. There is no occafion to mention any more articles of this famous treaty, fince
from thofe already given, it is fufficiently evident, that the trade
was fettled upon a footing very advantageous to both parties :
and I cannot help wifhing, that each nation faw fo clearly their
mutual intereft in the obfervance of every article of this treaty, as
might tempt them to form, upon the fame principles, fuch a fo-
lid *Commercial Compact*, as fhould never be diffolved.

NOTWITHSTANDING the arts of French infinuation, our
traffic with SPAIN is very confiderable, and chiefly in the following articles.——We export to that country large quantities
of

of dried and falted fifh, called by them *bacalas*; likewife broad cloths, and woollen ftuffs of various kinds to a great amount; filk ftuffs, cutlery ware, warlike and naval ftores, particularly cables and anchors; alfo watches, wrought brafs, and prince's metal, toys, mathematical inftruments, cabinet work, particularly of mahogony, wrought and unwrought tin, leather, lead, corn, dry and falted meat, cattle, butter, cheefe, beer, hats, linen, vitriol, pepper, rice, and other products of our American Colonies; and, if we attended to it, we might fupply them with great quantities of timber from thofe Colonies, as the Spaniards, tho' they have in fome parts fine woods of excellent oak, yet from their inexpertnefs in felling trees, and want of roads, are in a manner entirely deprived of the ufe of them.

FROM SPAIN we receive the following articles : Wines, oil, vinègar, fruits of various kinds, viz. olives, raifins of the fun, raifins dryed with afhes, called by them *paffas de lexia*; raifins from ALMUNEGAR, a city on the coaft of ANDALUSIA, famous for that produce; chefnuts, almonds, figs, citrons, lemons, oranges, cocao-nuts, Spanifh pepper, pomegranates, fine wool, indigo, cochineal, materials for dying, kali, or barillia, and fofa, for the making of foap and glafs, chiefly from ALICANT; quickfilver; fome wrought filks, particularly from VALENTIA; and of late raw filk, balfam of Peru, vanillas, cake-chocolate of GUAJACA, falfaparilla, falted fea-brizzle, faltpetre, falt from CADIZ, falt from PORT ST. MARY'S, woollen counterpanes, and a remarkable fine fort of blankets from SEGOVIA, iron from BISCAY, fword blades, particularly from TOLEDO, gun and piftol barrels from GUIPUSCOA and BARCELONA, vermilion, borax, hams, fnuff from SEVILLE and the HAVANNAH, foap, formerly a confiderable article, but as we now make it ourfelves, only a trifle, tho' there is ftill much of it annually run into SCOTLAND; and feveral roots and drugs of the growths of SPAIN and AMERICA, employed in medicine.

I HAVE not fpecified the *logwood* as an article of *importation* from SPAIN; for however it may have been fuch formerly, we may now hope to fupply ourfelves with it; as it appears by the

6   XVI.

XVI. article of the prefent Preliminaries of Peace, that we have at length happily obtained the free and unmolefted liberty of cutting it in the Bay of HONDURAS, on condition of demolifhing all our fortifications erected there, and in other parts of Spanifh AMERICA. But I could wifh, that the liberty of cutting it had alfo been extended in exprefs terms to the Bay of CAMPEACHY. Thofe who know the value of this article, will receive great pleafure on feeing it now well fettled; for whatever our pretenfions were, we certainly had but a very difputable title to this important branch of trade; and this will even appear from the perufal of the memorial of the Board of Trade, laid before his Majefty GEORGE I. and drawn up exprefsly to prove that claim.

THE Spanifh trade to SOUTH AMERICA is carried on by annual fhips, ufually divided into three claffes, the *Flota,* the *Regifter Ships,* and *Galleons;* of which the following is the moft accurate account I could meet with.

THE *Flota* is a fleet confifting of three men of war, and fourteen or fifteen merchant fhips, from 400 to 1000 tuns burthen; they are loaded almoft with every fort of goods which EUROPE produces for export; all forts of woollens, linens, filks, velvets, laces, glafs, paper, and cutlery; all forts of wrought iron, watches, clocks, quickfilver for the ufe of their miners, horfe-furniture, fhoes, ftockings, books, pictures, military ftores, wines, fruits, &c. fo that all the trading parts of EUROPE are highly interefted in the cargo of this fleet. SPAIN itfelf fends out little more than the wine and fruit; this, with the freight, and commiffions to the merchant, and the duty to the King, is almoft all the advantage, which that kingdom derives from her commerce with the INDIES. This fleet is fitted out at CADIZ, and bound to LA VERA CRUZ: they are not permitted to break bulk on any account, till they arrive there. When all the goods are landed and difpofed of at LA VERA CRUZ, the fleet takes in the plate, precious ftones, cochineal, indigo, cocao, tobacco, fugar, and hides, which are the returns for Old SPAIN. From LA VERA CRUZ they fail to the HAVANNA in the Ifland of CUBA, which is the place of their rendezvous, where they meet the

Galleons.

Galleons. Thefe are another fleet, which carry on all the trade of TERRA FIRMA, by CARTHAGENA, and of PERU, by PANAMA and PORTOBELLO, in the fame manner as the *Flota* ferves for the trade of New SPAIN. When the Flota arrives at the HAVAN-NAH, and joins the Galleons and Regifter fhips, which affemble at the fame port from all quarters, fome of the cleaneft and beft failing veffels are difpatched to Old SPAIN with advice of the contents of thefe feveral *fleets,* as well as with treafure and goods of their own, that the court may judge what *indulto,* or duty, is proper to be laid on them, and what convoy is neceffary for their fafety.

REGISTER *fhips* are fent out by merchants at CADIZ or SE-VILLE, when they judge that goods muft be wanted at any cer-tain port in the WEST-INDIES. The courfe is, to petition the council of the INDIES for licence to fend a fhip of 300 tuns bur-then, or under, to that port: they pay for this licence 40,000, or 50,000 dollars, befides prefents to the officers, in proportion to the connivance neceffary to their defign. For tho' the licence runs only to 300 tons at moft, the veffel fitted out is feldom lefs than 600. This fhip and cargo are regiftered at the pretended burthen. It is required too, that a certificate be brought from the King's officer at the port to which the regifter fhip is bound, that fhe does not exceed the fize at which fhe is regiftered; all this paffes of courfe. Thefe are what they call *Regifter fhips,* and by thefe the trade of Spanifh AMERICA has been carried on principally for fome years paft: which practice has been thought as much to the prejudice of their trade, as it is contrary to all their former maxims for carrying it on.

LA VERA CRUZ is fituated on the fouth-weft part of the Gulph of MEXICO, and to the fouth-eaft of that city.

THE fleet which is called *the Galleons,* confifts of eight men of war of 500 tons each, defigned principally to fupply PERU with military ftores; but in reality laden, not only with thofe, but with every other kind of merchandize on a private account, fo as to be in too weak a condition either to defend themfelves, or protect others. Under the convoy of thefe are twelve fail of merchant fhips, not inferior to the Galleons in burthen. This fleet of the *Galleons* is regulated in much the fame manner with the *Flota*, and is deftined for the *exclufive* commerce of TERRA FIRMA, and the SOUTH-SEA, as the Flota is for that of MEXICO.

As foon as this *Galleon* fleet arrives at CARTHAGENA, expref-fes are difpatched to PORTOBELLO, and to all the adjacent towns, but particularly to PANAMA, that they may get ready all the treafure which is depofited there, to meet the Galleons at PORTOBELLO; at which place all the perfons concerned in the various branches of this extenfive trade, affemble. There is no part of the world where bufinefs of fuch great importance is negotiated in fo fhort a time; for in a fortnight the fair is over. During the fair, heaps of wedges and ingots of filver are thrown about upon the wharfs, as things of no value. The difplay of gold, filver, and precious ftones on one hand, and of the various and rare workmanfhip of the feveral ingenious fabrics of EUROPE on the other, are truly aftonifhing.

CARTHAGENA is fituated on the moft northern point of TER-RA FIRMA: PORTOBELLO and PANAMA are on the oppofite fides of the Ifthmus of DARIEN; the firft on the north-eaft fide, and the other on the fouth-weft.

THE whole trade between the EAST INDIES and Spanifh AMERICA, is carried on by one great Galleon, which arrives at ACAPULCO from the PHILIPPINE iflands, on the coaft of CHI-NA, in the month of December. They fee no other land in their whole voyage of 3000 leagues, which they perform in five months, than the LITTLE LADRONES. The fhip is laden with all the rich commodities of the Eaft, as cloves, pepper, cinna-mon, nutmegs, mace, china, japan wares, callicoes plain and painted, muflins of every fort, filks, precious ftones, rich drugs, and gold duft. At the fame time the rich fhip from LIMA

comes

comes in, and is not computed to bring lefs than two millions of pieces of eight in filver, (450,000 l. Sterl.) Several other fhips, from the different parts of CHILI and PERU, meet upon the fame occafion; and befides the traffic for the Philippine commodities, this caufes a very large dealing for every thing which thofe countries have to exchange with one another, as well as for the purchafe of all forts of European goods. The fair at ACAPULCO lafts fometimes for thirty days. As foon as the goods are difpofed of, the galleon prepares to fet out on her voyage to the PHILIPPINES with her returns, chiefly in filver, but with fome European goods too, and fome other commodities of AMERICA. I fpeak here, as though there were but one veffel on the trade with the PHILIPPINES; and in fact there is only nominally *one* trading veffel, the galleon itfelf, of about 1200 tons; but another attends her commonly as a fort of convoy, which generally carries fuch a quantity of goods, as in great meafure difables her from performing that office. The galleon has often above 1000 people on board, either interefted in the cargo, or merely paffengers; and there is no trade in which fo large profits are made; the captain of the veffel, the pilots, the mates, and even the common failors, making, in one voyage, what in their feveral ranks may be confidered as eafy fortunes. It is faid by the writer of Lord ANSON's voyage, that the Jefuits have the profits of this fhip to fupport their miffions.

THIS commerce to fo vaft a value, though carried on directly between different parts of the King of SPAIN's own dominions, enriches them in proportion but very little; the far greater part of every thing which comes from the PHILIPPINES, being the produce, or fabric of other countries. The Spaniards add none of the artificial value of labour to any thing. The Chinefe are largely interefted in this cargo; and it is to them they are indebted for the manufacturing fuch of their plate, as is wrought into any better fafhion than rude ingots, or inelegant coins. When this ACAPULCO *Fair* is over, the town is comparatively deferted; however, it remains for the whole year the moft confiderable port in MEXICO for the trade with PERU and CHILI, which is not very great.

The

The East-India goods brought here are carried on trucles to MEXICO, from whence what exceeds their own consumption is sent by land-carriage to LA VERA CRUZ, to pass over to TERRA FIRMA, to the islands, and some even to OLD SPAIN, tho' in no great quantity.

ACAPULCO lies two hundred miles south of MEXICO, on the SOUTH SEA. MEXICO, though no port, nor communicating with the sea by any navigable river, has a prodigious commerce, and is itself the center of all the trade that is carried on between AMERICA and EUROPE, on one hand, and between AMERICA and the EAST INDIES on the other; for here the principal merchants reside, the greatest part of the business is negociated, and the goods that pass from ACAPULCO to LA VERA CRUZ, or from LA VERA CRUZ to ACAPULCO, for the use of the PHILIPPINES, and in a great measure for the use of PERU and LIMA, all pass through this city, and employ an incredible number of horses and mules in the carriage: Hither all the gold and silver is sent to be coined; here the king's fifth is deposited; and here is wrought all that immense quantity of utensils, and ornaments in plate, which is every year sent into EUROPE. Every thing here has the greatest air of magnificence and wealth. The shops glitter on all sides with the exposure of gold, silver, and jewels, and surprize yet more by the work of the imagination upon the treasures which fill great chests piled up to the cielings, whilst they wait the time of being sent to OLD SPAIN.

THE trade between SPAIN and her colonies in AMERICA, which has been just described, is the most considerable part of their external commerce, and the great support of their navy; for, till our late breach with FRANCE, very few of their ships navigated into foreign parts; and the chief source that supplied the balance of their trade with other nations, arose from this branch. Their *internal* traffic is by no means proportionate to the numbers of their people, the natural advantages of their situation and climate, the abundance of raw materials which the country produces, and their INDIES supply them with; especially when we reflect on the many years of peace which they have enjoyed,

joyed, and that commerce was never so much confidered by the several European states, as it is in the present age.

THE great error of the SPANISH policy seems to be this; they never sufficiently attended to the truth of the following political maxim, That industry, manual labour, and the arts, are more beneficial, and truer sources of wealth to a state, than the richest mines of gold and silver. Dazzled with the spoils of AMERICA, they turned their whole attention to seize the exclusive possession of those seeming riches; they neglected agriculture and manufactures, and contracted a contempt for the mechanic, and even liberal arts; in consequence of which, the country becoming daily less populous, their maritime and military strength soon declined. Of late years the Spanish ministry hath been fully sensible of this fatal mistake, and hath endeavoured to raise a spirit of industry among the people, by promoting the establishment of manufactures, in various parts of the kingdom: But though they have tempted the people, by exemption from taxes, and many other privileges, yet the progress they have made is not so considerable as might have been expected.

THEIR most remarkable manufactures are the following; the woollen fabrics are carried on at SEGOVIA, where they made, in the year 1759, 7,400 pieces of cloth, of 30, 60, and 80 bars in length; also at *Valdemoro, Guadalajara, Saragosa, Agulada,* and *Barcelona.* The woollen manufactures owe much of their present establishment, as USTARITZ tells us, to the care and encouragement of the DUKE DE RIPERDA, who had the direction of them in the year 1724. The old silk manufactures are chiefly in *Andalusia, Valencia,* and *Murcia.* Those in *Catalonia* are more modern. The principal one of all is at *Talavera de la Reyna,* in NEW CASTILE, for the richest gold and silver tissues. At *Madrid* there is also a manufacture of tissues, lutestrings, and other slight silks. There is a manufacture of linen at *Corunna,* said to supply the King's table; another of linen at *Segovia.* At *Madrid* is lately set up a manufacture of porcelain, in the gardens of the King's palace of the *Retiro,* wrought by Artificers brought from SAXONY. There is likewise in that city a new manufacture of

good

good tapeftry, and of cards, as the fineft cards of all, which are
made at *Barcelona*, are there prohibited. The fabric of glafs is at
St. Ildefonfo, that of fwords is at *Toledo*, and thofe of iron in
Bifcay; that of paper at *Segovia*. The pottery fabrics are very
numerous and excellent, particularly that of *Talavera de la Reyna*.
The looms of filk, wool, and linen, in all the kingdoms, are
faid to be 20,000; but whether that account be exact, I cannot
prefume to fay.

THAT their manufactures are not now more confiderable, is
not *folely* owing to their indolence, and the other caufes above-
mentioned, but likewife to the oppreffive fpirit of that fuperftition which reigns there, under the mafk of religion. This will
be evident from the following extract of a memorial, prefented
by EMMANUEL DE LIRA, firft fecretary of ftate to CHARLES II.
which breathes fuch a fpirit of patriotifm and toleration, that I
perfuade myfelf it will be very acceptable to the reader. DE LI-
RA having, in his memorial, propofed the eftablifhment of a general company of commerce, in which all foreigners that pleafed
fhould be allowed to be fharers, adds,

" THERE is only one obftacle on our fide, that can prevent
the eftablifhment of the company. It is, I confefs, great, but
neverthelefs very eafy to be furmounted, efpecially by your majefty, when you are once informed, that the removing of that obftacle would be a means of remedying feveral abufes introduced
among us, and alfo of preventing the daily profanation of our
moft facred myfteries. This obftacle arifes from the law eftablifhed in thefe kingdoms, and from the decrees and edicts of the
holy tribunal of the Inquifition, againft the Jews, and againft
herefy!

" I KNOW, Sir, that it is the greateft glory of SPAIN, that it
is the only nation which keeps itfelf pure in the faith of the Catholic, Apoftolic, and Roman church; it is this which gives
your Majefty the juft title of Catholic Monarch, which you fo
worthily poffefs. I likewife know, that there is not a more holy,
nor a more falutary inftitution than that of the holy tribunal; but

M m   I

I shall endeavour to make it appear, that by granting the liberty of commerce to heretics, and even to Jews, no prejudice could from thence result to SPAIN, nor to the glorious title of Catholic King, nor to the laws and prerogatives of the Inquisition.

" My reputation is unsullied, and I flatter myself that nobody will suspect me, as to my soundness in the Catholic Faith. I am evidently a zealous and true Catholic, by presuming to propose to your Majesty to grant liberty of conscience in these your kingdoms, as such a liberty would prevent a great many profanations that are daily committed.

" Is it not a truth, Sir, that all the prisons of the Inquisition throughout all SPAIN are filled with Jews and heretics, who have profaned our sacraments, by receiving them as though they had been zealous and devout Catholics! Is it not likewise a truth, that an infinite number of others keep themselves concealed among us, and participate of those sacraments unworthily, and by way of derision. Such a thing never happens in countries where liberty of conscience is allowed to all. The greediness of foreigners after our wealth gets the better of their apprehensions of divine or human punishments.

" WE might grant to the nations trading to CADIZ, or SE-VILLE, or any other place where this company should be established, the free exercise of their religion for them alone, in the same manner as the Dutch, and many Protestant States and Princes, have allowed it to the Roman Catholics in their dominions, namely, not an open toleration. Thus foreigners, interested in, and members of the company, and their clerks and domestics, would have this advantage, which would render their abode in SPAIN very agreeable; foreign merchants who traded hither would be satisfied, and we should deliver ourselves from those enemies of our mysteries, who keep themselves concealed among us, and remove them from our temples and our altars; for as it is interest that inspires them with the courage to surmount all apprehensions and dangers, the same interest would draw them to that place, where they might in full security follow their superstitions.

I   " THE

" THE example of the church of ROME for thefe feveral ages paft may inform us, that it is not contrary to religion to tolerate a worfhip quite oppofite to ours; for it has given a fynagogue to the Jews, and it alfo allows the Greeks to worfhip according to their liturgy, without thereby forfeiting the name, or the fovereign title of being the immoveable feat of our religion. This example has been followed by the Grand Duke of TUSCANY, at LEGHORN, and by feveral other Princes in Chriftendom.

" THE Englifh merchants, notwithftanding their diverfity of religion, have the liberty of trading in our ports, fince the treaty concluded by the Conftable of CASTILE, and the minifters of JAMES I. King of GREAT BRITAIN.

" YOUR Majefty's father, of glorious memory, granted the fame thing to the Dutch, and even engaged, by the treaty of MUNSTER, to furnifh them with a convenient and honourable place for a burial ground.

" THUS, the moft difficult ftep is already furmounted. As to other points, juft precautions might eafily be taken to prevent the venom of herefy from infecting the heart of Spaniards."

LETTER XIV.

An ACCOUNT of the SPANISH MONEY.

Pecuniam probant veterem, et diu notam.

TACITUS *de Mor. Ger.*

THE SPANISH MONEY is in itself not easy to be understood, especially by those who are not merchants. The Spaniards make up most of their accompts, and form their calculations chiefly in these *two* Species, the REAL DE VELLON, and the MARAVEDI.

THE MARAVEDI is the lowest of the denominations of their copper money, and in this the *King's accompts* are kept; consequently the revenues of SPAIN, and the wealth brought from PERU and MEXICO, are annually computed by an integer of copper, that is *three times less than our farthing.*

THE REAL DE VELLON is the smallest piece of their *silver money*, the ninetieth part of the pound Sterling, and equals our *two-pence-halfpenny, and two thirds of a farthing.*

BUT though it be the most usual way in SPAIN to compute by the *Maravedi* and the *Real de Vellon*, yet there are several other methods of calculation still in force. Thus, pensions from the court, payments of the army, navy, &c. are set down in the register of the Spanish finances, in *Escudos* and *Ducados*, (or copper

per

per crowns and ducats) reduced to *Reals Vellon*. Some accompts of merchants, and of private persons, are likewise kept in this way; but few things are bought and sold there, but by the former computation of *Maravedis* and *Reals*. There are, besides, *provincial* ways of calculation, and denominations of money peculiar to them, still subsisting, being the remains of the usages of the old kingdoms.

But our English merchants traffic chiefly in *Pieces of Eight*, and compute usually by the *Piastre*, or old disused Piece of Eight, consisting of fifteen Reals and two Maravedis: or, if they reckon by *Pistoles*, they mean the *Pistole* of sixty Reals, the *common* Pistole, not the *gold* one of seventy-five, and ten Maravedis, otherwise called the *Doblon effectivo de Oro*.

In the office of *Decimal Rents*, as they call them, that is to say *Tythes*, belonging to the archbishop of TOLEDO, accompts are still kept in the obsolete denomination of *Dineros*, ten of which make a *Maravedi*. There are no less than fifty clerks in this office; and well there may: think only how *voluminous* accompts must be for above 30,000 pounds a-year, that are kept in a denomination, the value of which is more than *thirty times less* than our farthing!

The different monies, and ways of reckoning, still subsisting in the *provinces*, make it necessary, that every province should have a separate office in MADRID for its own convenience: and though they live in the same street, the clerks of *one* office know no more of the process of accompting in the *other*, than a Chinese or Laplander would do.

In the REAL HACIENDA, or Royal treasury, accompts are kept only in *Millions of Maravedis*.

But all the offices in SPAIN, whether ecclesiastical or secular, compute by some of the following denominations; either by Dineros, Cornados, Blancos, Crowns, or Ducats: but these are
antiquated

antiquated divifions, thofe of the *Maravedi* and *Real* being moft in ufe.

THESE fmall denominations, which the Spaniards love to compute by, muft, as you will eafily imagine, render their ac-compts very like themfelves, flow, tedious, and elaborate; but then they have this advantage, that they make their accomptants moft minutely exact. An error is much more eafily detected, where the fum is divided into fuch a number of equal parts, and perhaps into *fractions* infinitely nice.

OF their loweft denomination, called a *Maravedi*, three and one fifth make an Englifh farthing. Thirty-four *Maravedis* go to a Real de Vellon, and ninety Reals Vellon are equal to the Pound Sterling.

THEIR money writers make mention of *Maravedis of plate*; but thefe, though they might exift formerly, are now no more in being.

THE different exigencies of government, and the various expe-dients to fupport expenfive projects of ambition, under the pre-ceeding reigns, have occafioned more alterations in the value and in the currency of the Spanifh money, than in that of any other nation in the world, I believe; particularly from the year 1642 to 1688, and during the confufion and neceffities of the fucceffion war. In PHILIP IV.'s time, in 1642, things were in fuch confufion, that the Piece of Eight in Auguft paffed for twelve Reals, the Doblon for forty-five; in October the Piece of Eight went at twenty-five Reals, and the Doblon at eighty-nine; in December the Piece of Eight was at twenty-four Reals, and the Doblon at eighty-feven.

THE Prefident OURRY, who was fo diftinguifhed for his great abilities, was three times fent for from FRANCE by PHILIP V. to re-eftablifh the difordered finances of the Spanifh monarchy.

As.

As the Spaniſh money hath been ſcarce ever recalled, there
hath ariſen a confuſed multitude of imaginary ſpecies of coin.
They committed a great error, in not making, upon the union
of the ſeveral kingdoms, *one general coin, ſolely current throughout
the whole peninſula.* All theſe circumſtances plainly ſhew how
little the genius and diſpoſition of this people is turned to trade.
What could be more *uncommercial,* than a money ſtandard perpetually fluctuating, and there being one ſort of coin in Castile,
another in Catalonia, a third in Arragon, and ſo on?

The *Mints* of Spain were formerly many, namely, that of
Madrid, Seville, Segovia, Cuenza in New Castile, of
Saragossa, Barcelona, and Valencia. Of theſe the two
firſt only, I believe, are now remaining. It is ſaid there are *four*
American mints, that of Lima, Potosi, Mexico, and Gua-
timala.

In order to give the reader the cleareſt idea of this matter, I
will firſt begin with the Spaniſh *copper* money, then go on to the
ſilver, and cloſe the account with the *gold.*

1.　Of the Spanish Copper Money.

The Spaniſh Copper Money is, for the moſt part, a very con-
temptible ſort of coin; ſome of it ſtamped without either form or
regularity; and what is even ſtruck in a ſet dye, is far inferior to
the worſt of our halfpence.

Their Copper Monies are only four.
1. The Maravedi, 34 = to the Real Vellon.
2. The Ochavo, =2 Maravedis, 17 = to the Real Vellon.
3. The Quarto, =4 Maravedis, $8\frac{1}{2}$ = to the Real Vellon.
4. The Pieza de dos Quartos, =8 Maravedis, $4\frac{1}{4}$ = equal to the
Real Vellon.

In 1718, Philip V. ordered they ſhould coin milled Money
of pure Copper, making out of each pound 51 Quartos, 102
Ochavos, and 204 Maravedis.

THERE

THERE is mention made of *Maravedis* in a grant of the fite of the cathedral of SEGOVIA, by ALPHONSUS, in the year 1160, where they are called, as the grant is in Latin, *Morabetini*, which plainly fhews, that the coin itfelf, as well as the word *Maravedi*, is Arabic, though COVARRUVIAS thought it was Gothic. See Colmenares Hift. Segov. p. 110. For, the word *Maravedi* is a corruption from *Almoravedi*. They dropped the *Al*, and called this little Copper Money *Moravedi*, now vulgarly ftiled *Maravedi*. The Englifh took only their *calculation-cyphers* from the Arabs, but the Spaniards took the Arabic numerals, and their manner of computation likewife.

SMALL denominations, and minute divifions of money, were in all countries at firft probably owing to the great fcarcity of fpe-cie. But, however fmall the *Maravedis* may appear to us, being 34 to the Real Vellon, thofe who are acquainted with the Roman writers will remember, that the Latin TERUNCIUS was very near as fmall a denomination, being $\frac{7}{10}$ of our Farthing.

THE Computation, indeed, by *Reals Vellon*, is almoft the fame as the *Roman* by *Seftertii*.

	L.	*s.*	*d.*	
A Roman *Seftertius* was worth	–	–	0	0	2
The Real de Vellon,	–	–	–	0	0	2 $\frac{1}{4}$ and $\frac{1}{7}$

What can be well nearer? Does not this fimilitude almoft induce one to think, that the original of this computation of *Reals Vellon* came from ROME? and though the *Maravedi* is Arabic, the *Real* is Roman. So far is very certain, that the gold *Efcudo* was for many ages called the *Aureus*, and was current under that name down to the time of DON FERNANDO.

THE moft ancient Spanifh money was made in imitation of the PUNIC. As the Carthaginians had been abfolute mafters of SPAIN, it is no wonder the Spaniards fhould copy from their models. This ancient money had *characters* ftamped upon it, which no one has been able to explain to this day, and therefore they are called MEDALLAS DESCONOSCIDAS. *Antonio Auguftino*, the learned archbifhop of *Tarragona*, has taken infinite pains to

make

make them out; fee PATIN's L'Hift. des Med. p. 103. Jou-
BERT, Science des Med. Inft. 7.

THE Spanifh Copper Money is more like the firft rude monies
of a barbarous people, than the coin of a great and civilized nation. They have often feen the Roman money for ages paft; vaft
quantities of it are every day ploughed up, and brought to fale.
It is much they fhould never have attempted the imitation of the
Roman Brafs Coins, though they might defpair, perhaps, of exe-
cuting their *Denarii*, or their *Aurii*. But there has been always fomething in the genius of thefe people averfe to improvements.

STRABO fays, that the Spanifh *Silver* Money confifted of very
thin pieces, or laminæ, which had been three times refined in the
fire. This muft have been pure indeed, but wretched coin,
ftamped, and without any *alloy;* confequently their Iron or
Brafs Money moft probably was much more rude and barbarous,
fuch as CÆSAR fays our Britifh anceftors made ufe of in his time.
The *Quatros* of PHILIP V. are the beft that I have feen of the
Spanifh Copper Money.

ONE reafon, they fay, why their Copper Money is fo bafe a
Coin, is eafy to be affigned. When the expenfive projects of
ambition, in the preceding reigns, had at different times reduced the Spanifh finances exceeding low, it had been fometimes an
expedient to coin vaft quantities of Copper Money : the confequence of this is, that there is now in SPAIN at leaft ten times
more Copper Specie than the circulation requires ; and at length
it hath become fuch a burden, that merchants will rather allow
one and a half *per cent.* difcount, than receive payments in copper. This hath produced another effect, for as the quantity is fo
great as to be circulated in large bags, marked, of fo much in
tale, the miniftry of SPAIN is afraid of calling in this Copper
Specie to the mint, for its value to be reiffued in Silver, as they
imagine the ftate would be a great lofer by the deficiency. This
is Spanifh policy ; but, for my own part, I cannot fee why this

N n   evil

evil might not eafily be remedied; for, if the government would but confent to lay out the fmall fum of 20,000 *l.* Sterling in buying them up, they might fupprefs 20 millions of thefe Copper denominations, and the convenience thereby arifing to the internal traffic of the kingdom would much more than coun-terbalance the lofs. The Spanifh miniftry are at prefent much embarraffed with this grievance. The expedient they now talk of to get rid of the greateft part of it, is to collect it in facks, and fhip it off for the ufe of their colonies in AMERICA. In the provinces, almoft all payments are made in Copper, which ren-ders commercial tranfactions there very troublefome.

2. Of the SPANISH SILVER MONEY.

THESE are, (1.) The Real de Vellon, = to 34 Maravedis. (2.) The Real de Plata, = to 2 Reals Vellon. (3.) The Pefeta Corriente, = to 4 Reals Vellon. (4.) The Medio Real de Plata Colunario, = to 1 Real Vellon and $\frac{1}{4}$. (5.) The Real de Plata Colunario, = to 2 Reals Vellon and $\frac{1}{4}$. (6.) The Real de a Dos Colunario, = to 5 Reals Vellon. (7.) The Medio Pefo, = to 10 Reals Vellon. (8.) The Segovian, or Mexican Piece of Eight, or Dollar, or Pefo, = to 20 Reals Vellon; but if it hap--pen to be ftruck at *Seville* in the year 1718, its value is no more than 16 Reals Vellon, and the half of this Pefo no more than 8 Reals Vellon.

So that you fee the Spaniards have *eight denominations* of their effective Silver Specie; but they have likewife fome *imaginary* di-vifions, like that of our *Englifh Pound.*—Such are the *five* follow-ing.

1. THE Efcudo de Vellon, or copper, commercial, nominal Crown, = to 10 Reals Vellon.

2. THE Ducado de Vellon, or nominal Copper Ducat, 11 Reals and 1 Maravedi; ufed chiefly in computing marriage Portions,

tions, contracts, fines, and court penſions, and in rating all eccle-
fiaſtical revenues.

3. THE computed Dollar, or old Piece of Eight, commonly
called THE PIASTRE, of fifteen Reals Vellon, and two Maravedis. N. B. In commercial computations, where no particular
ſpecies is mentioned, you muſt reckon by this *Piaſtre*.

4. THE Ducado de Plata Nueva = to ſixteen Reals Vellon,
and ſeventeen Maravedis.

5. THE Ducado de Plata doble = to twenty Reals Vellon, and
twenty-five Maravedis, and $\frac{11}{16}$ of a Maravedi.

IN regard to their *effective* ſilver ſpecie, in the firſt place obſerve, that it has no impreſs of any royal head; that whenever
it has a ſhield, or coat of arms on it, it is coined in Old SPAIN,
if it be ſtruck before the year 1733; the American ſilver money
ſtruck before that period, having only the *croſs* and the *numerals*.
But ſince the year 1733, the American ſilver money has been the
ſame with that of OLD SPAIN.

THE *Real de Vellon* is the ſmalleſt piece of their ſilver coin;
obſerve only, that though it be of *Silver*, yet it is called *Vellon*
Money, that is *Copper* Money: the reaſon is, that it was *originally* a Copper coin, but when they came afterwards to ſtrike it
in *Silver*, they ſtill retained the old name. The effect of this
hath been, that when merchants ſay *Vellon* Money, they mean
Silver, and now call the Copper Cobre, or Calderilla.

THE Peſo Duro, Gourdo, Dollar, or famous *Spaniſh piece of
Eight*, is now tolerably well known in ENGLAND; there are four
ſorts of theſe *Dollars*; two ſquare, one of LIMA, and one of
SEVILLE; two of the round ſort, one with pillars, and one without pillars. There have been no ſquare Dollars coined ſince the
year 1733. PHILIP V. then ordered that they ſhould ſtrike only
the round and milled. The Dollars of FERDINAND VI. have
the arms of CASTILE and LEON on a ſhield quarterly; the arms

of

of FRANCE on an efcutcheon of pretence under a regal crown. The legend——FERDND. VI. D. G. HISPAN. ET IND. REX.

On the *reverfe*—two globes under a regal coronet, between two pillars, with coronets inftead of capitals, labelled with the motto PLVS VLTRA. Legend, VTRAQVE VNVM. Thefe are called *Colunario*, becaufe of the *pillars*; they weigh exactly one ounce of filver, and their proportion between the filver and gold, is exactly as 15 = 1; fifteen of thefe being equal to the Doblon de á Ocho, which is alfo exactly an ounce of Gold.— When the exchange of this piece is at fifty-two pence, the Eng-lifh gain four per cent.

As *Silver* has been fcarcer in ENGLAND than *Gold*, thefe Dollars have been imported there with great advantage, while the fmall Spanifh *Gold Crown*, of exactly the *fame value*, hath paffed unnoticed. The price given for them by the *Bank of* ENGLAND having been from five fhillings, to five and four-pence per ounce : and of late, till the taking of the HERMIONE, fo high as 5 s. 8 d. and 5 s. 10 d.

THE meaning of the name *Piece of Eight*, was originally owing to its value; it was a Real, or *Dollar*, of eight Reals of plate currency. But there being now *three* diftinct pieces of Eight, ftill in ufe, this hath bred fome confufion : the reafon of this va-riety is however eafily to be accounted for.——The old Piece of Eight was, as 1 faid, originally in value eight Reals of Plate ; this by currency in time loft fomething, almoft half a Real of Plate, and went at laft for fifteen Reals Vellon, and two Mara-vedis. But when they came to coin better fpecie, to make this Dollar a more valuable, and fairer coin, they added the value of *two Reals of Plate* to it, which brought it to its modern ftand-ard, namely twenty Reals Vellon.—Yet ftill, as many of the old pieces of Eight ftill remained, the merchants were fo bigot-ted to their old calculation of fifteen Reals, and two Maravedies, that they ftill kept up that computation, and it remains even now, though the pieces themfelves are now no more, and is

what

what they call reckoning by the *Piaſtre*. This accounts for two of the Pieces of Eight, that of twenty Reals, and the imaginary Piaſtre.

THE exchange of the *Piaſtre* is now at par, or forty pence. The *third* Piece of Eight is that of SEVILLE, of the year 1718, and was ſtruck upon the old principle of eight Reals of plate currency, or ſixteen Vellon, which it now goes for: but theſe are rare, and do not often occur. But remember, that the *three* Reals de á Ocho, or Pieces of Eight, are that imaginary one of fifteen Reals Vellon, and two Maravedies; of ſixteen Reals Vellon of SEVILLE, and the modern one of twenty Reals Vellon.

IN the year 1726, PHILIP ordered, that old Silver Pieces of Eight ſhould paſs for Nine Reals of *Provincial* plate, and one half, that is for nineteen Reals Vellon, one leſs than the preſent currency. At this time there was a general recall of the ſmaller ſilver monies to the Mint.

IN the year 1728, PHILIP ordered a junta to regulate the mints and monies, which ordained that the Reals à 8º. and à 4º. ſhould be round and milled at the edges, and of ſixty-eight Reals of Plate the mark: that the *old Real de a Ocho* ſhould paſs thenceforward for ten Reals of Plate, that is twenty Vellon; and the Real a Quatro for five Reals of Plate; the mark for eighty Reals; the ounce for ten Reals of Plate, or twenty Vellon, and ſo on.

Of the SPANISH GOLD MONEY.

THERE were anciently only four Spaniſh Gold coins, and theſe divided by a very fair and goodly proportion; the Doblon of eight, the $\frac{1}{4}$, the $\frac{1}{2}$, the $\frac{1}{8}$; exactly the equal and direct diviſions of an ounce of Gold; ſince that they have added a $\frac{1}{16}$: and their Gold Money ſtands thus:

1. The Eſcudito de Oro, or little Gold Crown ⚌ to twenty Reals Vellon.

2. THE.

2. The Efcudo de Oro, or large Gold Crown, equal to thirty-feven Reals, and twenty-two Maravedis.

3. The Doblon de a Cinco, or Gold Piftole, = to feventy-five Reals, and ten Maravedis.

4. The Doblon de á Quatro, or double Gold Piftole, = to 150 Reals, and twenty Maravedis.

5. The Doblon de á Ocho, or Gold piece of Eight, or four Gold Piftoles, = to 301 Reals, and fix Maravedis.

The Spaniards have alfo two imaginary fpecies in the Gold, *the Dobla de Oro*, or Double Ducat, = to fourteen Reals, and nine Maravedis—and is ufed only by phyficians and chymifts—and the commercial nominal *Piftole* of fixty Reals Vellon.

The *Doblon of Eight* was originally worth *eight Half Piftoles*, and thence took its name—*El Doblon de á Ocho Efcudos*. It is at prefent but one Real more in value, becaufe feventy-five multiplied by four, makes 300; but its currency is 301 Reals, and fix Maravedis. Obferve, that there are no pillars upon any of the Spanifh Gold Money.

In the year 1728, Philip ordered, that the *Doblon de á Ocho* fhould pafs for fixteen old Pieces of Eight, or twenty Provincial Dollars; the Doblon á Quatro for eight of thofe Pefos; the Doblon á Dos for four; the Efcudo for two, or twenty Reals of Plate.

There are three forts of the Gold Doblon á Ocho. (1.) The American, or of Lima, fquare, with the crofs, and the numeral. (2.) With the head of the Prince, as legend, PHILIP V. D. G. HISPAN. ET. IND. REX.——Reverfe, arms of the King, with this motto: TIMOR DOMINI INITIUM SAPI-ENTIÆ. (3.) The third fort has no imprefs of the Prince, but has the arms of the King under a regal crown, legend, PHILIP.

PHILIP. V. DEI. GRATIA. On the *reverse*, a crofs, with this motto: HISPANIARVM. REX.

HAVING now concluded the account of the Spanifh money, I fhall refer the reader to the following Table, which will fhow at one view, the reduction of all the fpecies of it into Englifh money; and it is hoped the Table will be found both new and accurate.

A TABLE, *fhewing the Value of* SPANISH COINS *in* ENGLISH MONEY.

Reals Vellon.	Maravedis.	l.	s.	d.	f.	
	1				1/2	Maravedi.
	2				2/3	Ochavo.
	3 1/3				1	Quarto.
	4				1 1/2	
	6 2/3				2	
	8				2 2/3	Two Quartos.
	12 2/3			1		
	25 1/3			2		
1	34			2	2 2/3	Real de Vellon, or Half Real de Plata.
1 1/4	42 1/4			3	2	The Pillar'd Half Real of Plate.
2	68			5	1 1/3	Real de Plata, or Real of Silver.
2 1/2	85			7		The pillar'd Real of Plate.
3	102			8		
4	136			10	2 2/3	The Real de a Dos, or curr Pefeta.
5	170		1	1	1 1/3	The pillar'd Real de a Dos.
6	204		1	4		
7	238		1	6	2 1/3	
8	272		1	9	1 1/3	The SEVILLE Half Dollar.
9	306		2			
10	340		2	2	2 2/3	The Real de a Quatro, or Medio Pefo, (i.e. Half Piece of Eight.) The nominal Efcudo Vellon is of the fame value. Nine of thefe make a Pound Sterling.
11	374		2	5	1 1/3	
11 and 1 Maravedis,			2	5	1 1/3	The nominal Ducado de Vellon, or Copper Ducat.
12	408		2	8		
13	442		2	10	2 1/3	
14	476		3	1	1 1/3	
14 and 9 Maravedis,			3	2	1/3	The nominal Doblo de Oro, or Gold double.
15	510		3	4		

Real

Reals Vellon.	Maravedis.	L.	s.	d.	f.	
15 and 2 Maravedis,			3	4	½	The old Piece of Eight, or Piastre nominal.
16	544		3	6	2⅔	The SEVILLE Dollar.
16 and 17 Maravidis,			3	8		The Ducado de Plata Nuèva, or nominal Ducat of new plate.
17	578		3	9	1⅓	
18	612		4			
19	646		4	2	2⅔	
20	680		4	5	1⅓	Real de a Ocho, Pèso Gourdo, or Piece of Eight; the little Gold Crown is of the same value.
20 and $25\frac{15}{16}$ Maravedis,			4	7	1	The Ducato de Plata Doble.
21	714		4	8		
22	748		4	10	2⅔	
23	782		5	1	1⅓	
24	816		5	4		
25	850		5	6	2⅔	
26	884		5	9	1⅓	
27	918		6			
28	952		6	2	2⅔	
29	986		6	5	1⅓	
30	1020		6	8		
31	1054		6	10	2⅔	
32	1088		7	1	1⅓	
33	1122		7	4		
34	1156		7	6	2⅔	
35	1190		7	9	1⅓	
36	1224		8			
37	1258		8	2	2⅔	
37 and 22 Maravedis,			8	4	1	The Escudo de Oro, or large Gold Crown.
38	1292		8	5	1⅓	
39	1326		8	8		
40	1360		8	10	2⅔	
41	1394		9	1	1⅓	
42	1428		9	4		
43	1462		9	6	2⅔	
44	1496		9	9	1⅓	
45	1530		10			
46	1564		10	2	2⅔	
47	1598		10	5	1⅓	
48	1632		10	8		
49	1666		10	10	2⅔	
50	1790		11	1	1⅓	
51	1734		11	4		
52	1768		11	6	2⅔	
53	1802		11	9	1⅓	
54	1836		12			
55	1870		12	2	2⅔	
56	1904		12	5	1⅓	
57	1938		12	8		
58	1972		12	10	2⅔	
59	2006		13	1	1⅓	

Reals Vellon.	Maravedis	l.	s.	d.	f.	
60	2040	0	13	4	0	The nominal or common Piſtole.
61	2074	0	13	6	2½	
62	2108	0	13	9	1⅓	
63	2142	0	14	0	0	
64	2176	0	14	2	2½	
65	2210	0	14	5	1⅓	
66	2244	0	14	8	0	
67	2278	0	14	10	2½	
68	2312	0	15	1	1⅓	
69	2336	0	15	4	0	
70	2370	0	15	6	2½	
71	2404	0	15	9	1⅓	
72	2438	0	16	0	0	
73	2472	0	16	2	2½	
74	2506	0	16	5	1⅓	
75	2540	0	16	8	0	
75 and 10 Maravedis,		0	16	8	2	The Doublon of Gold.
76	2574	0	16	10	2½	
77	2608	0	17	1	1⅓	
78	2642	0	17	4	0	
79	2676	0	17	6	2½	
80	2710	0	17	9	1⅓	
81	2744	0	18	0	0	
82	2778	0	18	2	2½	
83	2812	0	18	5	1⅓	
84	2846	0	18	8	0	
85	2880	0	18	10	2½	
86	2914	0	19	1	1⅓	
87	2948	0	19	4	0	
88	2982	0	19	6	2½	
89	3016	0	19	9	1⅓	
90	3040	1	0	0	0	
150 and 20 Maravedis,		1	13	5	2	The Doublon de a Quatro of Gold.
180		2	0	0	0	
270		3	0	0	0	
301 and 6 Maravedis,		3	6	11	0	The Doublon de a Ocho of Gold.
360		4	0	0	0	
450		5	0	0	0	
540		6	0	0	0	
630		7	0	0	0	
720		8	0	0	0	
810		9	0	0	0	
900		10	0	0	0	
990		11	0	0	0	
1080		12	0	0	0	
1170		13	0	0	0	
1260		14	0	0	0	
1350		15	0	0	0	
1440		16	0	0	0	
1530		17	0	0	0	
1620		18	0	0	0	
1710		16	0	0	0	
1800		20	0	0	0	

O o

Reals Vellon.	l.	s.	d.	Reals Vellon.	l.	s.	d.
1890	21	0	0	5490	61	0	0
1980	22	0	0	5580	62	0	0
2070	23	0	0	5670	63	0	0
2160	24	0	0	5760	64	0	0
2250	25	0	0	5850	65	0	0
2340	26	0	0	5940	66	0	0
2430	27	0	0	6030	67	0	0
2520	28	0	0	6120	68	0	0
2610	29	0	0	6210	69	0	0
2700	30	0	0	6300	70	0	0
2790	31	0	0	6390	71	0	0
2880	32	0	0	6480	72	0	0
2970	33	0	0	6570	73	0	0
3060	34	0	0	6660	74	0	0
3150	35	0	0	6750	75	0	0
3240	36	0	0	6840	76	0	0
3330	37	0	0	6930	77	0	0
3420	38	0	0	7020	78	0	0
3510	39	0	0	7110	79	0	0
3600	40	0	0	7200	80	0	0
3690	41	0	0	7290	81	0	0
3780	42	0	0	7380	82	0	0
3870	43	0	0	7470	83	0	0
3960	44	0	0	7560	84	0	0
4050	45	0	0	7650	85	0	0
4140	46	0	0	7740	86	0	0
4230	47	0	0	7830	87	0	0
4320	48	0	0	7920	88	0	0
4410	49	0	0	8010	89	0	0
4500	50	0	0	8100	90	0	0
4590	51	0	0	8190	91	0	0
4680	52	0	0	8280	92	0	0
4770	53	0	0	8370	93	0	0
4860	54	0	0	8460	94	0	0
4950	55	0	0	8550	95	0	0
5040	56	0	0	8640	96	0	0
5130	57	0	0	8730	97	0	0
5220	58	0	0	8820	98	0	0
5310	59	0	0	8910	99	0	0
5400	60	0	0	9000	100	0	0

A TABLE of ENGLISH and PORTUGAL MONEY, reduced to SPANISH Computation.

	l.	s.	d.	R. V.	Mar.
Sixpence	0	0	6	2	8¼
Shilling	0	1	0	4	17
Half a Crown	0	2	6	11	8½
A Crown	0	5	0	22	17
Half a Pound Ster.	0	10	0	45	0

Half

	l.	s.	d.		R. V.	Mar.
Half a Guinea	q	10	6		47	8½
A Pound Ster.	1	0	0		90	0
A Guinea	1	1	0		94	17
Moidore	1	7	0		121	17
A Pound and a Half	1	10	0		135	0
* A Six and Thirty	1	16	0		162	0
A Three Pound Twelve	3	12	0		324	0

* N. B. Six and Thirties, or PORTUGAL Pieces, exchange in this country at great lofs: They will give at CORUNNA only 152, or at moft 156 Reals; at MADRID fomething more. The par is 162 Reals.

LETTER

LETTER XV.

The STATE of AGRICULTURE.

THE Soil of SPAIN is naturally dry, and is rendered still more so, by reason of the great heats, which parch up the springs and brooks, and by the want of rain to refresh the earth at proper seasons. Of this a remarkable instance happened about five years ago, when it had not rained in CASTILE for nineteen months together.

THE general surface of the country, if you except the two CASTILES, is uneven, scarped, and mountainous.—It has been doubted by the Abbe de * VERAY, and others, whether there ever were any *mines* of silver in SPAIN, because the Spaniards at present work none: but this presumption has been ill founded. I am told, that it is a standing maxim of Spanish policy, not to work any of their mines in EUROPE, as long as those of AMERICA will supply them. It is a certain fact, that there are many *silver* mines dispersed throughout SPAIN, and at GUADAL-CANAL in ANDALUSIA in particular.—*Englishmen* have gone over there, and have examined the very ore, and have found it so promising, that some have been sanguine enough to offer to contract

* But a modern writer has well confuted this opinion.—His words are, " La prudence Espagnole, qui ne songe pas tant au present, qu'elle na pense aussi àl' avenir, ne veut pas qu'on y touche, tandis que celles des Indes auront dequoi fournir. Je trouve que c'est sagement fait à eux.

for

for the working of the mines.   But suppose the *moderns* had not examined into this point, would not the testimony of the *ancients* have been strong enough to prove it?   POLYBIUS, STRABO, and LIVY, all affirm it.   CATO imposed a tax upon the silver and iron mines, among the VERGISTANI :   See LIVY, Lib. 34.

NOTWITHSTANDING the inconvenience arising from the dryness of the soil, and the want of rain, yet, if the inhabitants were industrious, and applied themselves with assiduity to the cultivation of their lands, a general abundance might prevail, which is far from being the case at present, for in many places there is often great scarcity of *bread*.

THE genius of the people is doubtless naturally averse to toil and labour.   Give a Spaniard but his cloak, hat, and sword, his wine and his bread, and he cares not how little he works.   Another great obstruction to Agriculture is the immense number of lazy *ecclesiastics* in these kingdoms, and the perpetual succession of *holidays* allowed by the church, which deprive the state of *one third* of the labour, that it ought to receive from its subjects. To these let me add, the thinness of its population ; SPAIN in general, and GRANADA in particular, have never recovered that fatal blow of *the expulsion of the Moors*; the effects of which are felt still more, by the addition of civil and religious *celibacy*. When PHILIP, on one hand, banished to the amount of 800,000 industrious infidels, from a principle of religion, he ought, on the other hand, from a principle of policy, to have set open the gates of every nunnery and convent in his dominions.   I have heard the number of these useless, sequestered males and females, these dead limbs of the body politic, computed at no less than 200,000 ; but I believe the calculation much exaggerated.

BESIDES the bad consequences arising from religious celibacy, their thin population is in part owing to the sterility of their females; and above all, to the vast emigrations of their people to AMERICA.

To

To remedy these defects, the ministry, in PHILIP III's and PHILIP IV.'s time, offered vast premiums to promote marriage and agriculture. But their imprudent schemes of policy in other instances have rendered those patriot laws almost ineffectual.

ANOTHER unfavourable circumstance to agriculture is, there being no exportation of corn allowed in SPAIN from one province to another, except for the King's use, the exigencies of the fleet, army, and such occasions. In consequence of this bad policy, they are obliged to send to BARBARY and AFRICA, or to ENGLAND for corn; for, it is morally impossible but the harvest must fail annually in some one province or other, and then that province must be supplied from abroad. Indeed, the transportation of it to any great distance is almost impracticable; for their large rivers being left in their natural state, are not navigable.

FOR my own part, I am persuaded, that they look upon all such improvements, in some measure, *as sinful*. What shall we say *superstition* will not persuade men to, when we read the following curious deliberation of a council of state, in the reign of CHARLES II.?—When a company of *Dutch* contractors offered that Prince, to make the TAGUS navigable to LISBON, at their own expence, provided they were allowed a toll, for a certain number of years, upon such goods as were sent by water-carriage that way: for they intended to render the *Manfanares* navigable from *Madrid* to where it falls into the *Tagus*.—The Council of CASTILE having long deliberated upon that proposal, made at last this remarkable determination: " That if it had " pleased God, that these two rivers should have been navigable, " he would not have wanted human assistance to have made them " such: but, as he has not done it, it is plain he did not think it " proper that it should be done. To attempt it, therefore, would " be to violate the decrees of his providence, and to amend the " imperfections which he designedly left in his works."

BUT besides this defect in their *rivers*, they have opened very few *roads* for carriages; in many places there being scarce

6   room

room even for a mule to pafs by.   Another difadvantage to agriculture is, that where the land happens to be let to a tenant,
which is not often the cafe, the *fale of the eftate voids the leafe* ;
from whence comes their Spanifh proverb, *Venta defhâze renta.*
—*The fale frees you from rent.*   This is fo directly contrary to our
law, and the equity of the thing, that the difcouragement to the
farmer need not be infifted on.

THE military fpirit of thefe people, which has always prevailed, has no doubt given them a contempt for agriculture.
Whoever travels over SPAIN, will be grieved to fee fuch vaft
tracks of fine land, turned to fo little advantage ; great part of it
not tilled, and that which is, done in fo carelefs and flovenly a
manner, as to produce a ftarved crop of corn, even in fpots
where they might command the moft abundant harveft.   Their
corn is ufually choaked up with ftones, filth, and weeds of every
kind.   There cannot be a ftronger proof given of the fertility of the
foil in SPAIN, than its producing fo much as it doth, when you
confider how little labour they beftow upon it.   When they
plow, they fcarce do more than juft fcratch the furface of the
ground with a flight furrow ; after the firft plowing, they let the
earth lie for a few days, and then they *fow*, the *Wheat* in September, and the *Barley* in February : when this is done, they
feldom ufe the *Harrow*, but plow it over again, in order to cover
the feed.   Thus it ftands till June or July, at which time they
cut it down.   The Barley is rarely bound in fheafs, and the
Wheat not always. . Neither, however, are carried into *Barns* ;
but they lay it down on fome clean dry hillock, and then their
mules come with a drag, and tread or beat out the corn ; it is a
fhorter method than our *threfhing*.   The winnowing there is
done ftill eafier, by only throwing the corn up into the air.

SUCH is the general indolence of the inhabitants of this country, that many of them will neither reap nor gather in their own
corn.   I fhould except, however, the induftrious GALLICIANS,
who, with great numbers out of FRANCE, from AUVERGNE
and LANGUEDOC, annually travel over all SPAIN, to be its huf-
bandmen.

THE

THE corn, when cut down, ufually lies expofed upon fome dry high ground for a month or fix weeks : as it muft therefore be watched by night, they build fmall huts to lodge in. Thefe places being moft commonly in the neighbourhood of great towns, it is the evening diverfion of the Spaniards, at this feafon, to walk out to thefe *Eras*, (or Areas) as they call them, to form parties there ; fome fitting, others playing on the guittar, others finging and dancing *Sequedillas* or *Fundungos*. During the heats, the cool air of thofe rifing grounds is pleafant, and the fcene odd enough. They frequently ftay out late at thefe entertainments. The ladies of fafhion at MADRID fometimes partake of them.

STRANGE as this manner of treading out the corn upon the ground, and in the duft, may appear to us, yet I do not find that it receives any damage from this practice; for it is all of the hard fort, and their flour is fine and white, not inferior to any in ENGLAND. This method of treading out the corn is, however, undoubtedly not lefs ancient than the time of MOSES, as may be feen in Scripture. When the corn is thus trodden out, they carry it into the public granary, from whence it is difpenfed to the people, by particular magiftrates, a *board* being appointed for that purpofe : this they call *Junta de los Abaftos*.

LITTLE elfe is fown in SPAIN, but Wheat, Barley, and Rye ; to the mules they ufually give *chopped ftraw*, and thefe animals will undergo amazing fatigue, upon fuch poor food. The Spanifh horfe are likewife commonly fed with chopped ftraw, and it gives them the fineft coat imaginable ; but when they are upon hard fervice, they give them Barley; the richer fort, indeed, give their mules barley. The Spaniards make little ufe of oats, tho' there are fome few fields of it to be met with.

WHEN I fpeak of the Spanifh Agriculture, I mean the *general* ftate of it in SPAIN; for fome parts of the country are certainly much more tilled and improved than others; which muft be the cafe in all countries : thus, for inftance, when you pafs the SIERRA MORENA, or that craggy faw of mountains, by which you enter

into

into ANDALUSIA, the scene is agreeably changed, the country chearfuller, all tilled to corn, or planted with olives; the villages neat and clean; but even here industry is wanting; no inclosures, no trees, but vines and olives.

FROM CORDUBA to SEVILLE you pass over a ruder country, less cultivated, and abounding in olives, and some vineyards. The country, however, about GRANADA, MURCIA, VALEN-CIA, and BARCELONA, has been of late years very nobly culti-vated and improved: in that latter city, in particular, there is so much industry, that you would be apt to think the people were not Spaniards. In the environs, also, of the two former cities, the country is one continued garden, abounding with all forts of me-lons, gourds, pimentos, and garden herbs, interspersed with plats of corn, maize, rice, hemp, &c. all growing under the shade of mulberry-trees, which cover the whole country: they have peas, cauliflowers, fallads, beans, &c. fresh from their gar-dens, without the help of an hot-house, in the middle of our winter.

WITH regard to the other provinces; in BISCAY they attend chiefly to their *Iron* manufactures, and so of course pay less regard to agriculture. ASTURIAS is all mountainous and woody, ex-cepting where they have laid the forests waste for the supply of their navy. I say *laid them waste*, because, through their unskil-fulness in cutting and felling the timber, and a careless prodigality in the manner of doing it, they have cut down as much of the noblest wood, to build a few *men of war*, as would have served the Spanish navy for some years. A gentleman, who lately tra-velled that way, assured me, that the ASTURIAS, in this re-spect, had more the appearance of a plundered province, than of a country in the hands of its own masters.

THE two CASTILES are miserably cultivated; LEON worse; but some parts of GALLICIA are fine; and though their atten-tion to, and skill in agriculture, is by no means equal to that of the southern provinces of SPAIN, yet it has no mean appear-ance.

P p   ONE

ONE of the late minifters tried to introduce the *Englifh ftyle* of agriculture into SPAIN, within thefe few years; and fent for ploughs, harrows, and other implements and tools of hufbandry from LONDON. But when he came to teach his *Caftilian* peafants, the ufe and application of thefe ruftic arms, they had no lefs averfion to them, than the Spanifh troops have now to the *Pruffian military exercife.* They tried to work with them, but in vain. The DON will as foon quit his fkin, as his habits and prejudices. So they laid the tools down very quietly, and told the minifter, " Que no fe puede trabajar con inftrumentos femijantes " á los Ynglefes—*That it was impoffible to work with fuch tools as* " *the Englifh."*

WITH regard to *Climate,* the Spaniards certainly breathe the pureft air, well fuited to fuch conftitutions as are not fubject to *cholics,* particularly to what is called the *dry cholic.* It is too thin and fubtle to agree with confumptive difpofitions; but to fuch whofe conftitutions are found, and unimpaired by hereditary or acquired diftempers, there are few better climates in the world. In GALLICIA the air is more impregnated with vapours and moifture; but in general, there is neither mift nor cloud, and you have the moft ferene azure fky conftantly over your head, that can be imagined.

IN winter, the cold is not of fo freezing a nature as in ENGLAND, nor does it numb the extremities in the fame manner; but it is of a more piercing and fubtle kind; wherefore great care muft be taken at thofe feafons to guard well the breaft and lungs. Fire is as much wanted at MADRID, in the midft of winter, as in LONDON, and yet they ufe *braziers* in general, and but few *chimneys.* In June, July, Auguft, and part of September, the heats are very oppreffive; during the hours of heat, to be ftill, with as little light in the room as poffible, is the only way to be tolerably cool. Great care ought to be taken in regard to the *water* all over SPAIN, particularly at SEGOVIA, and ARANJUEZ; for in thofe places, if drank without proper caution, it will have the moft fatal effects. The fureft prefervative is to boil it, or to put an hot iron into it, before you drink it. The

water,

water, indeed, of MADRID, is excellent, particularly that of the fountain of the *Recoletos*. The court of SPAIN have given it the ftrongeft recommendation poffible, for they have fent water from MADRID even to Don CARLOS and Don PHILIP, as far as ITALY.

YOU may find fome *Trees* in SPAIN not very common in other countries. The olive tree, green oak, and mulberry tree, abound there ; you will meet with vaft forrefts of *fir* and *cork* ; of which latter they make ftools and benches, and apply it to many other domeftic ufes. There are fine woods of oak in ESTREMADURA and ASTURIAS ; fome few *palms* and *cedars* are likewife found. Then as to *Fruits*, there are figs, pomegranates, oranges, lemons, citrons, dates, capefs, walnuts, chefnuts, piftacho-nuts, raifins, grapes, peaches, nectarines, apricots, plums of all forts, pears, apples, mulberries, ftrawberries, currants, but, I believe, no goofeberries.

GARDENING, except in the neighbourhood of BARCELONA and VALENTIA, and fome other places on the MEDITERRANEAN coaft, is entirely neglected in this country. They have not even the idea of gentlemens country feats, with gardens about them, after the Englifh manner, except at the King's palaces, or fome grandee's old caftle. Yet, notwithftanding, their lettuce, fallads, afparagus, cellery, cabbage, fpinnage, endive, garden herbs, onions, garlick, carrots, turnips, melons, cucumbers, artichokes, &c. are good.—The honey of SPAIN, where there is fo much wild thyme, is equal to that of HYBLA.

VINEYARDS abound every where ; for they make neither *beer*, nor *cyder* ; *rum* is prohibited, and their *brandy* is a wretched fpirit, diftilled from *anifeed*. Foreign wines are very difficult to be had there at any price, except in the *fea-ports* ; even the fine wines of their own growth are by no means cheap, or eafy to be procured. What wine is fold of foreign growth, is chiefly fome poor *Claret*, or wretched *Frontiniac*. The wines that are native are remarkably ftrong ; they are preffed out in the ancient manner, fo often mentioned in Scripture, by the feet ; when thus troden out, they are immediately put into *hog skins*, fewed up, and pitched on the infide : the *pitch* is apt to give them a deeper tint, and a very rank tafte; this the connoiffeurs call tafting of the *Borracho*. There are many fine wines in SPAIN, the very names of which I know not : thofe that have fallen in my way are the following. 1. *Mountain*. 2. *Xeres*, or what we call *Sherry*, a town near CADIZ. 3. *Paxarete*, both dry, and fweet. 4. *Malaga*, in that country, what the Spaniards call Don PEDRO XIMENES, from the name of a famous vintner in that city. 5. *Malvafia*, in CATALONIA, what we call *Malmfy*. 6. *Tinta de Rota*, or what we call *Tent*. 7. *Peralta*. 8. *Montilla*. 9. *Guarnacha*, in CATALONIA. 10. *Fontcarral*. 11. *Mofcatel*. 12. *Ribadavian*. 13. *Maravella*. 14. *Seges*. 15. *Mancha*. This laft is the wine of Don QUIXOTE'S country : it is of the red grape, and what is chiefly drank, mixed with water, by the court and gentry at MADRID.

THE Spanifh horfe were always famous; thofe of ANDALUSIA are the moft beautiful, thofe of ASTURIAS the ftrongeft : the beft mules are the *Caftilian*, particularly thofe of LA MANCHA : but both horfes and mules are very dear in this country; fifty or fixty pounds for a mule is no extraordinary price. All travelling, carriage, &c. is generally performed by mules, not horfes. In many places, where the mules go with fafety, an horfe would fcarce ftand.

THERE are great plenty of oxen and cows, though the Spaniards make no *butter*, oil fupplying its place. They make likewife very little ufe of *cows milk*, *goats milk* being only to be had, even at MADRID. They have black cattle in great abundance, and large flocks of fheep. All thefe are ufually poor and lean, for want of pafture, though the flefh is not without its relifh, and the meat is certainly more fubftantial, more nutritious, than what is killed in ENGLAND.

THEY have immenfe droves of fwine, particularly about TALAVERA DE LA REGNA. As thefe are fed with chefnuts, the pork is of a moft exquifite flavour. Poultry in general, except

the

the turkics, are in this country lean and. dry.   There are great
quantities of game of all forts, hares, partridges, &c. but neither fat nor well flavoured.   The venifon is good, but inferior to
our own.   *Rabbits* breed and multiply aftonifhingly in SPAIN,
and are very good food; they were fo great a nuifance, in the
time of AUGUSTUS, that the Roman foldiers were obliged to de-
ftroy them, as STRABO tells us.   This made CATULLUS call
SPAIN *Cuniculofa Celtiberia*.   And BOCHART fays, that the name
of SPAIN came from the *Phœnician* SPANIJIAM, which fignifies
the land of rabbits.

FISH is fcarce ever feen in the interior parts of the country;
and what does come there is ufually brought in *fnow*.   They
have great multitudes of craw-fifh at MADRID.—But their chief
fupply of fifh is fent them by the Englifh from NEWFOUND-
LAND, the *falt fifh*, or what they call the BACALAO.   The
Spaniards themfelves indeed, near CALES, falt no inconfiderable
quantity of the *Thunnus*, or *Ton-fifh*; and very excellent it is;
though this is no new practice, but as old as the Roman times;
for the ELDER PLINY tells us, " Optima autem omnium in
" Europa funt *Gaditana Salfamenta*."

LETTER XVI.

To the Reverend Dr. K E N N I C O T T, *&c. &c.*

TO thofe, Sir, who, like you, are great proficients in the *Hebrew* and eaftern languages, there are perhaps few countries in the world that would afford them more pleafure than this of SPAIN, could they but have free accefs to all the oriental *manufcripts* it is known to contain.

YOU need not be informed, that when the empire of the MOORS flourifhed here, they had univerfities of note, at a time when all the Chriftian world, and the reft of SPAIN in particular, was buried in the moft difgraceful ignorance. The Chriftians themfelves made no difficulty of going to ftudy in thofe feminaries, to learn aftronomy and philofophy.

THIS country was the refidence of thofe learnéd Arabs, AVICENA, AVERROES, ALMANZOR, and MESSAHALLAH. It was here thofe able Jews wrote their comments, the Rabbins ABEN EZRA, MOSES BEN-MAYMON, A. ZACUTH, BENJAMIN, MOSES KIMCHI, and his fons DAVID and JOSEPH; with others, whofe names and works are fo humoroufly defcribed in that beautiful poem, your *Oxford Auctio Davifiana.*

BUT though there certainly are great collections of *Hebrew,* and other *Oriental* MSS. remaining in SPAIN, yet let me intreat you, Sir, not to raife your expectations too high, or fanguinely

I

to

to imagine, that you can derive any great acceffions to your *new Edition of the Bible*, from this part of the world. Not that I am without hope of obtaining fome valuable *collations* for your ufe hereafter: but that muft be the work of much time and application: patience and perfeverance are moft effentially neceffary in all your tranfactions with a Spaniard.

You no doubt are well aware, that thofe who glean after fuch men as XIMENES, MONTANUS, and PERE HOUBIGEANT, in this country, cannot expect to find much left, which they have not *collated*. But ftill I am perfuaded, from knowing the genius of thefe people, that a fkilful and diligent enquirer would difcover fome *Hebrew* MSS. which thefe great men never faw: fome have doubtlefs been brought hither fince their time, and fome probably efcaped their fearch.

But, in order that you may fee the ftate of this matter more compleatly, I fend you inclofed *two Letters*, tranflated from the original, written by a very learned and intelligent *Spaniard*. The *firft* will give you a full view of the ftate of the *Hebrew* and *Arabic* learning in this country; and the *fecond* contains a moft exact account of the *Complutenfian Polyglott*.

Having ufed my utmoft endeavours to procure you fome *collations* of fuch ancient Hebrew MSS. of the Bible, as I could get intelligence of in SPAIN, it is but reafonable, that I fhould give you, Sir, as fatisfactory an account as I can of the fteps I took for that purpofe.

There are but *two* principal obftacles to your procuring the *collation* of the Hebrew MSS. in SPAIN: thefe are, the abfolute neceffity of his Catholic Majefty's permiffion; and the difficulty of finding perfons of ability, learning, leifure, and what is more, humility fufficient for fuch a work: for, fhould you find out an ecclefiaftic able enough to go through this dry tafk, he may poffibly have too much pride to receive your pay; and then what motive have you left to engage him with?

BUT

But how difcouraging foever thefe obftacles may appear, yet notwithftanding, if there breaks out no war, and I have the opportunity of another year's ftay in this country, I am perfuaded I fhall have the fatisfaction of being inftrumental in removing them in great meafure.

Upon receiving advices from England in regard to your undertaking, I immediately wrote to fome of the Spanifh *literati* upon that fubject, and among others to Don Fr. Perez Bagar, a canon and treafurer of the church of Toledo : he fent me word, that he had by him between * twenty and thirty Hebrew MSS. of the Bible, written poffibly in the XIIth century, or not much later; and that there was one in particular, dated 1144. This account of his, however, proved erroneous ; for he told me afterwards, that he had only eight MSS. by him of the Hebrew Bible, with another in the church library : for, not having fufficiently examined the reft, he found that feveral, which he imagined to have contained the text, were only Rabbinical comments.

In obedience to my directions from England, I informed the Earl of Bristol of the nature, ftate, and utility of your undertaking, and endeavoured to induce him to move in it : but his Lordfhip replied, that he could not ; that his office was only *political*, and that he had nothing to do with what was foreign to his commiffion.

Upon this I wrote to England, advifing an application to be made to the Count De Fuentes, in order to obtain his Catholic Majefty's permiffion, that the Hebrew MSS. of the Bible in Spain might be *collated* for your work. That Count's chaplain called upon me foon after at Segovia, and affured me, that the Count De Fuentes had promifed to procure an application from the Romifh college of Cardinals to the King of Spain, for the Englifh to have the fame permiffion here, which they had in the *Vatican*. This I have heard no more of fince; and to tell you the truth, I did not believe at that time.

* See above, p. 83.

You

You will fee in my † catalogue of the ESCURIAL MSS, what there is in that place. While I was there, I had the good fortune to meet with the Count GAZOLA, one of his Catholic Majefty's great favourites, a Lieutenant-general, and his principal Engineer. He having afked me, if I had fucceeded in obtaining accefs to the Hebrew and other MSS. in SPAIN? I replied, that I had feen thofe of the ESCURIAL, in a very curfory manner, but none elfe; that as to fuch an accefs as I wanted, for the purpofes of *collation*, I defpaired of ever feeing that point accomplifhed. He replied, "Cou- "rage, mon ami, a mon retour á MADRID, je vous ferois cette "grace moi meme."——This I looked upon as a moft favourable incident; and accordingly, when I returned to MADRID, I drew up the inclofed Latin epiftle to Count GAZOLA, ftating the nature of your propofals, and defiring his affiftance in obtaining the King's permiffion.

AFTER this, I faw BAGER at MADRID, who came to defire me to fend to ENGLAND for fome books, which would be necef- fary to him in finifhing a work he had almoft compleated, en- titled *an Explanation of the Samaritan coins*, to which will be added an account of the Spanifh coins, called *defconnocidas*. At this interview we made a mutual agreement; I undertook to pro- cure the books, provided he would *collate* and fend me the *various readings* of thofe nine MSS. at TOLEDO. So that you have no- thing more to do, Sir, than to write a letter to him in form, re- quefting the *collation* of thofe MSS. for your work, in order that he might lay that letter before the chapter of TOLEDO, to obtain their permiffion.

P. S. Since my return to ENGLAND, I have little more to add, Sir, to this account. When I faw the Honourable Mr. HAY at LISBON, he very warmly efpoufed the caufe of your undertaking; and was fo obliging as to offer to keep fuch a literary correfpon- dence open during the war, if neceffary. But as we have now the profpect of peace before us, we are under no reftraints of that fort; and whenever you would have any correfpondence in SPAIN

† See above, Letter VIII. p. 155.

Q q renewed

renewed upon this subject, please to let me know your commands, and I shall very readily obey them.

EPISTOLA

Ad Excellentissimum Comitem DE GAZOLA, &c. &c. de Collatione Hebraicorum Manuscriptorum Veteris Testamenti.

CUM nos Britanni, Comes Excellentissime, orbi litterato nuperrimé enunciavimus, nos hodie novam suscepisse sancti et antiquissimi istius Fœderis editionem, magni Cardinalis XIMENIS quasi classico et exemplo accensi : ita et in eundem finem rationes publice proposuimus, et é prelo edidimus, collationem manuscriptorum sacri textûs Hebraici solummodo spectantes.

INCREDIBILE est dictu quo ardore et benevolentiâ tantum opus ab omnibus fere nostrorum hominum ordinibus statim excipiebatur. Academiæ, Oxonia, Cantabrigia, Dublinia suffragia sua perquam libenter detulerunt; nec votis tantum inanibus prosecutæ sunt, sed auro et argento oblatis liberaliter adjuvarunt. Idem dicendum est de Archiepiscopis, Episcopis, Decanis et Capitulis, Collegiis, et ut ne singulos memorem de permultis non minus propter religionem et doctrinam eorum insignibus, quam per stemmata et fastos majorum.

QUAMPRIMUM igitur, Comes Excellentissime, incoeptum et consilium hoc divulgari coepit, tantus ardor et cæteros Britannos apud exteras regiones aliosque populos peregrinantes corripuit, ut confestim manuscriptos codices Hebraicos ubique delitescentes exquirerent, eruerent, et felici quâdam indagine aucuparent.

AT ne exteri quidem, ne eorum gloriæ et laudi detraham, tanto operi, tam latæ et universæ utilitatis in rempublicam, in gene-

I   ris

ris humani commodum et ornamentum excogitato, ne ipfi exteri pro fuis viribus, pro fuâ humanitate nobis defuerunt; Præcipue Romæ, Florentiæ, Bononiæ, Mediolano, Genuæ, Venetiis, By-zantii.

In urbe vero ROMA, ubi artes et litteræ humaniores tantâ olim ubertate floruerunt, nec hodié defertæ funt, primi ordinis nobiles, et etiam ecclefiæ Catholicæ Romanæ principes, fuum operi auxi-lium et patrocinium humaniter et urbane præftiterunt. Eminen-tiffimus Cardinalis *Paffionéi* liberam collationis licentiam a fummo et S. S. Pontifice obtinuit, et Vaticani fores confeftim patefecit : hodieque omnes in celeberrimâ illâ Bibliotheeâ Hebraici manu-fcripti per Anglorum manus accuratiffimé excutiuntur in ipfo pala-tio, et dum vivus aderat, fub Eminentiffimi Cardinalis aufpiciis et ductu.

SED quorfum omnis tendit hæc oratio me roges forfan Comes humaniffime ? Aperiam ftatim, fi modo mihi veftram expetenti veniam eam clementer dederis. Tendit, vir doctiffime, ut eundem Angli in Hifpaniis indulgentiam inveniant, quam a fanctiffimo Papâ, et celfiffimo Cardinalium Collegio ROMÆ obtinuerunt : Teque, Comes Excellentiffime, patriæ meæ nómine oro et ob-teftor, ut eandem nobis veniam et collationis licentiam in his ter-ris patefacias, quam ubique alias terrarum orbis habuimus.

FREMANT licet Monachorum coenobia, et clament Sacri Officii fubfellia, tamen cum liberum patriæ meæ fpiritum et animum mecum afportaverim, tibi Comes Litteratiffime liberrime dicam quod fentio : quanquam enim nos Chriftiani in diverfa ierimus momenta fidei, tamen *eandem* ambo *fidem* profitemur, ad *eafdem* facras *fcripturas* provocamus : Æqué et communiter amborum intereft eofdem ex quibus haurimus fontes puros putofque confer-vare. Quis etenim vel fanus vel fobrius malit eam illam ignoran-tiam, eofque errores, qui ex ofcitantia librariorum libros facros invaferint, de fæculo ad fæculum perpetuare, a generatione in ge-nerationem confecrandos tradere ? Eam quam hodie licentiam *Romæ* Britannis Papa præftitit, *Matrito* certe non detracturus erit. Sed in eo non moramur.

REGIS

REGIS tantummodo licentia et auctoritas noftræ caufæ, noftræ quæftioni expetitur. Quis autem adeo fidens inventus erit, qui hanc caufam et quæftionem humillimé per Miniftros fuos ad Regem Catholicum deferat ? Excellentiffimus Legatus nofter Britannicus rei politicæ folum invigilat, neque his curis alienis vel tangi vel impediri poffit. Si de me dicerem, qui tantum vile quoddam litteratorum noftrorum in hac quæftione inftrumentum fim, et tanquam exilis patriæ meæ vox, hæc me nunquam aufurum fufcepturumve non diffiteor.

SIN autem patronum aliquem invenero, qualem te Comes Excellentiffime, fub cujus umbra protegar ; et ut verum dicam præftantiorem potioremve nec velim, nec potuerim : Quippe tu, qui architecturæ et pingendi artes præcipuo quodam amore femper fovifti ; ita cœteras fcientias, et litteras humaniores publicis ftudiis, publicâ benevolentiâ adeo profecutus fis, ut parum fciam ad cujus Patrocinium vel Mufæ vel Gratiæ potius confugerent : fub tali Ægide, fub hâc Minervâ, caufam hanc et partes mihi honorifice delatas me non deferturum fateor, et quoad potuerim executurum.

VALE, Vir doctiffime, et te D. O. M. per multos annos fofpitem fervet, et fi mea ulteriora vota fit fas adjungere.

SIT tibi † POESTANÆ gloria prima rofæ.

† He is publifhing the Ruins of the Ancient POESTUM.

L E T-

LETTER XVII.

An EPISTLE *to* Charles Christopher Pluer, chargé
des Affaires *from the Court of* Denmark *to that of* Madrid,
written originally in Latin by Don Gregory Mayans, *and
containing the present State of the* Hebrew *and* Arabic
Learning in Spain, *and where the principal MSS. in those
Branches are to be found.*

THE Arabic and Hebrew languages have always greatly .
flourished in Spain; nor is this extraordinary, for the Hebrew contains the Scriptures, and has interpreters, though
for the most part very trifling, yet highly skilful in that language.—Add to this, that the wealth of Spain ever attracted the
avarice of the Jews, whose numbers increased so much, that
their sons were even admitted to holy orders, until they were forbid by some statutes, particularly that of Toledo, in 1547. This
statute became necessary, for there were found in one single town,
of the diocese of Toledo, fourteen clergy, all Jews but one;
and in many other places a similar discovery was made of their in-
crease.—There is no doubt, but that these Jews not only studied
and improved their own language, the Hebrew; but even the
most learned Christians learnt eagerly that language, in order
to convert the Jews, especially after the *Council held at* Vienna,
in the year 1311, as we may gather from the *first* Clementine,
title De Magistris, where it was ordained, that in the Universities of Paris, Oxford, Bologna, and Salamanca, which
were

were then the moſt famed Univerſities, the *Hebrew*, *Arabic*, and *Chaldic* tongues ſhould be taught.

THIS was done with ſo much ſpirit at SALAMANCA, that from thence, as from the TROJAN Horſe, mere Princes went forth; men who underſtood all the *Oriental Tongues* incomparably well. Nevertheleſs in the time of FERDINANDUS NONIUS, the parent of Greek learning in this country, *Chaldee* and *Arabic* profeſſors were wanting at SALAMANCA, as you may ſee in N. CLEUARD's Epiſtles, p. 235.

As to the *Hebrew*, it is well known what hatred and averſion hath always ſubſiſted between the JEWS and us CATHOLICS; from whence it happened, that this hatred, which ſhould have been confined only to the perfidy of that people, hath been abſurdly exerted againſt the innocent *Hebrew* tongue itſelf, and its learned Profeſſors.

How much prejudice the ſtudy of the HEBREW created againſt ANTO. of LEBRIXA, a man of moſt eminent learning, you may learn from his *Apologia*, which is a ſcarce book; you may ſee ſome extracts of it in my *Specimen of a Library*, p. 33. The Letters of LEWIS VIVES will alſo tell you the ill treatment JOHN VERGERA, and other eminent Hebræans, met with here on account of their knowledge of the *Hebrew*. Read the complaints only of B. A. MONTANUS upon this ſubject, in his *Commentary de Varia Hebr. Lib. Scriptione et Lectione*, where he is treating of the diſcordance or agreement of different verſions.

WHEREFORE, although Cardinal XIMENES firſt ſet the example, and rouſed the minds of the Spaniards to the ſtudy of the Eaſtern Languages, and particularly of the *Hebrew*, yet as patrons and rewards for it failed after his death, and the prejudice ran againſt it, that moſt uſeful ſtudy began to be looked upon as a mark of infamy.

UPON this account, in the beginning of the ſeventeenth century, it was warmly diſputed among the Spaniards, whether or no the *Rabbinical Writings* ought to be read at all : This queſtion was warmly debated and fully explained by JOHN MARIANA, in his *Defence of the Vulgate* ; there he tells us, ch. 26, that ſcarce thirty ſcholars could be found in all SPAIN, to whom the *Rabbinical Writers* could be of any uſe ; and he adds, that his countrymen were not then ſo much addicted to the dry ſtudy of the Languages, as to ſtand in need of prohibitions, but rather of incitements. It is remarkable too, to obſerve what he wrote in his tract *De Rebus Societatis*, ch. 6.

THE ſame MARIANA, being conſulted by the *Inquiſitor General* concerning the *Rabbinical Writers*, anſwered, that he thought that the THALMUD, with its Gloſſes, ought to be forbidden to be read, as it had been already forbidden ; and that RABBI MENAHEM, *a Recanate* upon the *Pentateuch*, ought to be prohibited alſo ; and likewiſe the book ZOHAR, written by SIMEON BEN-JOCHAI, which book the JEWS vulgarly imagine was written before the time of CHRIST. MARIANA adds, that he believes, that there are many other *Rabbinical Writings* which he had never ſeen or heard of, the reading of which ought not to be permitted even to the learned: And he then gives us a liſt of ſuch *Rabbinical Writings*, as wiſe men might read with the permiſſion of the *Inquiſition*.

WHEREFORE when the reading of the *Rabbinical Writings* was thus forbidden, it is no wonder that their MSS. diſappeared ſo totally, as not to be found in private libraries ―― Nay even the printed *Rabbinical* Works were not to be had in the Bookſellers ſhops : In ſo much, that only a few of them are to be ſeen in the Library of the ESCURIAL, in that of the church of TOLEDO, and in that of the College of SAN ILDEPHONSO at ALCALA DE HENARES.

THERE are however in ſome of our Univerſities the profeſſors chairs ſtill remaining, in order to fulfill *nominally* the academic conſtitutions. In my time I remember two inſtances, when a Profeſſor's chair in one of them was to be filled up, that not one of *three* candidates was able to read a chapter of the Hebrew
Bible

Bible off hand. And yet, in the Univerſities of SALAMANCA, and VALENTIA, we have public Profeſſors of *Hebrew*; but theſe have no pupils; for how can that be learnt which is not taught. ——This therefore is the true ſtate of the caſe, the ſtudy of *Hebrew* in SPAIN was revived by XIMENES, and died with the diſciples of the great MONTANUS.

As to the ARABIC language in this country, I will be ſome-what more diffuſe upon that ſubject, becauſe there are more monuments and MSS. of it remaining, but which remain ſo, as to be almoſt hidden treaſures. The MOORS extended their Arabic language in proportion as they enlarged their conqueſts in SPAIN, as you may ſee in ALDRETI's *Origin of the Caſtilian Language,* chap. 22.

IT is no wonder therefore, that there were many in SPAIN who were not only ambitious of glory in arms, but in letters; eſpecially during the fierce contentions of ſo many petty rival Kings, and in a country the moſt fruitful of great geniuſes. The ARABS in SPAIN chiefly ſtudied Philoſophy, Mathematicks, and Phyſick: In the *firſt*, principally Logic and Metaphyſics; in the *ſecond*, Arithmetic and Geometry; in the *third*, Botany and Chemiſtry.

ABU-NAZAR, AL-PHATAH, a native of HISPALIS, or SEVILLE, who wrote about the State of Learning in SPAIN, has told us how many, and what great men among theſe *Arabs*, have left works behind them in that language.

EBN ALKHALIB MAHOMAD, BEN ABDALLAH left likewiſe, in four large folio volumes, an *Arabico-Spaniſh-Bibliotheque*, containing the lives of the ſeveral Caliphs, Generals, Philoſophers, Poets, and learned women, among the *Arabs*, who lived in SPAIN. Theſe two laſt mentioned excellent works, are both of them ſtill exiſting in the Library of the ESCURIAL. See to this purpoſe, *Nic. Antonii Bibliothec. Hiſpan.* num. 8, 9. the Preface to which work is a very learned performance.

AMONG

AMONG the Kings of SPAIN, ALPHONSUS THE WISE is almoſt the only one who had any regard for the Arabic language:
By his order ABRAHAM ABENZOHAR tranſlated out of Arabic
into the Spaniſh, HAZALQUI's book of *Judicial Aſtrology*: And
JUDAS, the ſon of MUSCE, tranſlated the entire book of HALI,
the ſon of ABENRAGEB, upon the ſame ſubject, which was afterwards tranſlated into Latin by ÆGIDIUS DE TEBALDIS. Beſides, JUDAS, the ſon of RABBI MOSES HACKEN, a canon of
TOLEDO, tranſlated into Latin, by the order of ALPHONSUS,
the Aſtronomical Works of AVICENA, from the Arabic: And
the ſame Prince ordered the book, concerning all kinds of *Aſtro-
labes* and their uſe, concerning the number and diſtances of the
ſtars, to be tranſlated from the *Chaldee* into the Spaniſh tongue.
This book that great man HONORETES JOHANNES ordered to be
tranſcribed from the Library at ALCALA DE HENARES, and to
be depoſited in that of the ESCURIAL.

THE Univerſity of SALAMANCA contributed greatly to the
increaſe of Arabic learning; for in that Univerſity there were
eminent Profeſſors of Phyſic, who ſtudied and followed the ſyſ-
tems of the Arabs: For the Arabs firſt raiſed that neceſſary art
into repute in EUROPE, when it was fallen to a very low ebb.
Theſe men firſt introduced the true practice of their art, by unit-
ing the knowledge of the cauſes of diſtempers, with the prudent
application of the propereſt remedies.

BUT when things were come to that paſs, that the *Chriſtians*
began to apprehend that the *Moors* would ſubdue their conquerors
in their turn, they took all the precautions to be ſecure againſt
them, which fear naturally inſpires. This was done many ways.
It only belongs to my preſent ſubject to ſay, that the uſe of the
Arabic tongue was forbidden to the Moors of GRANADA, as
FERDINADO VALOR tells us in that eloquent ſpeech, in which
he complains with great addreſs, of the perſecutions of his countrymen. *See Did. Hurt. de Mendoza, in his Hiſt. of the War of
Granada, Book* 1. Sect. 7.

R r   AT

AT VALENTIA likewife, in the year 1568, were publifhed the CONSTITUTIONS of the Archbifhop of VALENTIA, the Bi-fhop of SEGORVE, the Bifhop of DERTOSA, the Bifhop of ORI-HUCLA, the Commiffary General for Profelytes, the Inquifitor of VALENTIA, the Count de BENAVENTE, Viceroy and Captain-General of VALENTIA: And by thefe Conftitutions it was or-dered, that whenever the Moors fhould make a *Will*, it fhould be written in the Valentian or Caftilian tongues; if it was made in any other language, it fhould be void and of no force. Be-fides this, LEWIS BERTRAND, a man of a very fevere difpofi-tion, writing in 1579 to JOHN RIBERA, Patriarch of ANTIOCH, and a man of the higheft prudence; BERTRAND, fpeaking of the beft method of converting the Moors to Chriftianity, fays, that the Arabic tongue ought to be prohibited in the kingdom of VALENTIA, as it had before been in the kingdom of GRA-NADA: For fays he, the women and children continue in their unbelief, only becaufe they do not underftand the fermons of our Spanifh Monks and Confeffors. See the Letter at the end of *the Life of John Ribera, printed, Rome, 1734, and written by John Ximenez.*

BUT it is certain, that other men of great piety and difcretion, were of a different opinion in this matter. FERNANDO TALA-VERA, Archbifhop of GRANADA, as we are told by FR. BER. DE PEDRAZA, part iv. c. 10. of his Hift. of GRANADA, feri-oufly faid, That he would very willingly lofe both his eyes, pro-vided he could be fuch a mafter of Arabic, as to teach and preach the word of GOD with fkill: And he advifed the parochial priefts to learn that language, in order to inftruct the Moors. *See Jof. de Siguenza,* Part. iii. *of the Hift of the Jeromites,* c. 34. The Archbifhop too perfuaded PETER DE ALCALA, a Francifcan, to compofe an *Arabic Vocabulary,* from which moft excellent book you can only learn the *Arabifms* in our language. Concerning the fcarcity of this book, fee *Antiquit. Hifp. pr. Bern. Aldreti, Lib.* 1. *c.* 10. and my *Origenes.*

BESIDES, *Martin Perez de Ayala,* Archbifhop of VALENTIA, a man of uncommon learning and rare piety, in order to inftruct

new

3

new converts to Christianity in VALENTIA, ordered to be printed, in 1566, Institutes of the Christian Religion in the *Arabic* and *Castilian* languages; in two columns, one in the common, the other in the Italic character, that priests, who were ignorant of the Arabic, might know how to pronounce the Arabic words. Observe only, what a general ignorance of the Arabic prevailed in SPAIN at that time. That the Spanish clergy knew as little of it in the beginning of the seventeenth century, appears from the testimony of JAMES BLEDA, *in his Moorish Chronicle of* SPAIN, *page* 84. In the time of RODRIGO CARO, who published the *Antiquities* of SEVILLE in 1634, there was no one there who understood the Arabic tongue, as he tells us, Book I. chap. 23.

WHEN there were discovered some plates at GRANADA, with Inscriptions on them, in the year 1595, PEDRO DE CASTRO, Archbishop of SEVILLE, when he came to that *See*, invited thither THOMAS ERPENIUS, who was reviving the Arabic learning at that time: His design was, that ERPENIUS should have interpreted those *plates*; but he would not accept of the invitation, as JOHN VOSSIUS tells us in his panegyric on the death of that great man.

FROM such a total ignorance of the Arabic tongue, you may easily conjecture the contempt it lay under at that period. The Christians always burnt, in those days, whatever they found written in that language. If you look into the *Scaligerana, page* 30 *and* 144, you will find some account of this matter, given upon the authority of B. A. MONTANUS, who says, that the Arabic MSS. burnt in those days, in the several branches of learning, such as Philosophy, Divinity, Physic, and Mathematics, were then valued at above 100,000 *crowns*. The Moors fearing this, carefully hid their Arabic MSS. in the cavities of walls, or other obscure places.

THE *Manuscript-Burners* seemed to have been possessed with the same spirit, as OMAR, the Saracen Caliph, who burnt the Alexandrian Library. *See* ALBUPHARAJUS, *in his History of the Saracenic Dynasties, page* 181, and POCOCK's Translation, p. 119.

These

Thefe Book-burning Bigots feem to have imitated the example of JOHN ZUMARAGA, the firft Bifhop of MEXICO, who commanded every body to burn all the *Indian Hiftories* they could meet with, becaufe he thought all the fymbolic figures in thofe Indian MSS. were idols. *See* JEAN TURRECREMATA's *Hift. of the Indian Monarchy, Book III. chap.* 6.

THE MOORS, as I faid before, carefully hid their MSS. in the cavities of walls, or other obfcure places. By this means fome of them now and then appear, which have been found in the ruins of old houfes. This hath very often happened in my time, and particularly at *Bugarra,* which is a little town in VALENTIA, where, about twenty-fix years ago, were found fome Arabic *MSS.* covered over with fpartum, a Spanifh plant, to preferve them from the wet; and the whole was concealed by layers of bricks. Two of thefe *MSS.* I fent elegantly bound to JOHN V. King of PORTUGAL: Another I have by me, damaged by the wet, and wanting the beginning and ending, but I will fend it to DAVID MICHAEL, if he pleafes, to fhew him how willing I am to oblige him.

IN the year 1754, in a little town belonging to the Bifhopric of ALBARRACIN, a large city in ARRAGON, they found in the cavity of a wall, upon ftone fhelves, above 144 volumes of Arabic MSS. That thefe might be preferved, I defired Don FRANCISCO RAVÁGO, the King's Confeffor, to acquaint his Majefty with the difcovery. The King immediately ordered them to be fent for; and that part of them which could be found, has been taken care of. The common people in SPAIN imagine, that thefe Arabic MSS. contain fome fecret verfes, and that they are a fort of Magic Charm, by the help of which you may difcover hidden treafure; therefore, whenever they find thefe MSS. they hide them, and fet a great value upon them. Whenever they try the virtue of this charm, they always get a *Moor,* who can read the Arabic, and who pretends to milk a goat with a *fieve.* This cuftom the Spaniards learnt from the Moors, as you may fee in JOHN LEO's *Defcription of* AFRICA, *Book III.*

You

You fee that the Chriftians in SPAIN ceafed to fpeak the Arabic tongue, when they began to govern the Moors and hold them under fubjection : The Moors were then forbid the ufe of their own language, fo that in the end, the Arabic tongue became in this country a dead language. *See* ALDRETI's *Origin of the Caftilian Tongue, Book I. chap.* 13.

MANY of the Arabic *MSS.* were burnt ; and many were tranfported out of SPAIN into AFRICA.   Three thoufand Arabic *MSS.* were carried thither by one Ambaffador only, who came from ALGIERS to the Court of MADRID.   See JOHN LEO's Defcription of AFRICA, Book IV. p. 523.

ADD to all this, the want of Arabic types in the Printing-houfes in SPAIN, as you may fee in the royal licence prefixed to AL-DRETI's *Spanifh Antiquities,* and that in a time too, when I may fay, without any injury to the prefent, that there was more found learning ftudied than there is now.   Befides, we have no Arabic Profeffor in any of our Univerfities.   You cannot find, I do not fay an Arabic *MS.* but not even an Arabic printed book, in any of our bookfellers fhops : In no private library that I know of, is there an Arabic *MS.* to be feen.   Nor do I remember to have read of any in the printed catalogues of our moft celebrated *Spanifh Libraries*; fuch as thofe of Don ANT. AUGUSTINO, Don GABRIEL SORA, LORENZO RAMIREZ DE PRADO, the Marquez MONTALEGRE, EMMANUEL PANTOJA, ANDRES GONZALEZ BARCIA, all which I have by me.   The only perfon in SPAIN in my memory, who had any confiderable number of books in the Eaftern Languages, was Don LUCAS CORTEZ : His library was, after his death, fold by auction for a trifle.

BUT to fay the truth, nothing fo much prejudiced the ftudy of the Arabic and the Eaftern Languages in this country, as that pride with which gentlemen of the court have always treated the Profeffors of thofe tongues.   RODRIGO GOMEZ, of the houfe of SYLVA, when fomebody was praifed in his company for his great fkill in languages, afked if the man underftood the *Caftilian* tongue likewife ? Yes he does, replied the other.   Very well, says fays GOMEZ, that's enough ; it is the only language we fpeak at court; and as for all the reft, they are not worth puzzling one's head about them. And yet for all this, there are a great number of *Hebrew and Arabic* MSS. in the ESCURIAL Library. For the moft learned men in SPAIN, out of compliment to PHILIP II. prefented him with the beft and rareft books, to adorn that collection. But that I may confine myfelf to fuch books only as belong to my fubject, DID. HURTADO DE MENDOZA left his books by will to PHILIP II. which books were carried into the ESCURIAL Library in 1575, as Jos. DE SIGUENZA tells us, in his *Hiftory of the Jeromite brotherhood*, Book III. page 3. who fays, that there were among them many Greek, Arabic, and Latin MSS. There were of *Arabic* alone, in this legacy of MENDOZA's, about 400, relating to fcience and hiftory, as MENDOZA himfelf fays, in a letter of his to JEROM SURITA, which you may read in *The progrefs of Hiftory in the kingdom of* ARRAGON, *publifhed by* Don DID. Jos. DORMER.

BUT here let me take notice of three miftakes made by JAMES AUGUSTUS DE THOU, or him who wrote the *Thuana*. It is there faid, that DIDACO MENDOZA wrote the *Hiftory of the* INDIES, whereas ANTONIO DE MENDOZA wrote it. He confounds DIDACO with FERNANDO MENDOZA, the laft of whom died mad; for DIDACO died by the amputation of a leg, as ANTONIO PEREZ tells us.——Laftly, DE THOU fays, that the Spaniards are wont to die mad, which is a notorious falfhood.

B. A. MONTANUS gave alfo to the ESCURIAL Library many MSS. in Hebrew, Arabic, and Greek, as SIGUENZA tells us. I pafs over others, who gave fine Oriental MSS. to the fame Library. Befides, LEWIS FAXARDO, who was High Admiral to PHILIP III. took from the Turks, in one engagement, 3000 Arabic MSS. which were all placed in the ESCURIAL, as FR. DE LOS SANTOS tells you in the hiftory of that Convent.

BUT, to the irreparable lofs of the republic of Letters, the greateft part of the Oriental MSS. and particularly the Arabic, were burnt in the year 1674, as NIC. ANTONIO tells you in the preface

face to his *Spanish Bibliotheque*. The fire began June the 7th, and lasted fifteen successive days, as Los SANTOS relates. FAX-ARDO's MSS. were all burnt, except the *Alcoran*, and some few others.

YET still a great number of Oriental MSS. and particularly *Arabic*, remain there. And to speak of the Arabic only, there are in the ESCURIAL Library above 200 Arabic Grammarians, many more Rhetoricians, Orators, Poets, &c. MICHAEL CA-SIRI, a Syrian, the Royal Librarian, hath printed a catalogue of these, of which only the first volume is published. The title of it is, SPECIMEN BIBLIOTHECÆ REGIÆ, ARABICO-HISPANÆ, ESCORIALENSIS; the first sheet of which I now send you, which I received from the King's Confessor. When this work comes out, the republic of Letters will know what vast treasures lie hid in that monastery. So that the words of Master LEO, related by ANT. PEREZ, will seem almost prophetic; who said, that " the ESCURIAL collection of books would become hereafter a " noble monument of royal magnificence; but that it would not " be a library, but a sepulchre."

MANY learned men have complained loudly of this burying books alive, if I may be allowed the expression. MARIANA, in his tract *de Rege et Regis institutione*, *Lib.* III. *Cap.* 9. says, " The ESCURIAL Library is built over the *Vestibulum*, in length " 185 feet, and 30 feet broad: it contains many Greek MSS. " most of them of a venerable antiquity, which were brought " from all parts of EUROPE in great abundance. These trea- " sures, which are more valuable than gold, deserve to have a " freer access of the learned, to inspect and examine them. For, " what advantage can be derived to the public from such captives " as these, imprisoned as it were by royal authority?"

I pass over the complaints of others. Monsieur BAUTRU, when he came into SPAIN, and had seen the ESCURIAL Library, went to the King, and talked with his Majesty about it; and said, among other things, that the Librarian of the ESCURIAL was a very fit man to be entrusted with such a royal treasure.

Why

Why fo? fays the King. Becaufe, replied BAUTRU, as it is plain he has ftolé none of the books, you may be fure he will never diminifh your Majefty's treafure.

THE collecting thofe books together, was, in one refpect, very providential; for, where would they have been now, if they had not been preferved there? They are of no great ufe indeed, becaufe the cuftody of them is given to a fet of illiterate monks, who, as DEAN MARTI faid, envy others what they make no ufe of themfelves. JOHN BAPTIST CARDONA, Bifhop of DER-TOSA, when he wrote to PHILIP II. concerning this library, ad-vifed him "to chufe a Librarian for it, who was well fkilled in "the Latin and Greek tongues, and who fhould know tho-"roughly the claffical writers; for, as to the Hebrew and Ori-"ental tongues, your Majefty may eafily procure *Rabbins* for that "purpofe.   There are now at ROME fome *Rabbins*, who are "converted to Chriftianity, men of piety and learning, fuch as "ANDREW, JULLIUS, and PAULLUS, men of note there. Your "Majefty muft likewife fend for a PERSIAN, and a TURK, and "fo on for each foreign language.—There is now living one "STEPHANUS, brought up in SOLYMAN's court, and a great "favourite of his.   This man, who commanded two gallies, "was taken in an engagement at fea, and is now fupported by a "penfion from the king at NAPLES.   He would be a very proper "perfon, and would certainly be of more ufe to your Majefty, "than to the King of NAPLES, for his fingular knowledge of "Turkifh affairs."——No one would certainly fay, that the ESCURIAL Library was of no ufe in the time of MONTANUS, who was Librarian there.   But fuch men as he are ftill wanting, to make that collection truly ufeful.

THE *Hebrew* and *Arabic* MSS. in SPAIN are written either on *Parchment*, or on *Paper*; the antiquity of which latter you may gather from an *Inftrument*, ftill preferved in the Chamber of Royal Archives at BARCELONA.   This inftrument was drawn in 1178, and, from the nearnefs of the two periods, I conjecture, that this fine Spanifh writing-paper was made at the famous SÆ-
TABIS,

TABIS, afterwards called XATIVA, and now SAN PHILIPPE *. The GEOGRAPHUS NUBIENSIS, who wrote about the year 1150, or perhaps a little before, says, " SÆTABIS is a moſt beautiful " city, and its environs are ſo delightful, as to be made a pro- " verb of; they make their paper of a moſt incomparable fine- " neſs."——It is no wonder this city ſhould be ſo celebrated for its *Paper Fabric*, for CATULLUS has taken notice of its fine handkerchiefs, the *Sudaria Sætaba*, as he calls them: And PLI- NY tells us, *Lino Sætabi tertia in Europa dabatur palma*. SILIUS ITALICUS too, and GRATIAN, have ſung its praiſes.

FROM MSS. the tranſition to *Medals* is very eaſy. Count MI- GAZZI, now Archbiſhop of VIENNA, when he was at MADRID, Ambaſſador to the court of SPAIN, obtained, by my means, 320 Silver Coins, 11 Braſs Coins, and one Gold Coin, all of them *Arabic* monies, ſtruck in SPAIN, and in good preſervation: The interpretation of theſe, if publiſhed, would be a new thing, and highly acceptable to the learned.

You will not be permitted to collate any of our MSS. without the King's leave. We have, beſides, no Spaniard able enough to aſſiſt DAVID CLEMENS in collating an Oriental MSS. but CA- SIRI, and he has no leiſure for it.

From OLIVA, in VALENTIA, December 23d, 1758.

* This city, which is ſo often mentioned by the Roman poets and writers, was in VALENCIA, and ſtood on the banks of the river XUCAR: It was very finely built, and the ſituation of it was delightful. Unfortunately it declared, in the year 1706, for the Arch-duke CHARLES. The year following, the Count D'ASFELDT be- ſieged and took it, and put all the inhabitants to the ſword that bore arms; few eſcaped but women and children. The citadel capitulated ſoon after, where they made 800 Engliſh priſoners of war. PHILIP ordered the city to be razed and level- led with the ground, and, on the ſpot where it ſtood, they erected a column, with this inſcription—" HERE WAS ONCE A CITY NAMED XATIVA, WHICH, AS A PUNISHMENT FOR ITS TREASON, AND ITS REVOLT AGAINST ITS KING AND COUNTRY, HAS BEEN LEVELLED EVEN TO THE GROUND. In the year 1707, they rebuilt, by PHILIP's order, a new city on the ſame ſpot, and it is now called SAN PHILIPPE.

LETTER XVIII.

An EPISTLE *written by* DON GREGORIO MAYANS, *to the late* SIR BENJAMIN KEENE, *containing a full Account of the* COMPLUTENSIAN POLYGLOTT, *&c. &c.*

MAY it pleafe your EXCELLENCY! You having hinted to me, that you defired fome information concerning the COMPLUTENSIAN BIBLE, and thofe MSS. which the learned editors of that work made ufe of, if they were any where now in being, I fhall endeavour to give your Excellency all the intelligence on that point in my power.

DON ALVARO GOMEZ, who wrote the Life of Cardinal XI-MENES, fays, * " That XIMENES, fearing left the facred myfte-" ries of our religion fhould fuffer fome detriment, from the " Scriptures being ill underftood, began moft timely to be appre-" henfive, left the Spaniards fhould become entire ftrangers, and. " totally unacquainted with the books of THE OLD AND NEW " TESTAMENT."

† DON ANTONIO DE LEBRIXA tells us, in the preface to his *Apologia,* how defpifed and neglected the knowledge of the learned languages was at that time, and how little the profeffors of them were efteemed. This ftate of ignorance continued to the

---

* Book II. p. 36, 38.　　† *i. e.* ANTONIUS NEBRISSENSIS.

I.

days

days of Montanus, and Mariana*, and I wish it did not continue now.

Gomez adds, " That Ximenes, therefore, (in imitation of
" the great Origen, who with amazing diligence put together
" all the translations of the Bible then extant, and united them
" in those famed Hexapla) ordered an edition of the Bible to
" be set on foot, to remedy this evil.   In that edition, the books
" of the *Old Teſtament* are divided into three columns.   In the
" firſt column is placed the *Hebrew*, in the middle the *Vulgate*,
" in the third the LXX. and its tranſlation.   At the bottom of
" the page is placed the *Chaldee Paraphraſe*, with its Latin tranſ-
" lation.——But the *New Teſtament* has the moſt correct Greek
" text poſſible, with the *Vulgate*.   In the laſt volume is added a
" dictionary of Hebrew words and phraſes, admired by the ſkil-
" ful in that language.   This addition was much wanted in ſome
" Bibles, through the careleſneſs of thoſe who kept them, and
" was a great detriment to the reader.   This undertaking of
" Cardinal Ximenes was highly laborious, magnificent, and
" great; it not only required a man of his eminence, but of his
" abilities likewiſe, to ſurmount all the difficulties which at-
" tended ſuch a work: He therefore ſent for men of letters,
" well ſkilled in the Greek and Latin languages, to aſſiſt him.
" Theſe were, firſt, Demetrius Cretensis, by birth a
" Greek, whom Aubertus Miraeus tells us †, Ximenes had
" ſent for out of Italy, by offering a large premium.   Second-
" ly, Anto. of Lebrixa: It was owing to this man's ſole ad-
" vice, that Ximenes undertook an edition of that *Complutenſian
" Bible*, as Anto. tells us in his *Apologia*, which is a very valu-
" able work.   In that you will ſee the envy and ill will which
" this great reviver of Spaniſh learning experienced, for his en-
" deavours to make it flouriſh in the univerſity of Salamanca.
" In the beginning of his book, he thus addreſſes the Cardinal.

" May it pleaſe your Eminence! I am in doubt, whether my
" genius did not owe me a grudge, when it prompted me to

---

* See B. A. Mont. on Josua, and Mariana's Defence of the Vulgate, Chap. 8:
26. &c.   † Scriptor. Sæculi XVI. Cap. 45. P. 140.

" think

" think of nothing, but what was difficult, to attempt only
" great enterprifes, to publifh nothing but what occafioned
" me much hatred and ill-will. Had I given my time to vifiting
" my friends; had I fpent my night watchings in fable and poe-
" tical fiction; had I read or wrote hiftory; had I flattered the
" living or the dead; I might have had the united applaufe of all
" the Spains: But now, becaufe I labour after the meat which
" does not perifh, and, as Jerom fays, trace out on earth that
" knowledge which only abideth in Heaven; becaufe I am thus
" employed, I am called impious, facrilegious, a falfe Catholic,
" and I am in fome danger of being fummoned in chains to plead
" my caufe before the Inquifition as an heretic: there will not
" be wanting an accufer; there are thofe who are ready and wil-
" ling enough.——So that I may apply to myfelf very juftly thofe
" words of Ecclesiastes, He that increafeth knowledge in-
" creafeth trouble.—If, Sir, it is the duty of a legiflator to re-
" ward the wife and good, and to punifh the wicked and hereti-
" cal fubject,—What are you doing, great Cardinal, in that go-
" vernment, where, &c."

I omit the reft, becaufe I *dare not* tranfcribe it. This great
man, therefore, was one of the chief compilers of the Complutenfian Bible.

Gomez adds, " That Ximenes fent likewife for * Lopez
" Astunica, or De Zuniga, as we Spaniards write it; he
" fent alfo for Fernandus Pintianus, whofe Spanifh name is
" Fernando Nunez de Gusman, a native of Valladolid,
" which is vulgarly called Pintia. How eminent this man
" was for his knowledge in the Latin and Greek tongues, may
" be feen in Justus Lipsius, A. Schottus, N. Antonius,.
" and many others †." But whereas Gomez tells us, that Pintianus's works were in every one's hands in his time, it was not
fo in 1580.

* See Critici SS. Tom. ix. p. 2. col. 3552.   A. Schotti Hifp. Bibl. Tom. iii.
p. 584.   † De Thou, Lib. xi. p. 401. L. xxi. p. 727.

Gomez

GOMEZ adds, "That XIMENES fent for thefe men, who were
" eminent Greek and Latin profeffors, and whofe works were in
" every one's hands; and for ALPHONSUS, a Phyfician at ALCA-
" LA DE HENARES,* PAULUS CORONELLUS, ALPHONSUS ZA-
" MORA †, all eminent *Hebræans.* Thefe had been public pro-
" feffors of that language in their fchools, but having afterwards
" taken holy orders, they were very properly fent for by Cardi-
" nal XIMENES, to execute fo great a work, which would require
" their virtue, their learning, and their perfeverance. With
" thefe men the *Cardinal* confulted about the plan; promifed to
" fupport them moft liberally with money; and invited them fe-
" parately to undertake the work, by giving them large prefents.
" Above all, the *Cardinal* recommended to them the utmoft dif-
" patch, Left, fays he, as all human things are uncertain, you
" fhould lofe fo willing a patron to this work, or I fhould lofe
" fuch able affiftants, whofe company, and whofe labours, I va-
" lue more than the Archbifhopric of TOLEDO.—This fpeech of
" the Cardinal's had its effect, and thefe learned men never ceafed
" their labours till they had finifhed the work. They firft fent
" for all the MSS. of both Teftaments, which could be pro-
" cured, in order to fix the pureft new text, to amend the errors
" of the old, to fettle the true reading of doubtful paffages, and
" to explain the obfcure."

THE greateft part of thefe MSS. particularly of the Old Teftament, were fetched from the Jewifh fynagogues, and principally
from thofe of TOLEDO and MAQUEDA. Thefe were eafily to become at, becaufe the Jews had been driven out of SPAIN ten years
before, in 1492. Thefe MSS. were afterwards chained down to
the fhelves in the college of SAN. ILDEPHONSO, at ALCALA DE
HENARES, by the order of the CARDINAL, and yet, notwithftanding that caution, many of them were afterwards ftolen.

GOMEZ adds, " But the moft ufeful collection of MSS. to XI-
" MENES, was that of the *Vatican Library,* which were of a
" moft venerable antiquity."

* See COLMENARES Hift. SEGOV. p. 707.
† This man did the 6th volume of the Polyglott.

THIS

This appears plainly by a letter of the Cardinal's to Leo X. prefixed to the Pentateuch; "For," fays he, "we can fairly "teftify to your Holinefs, that our greateft care has confifted in "employing the moft able linguifts, and in procuring the moft "ancient and moft correct MSS. from all quarters. With incre- "dible pains we collected an amazing multitude of Hebrew, "Greek, and Latin MSS. It was to your Holinefs that we "owed the Greek MSS. for you very politely fent us the moft "ancient MSS. of the Old and New Teftament from that Apo- "ftolic library, and which were of the greateft ufe to us in this "work."——The fame Cardinal, in his preface to the reader, fays, "With regard to the Greek part of Scripture, you muft "know, that we did not take any vulgar or common MSS. for "to fix our text, but the moft ancient and moft correct, which "Pope Leo X. fent me from the Vatican; MSS. of fuch inte- "grity, that if you cannot credit thefe, you can credit none.— "To thefe we have added not a few, partly tranfcribed from "that moft correct MS. of Bessarion, fent me by the fenate of "Venice, and partly procured by me at vaft labour and ex- "pence.

"We have alfo compared Jerom's Latin verfion with many "MSS. of the greateft antiquity, particularly with thofe in the "public library of my univerfity at Alcala de Henarez, "which are in *Gothic characters*, and were written above 800 "years ago, and with fuch amazing exactnefs, that you cannot "difcover the omiffion of a tittle throughout; yet fome of the "proper names, which were wrong fpelt, by a miftake of the "copyift, we let remain defignedly as they were."

Besides the *Vatican* and *Venetian* library, Miraeus tells us, they made ufe too of the *Medicèan*.

Gomez adds, "Thefe Vatican MSS. were fent to the Cardinal "by Pope Leo X. who admiring the magnificent fpirit of Xi- "menes, conceived the greateft opinion of him; and that Pope "fent to him afterwards for his advice in matters of high import- "ance to the Romifh church, though the Cardinal was then in "Africa.

" AFRICA.——The verfion of the Seventy was done partly by
" Complutenfian fcholars, partly by DEMETRIUS, PINTIANUS,
" and ASTUNICA; and was fo happily executed, that nothing
" was omitted in the verfion, of the force of thofe Græcifms,
" which are fo frequent in the Seventy.

" AMONG the learned men called together upon this occafion,
" was JOHN VERGARA, who had *the Books of Wifdom* for his
" lot. He reftored the text of them in many places, as he has
" often faid himfelf; and when very old, he ufed to wifh for
" nothing fo much at his leifure, as to publifh fome fcholia on
" ECCLESIASTICUS; but his ill health prevented that defign."

THIS JOHN VERGARA was afterwards a canon of TOLEDO;
he not only tranflated the Books of Wifdom from the Seventy into Latin, but added a comment likewife *.—Yet this great man
was afterwards thrown into the *Inquifition*, in April 1534, by AL-
PHONSUS MANRICUS, Inquifitor General, as L. VIVES tells
ERASMUS, in one of his † Epiftles: But VERGARA got happily
out of that prifon again, and lived to 1558.

GOMEZ adds,—" They were employed in this work from the
" year 1502, more or lefs, fifteen years; that one may almoft
" fay, that the Cardinal's life, and the edition of this work, end-
" ed at the fame period.—It would take me up too much time
" to give a minute detail of the labour and trouble thofe Editors
" went through, in comparing and examining the MSS. while
" XIMENES in the mean while had perpetual avocations with the
" affairs of ftate."

THE Complutenfian Bible was begun in 1502, and began to
be printed juft ten years afterwards, in 1512: It was finifhed in
1517. This was the very year in which XIMENES died.—

GOMEZ adds,—" With regard to the whole expence of this
" edition of the Complutenfian Polyglott, you muft know firft,

* See DE THOU, Lib. xxi. c. 11.　　　† Tom. II. p. 676.

" that.

" that only feven Hebrew MSS. which are now at Alcala
" de Henares, were bought by Alphonsus Zamora, Pro-
" feffor of Hebrew, in different countries, at a no lefs fum than
" § 4000 crowns, as was heard from his own mouth."

List of Hebrew Manuscripts now preferved at Alcala
de Henares.

1. Hebrew Bible, written in the ninth century.
2. Ditto, written in the twelfth century.
3. One·volume of the Hebrew Bible, no date.
4. Hebrew Pentateuch, no date.
5. Two volumes of a Chaldee Bible.

List of Greek Manuscripts there.

1. Greek Bible, modern character.
2. Greek Pfalter, very old character.

Latin Manuscripts there.

1. Bible, in Gothic characters, almoft 1000 years old.
2. Bible, almoft as old, as appears by the character.
3. Bible in two volumes, twelfth century.
4. St. Paul's Epiftles, with a glofs.
5. The New Teftament, with notes.

Gomez adds,——" To fay nothing of the Greek and the La-
" tin MSS. the former of which came from Rome ; the latter
" from foreign countries, and from the feveral Libraries in
" Spain; particularly thofe in Gothic characters, which are
" above 800 years old, were brought to Alcala de Henares
" at a vaft expence.——Then, if you reckon the wages of the
" type-founders and amanuenfes, the rewards given to the learn-
" ed Editors, the fums paid to meffengers and agents, and
" other fervants; all this together will make the whole expence
" above * 50,000 crowns; which I have heard the oldeft peo-
" ple fay was the fum."

§ He means the Half Piftole ; it is almoft 2000 l.
* Above 20,000 l. fterling.

BUT

BUT as BENEDICTUS ARIAS MONTANUS publifhed our *Royal edition of the Bible*, and made ufe of fome Complutenfian MSS. which the Cardinal's editors could not do, it will not be improper here to give fome account of that very great man.

MONTANUS was born at FREGENAL DE LA SIERRA; *Sierra* fignifies in Spanifh a ridge of mountains, and therefore he was called MONTANUS; this village being under the jurifdiction of the city of HISPALIS, he therefore calls himfelf *Hispalenfis*. MONTANUS was the firft perfon who obtained a lawrel crown in the Univerfity of SALAMANCA in the year 1552. He was a man of the greateft probity, ftrongeft talents, and uncommon judgement; could write with a mafterly ftyle, either in profe or verfe, and had amazing fkill in languages: He was a mafter of the *Greek, Latin, Hebrew, Syriac, Chaldee, Arabic, French, Dutch, Englifh*, and *Teutonic* languages. MONTANUS fays himfelf, in his comment on *Ifaiah*, that he knew thirteen languages. Befides this, he was a good poet, as well as a great fcholar, and blended the Belles Lettres with his feverer ftudies. It was very fortunate therefore for SPAIN, that when the copies of the Complutenfian Bible began to be fo fcarce——(FOR there never were more printed of that edition than 600 volumes, that is, as I underftand it, about 100 copies; as appears by comparing the Letters of LEO X. to the Bifhop of AVILA, and the Archdeacon of CORDUBA. It was the printing fo fmall a number, that has made the book fo fcarce,) that it poffeffed fuch a man as MONTANUS, who in conjunction with PLANTIN the printer, could ftir up the mind of PHILIP II. to a greater work than that of the Complutenfian Bible, though not fo expenfive. For PHILIP II. though he loved fame, was very covetous of his money; yet he confented to this work in 1578, and fent MONTANUS into HOLLAND with orders to re-print the COMPLUTENSIAN BIBLE, with improvements. For MONTANUS had made ufe of *feven* Hebrew MSS. which XIMENES procured from VENICE, but could not make ufe of himfelf: And MONTANUS had likewife a MSS. Latin Verfion of the Chaldee Paraphrafe.

T t

BUT

But this undertaking procured Montanus many enemies; so that he was twice cited before the Pope at Rome to plead his cause against a charge of Heresy. His chief enemies were * Leo de Castro, a canon of Valladolid, Rhetoric Professor in Salamanca; and, what I am sorry to say, John de Mariana, otherwise a great man; who out of envy to his learning, or his interest with Philip II. accused him to the *Inquisitor General*; and has left many marks of spleen against Montanus, in his *Defence of the Vulgate*.

From the accusations laid to his charge before the Pope, Montanus easily cleared himself in an Apologia, or defence of himself, wrote on that occasion, as Colomesius tells us. This was written in Spanish; and when the English about that time made a descent at Cadiz, they found this work there, and carried it into England, and deposited it in the Bodleian Library, and preserved it as the greatest curiosity.

This is the same work which I desired your Excellence some time ago to procure for me out of England, and which you told me could not be found at Oxford. I still hope it will be found some time or other.——Montanus died in his own house at Campo Florido, in the year 1598, and the seventy-first of his age.

List of Manuscripts in the Cathedral Library at Toledo.

1. Latin Bible, in *Gothic* letter, upon parchment, large folio, written in 1026.

2. Latin Bible, beginning with Joshua, and ending in the seventy-eighth Psalm, in folio, large parchment, and *Gothic* letter.

3. Latin Bible, beginning with the second book of Maccabees, then follows all the New Testament, and that is followed by Tobias; folio, large parchment, old character.

* See De Thou, Lib. cxx. c. 18.

There

THERE are five Latin Bibles in all, one of them containing the third and fourth book of EXODUS.——Thefe are all written in the thirteenth century, and on parchment.

4. BIBLE in Latin, with an interpretation of fome Hebrew words, written on parchment, in the thirteenth century.

5. BIBLE in Latin, written on parchment, in the thirteenth century.

6. HEBREW Bible, containing all the Pentateuch, and the portions of the Pfalms and Prophets appointed for each Sabbath ; the Canticles, Ecclefiaftes, Lamentations, Efther, and Ruth ; written in the fquare Hebrew character, with the points-or vowels ; and with the Scholia of the Rabbins, on parchment.

OLIVA, June 1754.

Tt 2   L E T-

LETTER XIX.

Of the ROYAL FAMILY *and* COURT *of* SPAIN. *Of the present* GENIUS, CHARACTER, *and* MANNERS *of that Nation. Their* HUMOURS, DIVERSIONS, *and* LANGUAGE.

DON CARLOS III. by the ftile of his Catholic Majefty, King of SPAIN, was born in MADRID the 20th of January 1716. He was, proclaimed King of NAPLES May 15th, and King of SICILY Auguft 30th, 1734; entered SPAIN the 10th of Auguft 1759, and was proclaimed King in MADRID, on the 11th of September following. The Kings of SPAIN are never crowned: inftead of it, they make a public entry into MADRID, with great expence, pomp, and magnificence, which pleafes the people much more, as they have an uncommon paffion for fhews and pageantry. The prefent Monarch made his public entry July the 13th, 1760; for an account of which, fee Letter VII. p. 125. When he landed at BARCELONA, the Catalans ftiled him CARLOS *Tercero, el verdadero,* or CHARLES *the third, the true Prince,* to diftinguifh him from the former CHARLES III. the Auftrian Archduke, who was afterwards Emperor. The Spaniards had at that time fo few failors, that they had great difficulty *in manning* the fleet which brought him over.——In coming from BARCELONA to MADRID, he drove fo faft as to make great deftruction of the mules and horfes that attended him. It is no uncommon thing for the guards that attend the Royal Family in this country, when they travel, to break a leg, an arm, or a neck; and when

when this happens, his Majefty fays, *Murio en fu officio, he died in his duty*. A Mahometan, who made fome ftay at NAPLES, happening to fee the prefent King of SPAIN driving in this *Jehu* tafte, faid to a friend——" Sir, is it any wonder that we Turks " think you Chriftians quite mad?"—Though his Catholic Majefty is now in his forty-fixth year, yet fhooting is ftill his ruling paffion: He is the greateft *Nimrod* of his time; he facrifices every thing to this favourite pleafure; he was difgufted at his public entry, becaufe it hindered him of four days fport. He ftayed *three* days at TOLEDO, and killed *fix* wild mountain-cats, which, as I was well informed by thofe who had calculated the expence of that expedition, coft him exactly 1000 l. a cat. He is fo eager at this diverfion, that when the days are fhort, he often fhoots by *torch-light*, an improvement which our Englifh fportfmen are not arrived at. He is in his perfon tall, round fhouldered, big boned, of a dark brown complexion, fmall eyed, and has a very large prominent Roman nofe. From this defcription, it is eafily feen that he is very plain.—His drefs is as plain as poffible, too homely for a Prince; he commonly wears a plain cloth frock, a leather waiftcoat, leather breeches, boots, (always made in LONDON) a large pair of tanned gloves, and ufually carries a gun upon his fhoulder, and is attended by fervants, carrying guns, powder, fhot, water, wine, victuals, cloaths, &c. and frequently dead game, fuch as wolves, hares, rooks, gulls, &c. &c.——He rifes at feven in the morning, opens his own fhutters, writes what *letters* and *difpatches* he has to do, and then fets out, let it rain or fhine, for the *chace*, or rather *fhooting*, for he never hunts as we do in ENGLAND. It is his Catholic Majefty's conftant maxim, *that rain breaks no bones*, and for this reafon it never ftops or fufpends any thing he is engaged in, to the no fmall mortification of his attendants.——His *fuite* on thefe occafions commonly confifts of the Infant Don LEWIS, the great officer in waiting, ufually the Duke de LOZADA, the Body-Guards, and three or four coaches and fix, with which there is always a chirurgeon, in cafe of any accident. He returns from this diverfion before noon, and dines regularly at eleven of the clock, and always in public, attended by the foreign minifters, and other people of diftinction about the Court. He ufually eats of fix things, drinks

three

three times, and is not long at table.——After dinner he sets out to shoot again, and seldom returns till dark, or after. Then he hears his own Ministers of State for an hour, or assists at the *Despacho*, as they call it; after that he sits with the Queen Mother in her apartment, and goes to bed between nine and ten.——And this is the general and constant round of his Majesty's life. He goes in February or March every year, to the palace of the PARDO; in April to ARANJUEZ; returns in June to MADRID; sets out at the end of July for SAN ILDEPHONSO; goes in October to the ESCURIAL, and from thence, in November, to MADRID. He sometimes fishes for variety, and at other times has what they call a general *Battida*, which is the setting five or six hundred men to drive all the game they can meet, for many miles round, into toils of great extent; and then the King and DON LEWIS, (attended by the whole Court, ladies as well as gentlemen,) go and kill it. This makes great havock among the game, and is a very expensive diversion. The foreign Ambassadors always attend on these occasions.——

HAVING described his person, and way of life, I will now endeavour to give some idea of his temper, genius, and of the absolute power with which he reigns.——It has been imagined that he is a very weak prince, and of little or no understanding: It is a great mistake.—He has some parts, but is mulish and obstinate to the last degree; and by being constantly flattered, he imagines that he has more understanding than he really possesses. He is reserved beyond the common reserve of Princes, has no confident, and communicates his will only by his orders to put it into execution.—He can neither be led nor driven; all must come from himself. Those things to which he has applied, he is a very compleat master of: He talks Italian, French, and Spanish fluently. He is an exceeding good *turner*, and has turned a multitude of things in the wooden-ware way. He looks minutely into most circumstances.——He has made with his own hands, every part of a soldier's dress, in order to be a judge of the true expence of their uniforms.——He told the foreign Ministers one day, that he had made a pair of shoes, Not indeed, says he, very good shoes, but such as might be walked in.——He shoots at a

4   mark

mark with the greateſt accuracy ; and I have often lamented, that
he has not been preſented with *Patent-ſhot* by our Miniſtry: I am
not clear, that he would not have given up the *Logwood* trade for
it.—To ſhew with what deſpotic ſway he rules, it ſhould be conſidered, that he allows no Miniſter to remonſtrate or argue with
him.—He removed the Duke of ALVA from Court, who had
been the firſt Miniſter during all the late reign, and was very popular in the nation.—Though to ſave appearances, ALVA made
a formal reſignation in the month of December 1760. He baniſhed the Dukes of ARCOS and OSSUNA from MADRID, on account of their amours with the Actreſſes, and put an Actreſs concerned in the common priſon; he arreſted and baniſhed the IN-
QUISITOR GENERAL, and ſent him priſoner to a convent. He
engaged in the preſent war with ENGLAND, contrary to the ſentiments of his Miniſters, and in direct oppoſition to the voice of
the whole nation.——He married June 19th, 1739, MARIA,
AMALIA, CHRISTINA, daughter of AUGUSTUS III. King of
POLAND, and Elector of SAXONY ; ſhe was born November 24th,
1724, and died at MADRID September 27th, 1760.——I will
now give ſome account of her.

THE late Queen AMALIA was a remarkably tall woman, with
large bones and features, rather of a maſculine appearance; had
no pretenſions to beauty ; but then what ſhe wanted in charms,
was amply made up in ſpirit: The *Poliſh temper* was but too viſible in the *Spaniſh* Queen. It has been obſerved of late, and I
think with ſome truth, that the *Sovereign Ladies* of the NORTH
have moſt of them been poſſeſſed of uncommon portions of this
ſpirit: The late Empreſs of RUSSIA, the preſent, and MARIA
THERESA, have been quoted as examples of it. How far this may
be the effect of *climate*, I cannot ſay. AMALIA, who came from
POLAND, had certainly much preſence, fire, and ſtrength of
mind ; ſhe reſembled, in ſome reſpects, our Queen ELIZABETH ;
for as that Princeſs, when ruffled in debate, would ſometimes
expreſs her royal reſentment, by ſtriking her Miniſters with her
own hands ; ſo the late Queen AMALIA would ſometimes give
her Ladies of the Bedchamber a box on the ear. She was entirely governed by the *Dutcheſs of* CASTROPINIANO, a Neapolitan,

one

one of her *Camarera's*, who had gained a moſt unaccountable aſcendant over her. It was obſerved, that the Queen's ſpirit, and the rapacious diſpoſition of her *Confidante*, though they have often put his Majeſty's temper to the trial, yet never could diſcompoſe that phlegmatic ſerenity ſo inſeparable from his mind. He always preſerved on ſuch occaſions, that reſpect and civility which is due to her ſex. She had iſſue by his Catholic Majeſty, ſix ſons and two daughters.

1. PHILIP ANTONY, Duke of CALABRIA, diſqualified for the ſucceſſion, born June 14th, 1747.

2. CHARLES ANTONY, Prince of ASTURIAS, born in NAPLES, November 12th, 1748.

3. FERDINAND ANTONY, King of NAPLES and SICILY, born January 12th, 1751.

4. GABRIEL ANTONIO, Infant of SPAIN, born in NAPLES, May 11th, 1752.

5. ANTONIO PASQUAL, Infant of SPAIN, born in NAPLES, December 31ſt, 1755.

6. FRANCISCO XAVIER, Infant of SPAIN, born in NAPLES, February 17th, 1757.

1. MARIA JOSEPHA, Infanta of SPAIN, born in NAPLES, July 16th, 1744.

2. MARIA LUISA, Infanta of SPAIN, born in NAPLES, November 24th, 1745.

PHILIP V. who died July 11th, 1746, had four ſons by his firſt wife, MARIA, LOUISA GABRIELLE, daughter of the Duke of SAVOY: LEWIS I. Don PHILIP, and Don PHILIP PEDRO GABRIELLE, who both died young, and FERDINAND VI. LEWIS died in 1724, after having reigned ſeven months; FERDINAND died aged forty-ſix, Auguſt 10th, 1759, after having reigned twelve years and ſome months.—By his ſecond wife, ELIZABETH of PARMA, PHILIP had iſſue,

.*

1. CHARLES

1. CHARLES III. the prefent King of SPAIN.

2. DON PHILIP, who died young.

3. DON PHILIP, Infant of SPAIN, Grand Prior of CASTILE, Duke of PARMA, PLACENCIA, and GUASTALLA, born March 15th, 1720, married to LOUISA ELIZABETH of FRANCE, in 1739, by whom he has one fon and two daughters.

4. DON LEWIS ANTONIO JAYME, Infant of SPAIN, born July 25th, 1727; at prefent not married.

5. MARIA ANNA VICTORIA, the prefent Queen of PORTUGAL, born March 31ft, 1718, and married March 31ft, 1732.

6. MARIA THERESA, married in 1745 to the Dauphin of FRANCE, and died in childbed July 22d, 1746.

7. MARIA ANTONIA FERNANDA, born the 17th of November, 1729, married to the prefent Duke of SAVOY.

ELIZABETH FARNESE, the prefent Queen Dowager of SPAIN, was born October 25th, 1692. Her hiftory is extremely well known in EUROPE; fhe has had no fhare in government or political matters, fince PHILIP's death, whofe memory fhe pays fo much regard to, as to cry once every year on the day he died. On the acceffion of FERDINAND, fhe was banifhed to the palace of SAN ILDEPHONSO, where fhe remained with her fon the Infant Don LEWIS, till his prefent Majefty's acceffion; who very dutifully recalled her to Court, but, to her great regret, would never admit her to the *Defpacho*. As a DE MEDICIS by blood, fhe inherited the parts, fpirit, and ambition of that family: *Two* of her fons fhe made Sovereign Princes; her filent plans at the *Efcurial* frequently threw all EUROPE into convulfions, efpecially when carried into execution by the intriguing and bold hand of her favourite ALBERONI, and the knight errantry of RIPERDA.——She formed many fpirited, though unfuccefsful fchemes, to make her *third fon* a *third Sovereign*; and was at one time very near fucceeding, by the marriage of Don LEWIS with the Princefs of BRASIL.——She is of a middle ftature, dark complexion, has great fpirit in her countenance. Before fhe reached MADRID, in the route from PARMA, when fhe came to be married to PHILIP, and before fhe had feen the King, who went as far as GUA-

U u

DALAXARA to meet her, she gave a specimen of what she would be when a *real* Queen, which was truly a coup d'eclat.——The *Princess of Ursins* had been for some time the reigning favourite in SPAIN; she had acquired such an ascendant over PHILIP and his first Queen, that she absolutely governed all. When ALBE-RONI, on her death, proposed the match of the *Duke of Parma's* niece to PHILIP V. it was even by the order of the Princess of URSINS, that ALBERONI wrote to found the Court of PARMA on that subject. Nay, the Princess of URSINS did more, she even went herself to meet the new Queen, as far as the confines' of ARRAGON and NAVARRE; who in return for these civilities, or-dered the officer on guard to arrest that *Princess* by force, and carry her out of SPAIN into FRANCE; which order was imme-diately executed. The *politick* Italian Princess knew very well that SPAIN was too narrow to hold her, and any other lady who dared to be a favourite of PHILIP's at the same time—And there-fore thought the shortest process was to get rid of her at once. When you have made your use of the ladder by which you rise, the surest way in sound policy is to kick it down.——Most others would have attempted this, after they had been well seated in a throne; but few would have had spirit enough to have given such an order, in their very first steps and passage to it, and without even the knowledge or consent of that very Prince, whose fa-vourite she banished, and whose future Queen she was designed to be.

ANOTHER instance of this Lady's genius may be the following: It is well known that PHILIP V. resigned his Crown to his son LEWIS I. who dying within the year, PHILIP, at the instigation of this Queen, resumed the scepter again. But afterwards grow-ing, as every body has heard, out of his senses, in one of his fits, he sent a full resignation of his Crown and Government, with-out the knowledge of this Lady, to the Council of CASTILE: And when he thought the act irrevocable, he told ELIZABETH FARNESE of it, and added, " Je vous ai trompé, Madame! J'ai en-" voié hier ma resignation de la Coronne d'Espagne au Concile de " Castille." This, as you will easily imagine, sufficiently alarm-ed her Majesty :—But however she had the presence of mind in-stantly to send to the president of that Council for the resignation;

nor

nor had fhe only authority to command, but influence enough to be obeyed, for he fent it her immediately.

WHILE the late King FERDINAND was Prince of ASTURIAS, upon fome difguft, fhe fent a meffage to FARINELLI never to go and fing or play any more in the Prince's or Princeffes apartment. For the late Queen BARBARA was not only very fond of, but an excellent judge of *mufick*. But FARINELLI's anfwer does immortal honour to that *Mufician*. " Go, fays he, and tell the " Queen, that I owe the greateft obligations to the Prince and " Princefs of ASTURIAS; and unlefs I receive fuch an order from " her Majefty's own mouth, or the King's, I will never obey it."

THOUGH fhe is now feventy years old, fhe keeps the fame hours that PHILIP did, and turns night into day. When fhe gives audience, fhe is held up by two fupporters, being unable to ftand long; and though almoft blind, ftill retains her ancient fpirit and vivacity. Her ambition will probably never expire but with her breath: And whenever fhe dies, I am perfuaded her laft words to the King will be, " *Remember* TUSCANY *for* DON LUIS."

DON LEWIS ANTONIO JAYME, the King's brother, feems to be of a very different mold, without either his father's military genius, or his mother's ambition; of a pacific and quiet temper. He took a very early averfion to the *Crofier*, though made almoft as foon as born, a Baby-Cardinal, and an Infant-Archbifhop, for the two fees of TOLEDO and SEVILLE. Upon quitting however thofe dignities in the church, he referved to himfelf about 7,400 *l. per annum*, out of the former, and about 5000 *l*. out of the latter. He feems to have much more inclination for a *gun* than for a *fceptre*, and fpends moft of his time in field fports: He has a ftrong turn for *mechanics*, and when not employed in fhooting, is bufied in making watches and mathematical inftruments. He has fome tafte for *medals;* and the monks he has employed have made for him no inconfiderable collection of thofe antiquities.

THE Prince of ASTURIAS is a lively youth, and has begun his triumphs with great joy, over fome fparrows fhot by his own
hand.

hand. MARIANA tells us, B. 18. ch. 7. that this title of Prince of ASTURIAS, was given in imitation of our title of Prince of WALES.

FERDINAND, King of NAPLES, gives fair promises of being one day a very spirited Monarch.—— He put on Majesty the moment his father embarked for SPAIN, with as much dignity and ease, as if his plaything had always been a sceptre.

THE Princesses JOSEPHA and LUISA, are both marriageable; so that time will now soon discover whether they will add any new strength to the FAMILY COMPACT.

I cannot quit the *Court of* SPAIN, without observing the little pains it takes to be *popular*. They pay scarce any court to the *Grandees* of the kingdom. They express publickly their dislike of the country, and are always preferring NAPLES to it. They employ foreigners preferably to natives, in posts at home, and embassies abroad. Can any circumstance more compleatly shew the *despotism* of that Monarchy ?

THE *Ministry*, or those who compose their *Council of State*, which answers to our *Privy Council*, are

1. THE Duke of ALVA; a discarded, though an honest, old, and faithful Minister.

2. THE Marquez de VILLARAS, formerly known by the name of SEBASTIAN DE LA QUADRA.

3. THE Marquez de SALAS, absent.

4. THE Prince YACCHI, absent.

5. DON RICARDO WALL.

6. DON ALPHO. CLEM. DE AROSTEQUI.

7. DON PEDRO GORDILLO.

N. B. ALL these, as such, have the title of *Excellency*.

THEIR

THEIR *Secretaries of State*, and *Universal Dispatches*, are,

1. GENERAL WALL, first Secretary of State, Dispatch, and of War.

2. THE Marquez DEL CAMPO DE VILLAR, Secretary of State, and of the Dispatch of Grace and Justice.

3. DON JULIAN DE ARRIAGA, Secretary of State, and of the Dispatch of the Marine and INDIES.

4. THE Marquez SQUILACCI, Secretary of State, and of the Dispatch of the Treasury, Superintendant-general of the Copper, and its distribution.

OF all these, General WALL, and the Marquez SQUILACCI, are the only *two ministers*, in our sense of that expression; the former *first Secretary of State*, and the latter *first Lord of the Treasury*. SPAIN has, for many years past, been under the direction of foreign *Ministers*. Whether this hath been owing to want of capacity in the natives, or disinclination in the Sovereign, I will not take upon me to say; such as it is, the native nobility lament it, as a great calamity. In looking back for above a *century* past, I find the ministers employed to be nearly half natives and half foreigners. Thus, the Conde Duke D'OLIVARES was a Spaniard, of the house of MEDINA SIDONIA, Don LUIS DE HARO was his nephew, EMANUEL DE LIRA a Spaniard, ALBERONI an Italian, RIPERDA a Dutchman, the Marquez DE BEDMAR a Spaniard, the Marquis DE GRIMALDO an Italian, the Marquez DE ENSENADA a Spaniard, known by the name of CENON DE SOMODEVILLA, Don JOSEPH CARVAJAL a Spaniard, Mr. WALL an Irishman, and the Marquis DE SQUILACCI a Neapolitan.

IT is well known, that Mr. WALL raised himself to that eminent station, which he now enjoys, by means which are usually the ruin of most others, I mean gallantry and gaming. Not but that his parts and merit are otherwise very conspicuous. The *Marquis's* fort I take to consist in his abilities as a *Financier*, his understanding thoroughly *Ways and Means*, as we call it, and the making very ample provision for the crown. He has put the

6

King

King upon fome ufeful projeds, and upon others feemingly as detrimental.   Paving and cleaning the ftreets of the CAPITAL, and. making new roads, were works worthy of a minifter ; his edicts againft old hats and old cloaks, of no moment ; his negligence in bringing robbers and murderers to juftice, certainly culpable ; his eftablifhing a new manufacture of *Rappè*, ill executed, and ill dropped fo foon after it was fet on foot ; you rarely find a minifter a good tobacconift ; and by his difcouraging the manufactures fo entirely, he feems to me to fhew, that he does not underftand the true interefts of SPAIN.   As Superintendant of the *Copper*, I fuppofe he will take fome fteps towards removing that grievance †.   The beft thing, in my opinion, to be done with it, is to recal it, and give it to the owners of the *Anti-Gallican Privateer*.

THE Marquis DE ENSENADA, it is to be hoped, will never have influence enough, to be employed as a *Minifter* again.   He is the moft fworn and implacable enemy the Britifh nation hath in SPAIN, both from prejudice and principle.   He wears on a *Gala*, or court day, more diamonds, croffes, orders, ribbands, fillets, *&c.* than any Spanifh grandee ; fo that, like *Sinon* in the *Æneid*, he feems a * victim fled from facrifice.   His fall was chiefly owing to the intrigues of that able and great Minifter, the late Sir BENJAMIN KEENE ; a circumftance, which, if I can have my wifh, fhall one day be laid more fully before the public. The *Marquis* was recalled to court, upon the prefent King's acceffion, by means of the *Dutchefs of Caftropiniano* : he is ftill as ambitious as ever ; and if intrigue and gold can make him fo, will be a minifter again.

THE two *oldeft*, as well as the *richeft* families in SPAIN, are thofe of MEDINA CELI, and MEDINA SIDONIA ; the former take their title from a town in OLD CASTILE, near the river XALON : they were made *Earls* by HENRY II. of CASTILE, in 1368 ; *Dukes* by FERDINAND and ISABELLA, in 1491.   The old family-name was LA CERDA ; it is now CORDOVA.   ELI-

† See the Account of the Money, Letter XIV.
* Vittæque Deûm, quas *Hoftia* geffi.

I

ZABETH

zabeth de la Cerda, heirefs of that family, married Moses Bernard, Earl of Bearne and Foix. Their eftate is fuitable to the nobility of their blood, being above 80,000 pounds fterling per annum. They have certainly a good title to the crown of Spain, as being of the blood *royal*, and defcended from its ancient monarchs. The laft Duke of the Cerda line was Don Luis François de la Cerda, who was Viceroy of Naples, from 1692 to 1706, Counfellor of State, and firft minifter, in 1709, and Governor of the Prince of Asturias: his Dutchefs had alfo a penfion from Philip of 4000 piftoles *per annum*. But, notwithftanding thefe numerous marks of royal favour, this gentleman entered into a confpiracy againft Philip, and held a correfpondence with the Arch-duke Charles. The Marquis of Astorga, who was alfo in the plot, difcovering this on his death-bed, this Duke was arrefted by Philip's order, as he was coming to council, conducted firft to Pampeluna, and afterwards to Fontarabia, where he died.

The family of Medina Sidonia are fo called from a town in Andalusia. They were made Dukes in 1445. Their name is Gusman El Bueno; their eftate is above 60,000 pounds *per annum*; but neither this eftate nor the former affords to its poffeffor any thing like that annual income; for, being both charged with heavy incumbrances, they are, for the moft part, parcelled out into fmall mortgages, the rents of which the mortgagee receives, till the fum due to him is entirely paid. Thefe two dukedoms did, for many years, belong to the fame family, the Gusmans; whether they do now or not, I cannot fay. Though they had great connections with the Austrian family, yet during the Succeffion-war, the then Duke of Medina Sidonia adhered inviolably to Philip's intereft, and followed his ftandard to the laft.

As the Captain of the La Reyna, who fo bravely defended the Morro Caftle, at the Havanah, when taken by the Englifh in 1762, has been much talked of lately, it may not be unacceptable to fay fomewhat of that family.

Tue

THE VELASCO family have been for ages Conſtables of CASTILE, the higheſt poſt anciently in that kingdom, being *Generaliſſimos* of all its forces; but it is now only a bare title, yet one of great honour and eſteem, like the old JUSTICIARY of ARRAGON. They were made Dukes of FRIAS in 1491, and Earls of HARO in 1430, and Earls of CASTEL NUEVO, and Marquiſſes of VERLANGA. This office of *Conſtable of Caſtile* was inſtituted in 1382, by JOHN I. of CASTILE. This honour is not hereditary in the family of the VELASCOS, though, having deſcended in it from father to ſon for many generations, it has very naturally been thought ſo.

THE Spaniards have in general an olive complection, are of a middle ſtature, rather lean, but well made; they have fine eyes, gloſſy black hair, and a ſmall well ſhaped head.—Their cloaths are uſually of a very dark colour, and their cloaks almoſt black. This ſhews the natural gravity of the people. This is the general dreſs of the common ſort; for the court, and perſons of faſhion, have moſt of them adopted the French dreſs and modes.

As their natural air is gravity, ſo they have conſequently great coldneſs and reſerve in their deportment; they are therefore very uncommunicative to all, and particularly to ſtrangers. But when once you are become acquainted with them, and have contracted an intimacy, there are not more ſocial, more friendly, or more converſible beings in the world. When they have once profeſſed it, none are more faithful friends.—They are a people of the higheſt notions of honour, even to exceſs, which is a ſtill viſible effect of their antient love of *Chivalry*, and was the animating ſpirit of that enthuſiaſm. They have great probity and integrity of principle. As they perſevere with much fidelity and zeal in their friendſhips, you will naturally expect to find them warm, relentleſs, and implacable in their reſentments.

THEY are generous, liberal, magnificent, and charitable; religious without diſpute, but devout to the greateſt exceſſes of ſuperſtition. What elſe could induce them to kiſs the hands of their *Prieſts*, and the garments of their *Monks?*

Iʏ

IF they have any predominant fault, it is, perhaps, that of being rather *too high minded*; hence they have entertained, at different periods, the moſt extravagant conceits; ſuch as, that the ſun only roſe and ſet in their dominions; that their language was the only tongue fit to addreſs the Almighty with; that they were the peculiar favourites of heaven, inſomuch that when the arms of Proteſtants have prevailed over theirs, they have been ready to call GOD himſelf *an Heretic*. They formerly thought, that wiſdom, glory, power, riches and dominion, were their ſole monopoly; but the experience of two or three centuries paſt has contributed to ſhew the fondneſs of all theſe deluſions. The open and avowed attempts of its AUSTRIAN Princes, graſping at univerſal monarchy; the ſecret and more concealed ambition of the BOURBON line, with all their plans of refined policy, have been, as SHAKESPEAR calls it, like the baſeleſs fabric of a viſion. It has been owing to theſe lofty conceits, that they are ſtill poſſeſſed with the higheſt notions of nobility, family and blood. The mountaineer of ASTURIAS, though a peaſant, will plume himſelf as much upon his genealogy and deſcent, as the firſt grandee; and the *Caſtilian*, with his *Coat-armour*, looks upon the *Gallician* with ſovereign contempt.

NOTHING can ſhew the *ſang froid* of the Spaniards more ſtrongly than the following circumſtance, which, though it hath been often related, is perhaps not known to every reader. In the war that enſued between SPAIN and PORTUGAL, upon the revolution in favour of the Duke of BRAGANZA, the Portugueſe plundered the village of *Traigueros*, and left a centinel in it, while the troops paſſed on.—The centinel, to amuſe the time, played on his guitar, which happened to be out of tune. A Spaniard belonging to this plundered village, offended with the diſſonance of the ſoldier's muſic, came to the centinel, and civilly begg'd him to lend him the guitar; which being done, he tuned it, and returned it to the Portugueſe, with this ſhort ſpeech— *Now Sir, it is in tune,—Aora ſta templada.*

THE profeſſion of arms is their chief delight; to this darling paſſion, commerce, manufactures, and agriculture have been al-

X x

ways

ways facrificed. It never appeared more evident than in the *Succeſſion war*; the peaſant voluntarily forſook the plough, and ran to the Auſtrian or the Bourbon ſtandard. There was no occaſion for an haranguing ſerjeant, or for an officer and a *preſs-warrant*, to call him to the field of action. A la guerra, a la guerra, was all the cry.

IT has been imagined, from the events of the preſent war, that the Spaniſh are not good troops; but it is a great miſtake; there are no ſoldiers in the whole world that are braver than the *Spaniſh*. Thoſe who ſay otherwiſe only ſhew their ignorance of hiſtory. They have had the Dukes of BERWICK and BITONTO, the Counts DE GAGE and SCHOMBERG, the Prince of HESSE, the Marquis DE LAS MINAS, the Generals STANHOPE, PETERBOROUGH, and STAREMBERGH, the eye-witneſſes of their bravery. That they make but an indifferent military figure at preſent, is no juſt argument againſt them; long peace, long diſuſe, and bad generals, will entirely damp the martial ſpirit of any people. Let them only be diſciplined, and led on by his *Pruſſian Majeſty*, and I will anſwer for their doing as much execution as any troops in EUROPE, and particularly the cavalry. They bear all hardſhips with the moſt unremitting patience, and can endure heat, cold, and even hunger, with ſome degree of chearfulneſs. They have courage and conſtancy ſufficient for the moſt hazardous undertakings; and though naturally ſlow, yet when once put in action, purſue their object with great warmth and perſeverance.

BIGOTRY has been very prejudicial to the Spaniards, not only in religion, but in the arts and ſciences, and has grealy retarded their advancement in learning.—It is impoſſible that thoſe who are too blindly attached to the opinions of the *Antients*, ſhould make any great figure among the *Moderns*. ARISTOTLE, DUNS SCOTUS, and THOMAS AQUINAS, were a triumvirate more dangerous to the freedom of the mind, than thoſe of ancient ROME to its liberties. And it had certainly been much more ſerviceable to our own univerſities, if, inſtead of expelling and burning the

2   **works**

works of LOCKE, they had at that time set all ARISTOTLE and PLATO on fire.

THIS bigotry, in favour of the Antients, appears no where more strongly, than in their practice of physic. Thousands have died in SPAIN by following the prescriptions of GALEN and HIPPOCRATES, who might have lived many years, had they had an equal faith in SYDENHAM and BOERHAAVE.

To politics the Spaniards have a natural inclination; they understand and study the political interests of their country very thoroughly; even the most common peasants will sometimes make reflections on public affairs, that would be not unworthy of a senator in the CORTES.

To give an idea of a *Spanish University*, it will be sufficient to describe that of SALAMANCA; the rest being all similar, only inferior.

It consists of 24 professors, who have 1000 ducats each *per annum*. It has a small library, the books of which are all *chained*. There are 12 Divinity Professors, four for the morning, and four for the afternoon. There are other Sub-professors likewise, who have only 500 vellon crowns *per annum*. There is a Professor of the doctrine of DURANDUS, and one for that of SCOTUS. This last seems most requisite, for ERASMUS was nine years in understanding the *Preface* only. Besides the stipendiary Professors, there are others paid by the scholars; Cardinal XIMENES was originally so low, as to have been one of these. There is also the same number of Professors for the Civil and Canon Law, Physic, Philosophy, and Mathematics; as for Divinity, all these are under the direction of an annual President. Next to him, is the *School-master*, who is always a canon of SALAMANCA, and answers to our *Vice-chancellor*. These two officers have 8000 ducats each *per annum*. The revenues of this University are said to be 90,000 ducats *per annum*.——It formerly had 7000 scholars; but that number has been considerably lessened this many an age: however, one of their schools is still large enough to hold 2000

X x 2 .

people.

people.   The fcholars all wear much the fame drefs as the ecclefiaftics, have all the *Tonfure,* and the *Bonnet,* for hats are forbidden.   There are in SALAMANCA 24 colleges; but no fcholar can
remain in them longer than feven years.   The Bridge of ftone
at SALAMANCA, thrown over the river TORMES, is a moft noble
Roman work.

As to the *Language* of SPAIN, there are two different tongues
fpoken in it, the *Bifcayan,* and the *Romance,* or' Spanifh.   The
Bifcayan was moft probably the language of the ancient Spaniards; juft as the moft ancient *Britifh* tongue is ftill preferved in
our ifland, in the mountains of WALES, and the *Erfe* in thofe of
SCOTLAND.   The *Romance* is plainly, from its name, a corruption of the *Latin;* this is now called *Caftilian.*—The Spaniards
confound the B with the V, and the C with the Q, and fo did
their mafters the Romans; thus, they ufed BENERI for VE-
NERI, BIXIT for VIXIT, PEQUNIAM for PECUNIAM.---
The Spaniards love the D final, fo did the Romans; as prædad,
altod, marid, for præda, alto, mari.   In Spanifh this is almoft univerfal; as Verdad, Liberdad, Jubentud, for Veritas, Libertas, Ju-
ventus, &c.   In many inftances the Latin and Spanifh agree word
for word, and the Caftilian often writes the language of the *Bas
Empire,* without defigning it.——Indeed I am perfuaded, that
more light might be gathered from the *Spanifh* tongue, towards
difcovering what the *Roman* language was, during *the fecond Punic war,* than from any other quarter.

THERE is a great fimilarity between many of the Englifh and
Spanifh *words;* in fuch a cafe, let others decide which is the
lender, and which the borrower.   Thus, *Cafaca,* a *Caffock;
Mucho, Much; Rajas, Rags; Carpa,* a *Carpe; Capa* a *Cape; Gol-
fo,* a *Gulph; Falta, Fault; Carga, Charge;* a *Ropper;* from *Ar-
ropar* to cloath warm; to *vamp,* from *Avampier,* Spatterdafhes;
Arcabuz, Harquebufs; Cordwainers, from the French *Corduan-
niers,* becaufe the fineft leather at that time came from CORDOVA,
or CORDUBA; *Tabard,* a Cloak, from *Tavardo,* which fignifies
the fame; hence comes our miftaken Englifh fign of the *Talbot,*
for a *Dog,* when it ought to be, as it was originally, a *Tabard,*
                                                                    or

or Cloak.——Lord BACON fays, that as one inftance of the *copia* of the Spanifh language, we have no word fo expreffive, as their *Defenvoltura*, and *Defpejar*; though I doubt the truth of that remark. That it delights in long words, the *Ampullas* and *Sef-quipedalia verba*, is very certain; *Defpavilladeras* is rather too long for fo common a word as *Snuffers*. There are many words, fuch as, *Abandanamiento*, and others, of feven fyllables and up-wards. As there is fomething pompous and magnificent in the length of its words, and the found of them, fo there is alfo a pe-culiarity in the turn and manner of their phrafes and expreffions. We fay, *the King and Queen*, their expreffion is, *the Catholic Kings*, los Reyes Catholicos, meaning the fame thing. His Britan-nic Majefty figns *George Rex*, the Catholic Monarch, *I the King*. We fay, *Long may you live*, they fay, *May you live, Sir, a thou-fand years and more*. They ufe the *mentiro* very frequently, tho', to give the LIE in Englifh, or the *menterie* in French, would be reckoned an affront. They never ufe the word *cuerno*, or *cor-nudo*, without begging pardon firft of thofe they fpeak to; the *Italians*, I am told, do the fame. Don JUAN DE JAUREQUI has tranflated LUCAN into Spanifh verfe; though I have taken fome pains, I never could procure the book; BREBEUF's French tranf-lation of that poet has been always thought *Lucano ipfo Lucanius*. What then muft be the effect of *Lucan*'s rant, who was by birth a *Spaniard*, when heightened with all the pomp, found, and bom-baft fo natural to the Spanifh language? The Spaniards have an infinity of *Proverbs*; fome political, fuch as, *Con todo el mundo guerra, y paz con Yngalaterra*; that is, *War with all the world, and peace with England*. Some of them are very ftrange, as, *Mas quiero, que fe mueran feys Duques, que morirme yo.---I had rather fix Dukes fhould die, than die myfelf.*——*Un afno coxo, un hombre roco, y el demonio, todo el mifmo.---A lame afs, a red-haired man, and the devil, are all the fame thing*.

THE military turn of the Spaniards appears in moft of their di-verfions, and even in the very *terms* and language which they ufe at CARDS: *Hombre* in Spanifh fignifies a man, from whence comes what we call *Ombre*; the four principal cards are called *Matadores*, or *Murderers*, becaufe they win all others. *Spadillo* is
                                                                                    the

the *little fword*, or the ace of *Spades*, as we very properly call it; for *Spada* in Spanifh is a *fword*, and they are fo painted on their cards. *Bafto* is properly the ace of *clubs*, becaufe it fignifies a *club*. *Punto* is any point, of the fpear fuppofe. What we call *Manil* is in Spanifh *Malillia*; the deuce of the black fuits, or the feven of the red. The *Sin prender* was going to war without taking a King for an ally.

For thofe who have curiofity this way, it may not be dif-pleafing to fee a fpecimen of the *three languages* fpoken in their *Peninfula*, as the Spaniards call it; of the *Caftilian*, the *Bifcayan*, and the *Portuguefe*.

CASTILIAN.	BISCAYAN.	PORTUGUESE.
Padre nueftro, que eftas en los cielos: Sanctificado fea tu nombre; venga tu Reino. Sea hecha tu voluntad, afs en la tierra, como en el cielo: El pan nueftro de cada dia danofle oy. Y perdonanos nueftras offenfas, affi commo nofotros perdonamos a los que nos offenden. Y no nos metas en tentacion, mas libra nos de mal. Amen.	Gure aita ceni etan aicena; fanctifica bedi hire icena; ethor bedi hire refuma; eguin bedi hire vorondatéa, ceruan begala turrean ere. Gure eguneco oguia igue egun. Eta quitta ietza que gure, corrac, nola gus gorduney, quittazen baitrarega. Eta ezgaitzala far eraci tentationetan, baina delura gaitzac gaichtotic.	Padre noffo, que ftas nos ceos. Sanctificado feia o feu nome. Ventra a nos o teu Reino. Seia ferta a tua volundade, affi nos cielo, ceos, come na terra. O pao noffo de cada dia dano to oje nefto dia. Et perdoanos as noffas devidas, affi come nos perdoamos a nos noffos devidores. Et nao nos dexes cahir en tentafao, mas libra nos de mal.

The difference of thefe three tongues is vifible to the eye; the firft almoft *Latin*, word for word; the fecond barbarous, and the third a fad corruption of Latin and French.

The Spaniards frequently breakfaft as well as fup in bed; their breakfaft is ufually of *Chocolate*, *Tea* being very feldom drank by them. They drink little wine. Their dinner is generally

rally a *Pochero*, or beef, mutton, veal, pork, and bacon, greens, &c. all boiled together. If it be a richer, or more expensive mixture of meats and delicacies, it is then stiled an *Olla podrida*, or what we call an *Olio*. Temperance in eating and drinking is doubtless one of their virtues; you may see it in their proverbs; *Unas azeitunas, una salada, y ravanillos, son comida de los cavalleros;* that is, *Olives, sallad, and radishes, are food for a gentleman.* They are great devourers of garlick; they seldom change the knife and fork, but eat every thing with the same individual weapon; delicacy, in many instances I could give, not being their character.

The taste for *gallantry* and *dancing* prevails in Spain universally; they are the two ruling passions of the country. Jealousy, ever since the accession of the house of Bourbon, has slept in peace. It is observable, that in proportion as manners become more civilized, that furious passion always loses its force. *Dancing* is so much their favourite entertainment, that their gravest matrons never think themselves excluded by age from this diversion. You may see the grandmother, mother, and daughter, all in the same country dance : the English, on the contrary, give dancing to youth, and leave cards to age. The two most favourite and universal Spanish dances are the *Sequedillas* and the *Fundungo*: the first is something like our Hay; the second is a very ancient dance, and though originally *Roman*, yet the Spaniards have mixed somewhat of the *Moorish* along with it: they are excessively fond of it; it is danced by the first of the nobility, as well as by the common people. I shall not attempt a description of it, as I am sure your English ladies of fashion would not send to Madrid for a Fundungo-master, to teach it their daughters; nor indeed could I describe it altogether decently : let it suffice to say, that it is exactly the same with the *Pantomime dance of Leda* among the *Romans*.

Most of the Spaniards take their *fiesto*, or sleep after dinner; *mass* in the morning, dinner at noon, and the evening's airing generally finish the round of their day. Though it is the *etiquette* of the country for the men and women to wear in the street,

and

and at mafs, all the fame drefs, yet the ladies in private vifits wear
as much variety of drefs, and of a much richer fort, than thofe in
ENGLAND; but to a people of gallantry, the advantage of all
wearing the fame uniform in public, is eafy to be conceived.
The married ladies in SPAIN have each their profeffed lover, juft as
the Italian ladies have their *cicifbeo*. Their evening's airing is infipid to the laft degree; you fee nothing but a ftring of coaches
following one another, filled with people of fafhion: Here a Duke
and his confeffor; there a couple of fmart young Abbes *tête a
tête*; here a whole family grouped together, juft like a Dutch
picture, hufband and wife, children and fervants, wet nurfes and
dry altogether.——When they take their airing on *gala*, or court
days, all their footmen are then dreffed in laced liveries, with
plumes of feathers in their hats.——The number of fervants kept
by the *Grandees*, and people of the firft fafhion, is immoderate;
they have often put me in mind of thofe words of TACITUS——
familiarum numerum, et nationes; for the *legionary fervants* at ROME
began at laft to be almoft an equal burthen with the *legionary
troops*. Some of the Spanifh grandees retain to the number
of 3 or 400 domefticks; the Englifh Ambaffador here, in
compliance with the tafte of the country, keeps near 100. As
they go with *four* mules ufually, they have confequently *two* drivers, or poftilions; generally *four*, and fometimes *fix* footmen behind their coaches, befides an helper to take off a pair of mules,
when they enter MADRID, as they are not permitted to drive
with more than *four* there. In the hot weather they take out
the fides and backs of their coaches, for the fake of the air.
They ufe *fedan* chairs but very little, and when they do, they
have always *two* footmen, who go on each fide the hindmoft chair-
man, in order to hold them up, left they fhould fall; and *two* of
each fide the fedan, and *two* who follow behind with *lanthorns*,
though it be in the middle of the day: That is to fay, they have
generally *nine* fervants with a coach, and *ten* with a fedan, befides thofe who go before.——

THE town of MADRID, for as it is not an *Epifcopal fee*, I
think we cannot call it a *city*, is built on fome little hills in the
neighbourhood of a very indifferent ftream called the MANSA-
NARES;

NARES; which occafioned much wit, when PHILIP II. built that great bridge over it, called the PUENTE DE SEGOVIA: Some faid *the King fhould fell the bridge to buy a river*, &c.

CHARLES V. having recovered here of a quartan ague, firft made this a royal refidence; but how injudicioufly, needs not to be remarked. The *capital* of fo great and extended a kingdom, ought doubtlefs to be at SEVILLE; where, by means of the port, all the conveniencies and neceffaries of life, and every article of foreign commerce might be had with eafe. But the expence of removing the tribunals and the King's palaces, will probably now prevent any defign of making that city a new capital.

MADRID is furrounded with very lofty mountains, whofe fummits are always covered with *fnow*. It has no fortifications to defend it; it has no ditch, but is environed by a *mud wall*. Its gates, according to the tafte of that country, have their *locks* upon the outfide. There are very few good ftreets, except thofe of the *Calle Mayor*, the *Calle d'Atocha*, the *Calle Alcala*, and the *Calle Ancha*: The reft are long, narrow, and extremely dirty. The only good fquare is the *Plafa Mayor*, which is large and regular enough; but there being *balconies* to every window, it takes off much of its beauty.

THE houfes in MADRID are moft of them brick, with dry walls, *lime* being there very dear and fcarce; *ftone* is ftill more expenfive, becaufe it muft be brought from fix or feven leagues diftance. Houfe rent is at an exorbitant price; but that is not all, furniture is fcarce to be had, without paying extravagantly for it; and if you would have *glafs windows* to your houfe, you muft put them there yourfelf, for you will not find them.—— The houfes in general are wretchedly ill-built, for you will feldom fee any two walls upon the fquare: They are laid out chiefly for fhow, convenience being little confidered: Thus you will pafs through ufually two or three large apartments of no ufe, in order to come at a fmall room at the end, where the family fit. This is the general ftate of the houfes there; not but there are fome very magnificent palaces, built chiefly by *Viceroys*, returned

Y y　　　　　　　　　　　　　　from

from their governments, and by the principal *Grandees:* Thefe have courts, and *portes cochers*, though the others have not. The houfe which the late Sir BENJAMIN KEENE lived in, near the convent of the MARAVILLAS, was of this fort; large, mag-nificent, and expenfive: It was built by one of the defcendants of the famous CORTES; though it had been half burnt down, it would contain two or three hundred people with eafe: The Earl of BRISTOL hired it on his predeceffor's death; and it is fince taken by the Prince CATHOLICO. The houfes in general look more like prifons, than the habitations of people at their liberty; the windows, befides having a balcony, being *grated* with iron bars, particularly the lower range, and fometimes all the reft. A fingle family is not the fole tenant of an houfe, as is ufually the cafe in ENGLAND; they are generally inhabited by many fepa-rate families, who notwithftanding are for the moft part perfect ftrangers to each other. Thofe who can afford it, have a diftinct apartment for fummer and winter. Foreigners are very much diftreffed for lodgings in MADRID; there being only one tolerable *inn*, the FONTANA D'ORO; and the Spaniards are not fond of taking any ftrangers into their houfes, efpecially if they are not *Catholics.* There is no fuch thing as a *tavern* or *coffee-houfe* in the town; they have only one *news paper*, which is the MADRID GAZETTE: Their places of diverfion are the *amphitheatre*, built for the exhibition of the *Bull Feaft*, and the two theatres of LA CRUZ, and DEL PRINCIPE. The noife made by the itinerant bodies of pfalm-fingers in the ftreets, or the ROSARIO's, as they call them, is very difagreeable in the evening; the frequent pro-ceffions, particularly thofe of the HOST, troublefome; at Eafter efpecially, when the fight of thofe bloody difciplinants, the *Fla-gellantes*, is extremely fhocking.

NEXT to the King's palaces, one of the beft buildings that I can recollect in MADRID, is the *Imperial College of Jefuits*, which is indeed a very noble ftructure. There is no paffing the ftreets there commodioufly without a vehicle; for as they practice the *Scotch*, or EDINBURGH *cuftom*, of manuring the ftreets by night, they would be too offenfive to your feet, as well as your nofe, without a chariot by day. Upon the fite of the *old palace*, where

FRANCIS

FRANCIS I. was kept prifoner, built by CHARLES V. but deftroyed, is now erected what they call the *New Palace*, on the
fouth fide of the town.   The *Cafa del Campo* was built I believe,
by PHILIP III. as an afylum for his miftreffes.——The *Buen Retiro* was built by the Conde Duke D'OLIVARES, in PHILIP IV's.
time.——Some of the *Convents* are fine, particularly that of *Atoche*, or our *Lady of the Bufh* : In the church belonging to it,
they fing their *Te Deum* upon victories and other public occafions.
The convent of the *Salefas* is likewife a new and noble ftructure.
There is an order of *Canoneffes* in MADRID, which they call
Ladies of St. James.   The *Monafteries* and *Nunneries* in all SPAIN,
were computed by one of their writers in 1623, at 2,141, and
the number of religious of either fex, fhut up in them, at 44,915,
which is doubtlefs a very moderate calculation.

LETTER XX.

JOURNEY from MADRID to LISBON,
December the 17th, 1762.

AS his Catholic Majesty did not think proper to give *the Earl of Briftol* any anfwer, in relation to the queftion put to him by the *Court* of GREAT BRITAIN, we, who all held our-felves in readinefs for an abrupt departure, made the neceffary difpofitions for an immediate return to ENGLAND : accordingly the requifite *Pafsports* being obtained, STANIER PORTEN, Efq; *the Englifh Conful-general at* MADRID, led the way, and fet out, on the 16th of December, on his route for PORTUGAL. We fhould have been obliged to return that way, becaufe the war prevented our going through FRANCE, and the road to CORUNNA being not practicable for a coach, unlefs we had made a very wide de-tour, and taken the road to SAN JAGO DE COMPOSTELLA.——But his Britannic Majefty fixed that route, by ordering that a fhip (the *Portland Man of War*, the worthy Captain RICHARD HUGHES Commander) fhould fail directly for LISBON, and bring home the Englifh Ambaffador, and his retinue.——The *Conful* having gone the day before, in order to prepare the way for the *Ambaffador*, procure him the beft accommodations, and to give notice of his coming : His Excellency fet out on the 17th of December, without taking leave of the Court of SPAIN.

As

As the whole nation were averfe to a war with ENGLAND, the Spaniards beheld the AMBASSADOR's departure with the utmoft regret; it being their opinion, as well as the conftant maxim of PATINHO, Con todo el mundo guerra, y paz con Ynglaterra, *War with all the world, but peace with England.* Some faid, *Es por nueftros peccaos*; and others, *Es uno golpe politico*; that is, *It is for our fins*; and, *It is a political ftroke*; that is to fay, the court's doing, not a national war.

THOUGH the Ambaffador returned, without having taken leave of the *Court*, yet he received, on his departure, all the honours and civilities which were due to his rank and character. General WALL fent orders to all the Governors, and Commandants of every city or town the Ambaffador was to pafs through, that they fhould fhew him all the accuftomed honours and refpects due to the Ambaffador of GREAT BRITAIN.—Accordingly, at every place, the Governor waited on his *Excellency*, at his arrival, with a polite Spanifh compliment; the foldiers were drawn up under arms, the drums beating, colours flying, and the canon on the ramparts fired at his departure.

WE were to travel *fixty-three* leagues before we could get out of SPAIN, and pafs the GUADIANA at BADAJOS, which is the laft frontier city towards PORTUGAL; and then we had *twenty-nine* leagues remaining to ALDEA GALLEGA, a little village on the fouth fide of the TAGUS, where we were to pafs that river to come at LISBON. This will appear much clearer from the following route.

ROUTE *from* MADRID *to* LISBON.

		Leagues.
Firft Day,	NABAL CARNERO,	5
Second Day,	CASA RUBIOS,	2
	NOBES,	4
Third Day,	STA. OLAYA,	2
	TALAVERA DE LA REYNA,	7
	Carried over,	20

3   Brought

		Leagues.
	Brought over,	20
Fourth Day,	LA CALZADA,	6
Fifth Day,	NABAL MORAL,	4
————	ALMARAS,	3
Sixth Day,	JARAYSEJO,	4
————	TRUXILLO,	4
Seventh Day,	LA CRUZ DEL PUERTO,	3
————	MIAJADAS,	3
Eighth Day,	SAN PEDRO,	5
————	MERIDA,	2
Ninth Day,	LOBON,	4
————	TALAVERUELA,	3
————	BADAJOS,	2
	So far in SPAIN.	63
Tenth Day,	ELVAS,	3
Eleventh Day,	ESTREMOS,	6
Twelfth Day,	VENTA DEL DUQUE,	3
————	ARROYOLOS,	3
Thirteenth Day,	MOSTREMOS,	3
————	VENTAS NUEVAS,	4
Fourteenth Day,	ALDEA GALLEGA,	7
	Thefe laft in PORTUGAL,	29
	Total,	92

WE were to pafs two thirds of this way in an enemy's country, and the remainder in a dreary, barren, rocky foil, fomewhat, indeed, more fertile than SPAIN, but very little better in its accommodations. Befides this, the feafon of the year, which is ever unfavourable to travellers, was moft particularly fo to us at this juncture, as it rained almoft that whole fortnight without intermiffion; infomuch, that fome of the rivers were fo increafed, as to prevent a paffage; which happened to thofe who conducted the baggage-waggons, which were retarded fome days by the floods.—Add to this, the rigour of the feafon, and the cold, the ftormy winds to be naturally expected in that part of the year; and, at thofe feafons, the reftlefs toffing of the Bay of BISCAY. All which circumftances frequently put me in mind of thofe remarkable words of Scripture, *And pray that your flight be not in the winter.*

THE firft place worth your notice in this route, is the town of TALAVERA DE LA REYNA, in the kingdom of NEW CASTILE, on the banks of the TAGUS. It is the greateft manufacture of filver and gold filks, perhaps in the whole country. The late King FERDINAND protected and encouraged it much; but it is now finking, as moft of the reft of their manufactures are, under the uncommercial afpect of the minifter SQUILACCI. There is likewife a curious manufacture of earthen ware. Its ancient name was TALABRIGA. It was called DE LA REYNA, becaufe it belonged to Queen MARY, wife of ALONZO XII.

THERE is one hill, of a long, winding, and difficult afcent, before you come to JARAYSEJO; it is dangerous in fome parts; it employed us almoft a whole morning to furmount it; and one baggage-waggon fell down fome part of the precipice, but was got up again entire. There is likewife a very dangerous pafs of a mountain, about two leagues before you come to TRUXILLO: Your coach muft here be drawn up by oxen, and fupported by men, otherwife it is impoffible to get it over the mountain.— TRUXILLO is a city in the province of ESTREMADURA, ftanding on a hill, on the top whereof is a *caftle*, the country about it fruitful.—It was founded by JULIUS CÆSAR, and after him called TURRIS JULIA, hence corruptly TRUXILLO.

THE next place of note is MERIDA, the capital city of the province of ESTREMADURA, built on the banks of the GUADI- ANA, over which there is a moft noble bridge, the work of that great Emperor, as well as Builder, TRAJAN. There are here ftill to be feen many fine remains of *Roman antiquity:* In the market-

market-place is a large column, built entirely of *inscription* and *sepulchral* stones, crowned on the top with an antique statue; the *Walls* for the most part *Roman*; there are some remains of an *Amphitheatre*, *Aqueduct*, *Circus*, &c. all *Roman*. It was built by Augustus, given by him to veteran troops, and called Emerita Augusta, whence corruptly Merida.

Four leagues farther, on the banks of the same river, stands Lobon, where there is a *Castle*. It was antiently called *Lychon*, in Greek, signifying a wolf, which its present Spanish name does likewise.

The last city in Estremadura, on the frontiers of Portugal, is Badajoz, well fortified, has a fine bridge, a castle, and was anciently called Pax Augusta; whence its present name.——Here we took our last *adieu* of Spain; and were not a little pleased to find ourselves on *Portuguese* ground the next morning, at Elvas; where the Ambassador stayed all day, though it was only *three* leagues to it, in order to forward a messenger to England, and send his dispatches to the Honourable Mr. Hay, his Britannic Majesty's Minister Plenipotentiary at the court of Lisbon.——Elvas is a city in the province of Alentejo in Portugal. Being the frontier to Spain, it is the best fortified place the *Portuguese* have: It is also a *Bishopric*. There is a good *cathedral*, with a most elegant chapter-room. The Dean, who was a very polite ecclesiastic, was so obliging as to shew it us himself.

Six leagues farther, you come to Estremos, another fortified place, about two leagues from Villa-Vizosa; there is a castle on the hill.——The situation is beautiful, and the town has a clean, neat, pleasing appearance; it is remarkable for a fine manufactory of *earthen ware*.——It is most memorable for a victory obtained by the Portuguese, under the command of Count Schomberg, in 1663, over the Castilians, whose general was Don John of Austria, in their last invasion of that kingdom. ——They found in that Prince's casket, after the battle, very complete lists of the Spanish army, artillery, and offensive munitions

of

of war.—The court of LISBON, diverted at this incident, bad their Secretary of State write at the bottom of one of thefe lifts, *We certify, that the above lift is very exact, having found it after the defeat of Don* JOHN *of* AUSTRIA, *near Eftremos,* 8th June 1663.——The diftance of time between their laft and the prefent invafion being only one year fhort of a century.

THE next place of note is ARROYOLOS, ftanding on an eminence, with a good *fort* to it; it gives the title of Earl to the family of CASTRO.

THE 31ft of December we arrived at ALDEA GALLEGA. Here our difperfed parties united again with the greateft joy, having the beautiful profpect of that fine river the TAGUS before us, which is no lefs than twelve miles broad at that place, and which we were to pafs at fix o'clock the next morning, becaufe of the tide. And here we were glad to reft from all our fatigues; fome of us having fuffered very much from the length and labour of the journey.

WE arrived at LISBON about eight o'clock the next morning; where the Honourable Mr. HAY received the Ambaffador, and his retinue, and conducted them to his own houfe.

THE city of LISBON, built, like old ROME, on feveral little hills, is one of the fineft views from the water, that can poffibly be imagined; as you approach nearer to it, the tragical effects, the havock of that dreadful earthquake, cannot but touch every beholder with fentiments of pain. After landing, we paffed through fome ftreets, near a mile in length, where the houfes were all fallen on each fide, and lay in that undiftinguifhed heap of ruin, into which they funk at the firft convulfive fhocks. Not that the reader is to imagine, that the greateft part of that fine city fell on that fatal morning; fo far from it, that I believe not above *one fourth part* of it was deftroyed : for it prevailed more in one particular quarter, than the reft; and there the defolation was almoft univerfal, fcarce an houfe or building that was not thrown down. In the other parts of the city, fome fingle ill-conditioned, or ruinous buildings fell, but the reſt ſtood.—And there is ſcarce a ſtreet but you will ſee ſhores and props fixed to the buildings on each ſide, to prevent their falling even now; they having ſuffered ſo much from the ſhocks they had received. —Conſidering how much time has elapſed ſince the earthquake, very little has been rebuilt in proportion.—They have built a Cuſtom-houſe, an Arſenal, a Theatre, and ſome few other buildings. All agree, that the fire occaſioned infinitely more ha- vock than the earthquake. Thouſands of the inhabitants, unhap- pily, in the firſt confuſion of their fear, taking the ill judged ſtep of thronging into the churches; the doors of which being ſome- times ſhut by the violence of the crowd, and ſometimes locked by miſtake, when the fire ſeized the roofs of thoſe buildings, theſe unhappy ſufferers were moſt of them deſtroyed; ſome by ſheets of lead, that poured like a molten deluge upon their heads; others maſhed by the fall of the roofs, and the reſt burnt alive. One's imagination can ſcarce form a ſcene of confuſion, horror, and death, more dreadful than this.——After the ſhocks were over, the fire continued burning for many weeks; and it is thought, was one principal cauſe of their eſcaping the plague, as the putrefaction of the bodies was by that means much leſs.—— The calculation of the number that periſhed, as they kept no re- giſters, muſt be in great meaſure *conjectural*; but that thouſands and ten thouſands were deſtroyed, there is no doubt. The morn- ing on which it happened was moſt remarkably ſerene and plea- ſant, particularly about 10 o'clock, and in one quarter more, all was involved in this dreadful ſcene of terror and deſtruction.——As this event produced many changes, thoſe among the commercial parts of the city were not the leaſt remarkable. One, who yeſterday was at the eve of a bankruptcy, found himſelf to-day with *his books cleared*; and hundreds, who lived in eaſe and af- fluence, as ſoon as they had recovered from their firſt panic and diſmay, ſaw want and poverty ſtare them in the face.

THE calamities of PORTUGAL in general, and thoſe of the city of LISBON in particular, within the ſpace of ſo few years, cannot, I think, be paralleled in all hiſtory.—— An earth- quake, a fire, a famine, an aſſaſſination-plot againſt their Prince, executions upon executions, the scaffolds and wheels for torture reeking with the noblest blood; imprisonment after imprisonment, of the greatest and most distinguished personages; the expulsion of a chief order of ecclesiastics, the invasion of their kingdom by a powerful, stronger, and exasperated nation; the numerous troops of the enemy laying waste their territory, bringing fire and sword with them, and rolling, like distant thunder, towards the gates of their capital; their Prince ready almost to save himself by flight.——The Spanish ministry had already decreed the doom of PORTUGAL, and nothing was to be heard at the *Escurial*, but " Delenda est Carthago." Carthaginian, perhaps, or Jewish story, may possibly afford a scene something like this, but, for the shortness of the period, not so big with events, though in their final destruction superior. From that, indeed, under the hand of providence, the national humanity and generosity of GREAT BRITAIN has preserved the Portuguese: And it remains now to be seen, in future treaties, how that people will express their gratitude.

THOSE who are able to search deeper into human affairs, may assign the causes of such a wonderful chain of events: for my own part, I cannot ascribe all this to so *singular a cause* as that which a *Spaniard* hath done, in a famous pamphlet, printed lately at MADRID, and which the *Baron de Wassenaer* sent me this summer. It is entitled *a Spanish prophecy*, and endeavours to shew, that all these calamities have befallen the *Portuguese*, solely because of their connection with the *heretic* English. The great Ruler and Governor of the World undoubtedly acts by universal laws, regarding the whole system, and cannot, without blasphemy, be considered in the light of *a Partizan*. The rest of the pamphlet tends to shew, that his Catholic Majesty carried his arms into PORTUGAL, solely to give them liberty, and set them free from English tyranny.

SOME of the Churches, the Arsenal, the Theatre, and above all, the Aqueduct at LISBON, deserve the attention of every traveller; the center arch, for its height, being one of the noblest, perhaps, in EUROPE. One thing is remarkable, that during the earthquake this building stood the attack, though it received so
much

much shock, as that many of the key-stones fell several inches, and hang now only because a small part of the base of the key-stone was catched by the center's closing again.

THE Theatre is an elegant building, and judiciously disposed; their actors excel in the mute Pantomime; they played the *Maes-tro di Schola* incomparably well; the scenes had sentiment, character, connection with one another, and carried on the general design. Though the scenery and machines of our theatres are admirable, yet our Pantomime farces seem to have little or no meaning. Nor do I much wonder at it; Mr. GARRICK, who is certainly the greatest actor that ever trod the stage, must be too warm an admirer of Shakespeare and Nature, to have any relish for these extravagancies, and therefore cannot stoop to give much of his attention to them.

THE streets of LISBON are cleaner than those of MADRID, but disagreeable, from the continual ascents and descents you are obliged to make. Most of the houses have the *Jalousie*, or lattice. The women, though more beautiful, are not so much seen in public as the *Spanish*, and their head-dress is much prettier. There are few fires in chimneys in the rooms at LISBON; the want of them is supplied by wearing a *cloak* constantly in the house, or perhaps by a brazier; though the cold is sometimes very piercing.

THE view of the TAGUS, from those windows of the town which command it, is remarkably pleasing: The *Bean-cods*, or small boats, which sail with any wind or tide, and are continually passing; the river crowded with shipping of all nations; the coming in of a *Bahia* or *Brasil* fleet; the opening of the river towards the bar, with the castle of *Bellem* on the right, the King's palace, and the castle of *St. Julian's* on the left; all together form a fine and agreeable view. The passage of the bar is sometimes very dangerous, either in coming in or going out of the river, by the bank of sand which is thrown up by the winds and sea. We past it, however, with no difficulty, on the 19th of January, landed at FALMOUTH on the 28th, and arrived in LONDON the 5th of February, 1762.

F I N I S.

www.ingramcontent.com/pod-product-compliance
Lightning Source LLC
Chambersburg PA
CBHW021342110726
47900CB00005B/1575